DATE DUE

*The South
as an American
Problem*

~The South as an American Problem

EDITED BY LARRY J. GRIFFIN

AND DON H. DOYLE

The University of Georgia Press   *Athens and London*

© 1995 by the University of Georgia Press
Athens, Georgia 30602
All rights reserved
Set in Minion by Tseng Information Systems, Inc.
Printed and bound by Maple-Vail
The paper in this book meets the guidelines for permanence
and durability of the Committee on Production Guidelines for
Book Longevity of the Council on Library Resources.
Printed in the United States of America
99 98 97 96 95   C   5   4   3   2   1
99 98 97 96   P   5   4   3   2   1
Library of Congress Cataloging in Publication Data
The South as an American problem / edited by Larry J. Griffin
and Don H. Doyle.
p.   cm.
Includes bibliographical references and index.
ISBN 0-8203-1729-2 (alk. paper);
ISBN 0-8203-1752-7 (pbk.: alk. paper)
1. Southern States—History.   2. Southern States—Civilization.
3. Regionalism—Southern States.   4. Southern States—Race relations.   I. Griffin, Larry J.   II. Doyle, Don Harrison, 1946–.
F209.5.S64   1995   975—dc20   94-23969
British Library Cataloging in Publication Data available

∾ Contents

∾ Preface

DURING THE ACADEMIC YEAR 1992–93, ten Vanderbilt faculty members from a variety of departments met each Thursday afternoon to explore a topic of common interest, the American South and its often troubled relationship with the rest of the nation. Our goal was to understand how and why the South, at particular times and in a great many ways, became defined as an American problem. This project was sponsored by the university's Robert Penn Warren Center for the Humanities as part of its annual Fellows Program. The Humanities Center and its faculty seminars have provided a much needed meeting place for scholars interested in crossing the forbidding frontiers that divide academic disciplines. Neither our seminar on "the South as an American problem," which proved so enjoyable and illuminating, nor this collection of essays, the fruit of all those weekly meetings, would have been possible without the encouragement and support of the Center's then director, Charles E. Scott, and its assistant director, Mona C. Frederick. The editors and authors are pleased to express our gratitude for all that they and other Center staff members did to help get this project off the ground and to sustain it through the publication of these essays.

What our seminar came to call America's "southern problem" can be seen in the bitter tone and argumentative content of exchanges between nation and region and in every institutional and interpersonal expression of southern life. It has shown itself through the painful autobiographical explorations of southerners, black and white, who have searched for their identity and their place, striving all the while to "explain" and "tell about" the South. The Problem South has been both created in and perceived through disparate cultural prisms—ranging from mediocre Hollywood movies and television programs to some of the most profound fiction written in the twentieth century—that refract contradictory images and stereotypes, some seemingly favoring or justifying the South, others damning or ridiculing it. America's southern problem can be seen in the region's religious expressions and intellectual routines, its economic and political institutions, its migration patterns, and most starkly and tragically in its racial practices and struggles.

Because no one academic field, specialization, or perspective could be expected to grasp and make sense of this extraordinary diversity and complexity, our Fellows Program embraced a wide range of disciplines from its very inception. The regular seminar participants included the following Vanderbilt faculty members: Robert A. Margo (economics), Teresa A. Goddu, Michael Kreyling, and Eric J. Sundquist (all from English), David L. Carlton, Joyce E. Chaplin, Don H. Doyle (all from history), James W. Ely Jr. (history and the law school), Richard A. Pride (political science), and Larry J. Griffin (sociology). With the exception of Teresa Goddu and Richard Pride, both of whom had preexisting obligations, all wrote essays specifically for this collection. Academic guests to the seminar included historians Hugh Davis Graham (Vanderbilt), Neil McMillen (Southern Mississippi), and James Oakes (Northwestern) and the political scientists Earl Black (Houston) and Merle Black (Emory). Hugh Graham and James Oakes graciously agreed to revise their talks for publication here. We were also lucky to get an authentic nonacademic, Nashvillian John Egerton, to speak in our seminar and to contribute his insight to this volume. John Egerton dealt directly with America's "southern problem" in the 1960s and has since chronicled the travails of the South in a series of penetrating books and articles that defy topical pigeonholing. Disciplinary and university obligations prevented one original member of our group, Vanderbilt historian Jimmie Lewis Franklin, from participating as he and we had hoped. Although we missed his acumen and knowledge in the seminar, Jimmie Franklin revised his 1993 presidential address to the Southern Historical Association for publication here.

In addition to the Robert Penn Warren Center and its staff, others were essential to the completion of this book: Karen Orchard, the executive editor of the University of Georgia Press, encouraged and sustained this project from its very beginning; Kelly Caudle, the Press's project editor, engineered the book through tricky production waters; Grace Buonocore copyedited the manuscript with rare dedication and clarity; and Darren McDaniel and William Fletcher, both graduate students in sociology at Vanderbilt, respectively, provided valuable research assistance and proficiently compiled the index. We are pleased to acknowledge their contributions.

The South
as an American
Problem

∼ Introduction

WRESTLING WITH A THEME whose origins and ramifications are as pervasive as "the South as an American problem" virtually mandated that each contributor to this collection integrate historical and contemporary questions, fact and interpretation, and social science and humanistic analyses. Each of us brought to this task our personal experiences and the insights and viewpoints of our academic disciplines, and each specific topic we explored — slavery, for example, or the South's late economic development, or its portrayal in literature — therefore was examined from a number of scholarly traditions and with dissimilar research tools. All of us, in fact, had to transcend the rather narrow limitations of our respective academic disciplines — each with its own intramural blinders, debates, and jargon — and had to learn from one another and from intellectual perspectives other than our own. And learn we did!

We began our intellectual journey with only one strong and guiding preconception, that the American South, more than any other region of the United States, has often been defined — typically by those outside the region — as being at odds with the mainstream of American values or behavior and therefore has been constructed as a special problem. Because the fate of the nation was and remains unalterably bound to the fate of the region, however, "the problem of the South" has also always been America's problem, understood most often as a blight on the broader cultural and political landscape and something that must somehow be addressed and solved. Whether the meaning of the "problem South" has been imposed from without or defined from within, it has elicited analysis and proposals for redress throughout the region's and nation's history. Each contributor to this volume addresses a significant aspect of America's southern problem: how it has been perceived, defined, and constructed; the remedies offered in response to each characterization of the problem and some of the consequences of those solutions; how it was experienced by those closest to it and how that experience, in turn, became the basis of a strong and vibrant culture; and its possible demise.

Despite our common obsession, each author was free to develop his or her own argument no matter where it led. As readers will quickly see, the editors did not smooth over genuine differences in interpretation and outlook, nor did we fabricate a false consensus or impose any orthodoxy whatsoever on contributors. By allowing this group of strong and independent minds room to range in and out of their disciplinary confines, room to disagree among ourselves, and room to challenge conventional wisdom and polite or expedient fictions, we anticipated that a richer and more complete and multifaceted understanding of the problem South was likely to emerge. Our expectation has been more than satisfied.

Don Doyle and James Oakes, for example, do not understand southern slavery to be an American problem in precisely the same way, and John Egerton and Robert Margo do not appear to agree on the cause or perhaps even extent of the region's poverty that was so widely publicized in the 1930s. Because of these differences, we get a sharper view both of how slavery did and did not contradict America's normative order and whether the South's peculiar economic arrangements and retarded development really produced a unique problem. David Carlton, to cite another example, seems dubious of the proposition expressed by Larry Griffin that the South stood in opposition to much of America's self-idealizations. Carlton's essay and especially that of John Egerton also suggest that the problems of the South often have been truly America's problems and that, as C. Vann Woodward once intimated, the nation may have something of importance to learn from a region that itself has had to confront its past and its shortcomings and try to make amends for them.[1] Rather than being forced back to the age-old issue of southern distinctiveness, we are instead led to reflect on the relevance of the nation-region relationship for conceptualizing and interpreting the South and America.

Eric Sundquist tackles what is perhaps the archetypal icon of southern liberalism, Harper Lee's Atticus Finch, and asks us to look anew at what Lee was really doing in her novel. His essay can also be usefully contrasted with that by Hugh Graham. Graham agrees that southern whites were incapable of saving themselves or liberating African Americans through the sort of moderation and decency displayed by Atticus, but he further argues that the civil rights movement's appeal to classic American legalism and liberalism ultimately provoked and transformed massive federal intervention into the instrument of profound and unalterable transformations in the region's race relations. Joyce Chaplin and James Ely remind us, in quite distinct ways, that the South has not always been considered a problem for the broader culture, and both, again, expose the analytical limits of the question of the distinctiveness of southern life and social organization. In his contribution, Jimmie Franklin scrutinizes the oppressive weight of much of southern history on the bodies and psyches of African Americans, but he also convincingly develops the idea that blacks, as co-creators of southern culture, have rightly earned the sense of the region as their "place" as well. Michael Kreyling, finally, warns against substituting myth and image, especially the image of "community," for history in southern literary criticism: the result, he argues, is apt to be a debilitating collective amnesia about the very wellspring of the region's extraordinary outpouring of superb fiction, race and race relations. Taken as a set, then, the essays are as nuanced in tone and attitude, as varied, and as contrary as is the subject matter itself.

We of course are not the first group of scholars connected with Vanderbilt to confront the long antagonism between America and the South and to try to interpret the South's place in the broader culture. Seven decades earlier, the university housed John Crowe Ransom, Donald Davidson, Allen Tate, Robert Penn Warren, and others who came together to form, first, a literary group known as the Fugitives and, later, to advance the notion of the "agrarian" South and to defend that construction against the forces of "industrialism" and modernity in the North. The publication of *I'll Take My Stand: An Agrarian Manifesto*,[2] authored by Twelve Southerners in 1930, remains a major event in the history of southern thought. A group like ours at Vanderbilt University engaged in discussions of the South and its relation to the United States could hardly be unaware of, or refuse to acknowledge, the Agrarians' earlier presence. Still, we had no intention of either echoing or answering our predecessors, and it was purely accidental that this collection of essays also contains twelve authors.

The precedent, however, invites comparison. We were aware, as were the Twelve Southerners, that America's problem *with* the South was the other side of the coin that made America a problem *for* the South, at least for those southerners who had invested themselves in what they took to be the region's "natural" traditions and folkways. The title of our volume, however, may seem to promise a strikingly different tone from that of the Agrarians, whose line from the song "Dixie" evoked memories of the rebellion against the United States and propounded a continued separateness from America. The tone *is* different, as are the times in which we write and our group's biographies and sentiments. In motivation and execution, our project differs from that of the Agrarians nearly two-thirds of a century ago. Readers will not find here an embattled defense of the South as a beleaguered victim of northern arrogance or condescension. Indeed, several of the essays contain unflinching criticisms of the South, and some authors, in fact, are primarily concerned with genuine social or political problems that have been most glaring in the South. But while we did discover that our title raised a few hackles among those who perhaps might have preferred a sequel to the earlier manifesto, no one who reads very far in our book will come away thinking that we accept at face value the notion that the South has simply been out of step with the rest of the nation and thus needs correction. Out of step it was, often seriously so, but the South's definition as an American problem depended as much on what the nation made of the South as it did on the region's actual deviance from what was understood to be "real" Americanism. So even as we criticize the South, the rest of the nation also gets its fair share of reproach.

Understanding the South as an American problem allows us to see important epochs in American history, as well as the relationship between region and nation, in a new and useful light. Once the South was defined by Americans as a problem requiring remedial action, a social dynamic — really a dialectical process of problem formulation, solution, and reformulation — was unleashed: national solutions *to* southern problems were constructed and acted on by white southerners as problems *for* the South (more precisely, the white South). White southerners then moved to "solve" their "American problem" by propagating and adopting practices that created "new" problems for America now needing new solutions.

The South's racial practices have been the most enduring target of criticism over time and provide the best example of this dialectical process at work. By the 1830s, slavery, as James Oakes and Don Doyle demonstrate, was understood to pose economic, moral, or political problems for the nation. The northern abolitionist solution to this problem, emancipation, was unacceptable to the white South, and other national solutions, such as restrictions on exporting slaves to the western territories, though less drastic, were seen by whites in the region as almost as threatening to the "southern way of life." Both were construed by white southerners as a potential "problem" of the gravest magnitude. White southerners then dealt with their American problem by attempting to forge their own fledgling nation, the Confederacy. Secession, in turn, created a new problem for the United States, the dissolution of the Union, which provoked a bloody new solution, civil war.

The nation's southern problems of the 1860s—slavery and secession—were eventually solved by America at great cost, but only by leaving the South and the nation with a legacy of new problems, most of them revolving around the place of free African Americans in the new order. Again, America searched for and found a remedy, Reconstruction, which aimed at bringing newly freed blacks toward some kind of political and economic equality with whites. But again the northern solution created for white southerners a situation many experienced as a living denial of all they had been taught and all that they knew. So abhorrent were the "evils" of Reconstruction in the white southern mind that they would remain an obstacle to sectional reconciliation for at least two generations.[3] Using violence, fraud, and disfranchisement as their weapons in the 1890s, southern whites sought solutions to their problems with Reconstruction and its wrenching aftermath by instituting and consolidating a series of segregation laws and other rigidly enforced Jim Crow customs that defined the place and position of African Americans.

The dialectic of problem reformulation–solution–problem reformulation did not stop here, but it did change form, and its terrain shifted from Washington to virtually every plantation, hamlet, and town in the South. For an inexcusably long stretch of time, America abetted and buttressed the white South's solution to what it saw as its "racial problem," either actively, through U.S. Supreme Court rulings as to the constitutionality of legally mandated segregation (as James Ely shows so clearly), or passively, by simply pleading exhaustion, declaring the democratic experiment represented by Reconstruction an insolvable problem, and walking away, back to its own problems of empire, monopoly, class conflict, and immigration. For thirty or more years, what was politely known as the South's "domestic affairs"—its systematic racial subjugation of blacks—was no longer a problem to America. But it was, without doubt, a problem to African Americans throughout the country and experienced by those below the Mason-Dixon line with particular harshness. Many blacks campaigned tirelessly for renewed national commitment to America's founding ideas, especially equality before the law. To this the nation cynically turned a deaf ear. So African Americans found their own solutions to Jim Crow's South, first in massive migration out of it and then through organization and nonviolent direct action motivated by a deep desire for racial equality. Their herculean efforts finally began to affect the national conscience during and just after World War II. What was a trickle in 1941, when President Franklin Roosevelt averted a national civil rights march on Washington by establishing the Committee on Fair Employment Practices, became a stream in 1948, when the national Democratic Party added for the first time a civil rights plank to its platform. It was an unstoppable flood by the mid-1950s.

Concerted agitation against white supremacy was again perceived by white southerners to be a problem because it jeopardized decades-old southern practices and institutions. What may be called the "Second Southern Resistance" of the 1950s and 1960s was the white South's solution to this latest manifestation of its American problem. This "solution" was judged unacceptable to the nation, and America, viewing the white South's solution as the nation's new problem, again pressed for and got deep changes within the region during the "Second Reconstruction" of the 1960s.[4] In his essay, Hugh Graham chronicles many of these changes with sensitivity and skill. More recent signs of a white political revolt, now national in scope and centering on opposition to the civil rights agenda of the Democratic Party, indicate, as John Egerton suggests, that neither the South nor the nation has seen the end of this dialectic.[5]

Race is but the most poignant expression of how the South as an American problem became formulated and reformulated almost with each new generation. The region's economic institutions, such as one-crop agriculture and sharecropping, were once thought to be oppressive and impoverishing, a drag on the whole nation. Today, the South's economy is certainly more industrialized than it was a generation or two earlier (the state with one of the largest concentration of manufacturing workers is North Carolina), but it continues to present economic challenges to the rest of the nation. In its efforts to attract industry from overseas and from America's "rust belt," the modern South offers a bundle of economic incentives—governmental subsidies, low wages and taxes, and abiding resistance to labor unions—that are sometimes labeled unfair and thought to wreak economic hardships on businesses and workers in the rest of the nation.[6]

The South's alleged cultural backwardness and fundamentalist Protestant religion were also once understood to be problems because they bred intolerance and suspicion of modernity, creating a blight on what was thought an enlightened and progressive America. They, too, have a contemporary incarnation and meaning, now as threats on a national level to personal liberty and civic and religious pluralism. Although not exclusively southern in geographical location or social base, and eschewing traditional southern racism, the religious right is nonetheless centered in the South and finds its greatest support in the country's southern bible belt. And as it has interjected its cultural agenda into the modern political arena, the fundamentalist impulse, and by implication the South once again, have come to be seen as a problem to the Democratic Party and, more recently and in a very different way, to the Republican Party as well. For at least the last twenty years, Democrats have suffered stunning electoral defeats owing in part to the special antipathy many white southern voters register in protest against an entire bundle of social issues: equal rights for African Americans, women, and gays; abortion, sex education, and prayer in school; and, more generally, the decline of public and private morality and the destruction of what are thought to be traditional family arrangements.[7] The Republican Party, nationally and in particular in the South, has thus far largely benefited from these defections and fears. There are now potent signs, however, that its political alliance with the religious right may cost Republicans, too, electoral support, now from conservative pragmatists who fear the narrowness and purpose of those urging a "Christianized" America. So the dialectic continues: even in what Earl Black and Merle Black have identified as the politically "vital South,"[8] the region continues to present problems for the nation.

Is it possible, our faculty group often mused toward the end of the year, that the South of the 1990s—this seemingly homogenized, urbanized, and "Americanized" New South—could ever again be seen as an American problem? At first glance, that prospect seemed quite unlikely to us. Since World War II the South, for better and for worse, has lost much of what distinguished it as a region and as a distinctive problem. Whether one sees its race relations as having improved markedly or the rest of the nation's racial problems as heightening, for example, the South in either case no longer provides the kind of isolated problem it was thought previously to represent almost uniquely. Similarly, the late arrival of relative prosperity to what pundits began calling the Sunbelt, along with the agonizing economic decline of older industrial regions in the North, has left today's South less distinctive in terms of America's persisting poverty and less responsible for it. Even the century-old national political stigma of being a southerner has been transcended by three southern presidents since the 1960s. Perhaps of greater salience, the waves of popular culture, wherever their geographical origin, seem to ripple across the nation and break down regional peculiarities: New Yorkers dance to country music, Nashvillians eat bagels, and both watched the end of the popular and long-running television show "Cheers" with equal fondness.

It seems, then, that the nation and the region, and the relationship between the two, have been so transmuted in the last fifty years or so that whatever America's problems, they will never again be projected onto the South. But even as we reached apparent consensus on this point, we retreated from it. In grappling with this issue, we began to comprehend more clearly what we had only sensed from the beginning of our discussions. The South was never just a geographical entity or region, a collection of states below the Mason-Dixon line or even those, as the phrase went, "in rebellion" against the Union. Rather, as Joyce Chaplin intimates in her essay, since before there was an American republic, the South has been understood and portrayed mythically and metaphorically. In a way that is no less important for the admitted difficulty we have in articulating it, this mythic and metaphoric "South" transcends geography, history, and social arrangements. The editors of *The Encyclopedia of Southern Culture,* Charles Reagan Wilson and William Ferris, have also said as much: "The South exists as a state of mind both within and beyond its geographic boundaries."[9]

As we explored this theme further, we realized that even our guiding premise was substantially more complex than we first supposed. Americans have historically utilized the South and its problems as a means of defining and implementing their own national values and ideals. In C. Vann Woodward's phrase, the region therefore has served as "an American counterpoint" in the national dialogue about the meaning and purpose of America.[10] The South, we finally concluded, has been an American problem because it became the repository for problems that were really "American" all along and that were only thought to be peculiar to the region and antithetical to mainstream American values. Without pretending to predict the future, it is likely that the renewal of such a definition of the South is yet possible. The necessary raw materials— the current economic trends, cultural conflicts, and political battles we discussed earlier—are with us still, and the region, its present and its possibilities as well as its past, continues to capture more than its share of journalistic and academic attention.[11]

So we return to our final questions—can the South ever again be defined by America as a problem to the nation at large? will it continue to function as an American counterpoint?—in proper academic style: that is, with evasion, qualification, and an appeal to the necessity of definition. And having reached this point, it is obvious that the time has come for us to pass these questions on to others to ponder and answer for themselves.

Notes

1 C. Vann Woodward, *The Burden of Southern History*, rev. ed. (Baton Rouge, 1968).

2 Twelve Southerners, *I'll Take My Stand: The South and the Agrarian Tradition* (New York, 1930).

3 Even a white liberal as committed to racial progress as the Pulitzer Prize–winning newspaper editor Hodding Carter found Reconstruction to be an outrage against the South. Carter, *The Angry Scar: The Story of Reconstruction* (New York, 1959).

4 See C. Vann Woodward, *The Strange Career of Jim Crow* (New York, 1973).

5 Thomas B. Edsall and Mary D. Edsall, *Chain Reaction: The Impact of Race, Rights, and Taxes on American Politics* (New York, 1991); Paul M. Sniderman and Thomas Piazza, *The Scar of Race* (Cambridge, Mass., 1993).

6 James C. Cobb, *The Selling of the South: The Southern Crusade for Industrial Development, 1936–1980* (Baton Rouge, 1982).

7 Edsall and Edsall, *Chain Reaction*. Earl Black and Merle Black, *Politics and Society in the South* (Cambridge, Mass., 1987) and *The Vital South: How Presidents Are Elected* (Cambridge, Mass., 1992).

8 Black and Black, *Vital South*.

9 Charles Reagan Wilson and William Ferris, *The Encyclopedia of Southern Culture* (Chapel Hill, 1989), xv.

10 C. Vann Woodward, *American Counterpoint: Slavery and Racism in the North-South Dialogue* (Boston, 1971).

11 See, for example, the series of four long, thoughtful articles entitled "New South and Old" that appeared in the *New York Times* from July 31 to August 3, 1994. The reporter, Peter Applebome, commented on many of the issues that we have discussed here.

~ Why Was the South a Problem to America?

LARRY J. GRIFFIN

No REGION OF THIS NATION has been more intensively analyzed and inter-preted than the American South. This simple observation is significant to my purpose here because it naturally suggests both an obvious question and a re-lated but somewhat hazy inference. The question is, why has the South been so subjected to such probing scrutiny by friends and foes alike? The infer-ence is that many in and out of the academy have for more than two centuries thought about the South and its relationship to America because they find in those issues something meaningful to themselves and to their times. I return at the essay's conclusion to what I believe that meaning entails.

The answer to the "why" question I just posed and, indeed, the basis of whatever is meaningfully extracted from ruminations about the South might seem, at first glance at least, to rest with the general perception that the re-gion was for so long so discernibly different from the rest of America, "an alien member of the national family," in Fred Hobson's apt phrase.[1] Some-what as the Balkans or Egypt or what was then Siam may have been viewed by travelers a hundred years ago, the South was thought by Americans and foreign visitors alike to be remote, mysterious, possibly even a bit dangerous. Having spent a few years in Alabama during the 1930s, for example, the north-ern journalist Carl Carmer recorded his experiences in a way that perfectly crystallized this view of southern distinctiveness. "The Congo," he wrote, "is not more different from Massachusetts or Kansas or California."[2] One of the region's and country's greatest novelists, William Faulkner, turned such ab-surdities into fine southern sport. In *Intruder in the Dust*, Faulkner's charac-ter, Gavin Stevens, reflects on the North's "gullibility: a volitionless, almost helpless capacity and eagerness to believe anything about the South not even provided it be derogatory but merely bizarre enough and strange enough."[3] Carmer's claim, of course, is literary exaggeration, but the basic sentiment he expressed — that the South is a virtually unknowable "enigma" compelling attempts at interpretation — is nonetheless the meat and potatoes of generations of more thoughtful observers and critics.[4]

Southern distinctiveness, even exceptionalism, was certainly real and potent enough in many of its particulars to justify amply the scholarly and journalistic attention the region received. As sociologist John Shelton Reed remarks in the opening pages of his book *The Enduring South*, almost any facile generalization about the United States could once be easily confounded with a simple "Yes, but not in the South."[5] But the South has been understood by both natives and outsiders as something more than merely different from America, and the region has done more than elicit attempts at interpretation. It has also been celebrated and vilified with a fervor absent from meditations about other sections of this country.

Regional distinctiveness alone, even sectional crankiness, I submit, simply does not summon forth such passionate defenses and zealous condemnations.[6] New England, for example, was for many years portrayed as being importantly different from the remainder of America, as was (and is) the American West, but neither region was so thoroughly feared and censured, on the one hand, and or so unashamedly embraced and sentimentalized, on the other, as was the South. Henry Steele Commager has shed some light on why a "distinctive" New England was never transformed into a "problematic" New England. By the middle of the nineteenth century, he argues,

> New England monopolized the writing of history. Here was a society conscious of its traditions and of its role in creating the American tradition and its responsibility for preserving it; here prosperity had developed a leisure class, Harvard College furnished an intellectual center, a maritime tradition broadened horizons, a relatively homogeneous society gave cultural stability, and slavery did not impose an apologetic or defensive pattern on thought.[7]

Far from being in opposition to the nation, New England, in fact, had the internal resources, cultural hegemony, and moral self-confidence (or perhaps naïveté) to create, to a considerable degree, an image of America in which its own presence and activities were of defining importance. The South tried to do the very same thing, of course, but it failed for reasons explored later in this essay.

Finally, while I know of no systematic study of what may be called "comparative regional autobiography," I am willing to bet that southerners, black and white, lead all other Americans in committing to print the richness and depth of their self-imposed quests to understand and explain their homeland, of their searches for identity and roots, and of their anguish and hopes and despair. Just ponder the wonderfully evocative titles of some of these autobiographies, titles denoting place or color or pain or redemption: *South of Freedom; North toward Home; Born in the Delta; Coming of Age in Mississippi; Separate Pasts; Black Boy; Killers of the Dream; Lay Bare the Heart; The Desegregated Heart; A Season for Justice.*[8] Again, mere regional distinctiveness is, in my opinion, unable to explain such an extraordinary outpouring of brooding introspection.

Why, then, has the South been the subject of so much attention from within and without, be it excusing or damning or sorrowful? The answer, I think, has something to do with the understanding that the South historically has presented a special and troubling problem to American ideals, identity, and practices. An assertion so glibly made should immediately raise a whole host of questions. I will deal with only two here. First, and perhaps most obvious, is the question of how do we know, really *know*, that the South has posed a particular problem for the nation's collective understandings, aspirations, and well-being? Second, why has the South been somehow significantly problematic, not only within but also for the broader culture?

Both questions may appear naive, even self-evident, to those at all familiar with American history, with southern history, and with the interplay between the two. All we need do, some may say, is simply compile a list of what we know of the objective conditions of southern life, and of America's response to those conditions, to see that, and why, we know the South was a problem for the nation.

The South, after all, retained slavery two generations longer than did the rest of the Union and relinquished its "peculiar institution," as historians call it, only after losing a Civil War in which more than 600,000 Americans, north and south, died. Only the South organized itself by law, custom, and force through racial segregation and white supremacy for almost seventy years. In the first half of the twentieth century, the South, more than the rest of the nation, was understood to be economically impoverished: too many of its children, black and white, were uneducated and suffering from hunger, pellagra, hookworm; too many of its adults, white and black, were unskilled and trapped in a vicious cycle of sharecropping, debt peonage, and poverty. Only in the South were conditions of life so brutal and dispiriting that almost ten million of its citizens escaped the region through migration to the North, one of the largest voluntary mass movements of human beings ever witnessed. Only in the South was the use of thousands of U.S. Army troops required to get its public schools and colleges to open their doors to members of a minority race.

The list could be easily lengthened — night riders, chain gangs, the Klan, the closing of public schools to avoid desegregation, violent repression of labor unions — but I believe the point has been made. The South was an *American problem* — and not just a problem for itself — because for two centuries, some would plausibly argue, life in the region was so harsh and so at odds with the nation's self-understandings that America repeatedly had to step in and clean up the messes the South had intentionally or otherwise created. It had to solve the problem of the South, to remove the blight the South created on the broader American cultural and political landscape. So, the argument goes, there is nothing mysterious or difficult to understand about *why* the South was a problem for America.

The Problem South as a Social Construction

There is much to commend this view: the objective facts of the matter do speak for themselves, and they speak quite loudly indeed. That these facts represent exceedingly painful realities, realities that still today beckon much anguish and soul-searching, maybe especially for southerners, is incontestable. But if my academic discipline, sociology, has taught me anything, it is that very few things really are as they appear on the surface and that nothing much is quite so simple. So, baldly put, I do not think that the South was an American problem simply because of the objective conditions of the region or whatever factual discrepancies between region and nation as may have existed.

Stated formally, the objective facts of southern life and culture were necessary conditions of America's "southern problem," but they were not sufficient to induce it. After all, there were surely conditions in the North and in the country more generally that past Americans should have seen or did see as serious problems requiring attention. The inventory is virtually as long and damning as that I excerpted from the register of southern outrages: horrendous, almost genocidal, treatment of Native Americans as a conscious national policy bred of wedding racism to America's expansionist ambitions; deliberate legal and social discrimination against immigrants and ethnic minorities; second-class citizenship of women throughout the entire nation; brutalizing child labor; calculated ghettoization of African Americans and lacerating urban poverty; the violent frontier mentality in what was then the newly opened West. Some of these facts or conditions were, at least for a time, defined and acted on as social problems. But there is an essential difference between the South's "American" experience in this regard and that of other regions. In *An American Dilemma*, Gunnar Myrdal quotes a southern journalist, Edgar Murphy, who wrote just after the turn of the century to this effect: "Too often we find that when our Northern journalism discusses wrongs at the North or at the West, it criticizes the *wrongs,* but when it discusses wrongs at the South, it criticizes the *South.*" Myrdal, agreeing with Murphy, says that "this is a correct observation," adding, however, that "the explanation and, we must add, justification of this fact is, first that the Negro problem actually is a main determinant of all local, regional, and national issues . . . in the South, while this is not true in the North; and, second, that there is a 'Solid South' backing the 'wrongs' in the one region, while opinions are much more diversified in the North."[9] In no other case, I would argue, were social problems so intimately related, even equated, in the public mind to a particular region for so sustained a period of time that the region itself—rather than the objective conditions—became commonly understood as the "real" problem.

What I am saying is that objectively harmful or destructive conditions are not automatically defined to be social problems and that only in the case of the South were conditions equated with problems and problems then equated with region. The widespread perception that an objectively harmful or malignant social condition is a problem requiring public or governmental attention, in fact, is not a matter that is determined solely by consideration of the facts themselves. Rather, the belief that objectively harmful conditions are a salient and pervasive problem results from what is essentially a competitive political process of collective definition. Through this process, some facts, but not others, are imbued with a particular cultural meaning and thereby come to be collectively understood and acted on as social problems amenable to solution.[10]

The process of collective definition in a democratic polity works something like this. Suppose you encounter a condition that offends you or you believe wrong or perhaps harmful to yourself or to others. If the condition is embedded in social institutions, or if it is an accepted and valued part of cultural routines, or if powerful others benefit from its existence, you and your group will be relatively powerless to alter the condition. Therefore to remove or alleviate the offending or harmful condition, you must convince the public at large—or at least a large or an important segment of the public—that the condition is harmful or offensive or morally wrong, that it deserves social and political attention, that it is, in other words, a problem.

To imbue the facts and conditions with meanings that you believe would sway the emotions and actions of influential others, you would in all likelihood use whatever resources you have—access to the media and government officials, money, organizing talent, speaking and writing skills—to persuade the public and the politicians that the condition is a problem and that a solution must and can be found. You would attempt to portray your plight in such a way as to draw on the public's sense of justice and fair play, cultivate its sympathy, invoke its compassion, or speak even to its own self-interest. If your labors are successful, you will get converts who accept the meaning you have given to the facts and thus also begin to define the condition as a problem needing a solution. When enough of you define the condition to be a problem, *and* when you get those with the power to act on that understanding to do something such as pass laws, levy stiff penalties, twist arms, and even use force, finally, then we can say that the condition has been collectively defined to be a problem.

Success at collective problem definition, however, is anything but guaranteed. Persuading others to accept your definition of the situation typically is an expensive and time-consuming process: as I said above, it takes a variety of resources, and if you, the offended group, have few resources, or if you are unable to convince others to use their resources, you are unlikely to get the broader public and government officials to believe as you do. Remember also that there are usually many different conditions that adversely affect many other groups, and each of these groups is trying to do precisely what you are doing—to persuade others that the condition they suffer from or are morally offended by is an important problem worthy of redress. Given that there are limited societal resources with which to define and deal with problems, and almost limitless competition among aggrieved groups for the resources needed for problem definition (whether money or good will or moral outrage or time), some groups will lose, as is the case in any competitive process, and so some conditions will not be defined as serious, significant problems. This is true no matter how objectively harmful the condition because, insofar as the government and a vast majority of the public know and understand, those conditions simply are not problems or, at least, are not as serious as other, more pressing problems. In a word, you would have lost the political contest over the meaning of the facts.

Social conditions therefore become social problems through the expenditure of scarce resources in a competitive political and cultural struggle over the collective definition and meaning of a set of facts. I believe something like this has occurred throughout much of the troubled history of the relationship between the South and the rest of America. The South became an American problem through a political contest over the meaning and importance of the facts of both southernism and Americanism. As the United States, its people and its governing machinery, was pressed by what we call "social problems operators" to somehow "deal with" the South and what were understood to be the problems it created for the nation, Americans advanced a variety of less-than-flattering definitions of the South and its conditions, and the South countered with its own understandings of region and nation. In the course of this struggle both the South and America were importantly, if not exclusively, collectively defined and then acted on in idealized and mythic ways. Most often the South lost this contest in the public square, and in so doing thus became defined as an American problem.

Allow me to avoid possible misunderstanding here: the South undoubtedly supplied America with more than enough ammunition for the nation to make that collective attribution—the painful, even brutal, facts making up much of the region's history and culture. But it was what both the South and America periodically made of those conditions through the political struggle for meaning and definition that led at times to the collective perception that the region was a problem for America, not just the facts themselves. On some level of conscious awareness, this was the meaning of the region most widely accepted and disseminated to influential Americans, including many, no doubt, in the South itself.

So the question shifts from "what are the facts about the South?" to "what is the meaning of these facts?"; that is, to how the facts and thus the South itself were understood and propagated—socially constructed, in sociological parlance—by important members of the polity.[11] This question, in turn, pushes us still further into the realm of collection problem attribution, to the matter of how those influential publics acted on their definitions of the facts. What, then, did the region and the nation make of these facts of southernism and of Americanism? My answer, admittedly speculative, is that in the contestation over the meaning of nation and region the South became defined, sometimes quite strongly, sometimes less so, by southerners and nonsoutherners alike "in opposition" to America and therefore experienced, intimately or vicariously, as something profoundly (if only periodically) "opposite to" the broader culture.

The Oppositional South

To grasp why I claim that the oppositional nature of the South is the source of its definition as an American problem, I must first explain that by the phrase "in opposition to America" I wish to convey both literal and symbolic sectional conflict and an attitude of self-idealized and mythic "oppositeness."

Throughout much of the troubled history of the relationship between the South and America, the region and the nation have literally opposed each other. We have seen such opposition in the arguments on the floor of the U.S. Congress and in the halls of the U.S. Supreme Court from the 1820s to the 1970s; in the statements issuing from southern statehouses and legislatures for at least as long; in the development of the constitutional positions of "nullification" and "interposition," legal maneuvers designed to allow the South to evade federal authority; in the debates over the "free or slave" status of what was then known as the western territories—Missouri in the 1820s and "Bleeding" Kansas in the 1850s. We saw such opposition with exceptional and sorrowful clarity in Gettysburg, Vicksburg, Shiloh, and a thousand other tragic sites in the 1860s. We saw its literal meaning in three essential amendments to the U.S. Constitution and in other legislative acts passed during the Reconstruction period and then, almost a hundred years later, in the Civil Rights and Voting Right Acts of the 1960s. Again, in Montgomery, Little Rock, New Orleans, Ole Miss, Birmingham and dozens of other cities and towns in the 1950s and 1960s, we saw the literal meaning of America and the South in opposition.

We have seen the phrase's symbolic meaning—that is, the opposition of the South to America's self-understandings, if not to its laws and armies—in novels such as *Uncle Tom's Cabin* and in newspapers, lectures, speeches, and pamphlets for a century and a half; in the podiums of antislavery societies in the North and in the pulpits of churches and the classrooms of public schools in the South, where the virtues and necessity of Confederate nationalism and, later, white supremacy were extolled and promulgated; in songs such as Billie Holiday's "Strange Fruit," about a southern lynching, and in Nina Simone's "God Damn Mississippi," the title of which needs no explanation. We saw such symbolic opposition in Dayton, Tennessee, home of the famous Scopes "monkey" trial in 1925, and in the 1948 Democratic National Convention, where for the first time a major political party openly aligned itself with the yearnings of African Americans by adopting a civil rights plank as part of its campaign platform and thereby alienated a generation of white southerners. We see the symbolic meaning of "in opposition to America" even today in South Carolina, Georgia, Alabama, and other southern states, where in 1995 southerners who honor their understanding of the Old South and its traditions oppose other southerners who honor *their* understanding of America and its traditions, a seemingly never-ending battle over the meaning of the Confederate battle flag and other southern symbols. So it is that America and the South periodically have opposed each other in what may be fairly called grievous combat, indeed, sometimes even mortal combat.

The region's oppositional nature arguably extends to the collective historical experiences and self-understandings of southerners. Following the argument of the dean of southern historians, C. Vann Woodward, the history of the South can, in important particulars, be seen as the opposite of that mythologized in the idea of America.[12] Where America was conceived morally pure and innocent, providentially decreed by God to be "a shining city on a hill" and free of the Old World evils of tyranny and class privilege, the South was steeped in sin — guilty of the evils of slavery, of racial segregation, and of violent resistance to the democratization of race relations. Second, according to Woodward, where America was the land of prosperity and plenty, the South was poor, desperately bereft of economic opportunity and economic justice, and publically proclaimed to be the nation's "number one economic problem" by President Franklin Roosevelt in 1938. Woodward's final comparison between nation and region is that where America was victorious in its military quests (until at least the Vietnam War) and for a considerable length of time the global prototype for successful nation building, the South's fleeting attempt at nationhood was a dismal failure, shot down in defeat in the costliest war in terms of American (including southern) casualties this nation has ever fought. The region itself was militarily occupied by a "foreign" power for years (truly a unique event in American history) and politically "reconstructed" from without. In identifying the bases of southern identity in its oppositional history, it is as if Woodward took a photograph of America's idealized self-image and then offered us its negative as the picture of the historical ordeal of the South.

Finally, as historian George Tindall has shown with such insight, we have seen such opposition in the variety and content of the cultural myths southerners and nonsoutherners have jointly created about the South.[13] Myths, at least in this context, should not be understood as erroneous beliefs or delusional understandings. As Henry Nash Smith has argued, myths "exist on a different plane" than that of the empirical fact. They organize and crystallize knowledge about and understandings of their subjects and, in so doing, depict collective representations of culturally significant phenomena, or what the literary critic Mark Schorer has called "controlling images." Because myths fuse "concept and emotion," they also become both analytical devices that help us understand what something is and, implicitly, evaluative and exhortative devices that allow us to judge the "goodness" and "badness" of the mythologized subject.[14] By their very nature—they are formed through selective emphasis, simplification, and generalization—myths can degenerate into distorted cultural stereotypes and even exaggerated caricatures of the mythic entity that can mislead and misinform, even as they motivate and justify human action.

Now what are the myths about the South? Professional South-watchers have for some time collected a whole assortment of mythic ways through which the South has been defined and known. Let me simply extract from that long list several that express the controlling image of the South as a special problem. Fred Hobson has argued that the notion of the South as "benighted" predates the controversy surrounding slavery in the second quarter of the nineteenth century and is older even than the existence of the South as a culturally distinct region.[15] But the first full mythic expression of the oppositional South stems, of course, from the image of the slave South of antebellum times. Because it both so heavily conditioned the content of other myths about the South and functions as the exemplar of the power of myths to shape understanding, it deserves brief elaboration.

Constructed largely by northern abolitionists rightly horrified by the atrocities of slavery, and seen quite clearly by millions of readers of Harriet Beecher Stowe's "little book," this myth portrayed the South to be a land, in George Tindall's words, "of corrupt opulence resting on human exploitation."[16] In the myth of the slave South, we see a system of property ownership in which one race of southerners was exorbitantly rewarded for buying and selling humans of another race and in which black Americans were bred like cattle for the profit of slave masters, their families broken asunder as mothers, fathers, and children were sold into bondage; we see a labor system so brutal that "slackness" and "maligning" were punished by whippings and even death; we see a legal system in which sexual assault on a slave woman by a white man was defined to be "trespass"[17] and which therefore permitted white slave masters virtually unrestricted sexual access to slave women because slave owners could hardly trespass on their own property.

The end of slavery did not mean the demise of the pejorative and unflattering myths constructing, intentionally or otherwise, the South as an American problem. Other such myths rapidly followed: the myths of the poor white trash, "cracker," and redneck South; the myths of white supremacist and demagogic South; and the myths of the savage and benighted and Gothic Souths. The "American Dream," apparently, neither included nor described the South. The list could easily be extended, with each framing the understanding of the South in the same general way: the South is not only different from America but also seriously at odds with it, indeed, its mythic opposite.

The "American" South or the Oppositional South?

Lest my argument be dismissed by accusations of one-sidedness, excessive simplicity, or historical ignorance, I hasten to acknowledge that the relationship between America and the South was substantially more complex than that of opposition only. Indeed, for long stretches of time it seems to have been one of reconciliation, near-harmony, or at least mutual acceptance—the first thirty or so years after the Republic's founding, for example, and then again the period dating from Reconstruction's demise until the 1920s.[18] There are several tragic ironies here. Even as the controversy over slavery was heating up in the 1820s and 1830s, for example, it would have been unthinkable for Americans above or below the Mason-Dixon line to view the South as in any way defined "in opposition to" America. Region was bound to nation by innumerable commonalities: colonial tradition, revolutionary heritage, slavery, language, Protestantism, and political culture (especially the primacy of individual property rights), among others. The South was also integrated into America by a national system of transport, by national markets, and by national political institutions.

The South was not just "American," moreover, it was central to the creation of America. Indeed, in his 1986 presidential address to the Southern History Association, the historian Carl Degler persuasively argued that the America we experience today is the synthesis of North and South.[19] The nation's history, he argues, would have been radically different had the South, as a distinct cultural formation, not existed. Degler catalogs a number of ways in which this is true. Let me add just a few more. A southerner, Thomas Jefferson, authored one of the nation's defining documents, the Declaration of Independence, and another important American symbol known throughout the world, Cola Coca, was invented by an Atlanta druggist, John Pemberton. Southerners occupied the White House for 50 of the first 61 years of America's existence, and the South's most important agricultural crop, cotton, fueled the nation's economic growth and prosperity for decades before the Civil War. The American novel would be sorely impoverished without the more recent contributions of several dozen first-rate southern writers, and American popular music would be unrecognizable or, at least in the form of blues and rock and roll, bluegrass, jazz, and country, nonexistent. America's scorn for things southern, then, clearly has been highly selective. It absorbed and assimilated what it valued and, in so doing, has become a much different and much more interesting America.

The South, therefore, has always been "American" even as it has also been defined in opposition to America. This extends, finally, to identity and assimilation as well. Southerners could hardly have escaped being "American" as well as southern, a point made with special poignancy in a collection of essays edited in 1960 by Charles Sellers. Each chapter in that volume was written by a historian with southern origins, and each agreed, as Sellers puts it, "that the most important fact about the Southerner is that he [*sic*] has been throughout his history also American." The unifying thesis of the book, again in Sellers's words, is that

> [t]he authors believe that the traditional emphasis on the South's differentness and on the conflict between Southernism and Americanism is wrong historically. This distorted historical image, we believe, makes it harder for the South to understand both its Southernism and its Americanism, and hence to escape the defensiveness, prejudice, and belligerence of its regional self-preoccupation, while enriching the national life with many valuable elements of its distinctive regional heritage.[20]

If all of this is true, and I believe much is, what license have I to assert that the South has been defined in opposition to America and thus has consequently been understood to be a problem for America? How can there be both an "American" South, as I use that phrase in this context, and also and at the same time an oppositional South? Does not one negate the other?

I frankly see no necessary contradiction between Degler's or Sellers's claims and the argument I have been developing in this essay. Consider first the message intended by the volume edited by Sellers. That southern-bred historians felt themselves compelled in 1960 publicly to espouse and affirm the essential Americanism of their native region and its people is evidence enough, I think, that the contrary view had widespread currency in important quarters in both the North and South. As I have argued, the real intellectual issue here is not what the South and southerners *really* were (even if such a matter could be determined, which is unlikely within a constructionist view) but rather how the meanings of both (and of "America" and "Americanism" as well) had been constructed, debated, and fought over during periods of conflict between America and the South. Within the theoretical perspective I am using, then, the writing and publication of *The Southerner as American* may thus be seen as yet another salvo in this contestation over meaning and identity, this one issued by dissident southerners.[21]

Consider now another, and equally important, dimension of Degler's argument. His interpretation that the fusion of North and South created the America that we now know is itself premised on interregional conflict and hostility as well as cooperation and complementarity. The Civil War represents the most profound example of how this process worked. The war ended slavery, created the racial "problem" surrounding the place and position of newly freed slaves that still plagues this nation, and led to the Thirteenth, Fourteenth, and Fifteenth Amendments to the U.S. Constitution. Civil War pensions became the prototype federal social insurance program and thus formed America's conception of, and limits to, the modern welfare state, and the war's aftermath solidified and deeply entrenched capitalist economic institutions in the nation's social fabric and mightily fostered its subsequent corporate order.[22]

By forging North and South together in a way previously impossible, the Civil War and the cultural meanings placed on it, finally, politically unified the nation and committed it to the precepts of its founding. In a provocative analysis, Garry Wills argues that Lincoln's Gettysburg Address reinterpreted both the foundation and the future of America. There Lincoln "not only presented the Declaration of Independence in a new light, as a matter of founding law, but put its central proposition, equality, in a newly favored position as a principle of the Constitution." Moreover, according to Wills,

> [w]hat had been a mere theory . . . — that the nation preceded the states, in time and importance — now became a lived reality of the American tradition. The results of this were seen almost at once. Up to the Civil War "the United States" was invariably a plural noun: "The United States are a free country." After Gettysburg it became a singular: "The United States is a free country." This was a result of the whole mode of thinking that Lincoln expressed in his acts as well as his words, making union not only a mystical hope but a constitutional reality.[23]

To return now to Degler's general thesis: simply put, he posits that the North (and thus America) was deflected from its own likely historical trajectory because repeatedly it had to confront and contest an oppositional South. And it was partly but significantly through those clashes — from the constitutional crises surrounding slavery through secession and the Civil War to the modern civil rights movement and its attendant victories and stalemates — that Degler's synthetic America was made and remade.

Indeed, it is the very "Americanism" of the South and the "Americanness" of southerners that created both the need for and the possibility of an oppositional South and thus for the South to be an American problem. Precisely because the region shared so many constitutive principles with the nation, and because the two social formations were so deeply interpenetrated, social conditions and institutions that were essentially "American" in origin, scope, or practice, such as slavery or de facto racial oppression or cultural intolerance, could be and needed to be externalized, expunged from the "real" America and rendered a near-exclusive property of the "opposite other," here, of course, the South. Otherwise, the very idea of America would itself be undermined, delegitimated. If America, in other words, were simply the South writ large, then what Gunnar Myrdal called the "American Creed" — the democratic and Judeo-Christian precepts governing public discourse and cementing all Americans together[24] — would be seen to be not only incomplete or imperfect but also hollow and hypocritical, a lie from its very inception. Likewise, unless the South were subsumed within and under an America that served as the sole repository of things properly "American," there would have been no culturally valid way for the nation to judge the "Americanness" of the South. Even with a decentralized federalism fostering states' rights and discouraging central government interference in the domestic matters of states, America — its laws, creeds, and cultural self-idealizations — thus served in virtually every important respect as the standard against which the South could be, and was, judged, judged and found lacking, found to be oppositional.

Strategies of Problem Formation: The Oppositional South as a Case

Generally, the process of collective definition occurs in what is known as "public arenas" (or sometimes the "public square") — churches, the scientific and popular media, government organs, universities, organized interest groups, and the like — that perform gatekeeping and refereeing functions. Public arenas and institutions select which messages will be disseminated to the broader public, often adjudicate among competing claims and definitions through analysis, commentary, or hearings, and ultimately use their cultural or political authority to further define, promote, and legitimate some conditions as "problems" and delegitimate or redefine others by doing nothing.[25] The meaning of southernism and Americanism was, as I noted above, fought out precisely in such arenas throughout the nation.

What follows is a sampling of the content of the framing of a South in opposition to America, a problem South.

Consider first the controversy over slavery. The most famous abolitionist of them all, William Lloyd Garrison, pictured a "blood-stained" South guilty of "driving women into the field, like beasts, under the lash of the brutal overseer . . . stealing infants . . . trafficking in human flesh." Wendell Phillips, another celebrated abolitionist, described slavery in the South as "a daily system of Hell." Still another suggested that southern society was given to "dissipation, sensuality, brutality, cruelty, and meanness."[26] Slaveholding was understood as "a falsehood in theory; tyranny in practice; a violation of God's law, and a parent of abominations." "[T]he Mark of guilt is upon it."[27] What we see here is a South without valid moral anchoring, driven by cruelty, despotism, and greed.

Now to Reconstruction. Here is the language of the Military Reconstruction Act of 1867:

> [W]hereas no legal State governments or adequate protection for life or property now exists in the rebel States . . . ; and whereas it

is necessary that peace and good order should be enforced in said States until loyalty . . . can be established: Therefore

Be it enacted . . . That said rebel States shall be divided into military districts and made subject to the military authority of the United States.[28]

Listen also to the words of Thaddeus Stevens, an influential Radical Republican in the U.S. House of Representatives, who defined the South in his proposal that plantations be confiscated by the U.S. government and redistributed to the former slaves:

> Reformation *must* be effected; the foundation of their institutions . . . political, municipal and social *must* be broken up and *relaid*. . . . This can only be done by treating and holding them as a conquered people. Then all things which we can desire to do, follow with logical and legitimate authority. As conquered territory Congress would have full power to legislate for them. . . . They would be held in a territorial condition until they are fit to form State Constitutions, republican in fact not in form only, and ask admission into the Union as new States. . . . If their Constitutions are not approved of, they would be sent back, until they have become wise enough to purge their old laws as to eradicate every despotic and revolutionary principle — until they shall have learned to venerate the Declaration of Independence. . . . The whole fabric of southern society *must* be changed. . . . Without this, this Government can never be, as it never has been, a true republic.[29]

What we see here is a South conquered and occupied by its military victor, truly an "un-American" vision. What we see is a South whose social institutions were so abhorrent to America and so antithetical to the fulfillment of America's republican ideals as to require a decade-long experiment in social and political Reconstruction.

I wish to turn now to a discussion of southern culture, or, to put the matter more accurately, to the lack thereof, at least in the eyes of many northerners. During the 1920s, especially, the South was portrayed as ignorant, intolerant, hidebound in its traditionalism, and fearful of ideas, science, change, modernity. No one did more to foster that image than the influential Baltimore newspaperman and essayist H. L. Mencken. In his columns he cataloged and denounced "morons," "hill-billies," "peasants," and the "degraded nonsense which country preachers [were] ramming and hammering into yokel skulls." In reaction to Prohibition, which much of the South supported with zeal, Mencken said it was orchestrated by "Baptist and Methodist barbarians" in the South, adding that "no bolder attempt to set up a theocracy was ever made in the world and none ever had behind it a more implacable fanaticism." On the Scopes trial, Mencken accused the South of wanting "to put down learning by law." [30] Earlier, in his famous essay "The Sahara of the Bozart," he had said,

> [In the South] a poet is as rare as an oboe-player, a dry-point etcher or a metaphysician. It is, indeed, amazing to contemplate so vast a vacuity. One thinks of interstellar spaces, of the colossal reaches of the now mythical ether. . . . [I]t is almost as sterile, artistically, intellectually, culturally, as the Sahara Desert. There are single acres in Europe that house more first-rate men than all the states south of the Potomac. . . . If the whole of the late Confederacy were to be engulfed by a tidal wave tomorrow, the effect upon the civilized minority of men in the world would be little greater than that of a flood on the Yang-tse-kiang. It would be impossible in all history to match so complete a drying-up of a civilization.[31]

What we see here, and see without any varnish, is a South defined by its spiritual and intellectual barrenness, fanatical in its religious fundamentalism, uncivilized in the classic sense of the term.

Now, what of the South's economy? In 1938 a self-proclaimed friend of the region, President Franklin Roosevelt, asked members of the Conference on Economic Conditions in the South to analyze the South's economic plight: "My intimate interest in all that concerns the South . . . proceeds . . . from my conviction that the South presents right now the Nation's No. 1 economic problem—the Nation's problem, not merely the South's. For we have an economic unbalance in the Nation as a whole, due to this very condition of the South." In his letter to the conference, the president further pointed out "the problems presented by the population itself[,] . . . the problems presented by the South's capital resources, and problems growing out of the new industrial era": "There is the problem of labor and employment . . . and the related problem of protecting women and children in the field. There is the problem of farm ownership . . . and of farm income. There are questions of taxation, of education, of housing, and of health." [32]

What we see here from the president of the United States is an economically retarded South, a South dependent on America, a South dragging down America's economy and with it the entire nation. What we see, to be sure, is a problem South.

The context of my final example is the modern civil rights era, and the words come from Martin Luther King's extraordinary "Letter from the Birmingham Jail," written in 1963 to southern church leaders critical of King because his presence in Birmingham allegedly "provoked" violence. In referring to southern African Americans who had militantly, if nonviolently, challenged the South's Jim Crow laws, King said:

> One day the South will know that when these disinherited children of God sat down at lunch counters, they were in reality standing up for what is best in the American dream and for the most sacred values in our Judeo-Christian heritage, thereby bringing our nation back to those great walls of democracy which were dug deep by the founding fathers in their formulation of the Constitution and the Declaration of Independence.[33]

Here we see a South that stands defiant against American ideals, a South in opposition to the nation's founders and to its defining documents.

But both in its rhetoric and in its widely and routinely sanctioned institutional and folk practices, the South—or more precisely, the white, politically conservative South—gave almost as good as it got throughout this cyclical historical process of collective problem definition. It contested the meanings America placed on slavery and freedom by rhetorically constructing slavery to be a positive good for members of both races, to be natural and ordained by God, and to be the bulwark of the freedom and constitutional rights enjoyed by all white Americans. The South created its own myth of the Lost Cause to explain the Civil War as heroic sacrifice and honorific commitment to duty and family. It challenged America's definition of Reconstruction by redefining it to be nothing more than orchestrated villainy, corruption, degeneracy, and political debasement, and it then acted on those understandings by inflaming and unleashing the Klan of the 1870s. It contested America's understanding of white supremacy and condemnation of lynching by creating the myth of white southern womanhood: "pure," the very embodiment of all that was fine and honorable about the Old South, and desperately deserving "protection" from another of the South's mythic creations, the "black beast." The South further defended its position on race by portraying Jim Crow both as necessary for social harmony and as separate, yes, but also equal. It tested America's sense of democratic practice by establishing a one-party South, with the Democratic Party functioning not just as the political party in and of the South but also as the party *for* the white South. It challenged the meaning America placed on southern economic backwardness by blaming America for ruthlessly exploiting the region, deliberately cultivating the South as a dependent "colony." It contested America's definition of the good and civilized and cultured life by creating its own agrarian version of such a life: a harmonious, intensely personal, and religious South grounded by and in touch with nature and the land, obviously superior to the unnatural, dehumanized, money-grubbing industrial North.[34]

The South's cultural distinctiveness and identity, thus, was first forged and then honed by repeated political, legal, cultural, and even military contestation with America and with America's understanding of its own meaning. The making of the South, I submit, has much to do with its opposition to the nation. And it is this quality of the region—the oppositional nature of its very definition and existence—that I believe really lies at the root of why the South historically has been thought to present a special, and at times seemingly intractable, problem to American ideals and identity.

Malcolm X believed in the crucial matter of race that no real differences existed between the South and America. "As far as I am concerned," Malcolm said, "Mississippi is anywhere south of the Canadian border."[35] The experience of America during the last quarter of a century suggests that Malcolm may have been uncannily correct after all. Whether we direct our gaze toward Chicago, or toward New York, or, just yesterday, toward Los Angeles, we seem to see poignant and terrifying reflections of the "South," a South not now, of course, as a tangible place to be located on the map but rather as an image of something opposite to America. Whatever the merits of Malcolm's observations—and I personally believe them more on target than not—America never understood itself to be Mississippi. But, almost unconsciously perhaps, it did seem to understand that it needed Mississippi, and the South more generally, to be the "America" of its own ideals and aspirations. The South, in the final analysis, was an American problem, I believe, because only through wrestling with the nation's darker, contrary impulses and practices—its opposites—could Americans grasp the idea of America and what America might become and then be cajoled and pulled and pushed, however haltingly and however frequent the reversals, toward their own ever higher and deeper definitions of national identity and aspiration.[36]

Notes

I would like to thank Don Doyle, Darren McDaniel, Peggy Thoits, and fellow members of the "South as an American Problem" seminar for their comments. Throughout this essay, I discuss the "South" and "America" as if they were conscious human agents, and, unless my argument requires otherwise, I often present both as if they were seamless entities innocent of internal social conflicts. Usually, anthropomorphizing and homogenizing entire cultures and social formations in this fashion is considered bad social science, an evaluation with which I agree. Both conventions, however, serve useful purposes in this essay. Conflict really did exist between the "South" and "America," for example, and expressing that fact in the way I have chosen (and in the way chosen by Gunnar Myrdal and Martin Luther King in their writing, quoted later) allows me certain stylistic felicities and a form of shorthand that avoids endless repetition and needless elaboration. When I use these two terms, I often have in mind the "average" or "typical" American, African American, or white southerner; occasionally, I mean the "southern white elite." The context of specific passages makes clear, I think, the social group to whom I am implicitly referring.

1 Fred Hobson, *Tell about the South: The Southern Rage to Explain* (Baton Rouge, 1983), 9. Perhaps the most systematic historical study of southern distinctiveness is Carl Degler, *Place over Time: The Continuity of Southern Distinctiveness* (Baton Rouge, 1977). John Shelton Reed's *The Enduring South: Subcultural Persistence in Mass Society* (Chapel Hill, 1986) makes the sociological case for continued southern distinctiveness. See also the collection of essays edited by Kees Gispen, *What Made the South Different?* (Jackson, Miss., 1990).

2 Carl Carmer, *Stars Fell on Alabama* (1934; reprint, New York, 1952), n.p.

3 William Faulkner, *Intruder in the Dust* (New York, 1948), 152.

4 David Potter, "The Enigma of the South," *Yale Review* 51 (October 1961): 142–51. The literature on southern self-exploration is vast. Hobson's *Tell about the South* is a very good treatment of the multiplicity of (often contradictory) ways native southerners explained their region to themselves and to the nation. See also W. J. Cash, *The Mind of the South* (New York, 1941); David Smiley, "The Quest for the Central Theme in Southern History," *South Atlantic Quarterly* 71 (summer 1972): 307–25; George Tindall, *The Ethnic Southerners* (Baton Rouge, 1976), esp. chaps. 1–4; Michael O'Brien, *The Idea of the American South, 1920–1941* (Baltimore, 1979); and Daniel Joseph Singal, *The War Within: From Victorian to Modernist Thought in the South, 1919–1945* (Chapel Hill, 1982).

5 Reed, *Enduring South,* 1.

6 Compare, for example, Howard Zinn, *The Southern Mystique* (New York, 1964), with Richard Weaver, *The Southern Tradition at Bay: A History of Postbellum Thought* (New Rochelle, N.Y., 1968). More visceral denunciations and apologies are presented later.

7 Henry Steele Commager, *The American Mind: An Interpretation of American Thought and*

Character since the 1880s (New Haven, 1950), 284–85. On New England distinctiveness, see also George Pierson, "The Obstinate Concept of New England: A Study in Denudation," *New England Quarterly* 28 (March 1955): 3–17. On the American West, see Henry Nash Smith, *Virgin Land: The American West as Symbol and Myth* (1950; reprint, Cambridge, Mass., 1970).

8　Carl Rowan, *South of Freedom* (New York, 1952); Willie Morris, *North toward Home* (New York, 1967); Margaret Bolsterli, *Born in the Delta: Reflections on the Making of a Southern White Sensibility* (Knoxville, 1991); Anne Moody, *Coming of Age in Mississippi* (New York, 1968); Melton McLaurin, *Separate Pasts: Growing Up White in the Segregated South* (Athens, Ga., 1987); Richard Wright, *Black Boy* (New York, 1945); Lillian Smith, *Killers of the Dream* (New York, 1949); James Farmer, *Lay Bare the Heart: An Autobiography of the Civil Rights Movement* (New York, 1985); Sarah Patton Boyle, *The Desegregated Heart: A Virginian's Stand in the Time of Transition* (New York, 1962); Morris Dees with Steve Fiffer, *A Season for Justice: The Life and Times of Civil Rights Lawyer Morris Dees* (New York, 1991). Some of the autobiographical burdens of southernness are explored in Ruth A. Banes, "Southerners up North: Autobiographical Indications of Southern Ethnicity," in *Perspectives on the American South,* vol. 3, ed. James Cobb and Charles Wilson (New York, 1985), and Bill Berry, ed., *Located Lives: Place and Idea in Southern Autobiography* (Athens, Ga., 1990).

9　Gunnar Myrdal, *An American Dilemma: The Negro Problem and Modern Democracy* (New York, 1944), 45 (emphasis in original). Myrdal thus is himself framing the understanding of the South in a particular way here, as indeed he does for America as well throughout this book.

10　This general view of social problem formation and solution is explored in the sociological literature. See, for example, Richard Fuller and Richard Myers, "The Natural History of a Social Problem," *American Sociological Review* 3 (June 1941): 320–29; Herbert Blumer, "Social Problems as Collective Behavior," *Social Problems* 18 (winter 1971): 298–306; Malcolm Spector and John Kitsuse, "Social Problems: A Re-Formulation," *Social Problems* 21 (fall 1973): 145–59; Steve Woolgar and Dorothy Pawluch, "Ontological Gerrymandering: The Anatomy of Social Problems Explanations," *Social Problems* 32 (February 1985): 214–27; and Stephen Hilgartner and Charles Bosk, "The Rise and Fall of Social Problems: A Public Arenas Model," *American Journal of Sociology* 94 (July 1988): 53–78.

11　The basic sociological reference here—and the parent of the "collective definition" perspective on social problem formation I use in this essay—is Peter Berger and Thomas Luckmann, *The Social Construction of Reality: A Treatise in the Sociology of Knowledge* (New York, 1966).

12　C. Vann Woodward, *The Burden of Southern History,* rev. ed. (Baton Rouge, 1968), especially the first chapter, "The Search for Southern Identity."

13　My discussion of myth is heavily indebted to George Tindall's fine essay "Mythology: A New Frontier in Southern History," in *The Idea of the South: Pursuit of a Central Theme,* ed. Frank Vandiver (Chicago, 1964).

14　Smith, *Virgin Land,* xi, ix. Mark Schorer, "The Necessity of Myth," in *Myth and Mythmaking,* ed. Henry A. Murray (New York, 1960), 355.

15　Fred Hobson, "The Savage South: An Inquiry into the Origins, Endurance, and Presumed Demise of an Image," *Virginia Quarterly Review* 61 (summer 1985): 377–95. In addition to

Hobson and the key contribution by George Tindall referenced above, see Gerald Johnson, "The Horrible South," *Virginia Quarterly Review* 11 (April 1935): 201–17; George Tindall, "The Benighted South: Origins of a Modern Image," *Virginia Quarterly Review* 40 (spring 1964): 281–94; and the collection of essays edited by Patrick Gerster and Nicholas Cords, *Myth and Southern History,* vol. 2, *The New South* (Urbana, Ill., 1989).

16   Tindall, "Mythology," 5.

17   Melton McLaurin, *Celia: A Slave* (Athens, Ga., 1991), 93.

18   This is an old idea linked to but reaching beyond discussions of southern distinctiveness. See, for example, Samuel Mitchell, "The Nationalization of Southern Sentiment," *South Atlantic Quarterly* 7 (April 1908): 107–13; Pat Waters, *The South and the Nation* (New York, 1969), esp. 332–75; and John Egerton, *The Americanization of Dixie, the Southernization of America* (New York, 1974).

19   Carl Degler, "Thesis, Antithesis, Synthesis: The South, the North, and the Nation," *Journal of Southern History* 53 (February 1987): 3–18.

20   Charles Grier Sellers Jr., ed., *The Southerner as American* (Chapel Hill, 1960), v–vi. See also C. Vann Woodward, *American Counterpoint: Slavery and Racism in the North-South Dialogue* (Boston, 1971), who writes quite movingly of both black Americans and the white "Southern-American."

21   The example of *The Southerner as American* raises yet another complication, namely that the South was hardly a unified, undifferentiated whole. White southerners occasionally disagreed among themselves, sometimes violently, about the meaning of the South and the proper relationship between the South and American ideals. See, for example, C. Vann Woodward, *Origins of the New South, 1877–1913* (Baton Rouge, 1951); Lawrence Goodwyn, *Democratic Promise: The Populist Moment in America* (New York, 1976); Morton Sosna, *In Search of the Silent South: Southern Liberals and the Race Issue* (New York, 1977); and Carl Degler, *The Other South: Southern Dissenters in the Nineteenth Century* (Boston, 1982). What is important for my purposes here is not the absence of southern consensus about the meaning of the South, which my argument does not require in any case, nor the presence of southern self-criticism, but rather the existence of political and cultural contestation (whatever its regional locus) that advanced and defended particular images and definitions of both region and nation. This essential point was quickly grasped by David M. Potter. In responding to Sellers's insistence that the American identity worn by white southerners was their "real" identity and the southern identity was "false," Potter flatly stated, "There is abundant evidence that both images have been real." See Potter, *The South and the Sectional Conflict* (Baton Rouge, 1968), 31.

22   On the peculiar American form of welfarism that emanated from the war, see Theda Skocpol, *Protecting Soldiers and Mothers: The Political Origins of Social Policy in the United States* (Cambridge, Mass., 1992). Barrington Moore, *Dictatorship and Democracy: Lord and Peasant in the Making of the Modern World* (Boston, 1966), among others, argues the centrality of the Civil War for the institutionalization of American capitalism.

23   Garry Wills, "The Words That Remade America: Lincoln at Gettysburg," *Atlantic Monthly* (June 1992): 79. James McPherson, among others, has convincingly argued that the Civil War was America's "Second Revolution." See McPherson, *Abraham Lincoln and the Second American Revolution* (New York, 1990).

24   Myrdal, *American Dilemma,* 3–25.

25   Hilgartner and Bosk, "Rise and Fall of Social Problems."

26   Quoted in Hobson, "Savage South," 386.

27   Quoted in William Hesseltine and David Smiley, *The South in American History,* 2d ed. (Englewood Cliffs, N.J., 1960), 155.

28   Quoted in Paul Escott and David Goldfield, eds., *Major Problems in the History of the American South,* vol. 1, *The Old South* (Lexington, Mass., 1990), 561 (emphasis in original).

29   Quoted in Escott and Goldfield, *Major Problems,* 563, 565 (emphasis in original).

30   As quoted by Tindall, "Benighted South," 284, 285, 286.

31   H. L. Mencken, "The Sahara of the Bozart," in *Prejudices: Second Series* (New York, 1920), 136–37. Mencken directed his barbs at a large number of targets, not all of them southern by any means. But, as Tindall has argued ("Benighted South," 284), he seemed to take particular glee in skewering the South.

32   The National Emergency Council, *Report on the Economic Conditions of the South* (Washington, 1938), 1–2. The reaction by southern newspapers and politicians to the report is discussed in Steve Davis, "The South as 'the Nation's No. 1 Economic Problem': The NEC Report of 1938," *Georgia Historical Quarterly* (summer 1978): 119–32.

33   Martin Luther King Jr., "Letter from the Birmingham Jail," in *Why We Can't Wait* (New York, 1964), 94.

34   The references here are numerous. Some of the more important are George M. Fredrickson, *White Supremacy: A Comparative Study in American and South African History* (New York, 1981); Drew Faust Gilpin, *The Creation of Confederate Nationalism: Ideology and Identity in the Civil War South* (Baton Rouge, 1988); Eric Foner, *Reconstruction: America's Unfinished Revolution, 1863–1877* (New York, 1988); Joel Williamson, *A Rage for Order: Black-White Relations in the American South since Emancipation* (New York, 1986); I. A. Newby, *Jim Crow's Defense: Anti-Negro Thought in America, 1900–1930* (Baton Rouge, 1965); Weaver, *Southern Tradition at Bay;* Samuel S. Hill Jr., ed., *Religion and the Solid South* (Nashville, 1972); Earl Black and Merle Black, *Politics and Society in the South* (Cambridge, Mass., 1987); B. B. Kendrick, "The Colonial Status of the South," in *The Pursuit of Southern History: Presidential Addresses of the Southern Historical Association, 1935–1963,* ed. George Tindall (Baton Rouge, 1964); Twelve Southerners, *I'll Take My Stand: The South and the Agrarian Tradition* (New York, 1930).

35   Malcolm X with the assistance of Alex Haley, *The Autobiography of Malcolm X* (New York, 1965), 417.

36   What I am arguing here goes considerably beyond the sort of scapegoating of the South of which the North has often been accused. Projecting the ills of America on the South may relieve the psychological tension and guilt of northerners, but it does little toward developing and linking ideas of region and nation to patterns of associated behaviors that induce actual social change. And I am writing of behavioral and institutional change, not of a psychological mechanism. For an especially poignant expression of the scapegoating thesis, see C. Hugh Hollman, "The Southerner as an American Writer," in Sellers, *Southerner as American,* esp. 199.

∼ How American Is the American South?

DAVID L. CARLTON

There exists among us by ordinary—both North and South—a profound conviction that the South is another land, sharply differentiated from the rest of the American nation, and exhibiting within itself a remarkable homogeneity.
—W. J. Cash, *The Mind of the South*

IN ONE WAY OR ANOTHER, everyone who engages with the American South has to contend sooner or later with the proposition that the region is, at least on some levels, an intellectual construct. Throughout most of its history the South has never had clear or stable boundaries, and much sterile debate about the region's character has arisen out of differences over which places qualify as "southern" and which do not. The only political existence the region has ever had came during its brief fling with nationhood in 1861–65; but the relationship of Confederate to "southern" borders is problematic, to say the least. Moreover, it is a commonplace to acknowledge, with W. J. Cash, that there are and have been "many Souths," displaying a bewildering diversity of local cultures, ethnic, economic, and political.[1]

Nonetheless, all of us concerned with studying the region join Cash in his leap of faith regarding the existence of "one South": the assumption that there is a definable community by that name, one that is distinguishable from the remainder of the United States in significant and salient ways. Of these the most obvious have had to do with race: the southern states of the American Union were those for which Negro slavery was central to both economy and society and that after emancipation preserved white supremacy in its most elaborate American forms. Although peculiar institutions of race relations have generally been seen as basic to the "southern way of life," numerous other traits have also been offered as evidence of southern uniqueness: persistent poverty; the endurance of traditional behaviors, beliefs, and values; a deep political and social conservatism.

Of course, concern with the peculiar characteristics of the American South is hardly original to scholars. As Larry Griffin has shown above, lay understandings, some dating from the eighteenth century, have long seen southern Americans as distinct from other people, notably people from other parts of the United States, in a variety of respects, profound and trivial. My primary concern here, though, is not with the catalog of regionalisms beloved of the popular press and the creators of the *Encyclopedia of Southern Culture* but with the effort to deduce from these distinctions an *essential* "otherness" to the South, a regional character opposed to an "American" character. In other words, I wish to address the contention that the region is, in some fundamental sense, "un-American" — in Howard Zinn's phrase, "a sport, a freak, an inexplicable variant from the national norm[,] . . . a stranger to the nation."[2]

This theme, of the South as an American "Other," has run through a good deal of writing on the region. Its hold is attributable in large part to the influence on the American intellectual tradition of antislavery propaganda, especially in its Republican, free-labor form, which by 1860 was successfully arguing that the southern "slaveocracy," despite its role in bringing the nation into being, was intrinsically hostile to basic American values as defined by the Republican Party and its greatest theoretician, Abraham Lincoln. As Garry Wills and many others have argued, "America" was decisively redefined in the crucible of civil war — but in a way that relegated the slave South, once at the center of national identity, to its margins.[3]

More important, though, this sense of "southern exceptionalism" has arisen from the difficulties of reconciling the regional experience with what up to a few years ago were believed to be the "central themes" of American history. In his classic essay "The Search for Southern Identity," C. Vann Woodward offered a framework for understanding southern history based on three pairs of oppositions: an experience of failure in a land of success, of poverty in a land of abundance, of guilt in a land of innocence.[4] Since that time southern scholars have debated many of his propositions about the South, but they have overwhelmingly accepted his larger presumption: that the standard by which the South is to be judged is set by a unitary "American society," one shaped by a coherent national ideology and made up of citizens possessing a clear "national character."

How that presumption has shaped discourse about the "problem" of the South can be illustrated through reference to my own first encounter, as a college freshman in the mid-1960s, with the discipline of American studies. My introductory course in American studies, focusing on the antebellum period, began by constructing an ideal-typical "model" of American society in the Jacksonian age. According to the model, to be American was to live in a society characterized by political democracy, human equality, social openness, economic expansiveness, and a boundless optimism about the capacity of human beings to bring heaven to earth. Americans were by birthright Lockean in politics and psychology, liberal-capitalist in economics, individualistic in their relationships, placing their ultimate hopes, not in the life of the world to come, but in the incessant improvement of this world. In short, to be American was to be "liberal," to be "progressive," to have the values imputed by the "modernization" theorists of the time to "modern" people and societies.

Then, however, came the monkey wrench: If that is "America," what is the American South? And how does it relate to the larger nation? Partly out of a need to frame the issue for doltish undergraduates, our instructors presented us with two dichotomous solutions to the problem: the "one-culture" hypothesis and the "two-culture" hypothesis. The one-culture hypothesis stated that, peculiarities of slavery and race relations aside, white southerners essentially shared the characteristics and values of other Americans as outlined in the model. They, too, were frontier individualists, devoted to personal liberty, free markets, the single-minded pursuit of profit, and democratic politics (for whites). Was not Andrew Jackson, the "symbol for the age," himself a white slaveholding southerner?

This solution to the problem of fitting the South into a broader conception of "Americanness" was widely popular in the 1950s — and not simply to explain the slave South. Many thinkers of the time were devoted to the notion that there were no deep ideological divisions among Americans, that "consensus" was the central theme of American history, and that the consensus was "liberal." In their view, the South of "massive resistance" to civil rights reform, a reactionary region seemingly in defiance of the nation's deepest purposes, was in fact only a perverted version of the larger American society. Formalized white supremacy had corrupted the basically liberal instincts and institutions of southerners, went the argument; remove it, and southerners themselves would quickly, in Henry Grady's old phrase, "wipe out the place where Mason and Dixon's line used to be." Lockean liberalism, after all, had been inserted into the American canon by Thomas Jefferson and was thus as much "south-ern" as it was "American." Moreover, a later version of liberalism, that of the New Deal, had been broadly popular among southerners. Thus to commenta-tors such as the political scientist V. O. Key, the "conservative" South was an artifact of institutions twisted by racial obsessions; break the hold of white su-premacy, and an interracial alliance of ordinary southerners could join hands with their nonsouthern counterparts to make the New Deal coalition truly hegemonic. Nor would breaking the hold of white supremacy prove that diffi-cult. According to the Swedish sociologist Gunnar Myrdal, white southerners fundamentally accepted the set of values that Myrdal dubbed the "American Creed," values that they affronted with their own racial practices. Ending dis-franchisement, discrimination, and Jim Crow would simply bring southern practice into accord with southern — American — theory.[5]

In the eyes of consensus scholars, even that bedrock of southern "un-Americanness," slavery, was in fact assimilable to "American" values. Kenneth Stampp and Stanley Elkins treated southern slavery essentially as a form of liberal capitalism, an institution that could only resolve the contradiction of bondage in a free society by dehumanizing its victims. To other historians, even that resolution was doomed to failure; liberty-loving white southerners could never rest easily while denying liberty to blacks. Thus Louis Hartz ridi-culed southern proslavery thought as a logically self-contradictory attempt to defend a conservative social order in liberal terms. Because white slave-holders were heirs of Jefferson, argued Stampp, William Freehling, Charles Grier Sellers, and (earlier) W. J. Cash, the contradiction between slavery and the propositions of the Declaration of Independence left them so wrenched with guilt that they may actually have welcomed the end of slavery as a sort of unbought grace. To these historians, the lessons to be drawn from the "travail of slavery" were similar to those offered by Myrdal; by abandoning segre-gation, disfranchisement, and racial discrimination, white southerners would not only be doing the right thing, but they would also bring themselves into line with their own deepest values.[6]

Although the one-culture hypothesis comported with the mood of the con-sensus years of the 1950s, the major alternative, the two-culture hypothesis, gained strength in the 1960s in tandem with emerging intellectual challenges to liberal hegemony. "Two-culture" theorists argued that the antebellum South possessed a social order wholly different from that of the so-called free states, one founded upon precepts fundamentally alien to the liberal-capitalist principles that have historically been regarded as pervading "American" life. Since the 1960s this view has been identified preeminently with Eugene Genovese. Reasoning from the Marxist premise of a fit between a society's relations of production and its larger social organization and values, Genovese argued that the plantation generated a distinctively conservative social order pervaded by patriarchal social relations, for which the association of master and slave was only the model. The classically defined "American national character," then, was utterly foreign to the ruling class of the slave states, whose most thorough-going apologists, indeed, moved to reject "free society" and all its works.[7]

Thanks in large part to the force of Genovese's interpretation, the two-culture hypothesis about the slave South gained enormous popularity in the late 1960s. Since 1970, though, and in the hands of other scholars, it has ranged far beyond traditional concerns with slavery and race to embrace the proposition that the heritage of slavery shaped subsequent southern social development in general, along lines fundamentally different from those pursued by the larger American society. At the root of this broadening is the ambiguous legacy of the civil rights reforms of the 1960s. Whatever the civil rights movement failed to achieve, it was clearly successful at clearing away the old peculiarities in race relations that had in the eyes of consensus theorists disguised the essential liberal values of Thomas Jefferson's South. Not only did blacks gain access to facilities and institutions previously reserved for whites, by the end of the decade the very existence of racially defined institutions had been extinguished. New laws broke the informal color bars that had kept blacks out of all but the most humble jobs. Blacks were enfranchised, in the process helping to bring multiparty politics to the region for the first time since the 1890s. The heady rush of racial and political change, along with the economic buoyancy given the region by 1960s prosperity, seemed to suggest that the sole remaining obstacles to full southern integration into national life had been removed.[8]

What in fact happened was somewhat different. To be sure, southern racial patterns did become largely "Americanized" as institutionalized color bars collapsed and as, more sadly, racial issues took center stage in localities over the nation—a process John Egerton has termed "the southernization of America."[9] More important, though, it became quickly apparent that the hopes of earlier commentators—that southern politics would become more liberal, and southern economic and social life more progressive, once the institutional rigidities of race ceased to inhibit southerners' freedom of action—were not quite going to pan out. Although southern politics in the 1970s and

1980s have displayed far more fluidity than at any time since the nineteenth century, they have also shown signs of hardening into a new, racially polarized pattern, with the white majority lining up behind a Republican Party that is sometimes harshly right wing and paradoxically devoted to all the traditional symbols of southern white culture, from Southern Baptist piety to the Confederate flag. Public policy has continued to run in its old channels, resistant to public welfare spending, tilting toward business on labor and environmental issues, unwilling to alter regressive tax systems. While politicians have fiddled, the ancient problems of the South have burned on. High infant mortality, educational disadvantage, and economic insecurity have continued to plague southern lives; despite the drumbeating for the "Sunbelt," southern economic convergence with the remainder of the country, apart from certain pockets and fringes, has since 1973 slowed significantly.[10]

With these developments, an air of pessimism overtook a good many liberal and left intellectuals, both within and without the region, and led them to take a new look at the faith of such liberals as Sellers in the South's "Americanness." Still wedded to the notion that "liberal" values (though whether Lockean or New Deal is not always clear) are "American" values, they tended to regard the failure of the South to become more "progressive," in their sense, as evidence of a far more basic "un-Americanism" than they hitherto recognized. Noting in 1975 that the collapse of disfranchisement and single-party monopoly had failed to produce a "populist," interest-based southern politics, Numan V. Bartley and Hugh Davis Graham said of the South that "history seems to have placed a peculiar kind of hex on her, not as an immutable curse but as a pernicious source of devilment that confounds our more rational and optimistic predictions and masks deeply rooted continuity behind the symptoms of basic change." If to Bartley and Graham political reform ultimately failed to root out the worst aspects of southern distinctiveness, the fruits of urbanization proved equally frustrating to David R. Goldfield. According to Goldfield, social science theories depicting the city as an autonomous force engendering "modern" thinking in its inhabitants were confounded by the failure of the urban South to create a new society of secular, liberal southerners. "The prophecies have foundered," he contended, "because they assumed that Southern cities were distinct from their region. They were—and are—not."[11]

So, if commentators of the 1950s and 1960s had seen the South as an *American* place, one set apart by social and institutional peculiarities correctable through social tinkering or the inexorable progress of "modernization," those of the 1970s and 1980s increasingly saw the *region* as an autonomous entity, successfully resisting dissolution in unexpected ways crying out for explanation. Many historians and other social scientists began to seek that explanation in some sort of two-culture hypothesis. Of those available, Genovese's formulation of the slave regime's otherness seemed the most promising, for understanding not only the antebellum South but also the postemancipation South and even the contemporary South. This approach, to be sure, posed problems. Genovese's vision of the Old South rested firmly on the foundation of slavery, which had been destroyed in 1865; how could the superstructure erected on that base survive its destruction? The answer, as developed by a number of historians and other social scientists, was that although slavery was destroyed, the slaveholding class was not; rather, it carried its fundamentally conservative, patriarchal, and antimodern views into the postbellum years, and through its continued domination of land, capital, and political power it continued to fasten a traditional, authoritarian regime on the masses of the southern people. This argument was reinforced by the application to the South of Barrington Moore's notion of multiple "roads" to the modern world. According to Moore, the traditional elites of certain premodern societies, feeling themselves threatened by the rising liberal industrial powers of the North Atlantic, began in the late nineteenth century to "modernize" themselves, but with the difference that the process remained firmly under the control of the old elite and indeed was driven not by the flexible dynamism of a liberal society but by forced mobilization. Such societies, Moore argued, would tend toward fascism, rather than democracy, in their politics and would favor repressive forms of social organization.[12]

This was a formulation, it would appear, that could explain the enduring problems of the modern South. It was especially attractive in that it shifted the basis of southern "un-Americanness" from its no-longer-peculiar racial patterns to its larger culture and social organization. The poverty and powerlessness of so much of the southern population, black and white, were thus reinterpreted as products, not of racism, but of a pattern of class repression. Despite the abolition of slavery, the argument went, the landless in the countryside were not truly free; the systematic use of debt peonage tied them to the land, inhibiting both their geographical and their social mobility.[13] The poor records of southern state governments in spending on education was attributable to "upper-class" desires to keep the masses ignorant, docile, and cheap. The lack of economic opportunity persistently characteristic of the region was likewise an upper-class product. According to Jonathan Wiener, for instance, the ruling planter elite of Alabama opposed efforts to develop Birmingham, seeing the new industrialists as a threat to their control over labor. Where industrialization did occur, local elites deliberately pursued low-wage forms of industrialization and, to maintain their control, kept high-wage or unionized industry out. Industrial relations were patriarchal in nature, with cotton mill villages, lumber camps, and the like serving to extend the plantation system into industrial life. Finally, the aspirations of southern workers were squelched by an openly repressive use of the state against labor organization. Thus, while the non-South was following the "classic path" to the modern world through the cultivation of a free and open economic and social life, eventually moving in the New Deal era to create a political economy devoted to expanding the purchasing power of the masses, the South was creating a repressive social order enforcing poverty, deprivation, and powerlessness upon the bulk of its inhabitants.[14]

At first glance this argument appears to illuminate a great many of the darker corners of southern history. If to be "American" is to conceive of oneself and one's society as endowed with boundless opportunity for both material and social advancement, the South has persistently refused to follow the script. But does that refusal say more about the South or about the script? Is it really conceptually tenable to speak of "the South" as a place apart from "America"? Is it, indeed, conceptually tenable to speak of an "America" from which the South clearly diverges?

The newer assertions of southern otherness, I would argue, fail to confront these issues with any real rigor. To begin with, they selectively ignore the numerous ways in which standards and values commonly deemed "American" apply across regional boundaries. Most obvious, the South's society has been critically shaped by its status as a constituent region of the larger American polity. As such it has shared national legal, political, economic, and voluntary institutions with other parts of the country. Moreover, thanks to the outcome of the Civil War, not only was slavery abolished through federal force and constitutional amendment, but a uniform standard of citizenship was established by the Fourteenth Amendment. While the federal government was loath to interfere in the internal affairs of southern states after the end of Reconstruction, it retained an interest in maintaining some semblance of the "free-labor" society for which Union soldiers had fought and died.[15]

As a result, the best evidence we have indicates, black laborers, while hardly independent, did enjoy at least rudimentary freedom in the postbellum South. Agricultural workers moved about frequently, despite attempts by landlords to constrain their movements. The most striking manifestation of this freedom was the so-called great migration of blacks (and many whites as well) to the industrial North beginning about the time of World War I. While such flagrant abuses of power as debt peonage have been all too common in the South, these have been far from unique to the region; a government report in 1911 dealing with immigrant peonage found similarly widespread abuses in the non-South, and in more recent times the state most productive of peonage cases has been California. Peonage, indeed, can probably be best understood as an *American* practice, appearing wherever employers face problems of labor supply and readily bullied minority populations are available.[16]

Nor does the "un-Americanness" of southern industrial relations bear up too well under scrutiny. Despite W. J. Cash's characterization of southern cotton mill villages as "industrial plantations," mill workers were neither slaves nor any other sort of truly forced labor; they moved about quite freely and maintained a strong political voice. While village organization certainly had its paternalistic features, moreover, again that was hardly peculiar to Dixie, as the proliferating studies of northern textile communities in recent years attest. Rather, the peculiar combination of economic and political authority that we term "paternalism" seems to be a response by entrepreneurs (and workers) to problems frequently arising at an early stage of development of certain industries (notably textiles), problems of mobilizing, training, and retaining scarce labor while conserving scarce capital. Like peonage, such problems, and the devices used to deal with them, were particularly widespread in the South, but they were also common to the yarn mills of southern New England, the lumber camps of the upper Midwest, and the town of Pullman, Illinois.[17]

If the social base on which postbellum and modern southern society was erected displays at least somewhat recognizably "liberal" American characteristics (and "American" society recognizably "illiberal" ones), so has the ideological superstructure erected above it. As we have seen, white southerners had inserted the notion of natural rights into the Declaration of Independence and had been largely responsible for giving them legal force through the Bill of Rights. Antebellum white southerners defended their right to hold human property with arguments drawn largely from Locke and the Founding Fathers; George Fitzhugh's reactionary theorizing was far less important to their thinking than were appeals to states' rights and the Fifth Amendment.

With slavery's end the ideological allegiances of white southerners became even clearer. The "conservatism" of the modern southern elite has been not the conservatism of an aristocracy preserving traditional special privileges but the conservatism of laissez-faire, and its language that of natural rights and liberties. States' rights and the rights of individuals to choose their associates — such was the language used to defend segregation in the 1950s and 1960s. Such also has been the basic vocabulary with which white southerners have understood their broader social relationships. How this is so can especially be seen in the area of southern labor relations; however inequitable they may be in operation, their ideological underpinnings are thoroughly grounded in the philosophy of "natural rights." Antiunion legislation is couched in terms of the "right to work"; southern workers are lauded for their "individualism" when they shun unions and replaced in the name of "freedom of contract" when they do not.[18]

To be sure, notions of "aristocratic" privilege crop up frequently enough in southern life, especially with respect to white-black relations but occasionally in supercilious behavior toward poor whites as well. It has always been a well-nigh impossible proposition, though, for even the most paternalistic mill owner or local grandee to subordinate fellow whites in the same way that he might blacks. Since the eighteenth century whites have formed the majority of the southern population, and the males among them have insisted on recognition as equal members of the southern herrenvolk — in James Oakes's term, the "ruling race." The modern southern political order emerged from Reconstruction drenched with hostility to special privilege and devoted to (white male) democracy. After about 1900 disfranchisement and the rise of the one-party system compromised white democracy, but even during that period any would-be leader had to make some obeisance to white sentiment. The critical power of the common whites has historically been a major reason why the most self-conscious conservatives have persistently sought to evoke "individual liberties" in defense even of special privilege.[19]

If there is no bedrock southern hostility to classically liberal concepts of individual liberty, nor is there any particularly sustained antagonism to progressive change. The southern Agrarians' crusade against "progress," after all, was frustrated as much by the indifference or hostility of their compatriots as it was by Yankee ascendancy.[20] Over the last hundred years the South has industrialized at a faster rate than has the rest of the country. "Planter hegemony" notwithstanding, the region has developed a vigorous middle class, not simply in the Atlantas and Nashvilles but in the Gastonias as well, eager to pursue, in C. Vann Woodward's phrase, "the alien gods of mass and speed." Middle-class interests, furthermore, have extended in the twentieth century to government as well, particularly to the use of the state to mobilize investment in infrastructure and public education. Southerners have certainly been selective about change, as evidenced by repeated legislative assaults on Darwinian theory; but in this regard they are scarcely different from many of the other subcultures that make up the American mosaic.[21]

This last proposition points to what seems to me to be the more serious weakness in most arguments opposing "the South" to "America": their assumption of a unitary, classically liberal, "American" standard from which the South deviates. At this point the problem of the South intersects with a problem that for most of the past generation has plagued American studies in general, the discrediting of the older liberal consensus about the character of American life. Our understanding of our common country has become increasingly pluralistic, as blacks, women, and numerous other ethnic and minority groups have advanced their claims on our attention and forced major reassessments of such "American" themes as equality and opportunity.[22] Furthermore, those who have reinterpreted our national ideological roots in terms of republicanism have suggested that at its origins our national character was not inevitably classically liberal but was rather an unstable compound of liberal and conservative, individualistic and communal, optimistic and pessimistic, and that these tendencies have played off each other in American history up to the present day.[23] Along with these developments has come a dissolution of our old understandings about the basic beliefs of Americans. A generation of diligent social and labor historians has unearthed evidence of nonbourgeois social forms and resistance to the blandishments of modern liberal capitalism in the northern countryside, in small towns, and among working-class ethnic communities.[24] The ethnocultural obsessions and restrictive practices of southern politics now look less curious in the context of a generation of research into the history of American political institutions and behavior.[25] Industrial capitalism itself we see now as growing out of premodern social forms and values. Thus the forms of repression and paternalism that we find in southern labor relations look less unique than we formerly thought, and the Yankee entrepreneurs described, for instance, in Robert Dalzell's recent work on the Boston Associates look less like Schumpeterian "creative destroyers" than like cautious men backing into the future.[26]

So, one could argue that to be southern is, in a profound sense, to *be* American, that, in fact, to be a fragment in a bewildering mosaic of communities is the true essence of Americanism. This approach has underlain a more moderate solution to the problem of explaining continuing southern distinctiveness, in which white southerners, along with blacks, are understood using the typology of American ethnic groups. This line of reasoning was introduced in 1970 by the sociologist Lewis Killian, in a study dealing with "hillbilly" migrants to Chicago, and has since been advanced in numerous writings by the sociologist John Shelton Reed and his historian colleague at the University of North Carolina, George Tindall.[27] In their hands, southern distinctiveness becomes a mild phenomenon, having to do not with fundamental differences in outlook but with relative propensities, with statistically significant variations from the nonsouthern norm. It can be objected here that they continue to play an old southern game, namely, comparing a region called "the South," with certain reasonably coherent qualities, with a region called the "non-South," with little or no coherence whatever, indeed not really a "region" at all. Nonetheless, the ethnic approach does provide a way to understand the South as part of a vast, patchwork America, the components of which have been loath to allow their particularities to be eaten away by the corrosions of a liberal-capitalist order.

But *is* the South, all told, just one ethnic community among many? There are problems here. First, of course, the South itself contains two ethnic communities, white and black, along with other, burgeoning groups in Florida and the Southwest. Moreover, it receives numerous immigrants, many of whom assimilate with an ease that belies the particularistic implications of ethnicity.[28] Most important, though, and most troubling, is the peculiar relationship of white southerners to the nation's history. Unlike most other ethnic groups, white southerners were present at the creation of the nation; indeed, it was in large part their creation. White southerners helped provide its ideological underpinnings, established much of its fundamental law, and provided its first great unifying symbol in George Washington. Later, Andrew Jackson and Henry Clay helped lead in the creation of modern mass party politics, and southern political leaders have ever since, with some lapses, been fully integrated into national political leadership. Even that most "un-American" of southern institutions, its "peculiar institution" of slavery, was as late as the 1850s arguably as much an "American" as a "southern" institution and was so understood by the likes of William Lloyd Garrison and Frederick Douglass.[29]

One could conclude from the central position of white southerners in pre–Civil War America, as some commentators have done, that the white southerner is the quintessential American; certainly this is the view of the average modern southern white, whose well-known hypernationalism is strongly tied to just such an identification of "America" with Dixie. To draw that conclusion would be fundamentally wrong, but the paradox of the South as the "most American and the least American of sections" does point to a unique feature of the southern experience: that, beginning as one of the core communities of the Republic, it came to be *defined* as a peripheral subculture in the course of subsequent history.

Thus the construction of the South as an idea has been intimately related to the reconstruction of the American idea over time. For if the notion of a unitary American culture has become more problematic to us, our difficulty is attributable not simply to the increasing racial and ethnic diversity of the American people but also to a historical experience that reshaped the society that brought them together. If there is a core to the American experience, we can only understand it by taking account of how a nation founded by and for a rather exclusive group of settlers from northwest Europe, in which racial slavery, patriarchy, and natural-rights philosophy existed in uncomfortable symbiosis, could become the polyglot, contentious, freewheeling arena we claim today as our common country. In coming to grips with that transformation, the story of how the South became exiled to the American periphery contains important clues.

Critical to that story, of course, was the slavery issue and its increasing expression in sectional conflict through the first half of the nineteenth century. Political abolitionists and Republicans (plus independent critics such as Frederick Law Olmsted) made antislavery a force to be reckoned with by constructing a broad-ranging political, economic, and social indictment of the "slave power," declaring the South to be in the thrall of a backward oligarchy seeking to extend its malign sway over the free states as well. Only with secession, civil war, and the stumbling process by which the Union cause came to be identified with emancipation, though, did freedom truly come to be national and slavery sectional, and in very short order slavery came to be extinguished even in the South. White supremacy survived, to be sure, but as C. Vann Woodward long ago pointed out, the differences in racial attitudes between North and South were, even in the heyday of Jim Crow, as much differences of degree as of kind.[30]

In sum, I would suggest that the heritage of the sectional conflict alone would scarcely have left the South permanently defined as "deviant." Rather, while the political-military conflict was raging, the social-economic character of the nation was being quietly but profoundly redefined in a way that effectively sequestered the land of Jefferson, Madison, and Calhoun as a separate cultural community. The agents of this transformation were the institutions of American business culture. To be sure, the roots of that culture lay in the ideology of the American Revolution, as embodied in the Declaration of Independence, the Constitution, and the developing body of American law. But, as Gordon Wood has recently argued, the flood of entrepreneurial energies released by the Revolution quickly swamped the embankments that the Founders had hoped would channel them to serve their utopian ends. Like a rampaging torrent, American enterprise proceeded to carve new channels for itself in the nineteenth century, in the process remaking the bucolic, hierarchically structured landscape of 1800 into the urban, perpetually unsettled and changing one in which we now live. It was business that devalued revolutionary concerns with virtue and corruption, business that exalted in their stead concerns for individualism and self-interest. To the Founders, freedom of speech and freedom of religion were means to civic ends; to American business culture, the need to accommodate workers and customers of increasingly diverse values, along with the relentless pressure to break social conventions that restricted the introduction of new products and advertising, made these freedoms into private possessions and tolerance and self-fulfillment the supreme values. In the process, it subjected all traditional constraints, of religion, of social convention, of community cohesion, to relentless corrosion—to "the acids of modernity."[31]

But not altogether. While crucially shaping the core institutions and values of modern America, the nation's business culture also created and nurtured an extensive and variegated periphery. Immigrants participated as individuals in the arenas of modern urban culture, even as they formed premodern "urban villages" and perpetuated among themselves the faiths of Sicily and the Pale. Steelmakers erected monuments to modernity in midwestern valleys while gathering about them communities of pious Slavs who dutifully funneled their children into the mills. Above all for our purposes, as the channels of American enterprise shifted, the South became simultaneously integrated into the new national culture and in important respects isolated from it. As entrepreneurs remade American geography, they effectively (if unintentionally) sequestered the South from the full impact of the most dynamic features of American life while, in a number of subtle ways, reinforcing the region's most traditional characteristics. That process, as much as the Republican Party and the Union Army, has defined the South as an American subculture rather than *the* American culture.

The workings of that process, and its implications for the South and the nation, are complex, and any short explication can at best be sketchy; but the following brief historical account will, I hope, be suggestive. The decisive development was the rise of a vigorous and many-sided entrepreneurial culture in the late-eighteenth-century urban Northeast. Plantation slave agriculture, the dominance of which effectively distinguished the "northern" from the "southern" colonies of British North America, was itself an enormously successful form of business enterprise in prerevolutionary times, but that very success encouraged in the South the development of highly specialized institutions of economic life, institutions that in turn engendered a certain entrepreneurial complacency. While southerners were content to reproduce proven techniques on new ground, in an economic version of the Jeffersonians' vision of an indefinitely self-replicating republic, urban northern businessmen, faced with pressing problems resulting from shifting markets and international dislocations, began exploring new options, opening up new markets in the West and extending operations into new sectors, such as manufacturing.[32]

By the mid-nineteenth century, the South and the North (including the Midwest) had begun to develop separate sets of economic institutions. While the entrepôt cities of the plantation belt had stagnated, constrained by limited opportunities and a business climate lacking in entrepreneurial urgency, a series of diverse industrial city-regions had formed across what geographers would later dub the American manufacturing belt, concentrating entrepreneurial and technological skills into critical masses producing chain reactions of expansive development. The relative vigor of entrepreneurial life in the two regions was also reflected in the relative pace of economic integration, as seen most clearly in the respective regional railroad systems. On the eve of the Civil War the free states had the makings of a coherent rail system clearly oriented along an east-west axis, following the lines of westward migration; by contrast, the southern rail system, isolated at all points from the northern, was singularly lacking in internal articulation. When it finally gained a coherent structure, in the postbellum years, it would direct the flow of traffic largely to the north, with telling consequences.[33]

Once the slave system had received its death blows in the Civil War, the South found itself in the classic position of a latecomer to modern economic development and had to build a new set of business institutions from scratch. Unfortunately, it found itself now not only poor but incorporated into an economy that, like the railroads, was arranged along a northeast-northwest axis. Encouraged by the strategic interests of the great trunk lines, goods and services, people and ideas, traveled on cheap long-haul rates between East and West. Thus the South found itself isolated from many of the invigorating currents that were shaping the modern business culture of the nation. Entrepreneurs migrated west, not south, carrying with them both their expertise and their business connections back east; so did immigrant workers.[34]

Beside this ever swelling current of creativity the South was but a minor eddy. Few outside entrepreneurs ventured south; my own research on industrialists in the Carolinas indicates that the vast majority were native born. More important, these indigenous entrepreneurs, while hardly lacking in entrepreneurial *mentalité*, were men of narrow, chiefly mercantile, experience, without the kinds of mechanical or organizational skills that were transforming the American industrial order elsewhere. The South did indeed begin to industrialize at this time, but chiefly by appropriating technologies, such as those of the cotton textile industry, that had already been fully developed in the North and were thus easily transferred to a "backward" region. Such an industrialization could easily assimilate itself to the traditional character of the southern workforce, just as New England mills such as Amoskeag accommodated the cultures of their immigrant hands; thus it permitted the development of an industrial culture that needed relatively little of the flexibility and dynamism that were remaking American society elsewhere. It could not, on the other hand, do much to stimulate innovation or a strong expansion of economic opportunity. Studies of regional variations in inventiveness suggest, in fact, that as the South industrialized, it became distinctively *uninventive* relative to its manufacturing base.[35]

The region's inability to spin off new products and create new industries, in turn, limited opportunities in commerce. Like other urban centers on the periphery of the industrial core, southern cities served largely entrepôt functions and were limited by the capacity of their hinterlands to generate trade. Postemancipation changes in the character of southern agriculture, along with the beginnings of industrialization, expanded commercial opportunities and fostered strong urban growth as cities drew ambitious migrants from the

southern countryside. But the capacity of postbellum cities to generate development was limited by their commercial character and by the subjection of
urban destinies to the strategic concerns of metropolitan railroads and finan-
ciers. Moreover, even the most vibrant southern cities were lacking in the economic diversity of the great northern industrial centers. Immigrants, whether
from Europe or from elsewhere in the nation, stayed away. For all its energy,
the southern urban middle class remained provincial, comfortable in its prejudices, resentful of outside domination.[36]

Not only did the east-west orientation of American business culture inhibit people and ideas from going south, it inhibited northward movement as
well. As David Potter has pointed out, among the major factors producing the
North-South differential in railroad freight rates was a desire on the part of
the great rail systems of the manufacturing belt, comprising what was called
Official Territory, to encourage long hauls on their trunk lines; traffic enter-
ing their track from the South, on the other hand, was primarily unappealing
short-haul traffic.[37] More subtle was the phenomenon recently explored by
Gavin Wright, the existence until well into this century of a separate southern
labor market. Despite the presence of a huge reservoir of cheap labor, black
and white, virtually in their back yard, northern manufacturers filled their expanding needs for unskilled and semiskilled labor primarily from across the
Atlantic. Only during and after World War I did they seriously begin to exploit
southern labor sources, and they never exploited them to their full potential. Why this was so remains unclear. While some stress the role of peonage
in tying southern laborers to the land, as we have seen above peonage was a
weak form of systematic labor control, unable to prevent out-migration when
opportunity beckoned; moreover, it can hardly explain the parallel isolation
of southern white mountain folk. Nor can it be explained as a choice by southerners; black migration movements, most famously the "Exoduster" colonization of Kansas in the 1870s, were endemic in the post-Reconstruction South,
and when the choice to migrate became less costly in the twentieth century,
it became a live option. Wright's own explanation I find most plausible: the
social process of migration carved specific channels for itself that were only
altered under extraordinary circumstances. As we know, migration has typically followed a chainlike pattern, with firstcomers assisting new arrivals in the
process of adjustment; moreover, employers have found these chains useful as
informal means of screening workers and maintaining discipline in the workplace. As the North entered its great age of industrial expansion in the late

nineteenth century, its labor flows came to be defined along east-west, not north-south, lines and thereafter resisted change until the European war immigration disrupted the traditional flows. Thus migration flows carved channels that left southerners in a backwater; the consequence was to reinforce a "folkish" isolation among blacks and poor whites, while assuring their employers and landlords a stable labor pool that could be exploited in traditional ways, without indulging in the labor-saving innovation that was transforming the workplace elsewhere. As a result, as late as the eve of World War II, the rural South could still be plausibly characterized as a "folk" society.[38]

The above discussion admittedly only begins to explore the argument I wish to make. I offer it here because I think it suggestive of the ways in which the emerging business culture of the United States, even while including the South in a national culture and economy, served to define the region as a distinctive cultural community, one with a decidedly ambivalent relationship to the "core" and its values. That isolation, to be sure, has broken down significantly within the past half century. The abolition of freight rate differentials and, more important, the development of interstate highways and airline service have dramatically improved southern access to national markets. The increasing domination of American manufacturing by national and international corporations has created a branch-plant economy that has largely eliminated entrepreneurial and technological barriers to southern industrialization. A complex of events has breached the walls separating southern and nonsouthern labor markets. A more powerful federal government has imposed national standards of race relations and politics on a region long exceptional in both respects and, especially with its military bases, has itself become a major southern branch-plant industry. Postwar prosperity, along with a revolution in the countryside, has expanded cities and attracted new waves of immigrants from outside the region. Finally, by underwriting a sharp expansion of education, prosperity has created critical masses of (a new thing in the South) urban cosmopolitan *southerners*, clustering in major cities, university towns, and high-tech regions such as North Carolina's Research Triangle. The "American" values of equality, tolerance, and the primacy of individual ambition and personal fulfillment over social solidarity and eternal verities — these run rampant in the modern South as never before.[39]

Nonetheless, the heritage of having been a separate community dies hard and, if John Shelton Reed is correct, may even be self-perpetuating.[40] Although southerners have made some signal contributions to American business

(Camel and Lucky Strike cigarettes, Holiday Inn and Piggly Wiggly, Coca-Cola and Shoney's), they have generally done so in a context defined elsewhere, with results that have shaped the southern community in peculiar ways. Its Research Triangles notwithstanding, the region's population is not on the cutting edge of innovation, generally being content to take the relatively undemanding, if in the global economy increasingly uncertain, jobs offered by technologically mature industries.[41] Despite the expansion of educational institutions and of an educated class, schooling remains relatively little valued; one economist has suggested that, insofar as the contemporary southern economy can be treated as a unit, it is because southerners as a group are poorly educated even by current American standards.[42] The isolation of the southern community, finally, has left it perhaps the most "folkish" of major American subcultures, a heritage that historian David Potter some years ago nominated as the true "central theme" of southern history.[43]

None of these qualities, to be sure, is necessarily unique to the South. All over the United States one can find communities of similar sorts, in Mormon Utah, in the Hispanic Southwest, in the rural Midwest, and in the ethnic communities of smokestack America. As we now know from the work of social historians, the institutions and values of the modern age (and I have argued here that the old liberal synthesis about "American character" essentially identified it with a "modern" ideal type) not only can coexist with more traditional forms but can actually find them useful. The business institutions that have done so much to create modern America have thus often found it worth their while to foster traditional ways of life, especially among their workers, as a means of minimizing one of their more important sources of risk. The mill workers of early-twentieth-century Amoskeag, and the "urban villagers" of Boston and Chicago, can thus be said, mutatis mutandis, to resemble southerners both in their ambivalent relationship to the modernity that surrounds them and in their fundamental dependence on it. Much of the tension and conflict that pervade modern American life, moreover, can be said to stem from the constant pressure to renegotiate that relationship, as issues from abortion to affirmative action to the North American Free Trade Agreement constantly remind us that the peace between America's diverse subcultures and the single culture tying it together is ever an uneasy one.[44]

If southerners, then, as C. Vann Woodward once argued, have been the great naysayers to the various American myths of progress, of the fresh start, of the imperial self, they have not been the only ones by any means. If the South, in the end, can be called American, it is not because it conforms to an ideal-typical vision of a "liberal" American society. Rather, it is American because its people share with many other Americans, working-class, ethnic, and minority, a common experience, of making their way in a world that they have not fully made and to which they give at best ambivalent assent.

Moreover, one need hardly be a member of a regional, racial, or ethnic minority to feel that "American" ideals, in their exaltation of the individual over all claims of community, of tradition, of obligation, estrange individuals not only from their compatriots but also from themselves. If, as I've argued, "American" identity consists of both a "core" culture and a congeries of "peripheral" ones, it can also be argued that even the most cosmopolitan of us use those subcultures to provide ourselves with emotional anchors in the boisterous sea of American liberty, and that it is precisely our "will to believe" in them that gives them their continuing power over us. I have contended here that the South has legitimate historical claims to being a subculture apart from the mainstream, but in large part it continues to exist for southerners, and for other Americans as well, because we need it to exist. The historical dialogue between the idea of "the South" and the idea of "America" has had a real impact on the lives of millions, but it has also rendered mythically an American psyche at war with itself, a war within that continues to trouble the internal peace of our souls.[45]

Notes

1   W. J. Cash, *The Mind of the South* (New York, 1941), vii-viii. A penetrating, witty, and unsettling view of "the idea of the South" is Michael O'Brien, *The Idea of the American South, 1920-1941* (Baltimore, 1979), esp. 3-27, 213-27.

2   Howard Zinn, *The Southern Mystique* (New York, 1964), 217.

3   Garry Wills, *Lincoln at Gettysburg: The Words That Remade America* (New York, 1992). For a discussion of the "free-labor" indictment of the South, see Eric Foner, *Free Soil, Free Labor, Free Men: The Ideology of the Republican Party before the Civil War* (New York, 1970), 40-72.

4   C. Vann Woodward, "The Search for Southern Identity," in *The Burden of Southern History* (Baton Rouge, 1960), 3-25.

5   V. O. Key, *Southern Politics in State and Nation* (New York, 1949), 664-75; Gunnar Myrdal, *An American Dilemma: The Negro Problem and Modern Democracy* (New York, 1944), esp. 3-25, 458-62. David Southern argues that Myrdal's influence has progressively declined as the notion of a unitary, idealistic "American Creed" has come under assault; see his *Gunnar Myrdal and Black-White Relations: The Use and Abuse of "An American Dilemma," 1944-1969* (Baton Rouge, 1987).

6   Kenneth M. Stampp, *The Peculiar Institution: Slavery in the Antebellum South* (New York, 1956); idem, "The Southern Road to Appomattox," in *The Imperiled Union: Essays on the Background of the Civil War* (New York, 1980), 246–69 (a paper originally delivered in 1968); Stanley Elkins, *Slavery: A Problem in American Institutional and Intellectual Life,* 3d ed., rev. (Chicago, 1976), pt. 2; Louis Hartz, *The Liberal Tradition in America: An Interpretation of American Political Thought since the Revolution* (New York, 1955), 145–200; William Freehling, *Prelude to Civil War: The Nullification Controversy in South Carolina, 1816–1836* (New York, 1965), 49–86; Charles Grier Sellers Jr., "The Travail of Slavery," in *The Southerner as American,* ed. Charles Grier Sellers Jr. (Chapel Hill, 1960), 40–71; Cash, *Mind of the South,* 62–63.

7   Eugene D. Genovese, *The Political Economy of Slavery* (New York, 1965); idem, *The World the Slaveholders Made: Two Essays in Interpretation* (New York, 1969).

8   Such was certainly the expectation of such commentators on southern politics as V. O. Key. See *Southern Politics in State and Nation.*

9   John Egerton, *The Americanization of Dixie: The Southernization of America* (New York, 1974), 1–25. Egerton's position, though, was anticipated in 1964 by Howard Zinn, who espoused a darker version of the one-culture argument. The South, he proclaimed, was a "mirror" of the nation, the projected image of a disfigured society that refused to admit the truth about itself. See Zinn, *Southern Mystique,* esp. 217–63.

10 Earle Black and Merle Black, *Politics and Society in the South* (Cambridge, Mass., 1987); James C. Cobb, "Beyond Planters and Industrialists: A New Perspective on the New South," *Journal of Southern History* 54 (February 1988): 45–68; Bruce J. Schulman, *From Cotton Belt to Sunbelt: Federal Policy, Economic Development, and the Transformation of the South, 1938–1980* (New York, 1991). For a journalistic discussion of the paradoxes of the contemporary South, see Peter Applebome's four-part series entitled "New South and Old" in the *New York Times,* July 31–August 3, 1994.

11 Numan V. Bartley and Hugh Davis Graham, *Southern Politics and the Second Reconstruction* (Baltimore, 1975), 184–200; David R. Goldfield, "The Urban South: A Regional Framework," *American Historical Review* 86 (December 1981): 1009–34.

12 Barrington Moore Jr., *Social Origins of Dictatorship and Democracy: Lord and Peasant in the Making of the Modern World* (Boston, 1966).

13 Pete Daniel, *The Shadow of Slavery: Peonage in the South, 1901–1969* (Urbana, Ill., 1972).

14 Jonathan M. Wiener, *Social Origins of the New South: Alabama, 1860–1885* (Baton Rouge, 1978), esp. 137–85; Cobb, "Beyond Planters and Industrialists"; James C. Cobb, *Industrialization and Southern Society, 1877–1984* (Lexington, Ky., 1984); Dwight B. Billings Jr., *Planters and the Making of a "New South": Class, Politics, and Development in North Carolina, 1865–1900* (Chapel Hill, 1978); Philip J. Wood, *Southern Capitalism: The Political Economy of North Carolina, 1880–1980* (Durham, N.C., 1986).

15 Steven Hahn, "Class and State in Postemancipation Societies: Southern Planters in Comparative Perspective," *American Historical Review* 95 (February 1990): 75–98.

16 Gavin Wright, *Old South, New South: Revolutions in the Southern Economy since 1865* (New York, 1986), esp. 64–66; William Cohen, *At Freedom's Edge: Black Mobility and the Southern White Quest for Racial Control, 1861–1915* (Baton Rouge, 1991); Daniel, *Shadow of Slavery,* 107, 189.

17   The notion of southern cotton mill villages as "industrial plantations" was introduced by
     Cash in *Mind of the South,* 205-7. For an expanded version of the above argument, see
     David L. Carlton, "Paternalism and Southern Textile Labor: A Historiographical View," in
     *Race, Class, and Community in Southern Labor History: Selected Papers, Seventh Southern
     Labor Studies Conference, 1991,* ed. Gary M. Fink and Merle E. Reed (University, Ala., 1994),
     17-26. See also Philip Scranton, "Varieties of Paternalism: Industrial Structures and the Social
     Relations of Production in American Textiles," *American Quarterly* 36 (summer 1984): 235-57.

18   On the "liberal" proslavery argument, see James Oakes, *Slavery and Freedom: An Interpreta-
     tion of the Old South* (New York, 1990), 56-78; on segregationist thought, see, for instance,
     W. D. Workman, *The Case for the South* (New York, 1960). On labor relations, see Carlton,
     "Paternalism."

19   Oakes, *Slavery and Freedom,* 127-36; James Oakes, *The Ruling Race: A History of American
     Slaveholders* (New York, 1982); J. Mills Thornton, *Politics and Power in a Slave Society: Ala-
     bama, 1800-1860* (Baton Rouge, 1978); Lacy K. Ford Jr., *Origins of Southern Radicalism: The
     South Carolina Upcountry, 1800-1860* (New York, 1988); Michael Perman, *The Road to Re-
     demption: Southern Politics, 1869-1879* (Baton Rouge, 1984); David L. Carlton, *Mill and Town
     in South Carolina, 1880-1920* (Baton Rouge, 1982).

20   See Paul K. Conkin, *The Southern Agrarians* (Knoxville, 1988).

21   Wright, *Old South, New South,* 60-64; Carlton, *Mill and Town,* esp. 13-39; Don H. Doyle,
     New Men, New Cities, New South: Atlanta, Nashville, Charleston, Mobile, 1860-1900 (Chapel
     Hill, 1990); George Brown Tindall, "Business Progressivism: Southern Politics in the 1920s,"
     in *The Ethnic Southerners* (Baton Rouge, 1976). The Woodward quote is from C. Vann Wood-
     ward, *Origins of the New South, 1877-1913* (Baton Rouge, 1951), 124.

22   For instance, see Edmund S. Morgan, *American Slavery, American Freedom: The Ordeal of
     Colonial Virginia* (New York, 1975).

23   For two recent, broad-ranging syntheses, see Gordon S. Wood, *The Radicalism of the Ameri-
     can Revolution* (New York, 1992), and Charles Grier Sellers Jr., *The Market Revolution: Jack-
     sonian America, 1815-1846* (New York, 1991).

24   Herbert G. Gutman, *Work, Culture, and Society in Industrializing America* (New York, 1976);
     Steven Hahn and Jonathan Prude, eds., *The Countryside in the Age of Capitalist Transforma-
     tion: Essays in the Social History of Rural America* (Chapel Hill, 1985).

25   Walter Dean Burnham noted early the parallels between political disfranchisement in the
     South and moves elsewhere to "purify" politics. See *Critical Elections and the Mainsprings of
     American Politics* (New York, 1970), 78-80.

26   Carlton, "Paternalism"; Scranton, "Varieties of Paternalism"; Robert F. Dalzell Jr., *Enterpris-
     ing Elite: The Boston Associates and the World They Made* (Cambridge, Mass., 1987).

27   Lewis Killian, *White Southerners* (New York, 1970); John Shelton Reed, *The Enduring South:
     Subcultural Persistence in Mass Society* (Lexington, Mass., 1972); idem, *One South: An Ethnic
     Approach to Regional Culture* (Baton Rouge, 1982); George Brown Tindall, "Beyond the Main-
     stream: The Ethnic Southerners," in *Ethnic Southerners,* 1-21.

28   John Shelton Reed, "The South's Mid-life Crisis," in *My Tears Spoiled My Aim and Other Re-
     flections on Southern Culture* (Columbia, Mo., 1993), 42-53, qualifies his earlier embrace of
     the "ethnic" model.

29   Morgan, *American Slavery, American Freedom.* On abolitionist attitudes toward America, see,

for instance, James Brewer Stewart, *Holy Warriors: The Abolitionists and American Slavery* (New York, 1976), 33–73, and Frederick Douglass's oration "What to the Slave Is the Fourth of July?" in *The Frederick Douglass Papers,* ed. John W. Blassingame, ser. 1, vol. 2 (New Haven, 1982), 359–88.

30 Foner, *Free Soil, Free Labor, Free Men;* C. Vann Woodward, *The Strange Career of Jim Crow,* 3d rev. ed. (New York, 1974).

31 This analysis draws on a number of sources, including two wide-ranging interpretations of American history: Wood, *Radicalism of the American Revolution,* and Christopher Lasch, *The True and Only Heaven: Progress and Its Critics* (New York, 1991), notably his comments on the connection between capitalism and modern American culture on 518–22.

32 This paragraph owes a great deal to the suggestions of Thomas Doerflinger in *A Vigorous Spirit of Enterprise: Merchants and Economic Development in Revolutionary Philadelphia* (New York, 1986), 344–64; see also Peter A. Coclanis, *The Shadow of a Dream: Economic Life and Death in the South Carolina Low Country, 1670–1920* (New York, 1989), and David F. Weiman, "Staple Crops and Slave Plantations: Alternative Perspectives on Regional Development in the Antebellum Cotton South," in *Agriculture and National Development: Views on the Nineteenth Century,* ed. Lou Ferleger (Ames, Iowa, 1990), 119–61.

33 Diane Lindstrom, *Economic Development in the Philadelphia Region, 1810–1850* (New York, 1978); David R. Meyer, "Emergence of the American Manufacturing Belt: An Interpretation," *Journal of Historical Geography* 9 (April 1983): 145–74; idem, "The Industrial Retardation of Southern Cities, 1860–1880," *Explorations in Economic History* 25 (October 1988): 366–86; David L. Carlton, "Urbanization," in *Encyclopedia of the Confederacy* (New York, 1993), 4:1641–48; George Rogers Taylor and Irene D. Neu, *The American Railroad Network, 1861–1890* (Cambridge, Mass., 1956).

34 On the prominence of migrants, frequently with outside connections, in midwestern manufacturing, see Donald L. Kemmerer, "Financing Illinois Industry, 1830–1890," *Bulletin of the Business Historical Society* 26 (June 1953): 97–111.

35 The foregoing paragraph is largely based on the author's research in progress. Apart from *Mill and Town,* 40–81, the principal published statements to date are David L. Carlton, "The Revolution from Above: The National Market and the Beginnings of Industrialization in North Carolina," *Journal of American History* 87 (September 1990): 445–75, and David L. Carlton and Peter A. Coclanis, "Capital Mobilization and Southern Industry: The Case of the Carolina Piedmont," *Journal of Economic History* 49 (March 1989): 73–94. On the developing southern lag in inventiveness, see Robert Higgs, "American Inventiveness, 1870–1920," *Journal of Political Economy* 79 (May–June 1971): 661–67, and David L. Carlton and Peter A. Coclanis, "The Uninventive South? A Quantitative Look at Region and American Inventiveness," *Technology and Culture* 36 (April 1995): 220–44.

36 Goldfield, *Cotton Fields and Skyscrapers: Southern City and Region, 1607–1980* (Baton Rouge, 1982) overstates the case. Doyle, *New Men, New Cities,* shows how entrepreneurial vigor could vary among southern cities, with old coastal ports, especially, declining in the postbellum years while interior towns expanded. The fiction of the southern writer Peter Taylor captures with richness and subtlety the complex mixture of modernity and provincialism characteristic of the elites of even the more successful of southern cities.

37 David M. Potter, "The Historical Development of Eastern-Southern Freight-Rate Relation-

ships," *Law and Contemporary Problems* 12 (summer 1947): 416–48, esp. 442.

38 Wright, *Old South, New South,* 64–80.

39 Wright, *Old South, New South,* 239–74; Mancur Olsen, "The South Will Fall Again: The South as Leader and Laggard in Economic Growth," *Southern Economic Journal* 49 (April 1983): 916–32; Schulman, *From Cotton Belt to Sunbelt;* David R. Goldfield, *Promised Land: The South since 1945* (Arlington Heights, Ill., 1987).

40 John Shelton Reed, *Southerners: The Social Psychology of Sectionalism* (Chapel Hill, 1983).

41 Cobb, "Beyond Planters and Industrialists," 66–68; Barry Bluestone and Bennett Harrison noted in 1982 that, "Sunbelt" talk notwithstanding, southern plants were slightly *more* vulnerable to plant closing than northern. Barry Bluestone and Bennett Harrison, *The Deindustrialization of America* (New York, 1982), 9–10. On the impact of chronic insecurity on southern textile workers, see Jeffrey Leiter, Michael D. Shulman, and Rhonda Zingraff, eds., *Hanging by a Thread: Social Change in Southern Textiles* (Ithaca, N.Y., 1991).

42 Timothy Bartik, remarks on panel discussion, Vanderbilt Alumni Reunion, 1988, reprinted in Fay Wirth Renardson, "Is There a Southern Ascendancy? Reflections on a Century-Old Question," *Vanderbilt Magazine* 73 (fall 1988): 7–13; Bartik's comment appears on p. 8.

43 David M. Potter, "The Enigma of the South," in *The South and the Sectional Conflict* (Baton Rouge, 1968), 3–16.

44 Tamara K. Hareven, *Family Time and Industrial Time* (Cambridge, Eng., 1982); Herbert J. Gans, *The Urban Villagers: Group and Class in the Life of Italian-Americans* (Glencoe, Ill., 1962). For one consequence of this ambivalence, see James Davison Hunter, *Culture Wars: The Struggle to Define America* (New York, 1991).

45 For an example of how estrangement from modernity worked to create the regionalist movement of the early twentieth century, see Robert L. Dorman, *Revolt of the Provinces: The Regionalist Movement in America, 1920–1945* (Chapel Hill, 1993). A different (and somewhat less angst-ridden) discussion of the formation of regional identity appears in Reed, *Southerners.*

∼ Climate and Southern Pessimism: The Natural History of an Idea, 1500–1800

JOYCE E. CHAPLIN

CLIMATE HAS LONG HAD A powerful and negative role within the historiography on the American South. So seemingly preeminent was climate's influence that Ulrich Bonnell Phillips opened his *Life and Labor in the Old South* (1951) with the command: "Let us begin by discussing the weather, for that has been the chief agency in making the South distinctive." The weather was a given, an independent variable that, Phillips claimed, led to staple-crop agriculture, thence to slavery, thence to the sectional controversy and the "race problem" that are the central features of southern history. If scholars have identified the South as a problem for American history and society, the region's problematic status has seemed to rely on a physical, that is, real or tangible, basis in irrefutable meteorological data.[1] Though Phillips and many subsequent scholars have identified the South as a problem by beginning with the weather, they have rarely begun at the chronological beginning, that is, with the history of the English colonies that later formed the states of the South. An examination of early Anglo-American attitudes about nature in the southern colonies (from the earliest English exploration and colonization in the late 1500s through the beginnings of the independent Republic in the late 1700s) demonstrates how southern climate was not then perceived as the powerful, independent variable it would become within antebellum historiography. Rather, contemporaries believed that nearly any American climate, north and south, could make its region distinctive, and they maintained that human character and agency could nevertheless prevent any climate from being or creating a problem.

Most studies of southern distinctiveness pay little attention to the colonial period, or they present decontextualized evidence from this era in order to

explain the antebellum or postbellum eras. There is, therefore, little understanding of how a language that critically assessed the southern climate took
shape before the antebellum period. And this itself is a problem, because if the
southern climate *was* an overarching force, it should have been so from the
outset of English settlement. Unless climate seemed to have effects during
the colonial period that were roughly similar to its later powers — that is, that
climate made the region not only distinctive but endowed with intractable and
unwelcome cultural practices — it would be difficult to stand by a contention
that climate was a material power that stood above the human culture of the
southern region and shaped it for the worse, made it a problem.

The Distinctive South/The Problem South

Was the negative effect (or perceived negative effect) of climate roughly continuous from the colonial period onward? Let me answer the question by
moving backward, from the most recent era back toward the settlement of the
southern colonies. The late nineteenth and twentieth centuries have yielded
empirical and quantifiable evidence for the effects of southern climate; this
is the case with studies of productivity under warm conditions and of the
way in which the existence of air-conditioning has been coterminous with the
emergence of a more economically and culturally vigorous new South. Such
evidence is not abundant for the earlier part of the nineteenth century; scholars therefore interpret subjective statements on the part of contemporaries to
imply that physical conditions in the antebellum South were discouraging or
debilitating. By uniting the two kinds of study (empirical and subjective) for
the entire modern period of southern history, scholars have established cultural studies of the "lazy South": a place where climate held power over person
and personality, where a long growing season and summertime heat promoted
agricultural wealth alongside illness and lassitude — the latter especially in eras
before air-conditioning. Climate induced a kind of fatalistic acceptance, evident in contemporary statements, that a hot and fevered environment had ill
effects on humans. The key assumption is, therefore, that verbal expressions of
despair over the southern climate were early, albeit nonquantifiable, evidence
of what science would later claim about hot climates.[2]

These statements may, however, have been parts of a construction of an
idea of southern distinctiveness that did not necessarily prove any southern
debility or backwardness. Some scholars have indicated that southerners had

ambivalent (that is, not consistently negative) opinions about their climate; furthermore, southerners were clearly ambivalent about one of the most empirically verifiable aspects of their climate, endemic disease. Thus, residents of parts of the South that had yellow fever (such as New Orleans and Charleston) were remarkably sanguine about their prospects for survival, blaming high mortality rates on unassimilated visitors. In addition, southern doctors who emphasized the distinctiveness of their practice may have been as much interested in their professional advancement — as investigators into or practitioners of a specialized form of medicine — as in defining genuine and practical differences between northern and southern forms of therapy.[3]

The ambivalence over climate's effects in the southern colonies is even more apparent. To be sure, some studies have emphasized the role of disease in the colonial South as a debilitating factor in early settlement. Historians of the seventeenth-century Chesapeake have asserted that a warm climate fostered diseases such as typhoid and malaria, that such maladies guaranteed frequent mortality, and that the resulting demographic disaster initially weakened family and community life in the region. In a similar way, economic studies have identified southern climate as the comparative advantage that encouraged investment in land and labor, which resulted in commercial agriculture and slavery. But other scholars have pointed out that colonists' interpretations of the climate and its consequences (such as disease) are as important in understanding the early South as the physical conditions themselves. Such a balanced view follows recent warnings that the study of climate's impact on human culture must include the cultural meanings ascribed to the climate.[4]

This is the balance that the cultural studies of a problematic South have yet to achieve and that this essay attempts. I wish foremost to establish a balance in the assessment of contemporary statements made about climate in the southern colonies. There has been some attention to the negative statements, which privileges them as the last word on the subject, as evidence of fear of warm climates and apprehension of the questionable behaviors that characterized people who lived in hot places. But many opinions were voiced about climate in the early South, generally agreeing that climate played a role in making the region distinctive but not concluding that its distinctiveness was a problem. Both visitors to the region and residents contributed to this debate. I have elsewhere pointed out that travelers' accounts of the South should be interpreted very carefully;[5] in this essay I focus on the assessments of whites who settled in or were born into the southern colonies or states.

Residents of the southern colonies did not assume that climate made their region a problem for three main reasons. First, not just heat but any extreme of climate—including coldness—was held to be dangerous. Second, contemporaries believed that, despite the dangers of any extreme climate, hot environments still had the advantage over colder ones because they offered greater potential for vegetal and mineral wealth. Third, and most important, settlers believed it the duty of humans to resist and rise above the ill effects of material surroundings, whether induced by heat, cold, damp, or aridity; they did not assume that the relationship between climate and humanity was unidirectional and inescapable. What is remarkable is, rather, how they felt they should be able to modify climate's effects on them, although they were dogged by the fear that they might not always prove their mastery over climatic forces.

If fatalism is a *conviction* that humans are weak, the position of early white southerners in relation to climate was, accordingly, not fatalistic. Their stance instead reflected pessimism, a *fear* of human weakness. Early southerners' pessimism showed itself in fear that, while some individuals might rise above the deleterious effects of southern climate, others would prove unequal to the task. Over the course of the period of English settlement in America, whites even deepened their pessimism. They moved away from a hope that humans might control nature toward a view of humanity that emphasized possible human damage to the natural order. In their darkest moments, whites even suspected that they might have ill effects on the climate, which would then, in turn, hurl newly worsened forces back at them. Especially in relation to activities they once had assumed would improve their material surroundings (cutting timber or cultivating the soil, for instance), whites now feared that these actions would affect the climate in ways more harmful than beneficial.

This position had little concern for the natural environment itself, unlike contemporary ecological views. Southerners focused on humanity rather than on nature. They used nature to explain themselves; the physical world was a testing ground for human ability and character. Given this ambivalent stance, it would be foolish to claim that southerners never despaired over their warm climate and its negative effects on them—especially climate-related disease and death. But such gloom was not always present, nor does it fully explain attitudes toward climate, which must be placed within the full context of attitudes toward nature. The concepts that early southerners used to make sense of their physical atmosphere were common property in the early modern era and explained regional distinctions generally, not specifically in the southern portion of North America. Comparable assessments of climate and its relation to humans could be found in New England. Furthermore, inhabitants of one southern colony might insist that their province's climate differed from that of others.

In short, early southern ideas of climate explain a distinct southern identity only in the way that every other colonial region expressed its distinctive character. There was, as yet, no South that used climate to argue for its larger regional identity, nor was there always a sense that climate could make southerners as a group unique. A specific, southern climate was not yet the problem—universal, corrupted human nature was. Southerners had simply inherited, along with everyone else, a post-Adamic duty to struggle with and rise above natural forces. While this early criticism of settlers was possibly an ancestor of the later rhetoric that shamed southerners for their climatically induced backwardness, it was nevertheless a critique that took as its target the universal characteristics of humanity, not the parochial characteristics of a geographical region.[6] Early white southerners were rarely resigned in the face of natural forces and insisted that there was a dynamic relation between specific place and person, an insistence that revealed a pessimistic view of human nature, one that eventually admitted how climatic changes were due as much to human action as to natural influences.

Early Attitudes toward American Climates

The concept of a "South as an American problem" would have been unfathomable to colonists of English-speaking America. If the problematic South (in full flower by the nineteenth century) represented a struggle for cultural definition between North and South—or between America and the South—any comparable struggle in the colonial period took place between the Old World and the New. To Europeans, that is, America seemed "southern" all over: it was an alien place with exotic phenomena that appeared to threaten a culture (western Europe) that was the standard. Any attempt to make sense of English assessment of southern climates must place this assessment within the argument of the Old World versus the New, of England versus America. English opinion of the southern regions of North America fell into two phases. First, the English formed their initial perceptions about the New World in terms of the extremes in its climate, an extremity that was both a real phenomenon and a shorthand way of denoting the difference between England and America.

Second, English settlers articulated specific understandings of the various portions of America that they settled; by the mid-1600s, therefore, colonists of the Virginia province began to explore the meaning of their immediate environment, a process later replicated in Maryland, the Carolinas, and Georgia.

Anglo-southern interpretation of climate depended on assumptions derived from the European understanding of nature: that humans existed in synchrony with their climate, that America posed challenging extremes of climate, but that warm zones of the New World were especially worth braving because their heat generated wealth. Central to the Europeans' interpretation of nature was the assumption that human populations—like plants and animals—were adapted to their various native climates. It was this view of connection between humanity and nature that formed the background to all thought about climate. This interpretation first explained the tasks all New World settlers would face and was only later significant in defining the southern region as climatically distinctive.

This essay cannot give an exhaustive analysis of early modern views of nature, but some summary in terms of climate is in order. From the sixteenth century through the eighteenth, climate had two meanings, one much narrower than the current definition, the other far more inclusive of natural phenomena. The word was most often a synonym for latitude: a climate was a zone described by its latitudinal position on the globe. (Thomas Jefferson punned on this meaning when, in his *Notes on the State of Virginia* [1785], he opened the section on climate with the words "under the latitude of this query.") One sixteenth-century text specified that each "Climate" varied from the equinoctial by thirty minutes, a measure that yielded approximately twenty-one parallels in each half of the globe. Each latitude had certain attributes because of its relation to the sun and planets above.[7]

To some extent, the idea of latitude encompassed a straightforward atmospheric or meteorological conception of climate that would now be familiar. But early modern ideas about nature tended to disdain explanations that were simple, stressing instead how all material phenomena were linked in complicated patterns: latitude affected temperature and moisture, which stimulated plant life and diseases, which then had effects on humans who ate the plants or got the diseases—effects that were tangentially related to climatic influences. Accordingly, the English used the word *climate* in a second way, to explain a network of natural forces within a geographically defined zone; a climate could mean a topographical microcosm affected not only by its latitudinal position but also by local influences such as distance from a seashore, presence or absence of urban centers, or geographical elevation. Here the influence of the Hippocratic text *Airs, Waters, Places* was paramount in early modern interpretation of geographical location and the resulting condition of human bodies. One sixteenth-century work of natural philosophy thus discussed how the "Clymate and Parallele" of a place said much about its "waters" and "windes," as well as "mannes helth" and "maners." In this second definition, in which climate simultaneously meant latitude, region, and environment, the word had already acquired the vague and metaphorical meaning that facilitated its use as a describer for other contexts—for example, climates of opinion.[8]

One European view of climate was clear: a fear of extremes, of both heat and cold. Apprehension of hot climates had a long European history. Hot zones were associated with fevers, swamps, deserts, poisonous serpents, predatory animals, and barbaric peoples. The modern sense that tropical and subtropical zones teem with microbes, vermin, and incivility is undoubtedly unfair but hardly new. These attitudes drew on classical assessments of hot places like Persia and Egypt; such opinions were then applied to America and enjoyed a long life there.[9]

Lingering suspicions about warmer zones in America were improvements, at least, on an earlier and enduring prejudice about the torrid zones, that they could not be populated by humans but instead remained deserts inhabited by wild and baneful beasts. Classical philosophy, especially as conveyed by Saint Augustine's glosses on ancient learning, had held that the regions around the equator were too hot to sustain human life and that the antipodes were similarly desolate of people. Europeans were therefore astonished when reports from Magellan's voyage around the southern tip of the New World insisted that the southern regions were inhabited. Classical learning about the globe soon became risible, both because the ancients had not known about America and because they had not even understood the known world's anatomy and characteristics. Richard Eden, the earliest English translator of continental European texts that described America (including Antonio Pigafetta's 1526 account of Magellan's expedition), conveyed Sebastian Munster's influential opinion that Ptolemy, the ancient world's foremost geographer, "knew nothing of *America*." In the English translation of Jose de Acosta's 1590 history of America, the English could read the definitive truth: "[C]ontrarie to the antient and received Philosophy . . . the regions which they call the burning zone, is very moist, and in many places very temperate." Further, the burning zone was "well inhabited," and even the antipodes boasted human population.[10]

As a long-standing and extremely harsh opinion about hot climates was softened in the late 1500s, Europeans who explored and described America also stressed a favorable aspect of warmer climates, that such places were sources of incredible riches. The sun was supposed to be a great incubator of animal and vegetable life and was even conceived of as an active influence on minerals. A loose association of warm regions (such as India or Africa) with precious stones and with gold took specific shape as a belief that the sun must nourish such minerals within the bowels of the earth, hence the Spanish pursuit — and gain — of empire in South America. Denizens of cooler parts of Europe also sustained hopes of wealth in warm colonies. The medieval myth of Saint Brendan's exploration of regions to the west of Ireland had been an early indication of this English expectation. The legend stressed the warmth and fertility of the unknown lands beyond Iceland. Because there was no winter there, the region's sheep "were ye whytest and gretest" ever seen — an interesting example of how the exoticism of a climate was expressed through its effects on a homely English beast. More empirical texts that described post-Columbian America tended to repeat the supposition that any portion of the New World that lay south of northern Europe must contain rare woods and herbs, gold mines, pearl fisheries, and deposits of jewels. Braving the elements of warm regions — their fevers and serpents — could therefore be worth the risk for any intrepid Briton.[11]

If warmth was associated with danger and wealth, coldness was associated with danger and poverty. For this reason, many early English tracts on America praised southern regions and criticized northern ones. A legend on Sebastian Cabot's world map of 1544 deprecatingly described the northerly area Cabot had explored for the English as "very sterile." This was a prospect that caused English apprehension about financial investment in northern zones. One 1541 account of North America reported apologetically its supposition "that ther is no riches of gold, spyces nor preciose stones, for it stondeth farre aparted from the equinoctiall whereas the influens of the sonne doth norishe and bryng fourth gold, spices, stones and perles." Strained apologies for North America (even for parts below the Arctic) continued to appear in English accounts, especially as it became clear that the Spanish claim to Florida blocked English access to warm portions of the northern New World. Much explanation was needed to assure potential investors that the remaining, cooler areas were not devoid of promise. Under these circumstances, Newfoundland, even, was described in 1578 as "temperate" — its coldness blew in from the north and was not the true "nature of the Climate" itself.[12]

The English struggle with cold remained characteristic of early venturing in America. If Spanish exploration at the start of the sixteenth century had shattered the classical contention that the equatorial and antipodean regions were uninhabited, the English had the distinction of pointing out the same about Arctic regions at the end of the century. Richard Eden emphasized how the heroic English had voyaged to "the frosen sea" that was "vnknowen to the Antiques, euen vnder and farre within and beyonde the circle Artike, where they thought that no lyuynge creature coulde drawe breath." At first this was so incredible to Europeans that English accounts hypothesized that humans could not live north of the temperate zone — only the most degenerate animals could survive there. Dionyse Settle concluded that the Inuit whom Martin Frobisher encountered could not really live in the north, which was "barren and unfertile," and that they must migrate north to hunt during each summer, returning later to their southerly "Winter stations."[13]

Even as the English struggled to justify their northern ventures, they still longed for the warmth that would sustain them and fatten their sheep. Because America seemed to have more extreme climates than Europe, and because Iberia seemed to have taken up all the New World's warmer regions, the English constantly expressed a forlorn desire to find a promising corner for themselves, between the "frozen Pole" and "burning Zone." Still, cold and not heat was the salient problem for sixteenth-century English venturers in America. This was why George Calvert, first Lord Baltimore, moved his Catholic settlers from Newfoundland to what would become Maryland, complaining in 1629 that the former region had "ayre so intolerable colde" that his house became a veritable "hospitall" for his ill and dying followers.[14]

English Bodies in American Places

In the late 1500s and early 1600s, concerted English settlement of America had finally begun. Temperate zones were most prized and included, in contemporary terms, northern Norumbega and southern Virginia — constituting most of the eastern coast of North America. Even if temperate, such areas were still alien to English bodies; the differences between the Old World and the New were still significant. Whatever climate they settled, English colonists had to adapt themselves to it, as human populations did everywhere. Eden explained that "all the inhabitauntes of the worlde are fourmed and disposed of suche complexion and strength of body, that euery of them are proportionate to the Climate assigned vnto them, be it hotte or colde." A contemporary cosmography emphasized that learned men must understand, as Galen and Hippocrates had taught, how each "Clymate" had its own distinctive forces that influenced the people within it. Not only extreme climates forced adaptation. Regional distinctiveness existed everywhere. Ulster and Cambridgeshire were in the same temperate latitude, but a native of the Irish region was not prepared for life in the malarial fens along the River Cam. Human adaptation to climate was both physical and mental: the sinews, or fibers, of the human body changed; humoral temperament became unbalanced then readjusted; susceptibility to diseases altered; bodily change created demand for different foodstuffs; temperature affected capacity for intellectual activity and military rigor.[15]

Belief that latitude influenced human character originated in classical thought, especially that of Aristotle and Ptolemy. The ancients had taught that the terrestrial globe was positioned beneath celestial spheres; the heavens influenced the latitudes of the earth below them; different stars overhead made one zone different from another according to its season and geographical location. The most important division of latitudes was by zone: temperate, tropical, and polar. In each, the heavens determined climatic differences. Torrid latitudes were most affected by the sun and by other bright stars such as Venus. Temperate zones were most familiar to Europeans, who of course assumed that tropical and Arctic areas harbored exotic phenomena. Some classical theory made common-sense observations about planetary influence: the sun's operation on warm areas made these more fertile. But the doctrine of planetary influence was also the basis of astrology, a belief that the planets affected the humans born under their specific patterns. Venus's presence in southern zones (such as Spanish America) was supposed, for instance, to make the inhabitants more passionate. Belief in planetary influence was part of learned culture during the Renaissance; if its power waned during the seventeenth and eighteenth centuries, its tenets nevertheless remained in popular or folk culture into the nineteenth century.[16]

Although regions within the same band of latitude shared characteristics, geographical and astrological differences created variation. Areas parallel to each other (Spain and Virginia, for example) were supposed to have similar climates but also differed from each other. It was because of this conception of microclimates that Europeans feared transferring themselves to America. A different climate — even one in the same latitude — required effort and discomfort for physical adjustment to take place; an ideal of colonial heroism that was not specific to southern regions took shape. William Bradford, for instance, brushed aside denunciations of Plymouth Plantation's deficiencies, including its plentiful mosquitoes: "They are too delicate and unfit to begin new plantations and colonies, that cannot endure the biting of a mosquito. We would wish such to keep at home till at least they be mosquito-proof." In a similar way, John Smith dismissed those "infirmed bodies" who "complaine[d] of the piercing cold" of North America's winters, which he labeled a "silly complaint" because the problem was easily overcome by a little effort.[17]

Latitude was one environmental variable among the many that could affect colonists. Northern and southern peoples were assumed to be different because one group acquired its characteristics from exposure to cold weather and its physical influences, the other from warm weather and its effects. The English took pains, unsurprisingly, to explain that their cool climate made them superior to denizens of warm zones. One sixteenth-century report explained that because Spain was "neere ye Tropike of Cancer," its residents would be "better able to tolerate Phoebus['s] burning beames" in southern America — another consolatory remark about the lack of easy English access to the warmest, richest New World zones. A warning from the 1590s stated that southern climates were "offensyve" to English "boddies," which could not "prosper in dry and scalding heates." Warmth was not, however, a unique danger; the English thought that both extremely cold and extremely hot climates encouraged lassitude and barbarity in their populations. Some commentators, indeed, believed warmth was, in general, more healthy than cold. William Cuningham maintained (using as his authority the Muslim doctor known to the West as Avicenna) that *tropical* air was the healthiest because it had no variation. What was truly dangerous, Cuningham pointed out, was mutation, either because the climate itself changed or because travelers who passed through different latitudes placed their bodies under great stress.[18]

Variation remained the main culprit throughout the early modern period. This was why moving to America was a problem. In defense of attacks on the Chesapeake that stressed the region's sickliness, John Hammond stated that "change of ayre does much alter the state of our bodies: by which many travellers thither may expect some sickness, yet little danger of mortality." Scholars have interpreted Hammond's diatribe as a calculated promotional tract, but his contentions were not far off from what any English observer would say about placing English bodies in America. Travel to the New World could be expected to bring illness to all, but most would survive and adjust. Throughout the era, however, the English rarely concluded that climate (outside the tropics and the Arctic) had a permanent influence that people could not alter. Rather, they assumed that the connection between climate and culture said as much about humanity's ability to rise above natural forces as about its submission to them; this was why heat and cold tested human resources and why extremes of temperature measured the extremes of human endeavor. As a Virginia almanac for 1776 later put it: "The climate inclines some nations to contemplation and pleasure; others to hardship, action, and war; but not so as to incapacitate the former for courage and discipline, or the latter for civility, politeness, and works of genius."[19]

When early settlers of the southern colonies spoke of climates and their varying effects on humans, therefore, they harked back to ancient definitions of latitudes, stars, and human character. Being born under a certain latitude could even determine susceptibility to disease—even to the disease most closely associated with America, syphilis. (One medical text, published in London in 1590, argued that the stars at one's birth could create propensity for syphilis.)[20] But if astrological assumptions informed thinking about climates and about climatic effects on humans, criticism of astrology provided an important counterbalance. Christian doctrine denounced reductionist, material explanation of the human condition. The stars and other material forces could not overshadow human sin and divine providence—belief in their overarching power was a heretical fatalism. Antiastrological sentiment appeared in colonial almanacs, even though these were the written works that also carried astrological information. In 1776, for instance, the *Virginia Almanack* issued a challenge to "all the *ass-trologers* and *conjurers*" to prove the "*starry* influences." In the face of repeated denunciations, therefore, the astrologers' insistence on latitudinal differences among people was softened.[21] Sin, virtue, social status, gender, patterns of diet, and dress all interacted with astrological forces to create specific human characters. This was the intellectual context of pessimism and climates, one that stressed the importance of human actions and capacities. A despairing comment on the inability to rally oneself under the effects of the hot sun or of passionate Venus was as much a comment on human frailty as on climatic power; nature and human character interacted, but the former was not supposed to be more powerful than the latter.

An optimistic faith in humanity was nonetheless balanced by pessimism over the possibility of failure. Both the latitude and the smaller climate of a place could challenge human striving. Human capacity to improve self and society—regardless of natural forces—had long shaped the rhetoric of colonization, as Bradford's comments on mosquitoes showed. Promotional literature that encouraged colonization often denied climatic difficulty and instead praised the southern colonies' temperate nature and easy climate.[22] Views of the colonies that did not fall within this promotional genre just as often stressed how southern latitudes were not Edenic but would test the mettle of English men and women. Hammond accordingly explained that Virginia was "a modell on which industry may as much improve it self in, as in any habitable part of the World; yet not such a Lubberland as the Fiction of the land of Ease." John Archdale similarly warned in 1707 that Carolina needed "laborious Hands" to recover "a Wilderness possess'd by Wolves, Bears and barbarous Indians."[23]

Such a view emphasized how danger lay in nature; even if the English were healthy and vigorous within their mother country, physical adaptation to a southern climate could trip up unwary intruders. Human action could either stimulate or prevent the natural world's effects. This was as much admonishment as encouragement: people were supposed to combat nature's ill effects and thus prove themselves masters of nature rather than slaves to it. This message was especially powerful in the seventeenth century because it interacted with early colonists' expectations that they would provide order over America's rude and uncultivated resources—which its natives did not seem to have done. John Smith said disparagingly of the Powhatan Indians that their agriculture could not feed them throughout the year: "Neare three parts of the yeare, they . . . live of what the Country naturally affordeth from hand to mouth." As Adam's heirs, humans were duty bound to cultivate the earth. They were rewarded by having that earth grow tamer, more fruitful, milder as they imposed an artificial order upon it. Indeed, the message that the postlapsarian generations were to improve wild nature reinforced a sense that human resignation to natural influences was sinful.[24]

Early in the history of colonization, Europeans insisted that they could establish a beneficial, disciplined form within nature. Often this program to exploit nature emphasized the economic benefit of such actions. Felling trees and farming land would provide commodities and, therefore, profits. But colonists also held that their actions would improve natural phenomena in ways that would provide both economic and noneconomic advantages: land brought under cultivation would become more rather than less productive, forests would cease to emit dank air after their trees were cleared or thinned, wild fruits would be larger and sweeter once tended by human hands, drained swampland raised the production of grain and lessened the prospect of fevers. A 1682 tract on Carolina warned that "the uncultivated Earth" of that colony, "covered for the most part with large shading Trees, breathes forth more nitrous Vapours, than that which is cultivated." Landon Carter concluded in the early eighteenth century that "fresh new rich lands" in America (or elsewhere) inclined to "Sowerness" until they had been well cultivated. Toward the end of the century, David Ramsay stated that unimproved swampland was vanishing in low-country South Carolina; Bernard Romans wrote that this phenomenon was, in Florida, responsible for the diminution of disease.[25] These statements were meant to encourage pioneers; equally, such assessments could shame those whites who, like the Native Americans, did not create a highly visible and artificial ordering of nature.

Just as latitudinally defined climates interacted with humans, so too did smaller climates within these latitudes. The galaxy of personal characteristics that modified astrological forces in shaping character could also, for instance, determine susceptibility to climate-specific diseases. Medical theory had the most to say on this point, especially seventeenth- and eighteenth-century neo-Hippocratic theories that recounted how the air, water, soil, and weather influenced the body. Each region's own array of earthly conditions shaped the people who had settled in it; moving to another climate would necessitate new adaptation among people who had been accustomed to different atmospheric conditions. The north-south distinction was not always the important one. When one of Virginia's first governors, Thomas West, Baron De La Warr, fell ill of an "Ague," then "Flux," "Crampe," "Gout," and "Scurvy," he concluded that Virginia and its climate "ill agree with the state of my bodie" — with no mention of how a southerly heat might be involved in his poor health. Although De La Warr suspected that he needed to return to "the naturall Ayre" of his "Countrey" for a complete recovery, he went for temporary relief, significantly, to Nevis: a place located south of Virginia, but with its "Orenges and Lemons" and famous "Bathes" it was a place whose warm climate refreshed rather than sickened. Likewise, John Smith blamed De La Warr's ill health — and eventual death in 1617 — not on Virginia's warmth but on its general underdevelopment: "[T]his tender state of Virginia was not growne to that maturitie, to maintain such state and pleasure as was fit for such a personage."[26]

Southern Climates

By the late 1600s, even personages such as De La Warr managed to survive in the southern colonies; a creole population would then emerge at the end of the century. Combined with similar evidence of survival in New England, creolization in the Chesapeake seemed to show that English bodies might adjust to and thrive in North America. At this point, settlers began to explicate the specific climates of the colonies rather than debate the comparison between Old and New World environments. Despite historians' recent emphasis on how settlers survived New England better than the southern colonies, this was only one topic of interest to the observers of the colonies. Indeed, in some ways, interest in the southern colonies was stronger and hopes for them higher. This had partly to do with the lack of English settlement in the extreme north and with the acquisition of valuable colonies in the Caribbean. The subsequent profits made from tobacco and sugar heightened English optimism over the continued and growing settlement in the south.

Optimism had to be balanced with fears of what southern climates might do to the human settlers who, unlike tobacco or sugar, did not always flourish under warm conditions. Since the 1500s, colonists had feared the baleful effects of the warm, un-English climates that awaited them in America. Because the English had scoffed at the hot-tempered, passionate, and luxurious Spaniards who settled in warm zones of America, they had next to consider whether they might Hispanicize themselves by adapting to warm climates. Even the most exaggerated opinions of heat survived the Enlightenment, which indicated how these fears colored the rhetoric of colonization. One early-eighteenth-century discourse on witchcraft observed that, though witches could raise "Tempests," they could do so only in places — such as the Caribbean — suited for such storms. Similarly, John Lawson claimed that Carolina rattlesnakes grew more venomous whenever the weather was hot.[27]

Colonial whites nevertheless refused to believe that all people in southern regions would suffer climate's ill effects; human behavior could either prevent or invite illness and bodily change. Disease — an outcome of climate's complex and multiple effects on individual humans — was an important measure of personal ability to adapt to new places. Though settlers and creoles who were already "seasoned" against local maladies might sympathize with the suffering of newcomers, they also exhibited a tough-minded and judgmental attitude toward those who failed to recover quickly from the seasoning. Individual behavior was indicted for prolonged or dramatic cases of illnesses; blaming the victim was common practice even in the case of diseases for which behavior could have done nothing to affect acquisition and recovery. Syphilis continued to pose an interesting conundrum to settlers. Even into the eighteenth century, nonsexual behavior was still seen as an important influence on susceptibility. John Lawson said that in Carolina the local pox was spread by drinking rum, being exposed to cold, having wet feet, and eating pork.[28]

Given that the southern colonies did have virulent disease cultures that were related to the environment, colonists' willingness to blame suffering on human behavior and not the climate is striking. Even the high death rate at Jamestown met with this opinion. John Smith chastised Virginia settlers for their illness and their deaths; he said that the settlers had foolishly eaten "hideous Serpents" and had, through "their [sexual] incontinency," contracted "the Indian disease, we call the French Pox." Criticism of behavior continued throughout the colonial period. Southern creoles admonished one another to dress properly, to eat, drink, and otherwise use their bodies with an eye to their health, not their gratification. In 1724, Hugh Jones identified both Virginia's weather (winter cold and damp) and Virginians' behavior (the "eating too plentifully of some delicious fruits") as factors that led to "feavers and agues," which constituted "the country distemper, a severe fit of which (called a seasoning) most expect[ed], some time after their arrival in that climate." Landon Carter lambasted members of his family and people in his household for their refusal to look after their health; he lamented how one "obstinate fool" weakened himself and worsened his malaria by refusing to fast and to take emetics. William Byrd II berated himself in 1730 for bringing on a fever one summer because he "had eat[en] so much fruit and so much milk the preceding summer, that [he] had chilled [his] stomach exceedingly." Byrd clearly blamed his own actions, specifically absolving his colony's "clymate" for his sufferings.[29]

By the second quarter of the eighteenth century, these blandishments were bundled up into the medical concept of temperance: the intemperate rashly weakened themselves, perversely making themselves prey to climatological distempers. Georgia's trustees insisted that settlers of their colony avoid the corrupting habits that undermined health elsewhere in the southern colonies; James Oglethorpe stated that "the Mortality in America" was due chiefly "to distilled Liquors." Bernard Romans also claimed that intemperance, not climate, killed British settlers in eighteenth-century Florida. In Charleston, Henry William DeSaussure maintained that only the "intemperate" sailors died of yellow fever. David Ramsay admonished Carolinians that continued "industry and temperance" would improve their health. The concept of temperance did begin to hint at a particularly insidious relation between heat and bad habits. Ramsay specified, for instance, that immoderate drinking would promote fevers by heating human constitutions already warmed by the climate, whereas moderate habits would cool the body and banish fevers.[30]

Southern residents therefore continued to fear that not all of their cohort might bear up under their climates' burdens. Care was needed to promote habits of temperance and industry. Danger lurked everywhere, and even the *positive* effects of a southern climate could be threatening. The Edenic interpretation of the southern colonies was curse as well as blessing. Human duty to cultivate the earth might be undercut, for instance, by the agricultural plenty showered down by a warm climate. Such a benefit invited laziness and improvidence rather than industry and forbearance. Here, southerners made explicit their peculiar mixture of hope and pessimism over their environment. Both tendencies appeared in Robert Beverley's assessment of Virginia. Beverley admired the way in which Virginia's "kind Climate" had enabled its aboriginal residents to live "without toiling and perplexing their mind for Riches." But he contrasted Native American simplicity with English improvidence; the colonists "spunge upon the Blessings of a warm Sun, and a fruitful Soil, and almost [be]grutch the Pains of gathering in the Bounties of the Earth." Beverley's point seemed to be that physical conditions that were advantageous to migratory savages were hurdles for civil, English peoples to overcome. William Byrd II also expressed contradictory assessments of southern climes: "[T]he more [settlers] are befriended by the soil and the climate the less they will do for themselves."[31]

Individual ability was not the only measure of human effort; the character of society and government might either develop or waste the promise of a fertile climate. This was why Samuel Wilson praised Carolina in 1682. The new English colony had the same "nature with those Delicious Countries about Aleppo, Antioch, and Smyrna" but also had "the Advantage of being under an equal English Government." The authors of *The Present State of Virginia*

(1697) stated of that colony: "As to all the Natural Advantages of a Country, it is one of the best, but as to the Improved ones, one of the worst," owing to the "narrow, Selfish Ends" of its governors and the "Obstinacy of the People." John Archdale in 1707 contrasted Carolina with its latitudinal counterpart, the Mediterranean, which was hampered by "Ill Government." Looking back on the early settlement of his own colony, Beverley concluded that Jamestown's infamous *"Starving Time"* resulted not from any "Fault in the Climate" to produce proper food but from "the Foolishness and Indiscretion of those who assumed the Power of Governing." [32]

John Lawson made an interestingly equivocal remark when, in a single sentence, he gave both praise and warning to colonists for their exploitation of their warm surroundings. He urged planters to make experiments and improvements, the better to be "acquainted with the Nature of the Earth and Climate"; they would be rewarded when they "arrive[d] to the Crops and Harvests of *Babylon*." Lawson evidently meant to evoke an image of ancient splendor, but his choice of barbaric and doomed Babylon revealed an uneasiness that luxury, sin, and destruction might, in warm latitudes, be associated with improvement and wealth. Wealth without personal striving was a problem. Increasingly, from the early eighteenth century onward, settlers of new areas in the South compared themselves with their seemingly more diligent counterparts to the north: "Should they be as Industrous as the Northern Colonies, Riches would flow in upon them." But this assessment of the frontier South of course competed with images of the settled regions that emphasized the Tidewater's remarkable existing wealth. [33]

If this accumulation of images about warmth, wealth, and lassitude seemed a portent of later conclusions about the South, it is important to remember other indications that this was not a clear line of development. First, the debate over Old and New World climates was revived, this time by its more familiar proponents, George Louis Leclerc, Comte de Buffon, and Cornelius de Pauw. By the eighteenth century, new speculation about the effects of climate on human population was again stating conclusions about the characters of northern and southern peoples; the theory of Charles Secondat, Baron de Montesquieu, was particularly significant in this regard, and climatic theorization enjoyed a new phase of development. Buffon and de Pauw had less to say than did Montesquieu about the north-south distinction. Instead, they postulated that the American climate—all of it—had ill effects on humans, as well as on the flora and fauna, either native or domesticated; all American specimens, from members of the colonial elite down to mere weeds, appeared degenerate when compared with the more vigorous stock seen in the Old World. Because it was directed at all of the New World, this hemispheric polemic acted as a temporary distraction from any assessment of American climates in more parochial terms, including any speculation about the characteristics intrinsic to southern regions. Further, Buffon contended that America was colder and more humid than Europe: "It will never produce anything but humid creatures . . . cold men and feeble animals." Such a statement must have vexed those who speculated about heat in the South. In the era of the Revolution and the early Republic, therefore, indignant whites from all colonies united against European speculation about their degeneracy; northern and southern Americans were not significantly divided on the means or meaning of their rebuttal of European theory.[34]

Second, southern colonists did not maintain that a warm climate necessitated slavery. True, contemporaries remarked that the fertility of southern areas prompted human greed for increased riches, which then led to the adoption of large labor forces in order to generate agricultural wealth. This opinion, however, was not equivalent to the later, antebellum apologia about how southern climates discouraged individual striving and necessitated forced labor. Individual striving was apparent in the colonial South; actual labor was not. Rather, whites' desire for wealth was met by adaptation to an economy of scale: they accumulated labor and expanded the production of merchantable goods. In this interpretation, desire for wealth, not willingness to enslave humans, was the primordial sin. Heat may have encouraged sloth, but it did not extinguish ambition, an ambition met by slavery and plantation agriculture, hence historians' conclusion that climatological justification of slavery was "convenient but formless and imprecise" during the colonial era. Only in South Carolina and Georgia, the rice colonies, did whites begin to argue that Africans were better fitted than Europeans to labor in the disease-ridden rice swamps. But this was an extremely place-specific theory, of no interest to slaveholders outside the low country of the lower South, and it was not yet the general association between heat and slavery that southerners later made.[35]

Rhetoric about the need to improve nature nevertheless continued. Indeed, Enlightenment-era ideals of progress probably strengthened the message, as did republican boosterism during and after the Revolution. By the mid-eighteenth century, however, some colonists had taken up another view, one that stressed that climate might naturally change without human assis-

tance. This interpretation downplayed human agency in material transformation and weakened the older view of humanity's heroic struggle with an un-
bending nature. At this point, the ability of British people to settle in America
was no longer a question, as it had been in the 1500s and early 1600s; nor
was there apprehension over the prospect of adapting to southern climates, as
had been the case in the seventeenth century. Now the question was whether
settlers affected the climate, rather than how it affected them. Landon Carter
feared, for instance, that Virginia was growing colder and less suited to commercial agriculture: "This climate is so changing [that] unless it returns to his
former state Virginia will be no Tobacco Colony." A few decades later, Jefferson speculated that Virginia was simply losing extremes in its weather patterns
and would eventually "become much more moderate." By 1808, the Medical
Society of South Carolina was discussing "the changes which the soil and climate of Charleston, and of South-Carolina, generally, ha[d] undergone" since
colonization began.[36]

More tellingly, southern colonists asked themselves whether recent changes
in climate were the results of more than a century of Euro-American transformation of the environment. Such a view not only underscored the continuing
pessimism over humanity's relation to nature but revealed an erosion, as well,
of earlier and more hopeful assumptions that humans could overcome material
obstacles, assumptions that had rallied colonists in the sixteenth and seventeenth centuries. An increased gloominess emerged slowly from ideas that
humans might misuse natural resources. This was a constant refrain in Robert
Beverley's *History and Present State of Virginia* (1705) — written barely two generations after the emergence of a creole population in America. Beverley castigated Virginians for "inordinate and unseasonable Use" of "Native Pleasures"
and for "hardly making Improvements equivalent to that Damage." Lawson
agreed when he concluded that Carolina's Native Americans did indeed "still
possess the Flower of *Carolina,* the *English* enjoying only the Fag-end of that
fine Country." These views would be more at home with romantic assessments
of untouched nature than with Renaissance insistence on the need to order the
natural world.[37]

This shift heralded an even more skeptical view of humanity. No longer did
southerners simply assume that nature held potential danger for weak humans;
they also feared an active evil within themselves, a danger in their own actions.
Indeed, attributes of socioeconomic improvement that had before been lauded
were now regarded as paradoxical harbingers of trouble as well as benefit.

Jefferson, for instance, made meteorological observations in order to correlate them with human alteration in the natural environment—he, like others, suspected that deforestation had altered climate.[38] Improvements meant to facilitate rice planting in South Carolina and Georgia especially fit this pattern of intensifying pessimism. Unaware that mosquitoes acted as vectors for malaria and yellow fever, whites assumed that changes in the air itself were responsible for increases in disease; they blamed themselves for these changes when they observed how increased incidence of fevers accompanied proliferation of swamplands planted with irrigated rice. Engineer William Gerard De Brahm, for instance, believed that because trees had been felled around Savannah, mephitic vapors that had once been held back by greenery thereafter swept through the city.[39]

Human action altered climate, which then fostered the disease that infected humans. Thus pessimism underpinned southern perception of climate; indeed, the pessimism increased as the colonial period drew to a close. Throughout the early centuries of exploration and initial settlement in what would later be the South, a fear of human weakness or ineptitude warred with assertions of human ability to control climatic forces; a suspicion that people could have unwelcome effects on the climate intensified this fear in the second half of the eighteenth century. Still, the dominant tone was hectoring rather than resigned: residents should fight against any deterioration in person and place that might result either from climate or from human agency.

Whites in the southern colonies thus provided an interesting contrast to later views on the southern climate, especially the view conveyed by historians of the antebellum and postbellum South. If, as scholars have argued, southerners were, by the early decades of the nineteenth century, newly fatalistic in the face of climate, they had—probably under the pressures of supplying explanations for slavery—removed themselves from the more ambivalent stance of their ancestors. To proslavery southerners, apologies for slavery that pointed to the inescapable power of a warm climate and its inducements to commercial agriculture must have seemed appealing. Colonial pessimism may have provided the structure for later criticisms of the South. The warnings about how climate-specific wealth could erode virtue and diligence could, for instance, easily be translated into denunciations of slave-produced wealth and leisure.

It would nevertheless have been a surprise to the earlier free residents of the southern region that the South was later seen as a problem for American culture and history and that climate was supposed to be an important cause of the problem. True, they believed that climate made their colonies and states distinctive, but all white British Americans believed this of their own regions. Distinctiveness was undeniable, but it was not yet equivalent to a problem. For white settlers, the easily corrupted nature of humanity was the problem, not climate and its effects. Indeed, and paradoxically, the later blame that critics of the South would place on factors such as climate would have seemed, to earlier southerners, a weak-minded denial of human agency, a criticism of the region that did not hold its human residents fully responsible for whatever problems existed there.

Notes

I would like to thank David Armitage, Karen Kupperman, and John Harley Warner, as well as the members of the "South as an American Problem" seminar, for their comments on earlier versions of this essay.

1   Ulrich Bonnell Phillips, *Life and Labor in the Old South* (Boston, 1951), 3.

2   See David Bertelson, *The Lazy South* (New York, 1967); A. Cash Koeniger, "Climate and Southern Distinctiveness," *Journal of Southern History* 54 (February 1988): 21–44; and Raymond Arsenault, "The End of the Long Hot Summer: The Air Conditioner and Southern Culture," *Journal of Southern History* 50 (November 1984): 597–628. Bertelson's work has most to say about the colonial period; the other works do little really to examine the colonial period, a problem also evident in Fred Hobson's essay "The Savage South: An Inquiry into the Origins, Endurance, and Presumed Demise of an Image," *Virginia Quarterly Review* 61 (summer 1985): 377–95.

3   On southern medical practice, see John Harley Warner, "The Idea of Southern Medical Distinctiveness: Medical Knowledge and Practice in the Old South," in *Science and Medicine in the Old South*, ed. Ronald L. Numbers and Todd L. Savitt (Baton Rouge, 1989), 179–205; on yellow fever, see Jo Ann Carrigan, "Privilege, Prejudice, and the Strangers' Disease in Nineteenth-Century New Orleans," *Journal of Southern History* 36 (November 1970): 568–78, and Joyce E. Chaplin, *An Anxious Pursuit: Agricultural Innovation and Modernity in the Lower South, 1730–1815* (Chapel Hill, 1993), 93–108.

4   On the Chesapeake, see Lorena S. Walsh and Russell R. Menard, "Death in the Chesapeake: Two Life Tables for Men in Early Colonial Maryland," *Maryland Historical Magazine* 69 (summer 1974): 211–27; Darrett B. Rutman and Anita H. Rutman, "Of Agues and Fevers: Malaria in the Early Chesapeake," *William and Mary Quarterly*, 3d ser., 33 (January 1976): 31–60; Daniel Blake Smith, "Mortality and Family in the Colonial Chesapeake," *Journal of Interdisciplinary History* 8 (winter 1978): 403–27; and Carville V. Earle, "Environment, Disease, and Mortality in Early Virginia," in *The Chesapeake in the Seventeenth Century: Essays on Anglo-American Society*, ed. Thad W. Tate and David L. Ammerman (Chapel Hill, 1979), 96–125. For the idea of comparative advantage, see Peter A. Coclanis, *The Shadow of a Dream: Economic Life and Death in the South Carolina Low Country, 1670–1920* (New York, 1989), 31–47,

57-58. For studies of the South that consider contemporary attitudes, see H. Roy Merrens and George D. Terry, "Dying in Paradise: Malaria, Mortality, and the Perceptual Environment in Colonial South Carolina," *Journal of Southern History* 50 (November 1984): 533-50, and Rhys Isaac, *The Transformation of Virginia, 1740-1790* (Chapel Hill, 1982), 46-52. On the need to assume a flexible relationship between climate and culture, see David Hackett Fischer, "Climate and History: Priorities for Research," *Journal of Interdisciplinary History* 10 (spring 1980): 821-30, esp. 825-26.

5   Especially in the early modern period, travelers wanted to divert audiences as well as convey information; historians who credulously interpret travelers' accounts as early and transparent examples of sociological speculation simply transmit the accounts' entertaining exaggerations to new readers. See Chaplin, *Anxious Pursuit,* 71-91.

6   For one example of how a New Englander wrestled with climate, see John Canup, "Cotton Mather and 'Criolian Degeneracy,'" *Early American Literature* 24 (1989): 20-34. On how whites in low-country South Carolina and Georgia believed themselves to be surrounded by an atmosphere unique to them and different from other parts of the South, see Chaplin, *Anxious Pursuit,* 93-108.

7   Thomas Jefferson, *Notes on the State of Virginia* (1785), ed. William Peden (Chapel Hill, 1955), 73; William Cuningham, comp., *The Cosmographical Glasse . . .* (London, 1559), 73-74.

8   On latitude and climate, see the *Oxford English Dictionary,* 2d ed., s.v. "climate"; Karen Ordahl Kupperman, "The Puzzle of the American Climate in the Early Colonial Period," *American Historical Review* 87 (December 1982): 1262-89. On Hippocratic theory and its revival in the seventeenth and eighteenth centuries, see Andrew Wear, "Making Sense of Health and the Environment in Early Modern England," in *Medicine in Society: Historical Essays,* ed. Andrew Wear (Cambridge, 1992); James C. Riley, *The Eighteenth-Century Campaign to Avoid Disease* (New York, 1987). Quotation from Cuningham, *Cosmographical Glasse,* preface.

9   The most important work on this topic is Karen Ordahl Kupperman, "Fear of Hot Climates in the Anglo-American Colonial Experience," *William and Mary Quarterly,* 3d ser., 41 (April 1984): 213-40.

10 Edward Arber, ed., *The First Three English Books on America* (Birmingham, 1885), 8; Joseph Acosta, *The Naturall and Morall Historie of the East and West Indies,* trans. E[dward] G[rimestone] (London, 1604), A3ʳ (quotation), 32. See also Cuningham, *Cosmographical Glasse,* 67.

11 *The Life of St. Brendan* (c. 1520), in *New American World: A Documentary History of North America to 1612,* ed. David B. Quinn et al. (London, 1979), 1:56. See also Cuningham, *Cosmographical Glasse,* 190 (the second of the two pages so numbered).

12 From Quinn et al., *New American World,* 1:95; Roger Barlowe, *A briefe summe of geographie* (London, 1541), 215; Anthony Parkhurst's report to Richard Hakluyt the elder (1578), in Quinn et al., *New American World,* 4:9. See also William Bourne, *A regiment for the sea* (London, 1580), 192.

13 "The Life and Labours of Richard Eden," in Arber, *First Three English Books,* xli; Settle cited in Quinn et al., *New American World,* 4:214, 215; see also, in the same work, 296-97 and Cuningham, *Cosmographical Glasse,* 68.

14 On climatic extremes, see Acosta, *Naturall and Morall Historie,* 261; first quotation from a

poem by Richard Bingham in the preface to *A Trve Reporte, Of the late discoueries . . .* , by George Peckham (London, 1583), n.p.; Baltimore to King Charles I, August 19, 1629, Colonial Office 1.5, Public Record Office, Kew.

15   "Life and Labours of Richard Eden," xlii; Cuningham, *Cosmographical Glasse*, Aiiʳ.

16   On astrology, see Wayne Shumaker, *The Occult Sciences in the Renaissance: A Study in Intellectual Patterns* (Berkeley, 1972), 1–11, 42–53; Keith Thomas, *Religion and the Decline of Magic* (London, 1971), 335–424; Jon Butler, "Magic, Astrology, and the Early-American Religious Heritage, 1600–1760," *American Historical Review* 84 (April 1979): 317–46; and Herbert Leventhal, *In the Shadow of the Enlightenment: Occultism and Renaissance Science in Eighteenth-Century America* (New York, 1976), 13–65. On astrological and climatological thought in the Spanish colonies, see Anthony Pagden, "Identity Formation in Spanish America," in *Colonial Identity in the Atlantic World, 1500–1800*, ed. Nicholas Canny and Anthony Pagden (Princeton, N.J., 1987), 81–83.

17   William Bradford, *Of Plymouth Plantation, 1620–1647*, ed. Samuel Eliot Morison (New York, 1953), 144; John Smith, *Advertisements For the unexperienced Planters of New-England, or any where* (1631), in *The Complete Works of Captain John Smith (1580–1631) in Three Volumes*, ed. Philip L. Barbour (Chapel Hill, 1986), 3:291. It is not clear that Smith was referring to what would now be considered New England; it is more likely that he meant all the territory north of Spanish Florida — see 291 n.

18   Kupperman, "Fear of Hot Climates," 213–40; Dionyse Settle, *A true reporte of the laste Voyage into the West and Northwest regions . . . by Capteine Frobisher* (London, 1571), Aiiiʳ; [Edward Hayes and Christopher Carleill], "A Discourse Concerning a Voyage . . . ," (1592), in Quinn et al., *New American World*, 3:159; Cuningham, *Cosmographical Glasse*, 81–82.

19   John Hammond, *Leah and Rachel, or, the Two Fruitfull Sisters Virginia, and Mary-Land* (London, 1656), 10; David Rittenhouse, *The Virginia Almanack for the Year of Our Lord God 1776* (Williamsburg, [1775]), s.v. "May."

20   Philip Hermanus, comp., *An excellent Treatise teaching howe to cure the French-Pockes . . .* (London, 1590), 1, 61.

21   See Thomas, *Religion and the Decline of Magic*, 425–58; Shumaker, *Occult Sciences*, 16–27; Frances A. Yates, *The Occult Philosophy in the Elizabethan Age* (London, 1979), 33–34; Rittenhouse, *Virginia Almanack*, s.v. "January."

22   See Merrens and Terry, "Dying in Paradise," 534–39.

23   Hammond, *Leah and Rachel*, 10; John Archdale, *A New Description of That Fertile and Pleasant Province of Carolina* (1707), in *Narratives of Early Carolina, 1650–1708*, ed. Alexander S. Salley Jr. (New York, 1911), 306.

24   These were not views unique to the southern colonies. See Keith Thomas, *Man and the Natural World: A History of the Modern Sensibility* (New York, 1983), 17–50, 192–97; Cecelia Tichi, *New World, New Earth: Environmental Reform in American Literature from the Puritans through Whitman* (New Haven, 1979), chaps. 1, 2. Quotation from John Smith, *The Generall Historie of Virginia, New-England, and the Summer Isles . . .* (1624), in Barbour, *Complete Works*, 2:113.

25   Francis Jennings, *The Invasion of America: Indians, Colonialism, and the Cant of Conquest* (Chapel Hill, 1975), chap. 2; Timothy Silver, *A New Face on the Countryside: Indians, Colo-*

nists, and Slaves in South Atlantic Forests, 1500–1800 (Cambridge, 1990), 104–38; Samuel Wilson, *An Account of the Province of Carolina, in America* (1682), in Salley, *Narratives of Early Carolina*, 168; Jack P. Greene, ed., *The Diary of Colonel Landon Carter of Sabine Hall, 1752–1778* (Charlottesville, Va., 1965), 1:256; David Ramsay, *A Sketch of the Soil, Climate, Weather, and Diseases of South-Carolina* (Charleston, 1796), 8; Bernard Romans, *A Concise Natural History of East and West Florida* (London, 1775), 14–15.

26 *The relation of the right honourable the Lord De-La-Warre* (1611), in Quinn et al., *New American World*, 5:263, 264; Smith, *Generall Historie*, 2:263.

27 [Richard Boulton], *A Compleat History of Magick, Sorcery, and Witchcraft* (London, 1715), 1:16; John Lawson, *A New Voyage to Carolina* (1709), ed. Hugh Talmage Lefler (Chapel Hill, 1967), 134.

28 On place-specific theories of disease, see Anthony Grafton with April Shelford and Nancy Siraisi, *New Worlds, Ancient Texts: The Power of Tradition and the Shock of Discovery* (Cambridge, Mass., 1992), 159–94; Riley, *Eighteenth-Century Campaign*, chaps. 1, 5; and John Harley Warner, *The Therapeutic Perspective: Medical Practice, Knowledge, and Identity in America, 1820–1885* (Cambridge, Mass., 1986), 58–80. Lawson, *New Voyage*, 25.

29 Smith, *Generall Historie*, 2:299; Hugh Jones, *The Present State of Virginia, from Whence Is Inferred a Short View of Maryland and North Carolina* (1724), ed. Richard L. Morton (Chapel Hill, 1956), 84–85; Greene, *Diary of Colonel Landon Carter*, 2:765–66; Marion Tinling, ed., *The Correspondence of the Three William Byrds of Westover, Virginia, 1684–1776* (Charlottesville, Va., 1977), 1:429.

30 "Letters from James Oglethorpe," Georgia Historical Society, *Collections* (Savannah, 1848), 3:142; Romans, *Concise Natural History*, 12–13; DeSaussure to Ezekiel Pickens, September 10, 1805, Henry William DeSaussure Papers, South Caroliniana Library, Columbia, S.C.; David Ramsay, *A Review of the Improvements, Progress and State of Medicine in the Eighteenth Century* (Charleston, 1800), 33, 46–47; idem, *A Dissertation on the Means of Preserving Health in Charleston and the Adjacent Low Country* (Charleston, 1790), 7.

31 Robert Beverley, *The History and Present State of Virginia* (1705), ed. Louis B. Wright (Chapel Hill, 1947), 226, 319; Louis B. Wright, ed., *The Prose Works of William Byrd of Westover: Narratives of a Colonial Virginian* (Cambridge, Mass., 1966), 409.

32 Wilson, *Account of the Province of Carolina*, 169; Henry Hartwell, James Blair, and Edward Chilton, *The Present State of Virginia, and the College* (1697), ed. by Hunter Dickinson Farish (Williamsburg, 1940), 3, 4–5; Archdale, *New Description*, 283; Beverley, *History and Present State of Virginia*, 35.

33 Lawson, *New Voyage*, 80; Archdale, *New Description*, 290.

34 On Montesquieu, see Peter Gay, *The Enlightenment: An Interpretation*, vol. 2, *The Science of Freedom* (New York, 1969), 326–31; on Buffon and de Pauw, see Antonello Gerbi, *The Dispute of the New World: The History of a Polemic, 1750–1900*, trans. Jeremy Moyle (Pittsburgh, 1973), chaps. 1–5, quotation from p. 8.

35 See Larry Tise, *Proslavery: A History of the Defense of Slavery in America, 1701–1840* (Athens, Ga., 1987), 15–16, on the lack of any real proslavery argument during the seventeenth and eighteenth centuries; Winthrop D. Jordan, *White over Black*, 260–65, quotation from 261; and Chaplin, *Anxious Pursuit*, 117–30. Europeans involved in the slave trade to the Carib-

bean and Latin America had long made a climatological argument for slavery. See Philip D. Curtin, "Epidemiology and the Slave Trade," *Political Science Quarterly* 83 (June 1968): 190–216. This seems to have been less important in British North America, except for the narrow rice-growing coast.

36   Greene, *Diary of Colonel Landon Carter*, 1:433 — see also 2:634–35; Jefferson, *Notes on the State of Virginia*, 80; *Carolina Messenger*, August 9, 1808.

37   Beverley, *History and Present State of Virginia*, 156; Lawson, *New Voyage*, 61. On this general topic, see Silver, *New Face on the Countryside*, 139–85. Cf. William Cronon, *Changes in the Land: Indians, Colonists, and the Ecology of New England* (New York, 1983), 122.

38   Silvio A. Bedini, *Thomas Jefferson: Statesman of Science* (New York, 1990), 395.

39   William Gerard De Brahm, *History of the Province of Georgia with Maps of Original Surveys* (Wormsloe, Ga., 1849), 47–48. See also Joyce E. Chaplin, "Tidal Rice Cultivation and the Problem of Slavery in South Carolina and Georgia, 1760–1815," *William and Mary Quarterly*, 3d ser., 49 (January 1992): 59–61.

~ Slavery as an American Problem

JAMES OAKES

As LARRY GRIFFIN POINTS OUT in his essay, the seemingly simple proposition that the South is at once American and different from the rest of America leads to surprisingly complex conceptual difficulties. To be sure, in the three decades since Charles G. Sellers edited his collection of essays entitled *The Southerner as American,* scholars have become more comfortable with the idea that people have multiple identities and that tensions often develop as a result.[1] That someone could be a southerner *and* an American, with potentially explosive results, ought to be a straightforward proposition. Yet many historians continue to associate Sellers's approach to southern history with a "consensus" interpretation that wiped all serious conflict from the face of American history. Even a moment's reflection dispels this characterization. In an important series of articles written just before *The Southerner as American* was published, Sellers located the basis of antebellum political conflict in a fundamental social cleavage that pitted those who stood to gain the most from capitalist development against those who had the most to lose. To Sellers, then, the fact that southerners were Americans meant that they had inherited all the political turmoil, class divisions, and moral dilemmas that marked the Jacksonian era as a whole.[2]

To appreciate this is to confront the complexity of southern history, and with it the recent tendency to wipe that complexity away through a series of semantic maneuvers that define the North and South as fundamentally different from each other—the assumption being that difference is an adequate explanation for conflict. This process of simplification proceeds along two different trajectories. The first is driven by the contemporary impulse to view all major political and social issues as at bottom *cultural* rather than structural. Hence the prevailing obsession with southern cultural distinctiveness simultaneously exaggerates the differences between northerners and southerners before the Civil War while obscuring the political and economic bases of the sectional conflict.

The second trajectory approaches the structural antagonism of North and South by means of a grossly oversimplified definition of capitalism as "wage labor," a maneuver that automatically eliminates the most substantial analytical problems. Capitalism and slavery become fundamentally antithetical, *by definition*. Hence the imposing historical question — What was the relationship between the development of modern slavery and the development of capitalism? — is pushed off the agenda. Serious historical analysis gives way before a clever verbal device. There is no room, in this simplified analytical universe, for a historical understanding of capitalism as something that developed over centuries, that manifested itself differently at different stages of its development. Still less is it possible to relate this historical process to the parallel development of slavery in the New World. In the resulting game of historiographical roulette, you have only two choices: either you cast all your bets with the argument that slavery was simply "capitalist," or all your chips go down on the claim that slavery was fundamentally antithetical to capitalism. With that, the complexity of slavery's changing relationship to capitalism simply disappears.

But what if you define capitalism as something more than wage labor, as something that begins with the emancipation of the serfs and includes the rationalization of agriculture, the spread of rational philosophy and Protestant theology, the transatlantic fetishization of the commodity, the emergence of a bourgeois society marked by novel patterns of social reproduction, the rise of the liberal state, the growth of wage labor beginning in the late eighteenth century and culminating — but not ending — in the astonishing development of cities and industry in the late nineteenth century? Once capitalism is understood in such historical terms, the relevant issue ceases to be whether slavery was or was not "capitalist" and becomes, instead, the relationship between the development of capitalism and the rise of modern slavery.

If "free labor" is inadequate as a definition of capitalism, "unfree labor" is even less useful as a definition of slavery, particularly in light of recent scholarship. As comparative history and sociology have become more sophisticated, the definition of slavery has become more subtle and a good deal more abstract. By the 1980s Orlando Patterson was offering a book-length definition that applied to hundreds of different cultures across the entire sweep of human history. Yet there was an intriguing twist here, for this was a definition with its own cul-de-sac, a definition that, by the very breadth of its abstraction, required its users to turn around and go back to the particulars of every time and place in which slavery appeared. Everywhere, Patterson told us, slavery was understood as "social death," which meant that everywhere, slavery depended on the meaning of social life.[3] It is abundantly clear, however, that social life has been defined in many different ways throughout human history. Thus, if full social life in Athens was defined as participation in the polity, social death in ancient Greece was defined as exclusion from the polity. Similarly, if social life in Africa was defined as membership in the kinship system, social death, or slavery, in Africa was defined as exclusion from the kinship system.

Herein lies the importance of seeing liberal capitalism as something that develops over time and slavery's dialectical relationship to that process of development. Simply put: capitalism brought into existence entirely new forms of social life and as such redefined the meaning of social death. To be enslaved in the modern world was to occupy the paradoxical position of an "outsider" within the very process of global capitalist development of which modern slavery was a part. In the southern United States this paradox was especially acute. The slaves were a species of private property but were themselves incapable of legally owning property. Their working lives were devoted to the production of marketable staples, but they had no legal claim on the fruits of their labor. They could be contracted for work or for sale, but they could make no contracts of their own. In short, southern slaves were thoroughly embedded in and at the same time absolutely removed from the historical process of capitalist development. And far from being peripheral curiosities, these contradictions were fundamental to the definition of slavery in the American South. From them arose the cataclysmic sectional tensions that ultimately destroyed the Union. Thus slavery may have been historically ubiquitous, and liberal capitalism may be larger than any one nation, but what made slavery an American problem was the historically specific relationship between slavery and liberal capitalism in the United States, a relationship that changed dramatically over time as both slavery and liberal capitalism continued to develop.

I am tossing around quite a few big abstractions here: Slavery, Capitalism, and Liberalism. Even to define their contours demands careful scholarship and a good deal of time. If I am to approach the issue here with any degree of intellectual integrity, I will need a shortcut: an example, an incident, a case study that will, in a relatively brief narrative, address some of the most important issues raised by the problem of slavery in American history.

Colonial Georgia makes a good case study, if only because it was so anomalous. It was the last of the slave colonies to be established in British North America and the only one in which the development of slavery provoked serious political divisions and extended public debate. Nowhere else in America were the origins of slavery so self-consciously observed by the white settlers who lived through the process, and so nowhere else were the assumptions of the advocates and opponents of slavery so clearly articulated.

Georgia was to be a patriarchal utopia, undemocratic yet benevolent. The power structure was centralized and authoritarian, but the focus of life was to be communal. Leaders were selected without reference to popular opinion — unlike every other colony in British North America at the time, Georgia was to have no representative assembly. But the leaders were prohibited from activities designed to enhance their own personal wealth. Settlers were subject to economic restrictions unparalleled in other colonies, but the restrictions were devised for the protection of the "worthy poor." Specifically, there were to be no slaves, and private property was banned. This was to be an antislavery patriarchy. Justified on both philanthropic and military grounds, the initial organization of the colony was almost feudal. Thus the distribution of land was determined by considerations that were simultaneously strategic and economic, and land could be transferred only to male heirs.

What power was not vested in the trustees James Oglethorpe simply assumed to himself. He was the first in a series of one-man rulers of Georgia, arousing both resentment and dependence among the settlers. Like a true patriarch, Oglethorpe preferred to exercise his authority informally. Indeed, he ruled Georgia for some time with no formal grant of power. He disliked routine paperwork, gave orders verbally, and put trusted friends into positions of great authority. Yet he was in no way a disorganized administrator. James Oglethorpe had a clear vision of the kind of society he was striving to build, and his informal style of leadership was as much a part of that vision as was his authoritarian — some said tyrannical — rule.

Alas, utopian schemes depend on committed participants, and Oglethorpe's plans soon bent beneath the strains of internal dissension. Within six months after arriving, in early 1733, some Georgians began to resent the trustees' restraints. Savannah residents revealed themselves to be nearly as unmanageable as Jamestown's settlers had been a century earlier. They violated the ban on rum, they refused to live in the small settlements Oglethorpe had set up as a barrier around Savannah, they complained about the restrictions on landholding, and some began to bring slaves into Georgia while Oglethorpe was visiting England. He expelled the slaves upon his return, declaring at one point "that as long as he had any thing to do with the Colony, there should neither be Allowance of Negroes nor Alteration in the Titles of Land."[4]

If the predispositions of the English settlers rendered Oglethorpe's plans problematic, the settlement of the Salzburgers breathed new life into those plans. Invited to Georgia by the trustees, they began arriving from the Archbishopric of Salzburg in March 1734. Under the strong and effective leadership of the Reverend Johann Martin Bolzius, these persecuted German Lutherans came closer than any other group to implementing the utopian schemes conceived by English reformers for the relief of Britain's debtors. Others tried to meet the ideal as well, notably the Highland Scots, whose own community of Darien was located on the Altamaha River, south of Savannah.

According to the policy established by the trustees, each of these immigrants was allotted a plot of fifty acres plus the tools needed to work it. None of the lands could be sold, and if residents failed to meet any of a number of strict use requirements, the plots would revert to the trustees. Nobody was allotted more than five hundred acres for the first twenty years of Georgia's existence, and before 1752 fewer than 12 percent of all land grants were over fifty acres. Larger tracts were distributed only in the late 1740s, especially during the last five years of the trustee period. By then, more and more large plantations were established while the ideals of the trustees were withering.

There were several reasons for this. The lands upon which settlers were placed were frequently poor and unproductive. Silk and wine production, the chief enterprises encouraged by the trustees, were not spectacular successes in Georgia, and the colony's economic basis remained unsteady. But it is hard to tell whether it was outright failure or the absence of an economic boom that provoked the most complaint. Englishmen and Lowland Scots, often from neighboring South Carolina—where rice production by slaves was then a thriving enterprise—pressured most insistently for lifting Georgia's bans on slavery and private property.

The trustees, backed up by the Salzburgers and the Highland Scots, resisted the pressure from the planters and merchants and argued forcefully against the introduction of slavery into Georgia. The Germans and Scots had proved themselves to be hard workers. They did produce silk, although not in quantities large enough to sustain an economic boom. And the Salzburgers had personally disproved the claims of white Carolinians that only black slaves could grow rice. These poorer Georgians feared the competitive threat of slave labor. The ban on slavery had raised artisan wages in their colony to one of the highest levels in North America.

Indeed, the high cost of labor in Georgia was a common complaint among those who sought to introduce slavery into the colony. They stepped up their attacks on the trustees, ostentatiously violating Georgia law by bringing slaves into the colony. They published harsh attacks on Georgia's leaders and petitioned British officials in London to force the trustees to back down. In so doing they produced an extraordinary series of documents, the closest thing anywhere in American history to a public campaign for the establishment of slavery where it had already been outlawed.

In late 1738, not six years since Oglethorpe had established the colony, 117 settlers petitioned the trustees to alleviate their "*present* Misfortunes and this *deplorable* State of the Colony." Arguing that their proximity to a booming slave economy put Georgians at a competitive disadvantage, they cited two problems that needed particular attention: "*1st* The Want of a free Title or Fee-simple, to our Lands; which if granted, would both induce great Numbers of new Settlers to come amongst us, and likewise encourage those who remain here chearfully to proceed in making further Improvements"; and second, of course: "The Want of the Use of Negroes, with proper Limitations; which if granted, would both occasion great Numbers of white People to come here, and also render us capable to subsist ourselves, by raising Provisions upon our Lands, until we could make some Produce fit for Export."[5]

More interesting than the fact of such petitions was the set of assumptions on which they were based, the rhetorical traditions from which they emerged. At the crude end of the spectrum, the proslavery Georgians appealed to blatant self-interest, at one point ridiculing a preacher who had supported the ban on slaves by claiming "that he never desir'd to see Georgia a Rich, But a Religious Colony."[6] Time and again they contrasted the flourishing state of South Carolina with the misery of Georgia.

Like so many eighteenth-century Anglo-Americans, however, Oglethorpe's enemies associated material prosperity with political freedom. Thus by the early 1740s the front line of their assault was on the patriarchalism of Georgia's government. The economic restrictions were bad enough, the petitioners argued, but while they "labour'd under those Difficulties" in supporting themselves, their "*Civil Liberties* received a more *terrible* Shock." They complained that Oglethorpe had left them at the mercy of a "*Dictator*" whose high-handed execution of justice had terrorized the entire settlement and sent dozens scurrying across the border into the "*Land of Liberty*," South Carolina. And when the polemics reached fever pitch, they took to ridiculing Oglethorpe as a "*Perpetual Dictator*" who had taken it upon himself to decide what was best for the settlers of Georgia. The sarcasm is heavy handed but once again revealing of the assumptions of those who supported the introduction of slavery. (Notice, incidentally, the dripping disdain for classical republican virtues.) Let me quote them at some length:

> we have seen the ancient Custom of sending forth Colonies, for the Improvement of any distant Territory, or new Acquisition, continued down to ourselves; but to Your Excellency alone it is owing, that the World is made acquainted with a Plan, highly refined from those of all former Projecters. They fondly imagin'd it necessary to communicate to such young Settlements, the fullest Rights and Properties, all the Immunities of their Mother Countries, and Privileges rather more extensive: By such Means indeed, these Colonies flourish'd with early Trade and Affluence; but Your Excellency's Concern for our perpetual Welfare, could never permit you to propose such transitory Advantages for us: You consider'd Riches like a Divine and Philosopher, as the Irritamenta Malorum, and knew that they were disposed to inflate weak Minds with Pride; to pamper the body with Luxury, and introduce a long Variety of Evils. Thus have you *Protected us* from ourselves . . . by keeping all Earthly Comforts from us: You have afforded us the Opportunity of arriving at the Integrity of the *Primitive Times,* by intailing a more than *Primitive Poverty* on us: The Toil that is necessary to our bare Subsistence, must effectually defend us from the Anxieties of any further Ambition: As we have no Properties, to feed Vain-Glory and beget Contention; so we are not puzzled with any System of Laws to ascertain and establish them: The valuable Virtue of Humility is secured to us, by your Care to prevent our procuring, or so much as seeing, any *Negroes,* (the

only human Creatures proper to improve our Soil) lest our Simplicity might mistake the poor *Africans* for greater slaves than ourselves: And that we might fully receive the Spiritual Benefit of those
wholesome Austerities; you have wisely denied us the Use of such
Spiritous Liquors as might in the least divert our Minds from the
Contemplation of our Happy Circumstances.[7]

Behind this sneering contempt lay a set of remarkably ordinary assumptions, widespread among Anglo-Americans, about the unique freedom of the
English people in the eighteenth century. Thus proslavery advocates appealed
to "ye famous Declaration of Rights made by our Fore Fathers at ye Glorious
Revolution" of 1688.[8] Another of slavery's supporters solemnly predicted that
"the Genious of the *British Nation*, so remarkably zealous for *Liberty* and the
Rights of Mankind, [would] never suffer *British* Subjects . . . to be depriv'd of
publick Promises of the *natural* Liberties of *British* Subjects." "As we are on a
Frontier," he added, "where our Lives and Fortunes may more frequently come
into dispute than other People's; our Privileges and Supports should be pro-
portionably greater; for who would venture his Life to secure *no Property*, or
fight to secure to himself *Poverty* and *Misery*."[9]

At first the trustees were contemptuous of such arguments, dismissing out
of hand "*Those*, who, to gratify the greedy and ambitious View of a few Negroe
Merchants, would put it into their Power to become sole Owners of the Province, by introducing their baneful Commodity."[10] Even the modest success of
the Germans, Thomas Jones argued in 1741, exposed them to the "Envy and
Hatred" of "Negro-Mongers" and those who sought "the extirpation of the
Colony."[11]

However, while South Carolina's economy was booming, Georgia could
barely sustain its tiny communities of hardworking Germans and Scots. By the
1740s immigration to Georgia virtually came to a halt, philanthropic contributions dried up, and the colony was kept afloat by parliamentary grants — the
only ones given out in North America — justified because of Georgia's strategic military position. Eventually even the trustees' interest waned. Late in the
decade they liberalized the bans on slavery and private property. So did the
resistance of the Salzburgers diminish with their realization that after twenty
years in America they remained poor subsistence farmers, while all about them
colonists were growing rich with the profits of slavery and land speculation.
In 1752, the trustees removed the bans altogether and relinquished control of
the colony to the Crown, one year before their grant ran out.

Georgia's new regime went to work swiftly. The mercantilistic restrictions were lifted; a representative assembly was established. Private property, an elected legislature, and slavery replaced a closed economy, patriarchal government, and relative social equality. As Georgia approached the revolutionary era, a new vision emerged, as utopian in its own way as Oglethorpe's had been. This was the liberal vision of a free society, peopled by virtuous, independent citizens, proud of their liberties and their balanced government, jealous of their rights as Englishmen, especially their property rights, upwardly mobile, and increasingly dependent on the labor of black slaves. Contemporaries could only marvel at their achievement. After the trustees relinquished their power, opening the door to slavery and private property, Georgia was said to have grown into "one of the most free and happy countries in the world," in the words of one observer. "Justice was regularly and impartially administered, oppression was unknown, the taxes levied on the subject were trifling, and every man that had industry became opulent."

So the "problem" of slavery in Georgia, as in America, reduces once again to a familiar paradox: in the century before its independence from Great Britain, America simultaneously committed itself to freedom and to slavery. The contradiction was epitomized in the galvanizing words of the Declaration of Independence — "we hold these truths to be self-evident, that all men are created equal" — written by a Virginia slaveholder and repeated endlessly by countless slaveholders at Fourth of July celebrations across the antebellum South.

Now if you paid close attention to the last paragraph, you may have noticed the intellectual sleight of hand as I moved from one paradox, slavery and freedom, to another, slavery and equality. Orlando Patterson has argued that, beginning in ancient Greece, slavery has always generated and sustained the West's unique commitment to freedom and that the paradox of slavery and freedom is therefore built into the nature of slavery.[12] But equality and freedom are not the same thing. Notwithstanding the Stoic and Christian beliefs in the spiritual equality of humankind, the secular principle of fundamental equality *here on earth* is very much a modern idea. Indeed, it was popularized in America at the same time that slavery was. To understand why slavery and the idea of human *equality* developed simultaneously, we have to go back for another look at the development of early American capitalism. Simply put, we cannot resolve the paradox of slavery and freedom in America until we first confront the paradoxical relationship between capitalism and human equality. To do this we need to shift our attention from Georgia's internal problems to the larger context within which Georgia developed.

Confronted with the Declaration's astonishing proposition of fundamental human equality, historians have gone off in two different directions in search of an explanation. The first and most common route is to argue that the inequalities in eighteenth-century America were paltry in comparison with those of Europe: most free men owned their own land, and this simple fact restricted the amount of inequality that was possible in colonial society. It is this *relative* equality that is said to explain the saliency of Jefferson's proposition. More recently, skeptical historians, armed with big equations and bundles of data, have suggested that in the decades preceding the American Revolution the distribution of wealth in colonial society was becoming *less* equal, that the rich were getting richer at the expense of an expanding number of poor people. For these skeptical historians the doctrine of human equality was a radical revolt against the *decline* of social equality in the prerevolutionary years.

Both of these explanations — relative versus declining equality — presuppose a suspiciously transparent relationship between ideology and practice. Americans came to believe in equality either because there was so much equality or because they were losing the equality they had previously enjoyed. But there is no reason to believe that cultures work that reflexively or that ideology corresponds so directly to some presumably objective social reality. In fact, neither argument captures the nature of social change in eighteenth-century America. At issue was neither the relative equality of Americans nor the increasing maldistribution of wealth; at issue were the historically new forms of inequality that were developing rapidly by the third quarter of the eighteenth century and their paradoxical relationship to the principle of human equality.

Georgia's slave society emerged in the context of several other dramatic social transformations in the British colonies. We know, for example, that in rural households across eighteenth-century America women's work was redefined so that it no longer counted as "labor" at all. Men now "worked" because they alone produced the surpluses that were sold for cash beyond the family farm. By removing women's subsistence work from the central place it had once occupied in the process of social reproduction, by defining as labor only that work that generated cash in the marketplace, gender relations were dramatically transformed: they were not equal; they were not "more" or "less" equal than they had once been. They were different.[13]

In the same years apprenticeship contracts were transformed and ultimately disappeared altogether. Traditionally apprenticeship was a system of education and social reproduction: the young man or woman was put to work under a contractual arrangement designed to teach the skills of, say, housewifery or artisanal craftsmanship and also to reproduce the hierarchical social order from which the young people emerged. By the third quarter of the eighteenth century, however, apprenticeship had been effectively transformed into a system of contract labor. Young women sold their labor power as domestic servants, seamstresses, or laundresses, young men as unskilled workers with few prospects for advancement. As with the transformation of gender relations in the colonial household, the shift from apprenticeship to wage labor cannot be reckoned in quantitative terms as an "increase" or "decrease" of social inequality. As a system for organizing a labor force, contracts based on wage work were qualitatively new to late-eighteenth-century America.

At first glance slavery contradicts this pattern—if only because wage labor and slavery are such profoundly different systems of social organization. Yet in important ways slavery was very much a part of this larger story. The first slaves had arrived in North America in 1619, but slavery did not replace indentured servitude as the dominant system for organizing plantation labor until after 1680. The system's expansion, at least as measured by the importation of slaves, grew steadily thereafter and peaked in the third quarter of the eighteenth century. And, as I argued in my last book, this expansion was closely tied to the spread of capitalist social relations in the Atlantic world. Modern slave societies came into existence to feed the expanding consumer demand of capitalist society. In fact, it is a commonplace among historians that Georgia's initial social experiment failed precisely because the trustees never found a commodity that they could produce cheaply enough and for which consumer demand was strong enough. Only with the introduction of slavery and private property did Georgians prosper by producing cotton, indigo, and rice for anxious customers in Great Britain and New England.[14]

Thus colonial American society was not characterized by real social equality, nor is there anything unambiguously significant about the inconsistent shifts in the distribution of wealth. Far more important was the development of several new forms of social inequality, all of which had this critical feature in common: each was associated with the dramatic development of a consumer society in Anglo-America. As family farms produced more and more marketable surpluses, as the number of workers living off their wages increased, and as growing numbers of African slaves were put to work producing cash crops, the number of commodities passing back and forth across the Atlantic world almost literally exploded.[15]

In this dramatically new setting—where the basic necessities of life were increasingly purchased rather than produced at home, where levels of consumption established a new hierarchy of social status, where freedom of "choice" was exalted in ways previously unimaginable—social life took on an entirely new appearance. More and more daily interactions took the form of commercial exchanges, exchanges not simply of luxuries but of necessities, and not simply of goods but of labor power itself. Money, the "universal equivalent," lent to those relations of commercial exchange an appearance of equity and voluntarism missing from the accompanying relations of production. Every sale was a contract entered into voluntarily and mutually agreed upon. Goods and services were exchanged for an equivalent amount of cash, and every dollar was equal to every other dollar. I offer it as a reasonable hypothesis, therefore, that several new forms of social inequality that developed in the eighteenth century, all of them tied to the spread of consumer exchange, made it possible for men and women to imagine for the first time that they were all, somehow, equal.

Slavery was an integral part of this process. Hence the specifically American paradox of slavery and human equality begins in the relationship between slavery and capitalism at a critical moment in the latter's historical development. Caught up in the world of burgeoning consumer demand, the slaveholders had become increasingly attached to marketable commodities, as has been exposed to us by their own probate inventories. It is no wonder the slaveholders themselves began to speak in the language made possible by the profoundly egalitarian appearance of exchange relations. In the face of the most inequitable relations of production known to human history, the slaveholders declared their commitment to the revolutionary proposition that all men were equally endowed with the fundamental rights of life, liberty, and property. The slaveholders had become liberals.[16]

What does that mean—liberals? There was one simple way to spot a liberal in eighteenth-century America. Anyone who opened a speech, introduced a pamphlet, or commenced an argument with an attack on the patriarchal belief in divinely ordained inequality was almost certainly a liberal. In a sense, that is what liberalism *was* initially: a powerful critique of patriarchalism. That is the way John Locke organized his *Two Treatises,* and well into the nineteenth century liberals continued to open their arguments with assaults on the evils of patriarchal government, whether monarchical, aristocratic, or simply tyrannical. Georgia's slaveholders did precisely that when they invoked the triumphant language of the British Declaration of Rights in their attack on Oglethorpe. Nor is it surprising that Oglethorpe's "Plan" for organizing Georgia society grated on the slaveholders' deepest political sensibilities.

Born as an assault on "organic" theories of society, liberalism has often been defended for its unutopian character or, conversely, criticized for lacking a social vision — a plan — of its own. The antiliberal complaint runs something like this: the declaration of fundamental human equality amounts to little more than equality of individual rights; individual rights are fundamentally "negative," that is, they tell us what we cannot do to one another rather than what we are obliged to do as members of a community. Liberal societies are thereby left to drift aimlessly in moral relativism and spiritual anomie, unable to define "the good" that would anchor us in the community and obligate us to preserve it.

By this standard slavery violated everything that liberalism stood for. The slaves had no rights, only obligations. Because obligations imply community, slave society was the very antithesis of an atomized collectivity of isolated individuals. As the most extreme form of subordination, slavery stood at the furthest possible remove from liberalism's opening premise of fundamental human equality.

Nevertheless, in Georgia the slaveholders were the colonists most likely to invoke liberal rhetoric, while the opponents of slavery, including the colony's founders, adhered quite strongly to a communitarian vision of the world. The same pattern persisted into the antebellum South. Few slaveholders abandoned the liberal rhetoric of rights; few openly rejected the Jeffersonian dictum of fundamental human equality. Outside a small circle of proslavery intellectuals and theologians, few slaveholders held up a divinely ordained hierarchy as the preferred alternative to Lockean or Smithean liberalism.

It is easy enough to appreciate how the slaveholders might see in liberalism a stanch defense of private property that was well suited to their needs. I have argued elsewhere that Locke himself found in the state of nature a virtually physical location for the slaves: outside society in a perpetual state of war. In M. I. Finley's definition of slaves as "foreigners," recast by Patterson as "social death," we can also see how American slavery was defined as "rightlessness" precisely because Americans defined social life by the possession of certain fundamental rights.[17]

Therein lies a problem, however — for the study of slavery, of liberalism, and

of the relationship between the two—for we have already seen that in orthodox terms liberalism is reckoned to be a "negative" philosophy, praised or
castigated for its *lack* of social vision, for the absence of any affirmative convictions about how social life ought to be ordered. Committed to the interests of
the individual over society, liberalism would seem to represent its own form of
social death—a world of atomized human beings for whom "society" has little
meaning except as a public form of solitary confinement. Notice the difficulty
this raises. If slavery is the negation of social life, and liberalism is itself a negative philosophy, we are left scratching our heads in a futile attempt to imagine
American slavery as the negation of negation. How can you be socially dead
in a world that is socially dead?

There is a deceptively simple answer, but it compels us to move beyond the
orthodox definition of liberalism. To understand what social death meant to
American slaves is to appreciate the breadth and power of the kind of social
life liberalism envisioned. Indeed, from Locke and his followers came the first
fully developed concept of "the social"—the view that human beings were the
products of their society and that their proper rearing was that which fitted
them for life in society. Liberalism, in short, was *not* a negative philosophy;
it did not repudiate community; it did not exalt the individual over society.
On the contrary, as was clear in eighteenth-century Georgia, liberals entertained a profoundly utopian vision of the world—a utopianism so deeply ingrained and so widely shared that it soon became all but invisible to most of
the Americans who ascribed to it. It is essential for the study of slavery as an
American problem that we recover liberalism's utopian vision. For if we fail,
we will remain deaf to the language within which slavery was discussed in early
America. Neither proslavery racism nor antislavery ideology will make sense
until we go back to the beginning and redefine liberalism as it developed in
the colonial era.

Consider rights rhetoric. Even if we reduce liberalism to the primacy of
rights, we are hard pressed to demonstrate the antisocial nature of the rights
that mattered most to eighteenth-century liberals. The case for the atomiz-
ing force of "rights" rhetoric is theoretical, not historical. Ask yourself why so
many of the rights Madison laid down in the first ten amendments to the Constitution were designed to defend public rather than private life. Is freedom
of assembly an invitation to withdraw into privacy? Can freedom of speech be
reckoned as anything other than a defense of social interaction and political
participation? Is freedom of the press a bulwark of atomized individualism?

The several rights guaranteeing free expression were seen by their advocates as the building blocks of deliberative democracy. They gave constitutional sanction to a "public sphere" in which citizens were encouraged to engage in various forms of reasoned discourse, including political criticism. The government itself was compelled to act publicly, in some cases through the device of constitutional rights—hence the right of habeas corpus, the right to due process in open court, including the right to be publicly charged with a crime and to be judged by representatives of the public, in a public trial. These were rights designed to protect the integrity of public life in a political system whose legitimacy had come to rest on "public opinion."

For a vigorous public sphere to develop, liberals committed themselves to much more than the sanctity of individual expression. Public life had to be conducted in ways that encouraged widespread participation through respect for the dignity of every citizen. So liberals were unusually concerned to construct a new set of manners. Conflicting opinions had to be tolerated. Hypocrisy, snobbery, and cruelty—both physical and psychological—became unacceptable vices; condemned as badges of inferiority, they inhibited the robust discussion that was the raison d'être of a public sphere.

Locke and his followers understood that participation in reasoned public debate required specific forms of child rearing and careful education. As we might say today, individuals had to be "socialized." Thus liberal ideology also emphasized the importance of a "private" life of family and work. Specifically, liberals argued that families should be bound together by affection rather than coercion, that children should be nurtured on love rather than fear, and that their rational faculties should be exercised from a very early age so that they could one day assume their place in society as responsible adults. Charles Taylor calls all of this "the affirmation of ordinary life,"[18] and it was one of the hallmarks of the liberal social vision. In the labor theory of value, as in the ideal of the affectionate family, liberal egalitarianism expressed itself in the cultural value it attributed to everyday experience. Indeed, liberals often argued that the public sphere stood as the protective barrier shielding private life from the intrusions of an overbearing government. But the private and the public were understood less in isolation than in relation to each other. If the public sphere was designed in part to protect the private life, the private sphere in turn was designed to prepare citizens for public life.

So the charge that liberalism was devoid of a social vision simply cannot stand. Imagine the kind of social life liberal rights and institutions created.

Capitalism, for example, is hard to conceive without the liberal commitment to private property and free labor. But liberals constructed much more than that—and much that was in tension with capitalism. A partial list would include affectionate families, educated citizens, religious toleration, dignified labor, government by reflection rather than by authority, status determined by merit rather than lineage, equal respect rather than divinely ordained hierarchy, respect that included concern for the emotional as well as the physical integrity of all human beings.

If this is what social *life* in liberal society is all about, we can now return to the subject at hand, to a renewed appreciation of the problem of social *death*, or slavery, in America. To be a slave in liberal America was to be denied both a public and a private life. The slave family was barely recognized in law; the "public" rights of speech, assembly, and the press did not apply to the slaves. The mutual respect of civil life was replaced, under slavery, with the systematic, even ritualistic, dishonoring of the slave. Slave labor was the epitome of degradation among liberals: it destroyed self-respect, it thwarted social mobility, it bred laziness and incompetence. The "badges of inferiority" so reviled in free society were among the hallmarks of involuntary servitude: slaves were physically abused and publicly humiliated in systematic rather than incidental ways. There is no better way to appreciate what it meant to be a member of a liberal society, to participate in liberal social life, than to unpack the meaning of social death in the American South.

If American slavery is now easier to define, so is the rhetoric of abolitionism easier to comprehend. For Thomas Jefferson the issue was straightforward. If "all men are created equal," if they are equally endowed with the rights of life, liberty, and happiness—then slavery was morally wrong and had to be abolished. But most abolitionist rhetoric went far beyond this simple proposition, invoking as well a whole series of moral indictments that were drawn directly from the utopian vision of liberal society. Slavery was cruel, both physically and psychologically. Slaveholders who professed their commitment to democracy and the principles of Jefferson's Declaration were rank hypocrites. Slavery degraded human labor, undermined the work ethic, and held untold millions in poverty and ignorance. It undermined family life, forced men and women to live together outside the bonds of marriage, exposed the privacy of the home to the intrusive authority of the master, and then barbarically destroyed the affectionate bonds that had formed between slave mothers, slave fathers, and slave children. By mandating the illiteracy of the slaves, the "peculiar institution" not only deprived them of unmediated access to the word of God, it also excluded slaves from participation in the public sphere.

In the conspicuous absence of these quintessential liberal arguments against slavery we can detect the great limitation of Jefferson's antislavery sentiments. He wanted to end the social death of slavery, but he did not want the freed slaves to participate in American social life. He could not imagine whites and blacks sharing the affection and intimacy of the private life, nor could he imagine free blacks participating as equals in the public sphere. Unwilling to tolerate the presence of blacks in American social life, Jefferson went out of his way to theorize a justification for the colonization of African Americans outside the boundaries of the United States. And in so doing, he laid the groundwork of the central theme of *proslavery* thought: that blacks were unsuited for freedom in America.

Consider Jefferson's racism carefully. He did not argue that blacks were inferior to whites in every way. As Garry Wills and others have pointed out, Jefferson acknowledged that Africans were born with a moral sense equal to that of whites; this was one of the most compelling reasons for their inalienable right to liberty.[19] Rather, Jefferson argued that blacks were inferior in two very specific ways: aesthetically and intellectually. Why these two? For Jefferson the aesthetic inferiority of blacks—both their physical appearance and their insufficiently restrained emotions—precluded intimate relations with whites and therefore made it impossible for blacks and whites ever to share their private lives as equals. Conversely, their intellectual inferiority rendered blacks forever incapable of engaging in rational discussion at the level of whites, of participating in the public sphere as equals. Thus unworthy of equal respect, blacks could only degrade American social life by their presence. So for all his avowed antislavery sentiments (and there is no good reason to believe them insincere), Jefferson nevertheless established the racist framework that would, by the nineteenth century, become the justification for continuing to hold blacks alone in slavery.

One way to appreciate this is by returning, briefly, to Georgia, a century after the collapse of the trusteeship. By 1860 the Jeffersonian combination of devotion to fundamental liberal rights and contempt for blacks resonated throughout the rhetoric of Georgia's leading secessionists. Robert Toombs complained of the North's repeated "violation of [Georgians'] constitutional rights," in particular the right of property—in slaves. Henry L. Benning stood on the universal "right to self-preservation." And where Oglethorpe's opponents had invoked the English Declaration of Rights, Thomas R. R. Cobb recited the classic Lockean triad. "Protection to the life, liberty and property of the citizen is the corner-stone and only end of government in the American mind," he argued.[20]

The catch, for Cobb, was in the word *citizen*. He took citizenship to be a token of membership in American society, and blacks were not members. As he enunciated his basic principles, Cobb declared, "*First.* This Constitution was made for white men — citizens of the United States; this Union was formed by white men, and for the protection and happiness of their race." It was not simply that blacks were inferior or that they were suited by nature for slavery but that they were *un*suited for freedom. Cobb argued, simply, that blacks could never participate as citizens in American public life. Nor could they share private lives as free men and women — quite the contrary. Henry L. Benning was not the only Georgian who argued for secession as the necessary means of avoiding apocalyptic racial slaughter. If the North had its way, Benning warned, if the "black Republicans" freed the slaves, "very soon a war between the whites and the blacks [would] spontaneously break out everywhere. It [would] be in every town, in every village, in every neighborhood, in every road. It [would] be a war of man with man," he added, in a dreadful echo of Jefferson himself, "a war of extermination." [21]

The assumption, also inherited from Jefferson, was that blacks and whites could not live together as equals, and since living together as equals was the core precept of American liberalism, blacks could never live in America as free men and women. For Jefferson that meant colonization, for Benning secession. But it does not require a great act of imagination to detect the same premise operating in the two different arguments.

Let that premise stand as my conclusion. Simply put: There are membership rules for Americans — rules that define what it means to participate fully in our social life. They are not distinctive to America, and they are far more elaborate than historians of American liberalism have ever appreciated. But slavery makes it hard not to see those rules, and this is why slavery — whatever else it was — was so *American* a problem. For more than anything else in our history, the struggle over slavery forced Americans to come to terms with their own identities. If you want to know what it means to be an American, think about what it meant to be a slave.

Notes

1   Charles Grier Sellers Jr., ed., *The Southerner as American* (Chapel Hill, 1960).

2   See, for example, Charles Grier Sellers Jr., "Who Were the Southern Whigs?" *American Historical Review* 59 (January 1954): 335–46.

3   Orlando Patterson, *Slavery and Social Death* (Cambridge, Mass., 1982).

4   Pat. Tailfer et al., *A True and historical narrative of the Colony of Georgia* . . . (1741), in *Tracts and Other Papers, Relating Principally to Origins, Settlement, and Progress of the Colonies in North America, from the Discovery of the Country to the Year 1776,* ed. Peter Force (Washington, D.C., 1836), 1:36.

5   Tailfer et al., *True and historical narrative,* 40.

6   Tailfer et al., *True and historical narrative,* 30.

7   Tailfer et al., *True and historical narrative,* 23, 1, iii–v.

8   Quoted in Clarence L. Ver Steeg, *Origins of a Southern Mosaic: Studies of Early Carolina and Georgia* (Athens, Ga., 1975), 99.

9   Quoted in Ver Steeg, *Origins of a Southern Mosaic,* 48.

10 Tailfer et al., *True and historical narrative,* 53.

11 "A State of the Province of Georgia, Attested upon Oath, in the Court of Savannah, November 10, 1740" (1742), in Force, *Tracts and Other Papers,* 1:18.

12 Orlando Patterson, *Freedom: Volume 1: Freedom in the Making of Western Culture* (New York, 1991).

13 Jeanne Boydston, *Home and Work: Housework, Wages, and the Ideology of Labor in the Early Republic* (New York, 1990), 1–29.

14 James Oakes, *Slavery and Freedom: An Interpretation of the Old South* (New York, 1990), chap. 2.

15 Oakes, *Slavery and Freedom.*

16 Lois Green Carr and Lorena S. Walsh, "Changing Lifestyles and Consumer Behavior in the Colonial Chesapeake," in *Of Consuming Interests: The Style of Life in the Eighteenth Century,* ed. Cary Carson, Ronald Hoffman, and Peter J. Albert (Charlottesville, 1994), 59–166.

17 Oakes, *Slavery and Freedom,* 63–65, 70–71. Moses I. Finley, "Slavery," in *International Encyclopedia of the Social Sciences,* ed. David Sills (New York, 1968); idem, *Ancient Slavery and Modern Ideology* (New York, 1980).

18 Charles Taylor, *Sources of the Self: The Making of the Modern Identity* (Cambridge, Mass., 1989), 211–302.

19 Garry Wills, *Inventing America: Jefferson's Declaration of Independence* (Garden City, N.Y., 1978), 223–28.

20 William W. Freehling and Craig M. Simpson, eds., *Secession Debated: Georgia's Showdown in 1860* (New York, 1992), 44, 144, 12.

21 Freehling and Simpson, *Secession Debated,* 8, 120.

∾ Slavery, Secession, and Reconstruction as American Problems

DON H. DOYLE

THE ORIGIN OF THE SOUTH as an American problem was rooted in slavery. It was well after the American Revolution, after Americans began to think of themselves as a nation supposedly sharing common values and principles, that it was even possible to think of the South as some kind of anomalous region at odds with those ideals. Slavery, above all else, provided the essential material with which critics fashioned the idea of a South opposed to the liberal values the Revolution crystallized. It was not so much that the South diverged to oppose the rest of the nation; rather, reformers in the northern states, particularly New England, suddenly came to condemn slavery—and with it the South—as contradictions to the ideals of the Revolution, the morality of Christianity, and the principles of America.

The crusade against slavery gained force in the North as a moral attack on the evil of slaveholding and later broadened into a general condemnation of the whole South because it rested on the flawed foundation of slavery. William Lloyd Garrison and the American Anti-Slavery Society based their radical appeal for immediate and total abolition not simply on the idea that the slave master was guilty of sin but on the belief that all Americans shared responsibility for this sin. It was an *American* moral problem, they insisted, embedded in the very Constitution that defined the nation. This moral attack on slavery was broadened by arguments pointing to its practical ill effects suffered not only by the slave but also by the entire society, which was tainted by slavery. Indeed, the charges that found greatest public support were those that cast slavery as a liability to people *other* than slaves. Slavery was evil, one argument went, because it degraded free labor and condemned the "poor white" masses to misery and the South to poverty. Slavery was counter to American republican ideals, another attack emphasized, because it supported an exclusive, selfish aristocracy that dominated southern politics and society.[1]

These arguments on the social, economic, and political repercussions of slavery pointed to problems southerners suffered, but nothing in the logic of these attacks demanded that slavery be treated as anything more than a regional problem and therefore no problem at all to America as a nation. Slavery, with all its implications, had to be seen as an expansive and insidious force that posed a menace to the whole Republic. This idea did not find a broad audience until the war with Mexico, which began in 1845 and ended three years later with a vast new empire extending into the Southwest. The war came to be understood by northerners ill disposed toward slavery as part of a larger design by which the "slave power conspiracy"[2] sought to expand its political power by adding slave states to the Union, from which more proslavery congressmen would come to control the nation's government. Ultimately, some northerners began to warn, the goal of this slave-power conspiracy was nothing less than to extend slavery throughout the North and thereby imperil the whole experiment in republican government.

An America with widespread slavery, antislavery forces argued, would become like the South, a society of privileged slave masters ruling a population of racially alien slaves (augmented, it was feared, by a reopening of the African slave trade). Below the aristocratic slave masters, a miserable class of poor whites would be squeezed out of the mainstream of economic opportunity and deprived of education. Slavery would drive out free labor and destroy the vital free institutions it fostered. Abraham Lincoln was among the early opponents of this slave-power conspiracy during the war with Mexico. America, he later warned in his famous "House Divided" speech, must "become all one thing or all the other" — all slave or all free.[3]

Whatever dire consequences slavery and its expansion posed to the nation, only the radical abolitionists advocated ending slavery where it already existed. To "free-soilers" slavery posed a problem to the nation outside the slave states, and the remedy was to *contain — not abolish —* it. Eventually, many free-soilers hoped, the containment of slavery in the southern states would lead to its gradual extinction, once the slave economy was denied satisfaction of its voracious appetite for new land and once the domestic slave trade was deprived of its western market. The important thing was to save the West — not the slave — from the evils of slavery.

Garrison and the radical abolitionists continued to focus on the personal immorality of slave ownership. They appealed to the conscience of Americans by exposing the brutality and cruelty inherent in the master-slave relationship. They invoked religious and humanitarian principles, as opposed to the more practical economic and political ideas free-soilers drew upon. The abolitionist remedy for this sin was total and immediate emancipation, not containment. Nor did they tolerate any plan of gradual emancipation of the slaves, particularly when that involved some kind of compensation to slave owners.

Before 1830 antislavery reformers in the South and North had attempted to define the problem within a morally neutral and racist framework. American slavery, they had argued, was an unfortunate accident of history, an inherited burden that reflected in no way on the morality of southern slaveholders or the South. Slave owners were excused as having no choice but to continue enslavement, the alternative being an unthinkable emancipation of a degraded black race in what was widely assumed to be a "white man's republic." Given this premise, the only solution they could imagine was a program of gradual, voluntary emancipation and colonization of freed blacks in Liberia, which would become a beacon of Christianity and democracy in the dark continent of Africa. One of the first lines of attack Garrison and other abolitionists had taken in their crusade was to challenge the prevailing moral defense of slavery as a curse visited upon innocent Americans by British slave traders before the Revolution, an idea Jefferson had long ago incorporated into the Declaration of Independence. Abolitionists also dismissed racial arguments that excused slavery as a "necessary evil," a view premised on the belief that letting Africans live free within a white society was unthinkable, either because it would threaten whites or because it would harm freed blacks. The sin of slavery in their view could not be excused because of its origins or the consequences of its abolition.

Once abolitionists defined slavery unequivocally as a moral sin, they exhibited little tolerance for more pragmatic, moderate, or conciliatory reformers, some of whom questioned the practicality of total and immediate emancipation or raised issues regarding the future of the freed slaves in America. "I do not wish to think, or speak, or write, with moderation," Garrison warned. "Tell a man whose house is on fire to give a moderate alarm; tell him to moderately rescue his wife from the hands of the ravisher."[4]

The master-slave relationship, as the abolitionists presented it in their literature and speeches, was inherently evil because it deprived the slave of free will and exposed the slave to horrible acts of physical brutality—whipping, branding, mutilation, and sexual abuse. Slavery reduced human beings to "things" and invited unspeakable cruelty. Among the most powerful images of slavery that antislavery forces projected were those depicting the sexual exploitation of slave women by licentious masters and the callous breaking of families by sale and migration.

These depictions of brutality, sexual exploitation, and shattered families all gained enormous force from new currents of thought that were emerging in a number of antebellum reform movements. In the newly invented penitentiaries and asylums for the insane, reformers had instituted new standards of humanitarian treatment for those who had been regarded as the most depraved members of society. Traditional methods of corporal punishment and public humiliation of criminals, for example, came to be denounced as barbaric atrocities by penal reformers who now wished to place them in isolation from society, where they would do penance and redeem their lives, ultimately returning to society as useful members of the community.[5]

The condemnation of physical brutality and sexual exploitation also gained force from new concepts of child nurture and sexual restraint that were being formulated within the urban middle class. At the heart of this new domestic culture was a rejection of the authoritarian patriarchal family within which men had once been urged to rule "family government" with an iron fist. Traditional advice to parents had likened child rearing to breaking horses and warned that softness would only encourage willful disobedience—"spare the rod and spoil the child." The authoritarian values that justified harsh, often brutal use of force were repudiated by those who argued that human nature was more "plastic," therefore capable of "Christian nurture" through persuasion and example rather than force. If slavery was defended as a domestic institution, and justified by the notion of slaves as childlike, the antislavery attack, at the very least, imposed new standards of paternal conduct.[6]

These newly minted standards of humanitarian, voluntary relations between people, whatever their social status, provided a moral yardstick against which slavery could be exposed as a moral evil, antithetical to Christianity, American principles, and decent family values. The litany of atrocities, from whipping to sexual exploitation, that abolitionists employed to generate public abhorrence of slavery would hardly have claimed much of a hearing within an earlier cultural context.

The abolitionist crusade made ample use of the depictions of physical cruelty and depraved immorality suffered by slaves, but the appeal drew not so much on the audience's sympathy for the slave as it did on a condemnation of *slave ownership* as a sin. Whatever injuries slavery brought to the slave, these were not necessarily problems the nation had to grapple with. Countering any concern for the slave victims were racial fears that white Americans north and south shared regarding the future of freed blacks in a "white man's country" and more hardheaded concerns about the consequences of abolition on the nation's economy. It was the abolitionists' mission to persuade their audience of the idea that slavery was a moral sin, one in which *all* Americans were implicated—an organic sin. The problem slavery presented to America, therefore, was its very existence within the nation, for it threatened the moral purity of the Republic. Accordingly, abolitionists made their case *against* the sin of slaveholding and not solely *for* the slave as victim. It was a tactic that would have profound influence on the eventual failure of Reconstruction.

This abolitionist wing of the antislavery movement pursued a campaign of moral suasion through public exhortation accompanied by a blizzard of tracts, books, petitions, and speeches. Like other reform movements of the time, opponents of slavery began from the premise that free citizens and their political leaders, once fully informed of the evils of slavery, could make a moral choice to condone or condemn it. Garrison's followers eschewed political remedies to pursue this strategy of persuasion and voluntary compliance. The American Anti-Slavery Society in 1834 avowed that its chief mission was the "overthrow of American slavery . . . mainly by showing to the public its true character[,] . . . its contrariety to the first principles of religion, morals, and humanity, and its special inconsistency with [the nation's] pretensions, as a free, humane, and enlightened people." By these educational means, it expected to "produce a just public sentiment, which [would] appeal both to the conscience and love of character, of . . . slave-holding fellow-citizens, and convince them that both their duty and their welfare require the immediate abolition of slavery."[7] Though most of the agitation for abolition would take place outside the South, the success of the cause depended, ultimately, on the slave owners themselves carrying out the "duty of all masters" and freeing their slaves voluntarily.

If the purpose of the abolitionist crusade was moral suasion of public opinion against the sin of slavery, it was not so clear just how those persuaded were supposed to act on their convictions, except to persuade others, eventually converting the only individuals who could do anything to remedy the sin—the masters themselves. Though abolitionists had to know this would ultimately require some kind of practical policy, some government program of emancipation, they deliberately avoided discussing the process of abolishing slavery and refused, at the same time, to focus the argument on the future of the freed slaves. "Do not allow yourself to be drawn away from the main object, to exhibit a detailed PLAN OF ABOLITION," Theodore Weld's instructions from the American Anti-Slavery Society read; "[l]et the *principle* be decided on, of immediate abolition, and the plans will easily present themselves."[8] For abolitionists slavery was a national problem, but its remedy was personal moral conversion.

This tactic, of course, conveniently allowed abolitionists to ignore vexing issues enmeshed in the constitutional protection of states' rights and individual property rights. It also owed much to Garrison's own anarchistic rejection of political action and government compulsion in any form. But he, more than any, was aware of the fundamental contradictions at work in a reform movement that began from a condemnation of coercion of one human by another. Unjustified force was the essence of the evil inherent in the master-slave relationship, but some policy of coercion also seemed integral to any plausible plan for emancipation. The vagueness and naïveté with which abolitionists tried to bridge moral sentiment and action were strikingly evident in the most popular statement of antislavery thought, Harriet Beecher Stowe's *Uncle Tom's Cabin*. In an afterword to the novel, Stowe posed the question so many of her readers had come to: "But, what can any individual do?" "There is one thing that every individual can do," she answered confidently; "they can see to it that *they feel right.*" "[Y]ou have another power," she went on; "you can *pray!*"[9] With that kind of counsel abolitionists seemed willing to leave the path between moral conviction and public action open to any number of possible courses.

If the abolitionist attack on slavery as a sin failed to address the practical problems of emancipation, the more pragmatic, political antislavery groups also neglected any serious consideration of what was to follow the end of slavery. Efforts to politicize the antislavery movement aimed at converting moral distaste for slavery into electoral support for parties or candidates who would advance restrictionist policies. This campaign initially found expression in single-issue political parties beginning with the Liberty Party in 1840, followed by the Free Soil Party in 1848. But it was not until 1854 that the Republican Party gave antislavery a viable political voice. In the Kansas-Nebraska

Act of that year, moderates tried to find a pragmatic solution to the question of slavery in the territories by turning the question over to the settlers themselves. The result was a travesty of popular sovereignty and a bloody preview of the Civil War. Out of the political earthquake the Kansas-Nebraska fiasco set off, the second party system collapsed and a new coalition, the Republican Party, emerged. With the opposition shattered or divided by the slavery question, antislavery finally found in the Republican Party a winning vehicle. But it was successful only insofar as Republicans advanced a moderate antislavery position limited to moral condemnation and territorial containment. Initially, the only problem southern slavery posed to the nation, in Republican eyes, was its expansion. In their moral condemnation of slavery, however, Republicans made good use of the ideological materials assembled by antislavery forces over the previous three decades. Lincoln and the Republicans ran in 1860 against slavery and all the social ills that grew from it within the South. In opposition to this version of the South, Republicans put forth a vision of industrious, free labor invigorating a prosperous, democratic society imbued with the spirit of improvement, a society to which slavery was antithetical. Republicans, more than any other antislavery voice, condemned slavery as an institution, criticized the South as a corrupt product of slavery, and framed both as a serious threat to the American experiment in republican government and free society.[10]

In a real sense the radical southern fire-eaters solved the Republicans' problem with the South by taking their troublesome region out of the nation. Secession in a stroke obliterated the moral concerns northern reformers had with the evil union with slaveholders. At the same time, it rendered obsolete the legal and political debate over the expansion of slavery and its menace to the free states and territories of the United States. Many opponents of slavery and the South recognized this and applauded the secession of the slave states. Separation would finally purge the nation of the sin of slavery. Garrison had long since denounced the Constitution as a "union with slaveholders" and had openly advocated secession of the North from the South.[11] How could he object to the South seceding? A pacifist and anarchist, Garrison could not conceive of force as a basis for human society. "At last 'the covenant with death' is annulled, and the 'agreement with hell' broken," he announced, criticizing all efforts to save the Union as "simply idiotic."[12] No southern fire-eater argued more forcefully for the South's right to secede than the abolitionist Wendell Phillips, who in the winter of 1861 lectured throughout the North on behalf of peace and disunion. "Standing with the principles of '76 behind us," he implored, "who can deny them the right?"

Not all abolitionists accepted secession as a means of purging moral evil from what remained of the Union. Some, like Phillips, thought slavery would end more rapidly in an independent South without "Northern bayonets calming the masters' fear." Secession would expose Confederate slavery to a vast border with a free and hostile United States; no fugitive slave law would protect them now. Others accepted disunion as preferable to any further compromise and protection of slavery, if that was what would be necessary to keep the slave states in the Union. Whatever their thinking, had it been up to most abolitionists in the winter and spring of 1861, the South might have seceded without war, and America's problem with the South would have been solved, or at least transferred to the arena of international diplomacy.[13]

Wars often force the parties engaged to justify their sacrifice, to demonize the enemy, and to confirm their own moral superiority. In modern wars fought with citizen armies, and particularly those fought by democratic societies, the success in defining a nation's purpose in war often determines success in war as much as military events alone. The process by which the North defined its purpose unfolded unpredictably after war commenced in the spring of 1861.

Abolitionists, who, prior to the fall of Fort Sumter, found themselves in an unlikely alliance with southern secessionists, began to recant once the shooting began. They sought to make the cause of Union and emancipation one, and they now welcomed the war as an opportunity for national moral regeneration. As Garrison, Phillips, and other leading abolitionists wriggled out of their earlier disunionist and pacifist sentiments, they broadened and redefined the American problem with slavery in patriotic and historical terms. Now they denounced slavery and the South as evil because they threatened to destroy the Union that had been born in the Revolution. Proclaiming the war a "Second American Revolution," one abolitionist urged: "The Revolution must go on to its completion—*A National Abolition of Slavery.*" Garrison explained his new allegiance to the Union cause with unflinching conviction: "[T]he one great cause of all our national troubles and division is SLAVERY: the removal of it, therefore, is essential to our national existence. What can be plainer than this."[14]

While abolitionists began to define the war as a crusade for emancipation and fulfillment of the American Revolution, Lincoln and most of the northern public were far from agreement. Rebellion, not slavery, was the evil the South now posed to the nation in the eyes of most Republicans. It was not at all clear that northern war aims would ever include emancipation of slaves; initially Lincoln seemed bent on doing all he could to assure just the opposite. With a cautious eye on the border slave states and another on ambivalent northern public opinion regarding slavery and race, he reassured Americans — south and north — that he had no intention of interfering with slavery and that it would be protected once the rebellion ceased. He did so in the hope of ending the war quickly and preserving the Union. As those hopes sunk in the gory reality of a long, bloody conflict, Lincoln gradually shifted northern policy toward the abolitionist position. Once again, he did so to bring a more rapid end to the war and preserve the Union. Lincoln was candid about his expediency in embracing emancipation: "If I could save the Union without freeing *any* slave I would do it," he explained in his famous reply to abolitionist Horace Greely, "and if I could save it by freeing *all* the slaves I would do it." [15]

The story is now familiar to most Americans: Lincoln, pursuing political, military, and diplomatic advantage — and responding to pressures from runaway slaves themselves — transformed a war with the limited aim of restoring the Union into a war against slavery. Lincoln's slow and morally ambiguous gravitation toward emancipation makes an easy target for criticism. It is often pointed out that the Emancipation Proclamation left the slaves under Union control still in bondage and theoretically freed only those under Confederate control and beyond federal power to set free. Had those rebel governments given up before January 1863, the proclamation guaranteed the safety of slave property there as well. No one was more forthright in admitting the calculated motives underlying the proclamation than Lincoln, who, even after transforming the war into an antislavery crusade, continued to speak in favor of a program of gradual emancipation by the states, federal compensation for slave owners, and deportation and colonization of freed slaves. Indeed, he incorporated such proposals into the proclamation should the slave states return to the Union. [16]

Whatever the moral ambiguity of Lincoln's strategy, the Emancipation Proclamation constituted a fundamental redefinition of the American problem with slavery and the South, and it marked a radical departure in the remedies offered. At the most basic level, the Emancipation Proclamation provided the nation with the first clear solution to the problem of slavery, that is, to simply abolish it by federal fiat. Abolitionism was brought from the radical fringe to the mainstream of national policy. Its leaders, who had begged Lincoln to make the war a crusade against slavery, found that their attacks on the slave-ocracy had won a surprising degree of public respect during the war. Once a despised fringe, ridiculed for its extreme views (which included racial and sexual equality, critics charged), the abolitionists had come to enjoy unprecedented honor from the press and politicians as the moral representatives of a growing segment of public opinion in the North.[17] Their appeals to white guilt over slavery had already been employed in the efforts to mobilize the northern military effort; the call of men to arms and the summons of women volunteers at the home front frequently joined patriotism and defense of the Union against the rebels to a general antipathy toward slavery and slave masters. As the bloody ordeal of war proceeded, the reports of death and destruction could now be justified by the higher moral cause the Emancipation Proclamation seemed to invest in the northern war effort. The transformation of a war against secession and rebellion into a war for freedom percolated down to soldiers on the front lines, who now marched to battle singing the abolitionist anthem "John Brown's Body" and Julia Ward Howe's famous "Battle Hymn of the Republic": "As he died to make men holy, Let us die to make men free."[18]

With the Emancipation Proclamation, Lincoln and the power of the national government had become *allied*—but not completely *aligned*—with the abolitionist position on slavery. The federal government, abolitionists argued, could emancipate the slaves under the extraordinary powers of a nation at war as a "military necessity." War provided an excuse to circumvent the nagging constitutional provisions for the protection of slave property and the right of states to regulate slavery. That protection, that right, they claimed, had been forfeited by the rebels. For the moment, radical abolitionists shrewdly accepted the military's definition of slaves as property and proposed wholesale confiscation of slaves as "contraband of war." This proposal may have aimed more at punishing the slaveholding rebels and breaking the back of their labor force than it did at helping the slaves, thousands of whom had long since taken the question of emancipation into their own hands by fleeing to Union lines.[19] In embracing this contraband policy, antislavery zealots showed they were as willing as Lincoln to argue from expediency when it came to emancipation.

Even as slavery was destroyed, its victims, the slaves, remained outside the central focus of concern. Emancipation found support among Republican moderates primarily as a strategy aimed at weakening the Confederacy's capacity to wage war and undermining pro-Confederate sympathies in Europe. Slaves constituted approximately half the Confederate labor force: "The very stomach of this rebellion is the . . . slave," Frederick Douglass pleaded. "Arrest that hoe . . . and you smite the rebellion in the very seat of its life."[20] If the Union could count on slaves to abandon their masters, it was not inconceivable that fugitive slaves and freedmen might also serve their master's enemy. The idea that runaway slaves would be employed by the Union army, and even armed as soldiers in a war for their own freedom, took the logic of the emancipation strategy one step further. A provision for the enlistment of blacks in the U.S. Army and Navy was incorporated into the final version of the proclamation.[21]

With the Emancipation Proclamation activated at the opening of 1863, the invading Union army became—willing or not—an army of liberation, everywhere undermining slave discipline, encouraging slaves to run away or rebel against their masters, and, in the process, disrupting the economy and social order of the Confederacy wherever it was penetrated. Although Lincoln denied any intention of inciting slave insurrection, it seemed to many, especially white southerners, that John Brown's maniacal dream of a slave uprising had become de facto federal policy. Out of a combination of humanitarian concern and military expediency, and against the manifest wishes of large numbers of northern soldiers and citizens (few of whom wanted to sacrifice lives for black freedom), Lincoln had managed to turn the war for union into a crusade for a "new birth of freedom."[22] The destruction of slavery was at once the remedy to the *moral problem* of slavery, as defined by abolitionists, and the solution to the *military problem* of defeating the rebellion and preserving the Union, as defined by moderates.

None understood the implications of emancipation better than Lincoln. With dread, but with what seemed for a time prophetic accuracy, Lincoln told an associate not long after the passage of the proclamation: "[T]he character of the war will be changed. It will be one of subjugation. . . . The South is to be destroyed and replaced by new propositions and ideas."[23]

The northern will to subjugate, destroy, and reform the South did not come from the abolitionists, many of whom retained a rather narrow conception of the "southern problem." With the rebellion finally defeated by April 1865, and with the passage of the Thirteenth Amendment (which placed the wartime expedient of emancipation into constitutional law), many were quite willing to pronounce the problem solved. Even the most zealous among the abolitionists declared victory and were prepared to retreat from the field of battle in triumph. Upon news of the passage of the Thirteenth Amendment, William

Lloyd Garrison gladly announced that his career as an abolitionist was over; he ceased publication of the *Liberator* and called for an end to the American Anti-Slavery Society (it would disband five years later). Garrison ridiculed proposals for further guarantees of civil rights, particularly voting privileges, for former slaves and did so with blatantly racist reasoning: "[A]s soon as the state was organized and left to manage its own affairs, the white population, with their superior intelligence, wealth, and power, would unquestionably alter the franchise in accordance with their prejudices, and exclude those thus summarily brought to the polls. Coercion would gain nothing."[24] But to others in the North, whatever their earlier misgivings about war and coercion, the war seemed to point clearly to an opposite lesson, that coercion might gain everything.

The idea of the South as a critical problem to the nation required reformulation once slavery and secession found their remedies. This reconfiguration still drew upon the large stock of condemnations of southern society and economy built up during the antislavery crusade. To these were added the bloody evidence from four years of war that the South was a proven menace to the safety of the Republic. The southern peril to the nation had been defeated but not destroyed, Radical Republicans insisted. The "wicked rebellion" that had plunged the nation into such a terrible war was the product not simply of a cabal of fanatical fire-eaters who, in a moment of crisis or some accidental opportunity, had gained momentary advantage. The South, many believed, had been led into secession and war by its planter aristocracy, whose power rested on control of land and black labor. This, the Radicals contended, was a social structure based on inherited privileges and inequality of a sort fundamentally at odds with American principles. The flaws of southern society, they believed, could not be remedied simply by the eradication of slavery. The powerful planter class would only legislate new means of labor control if the southern states were allowed to return to the Union, Wendell Phillips warned, "with the same theories, the same men to work them." The remedy for this type of problem would require more drastic reconstruction of the social structure.[25]

Radicals claimed to take their models not from some brave new revolutionary ideology but from the American past. In his 1865 speech before Congress, Thaddeus Stevens recalled the American Revolution, his version of which cast the southern slaveholders among the Founding Fathers as willful obstructionists to the true abolitionist spirit of the Revolution: "Our fathers repudiated the whole doctrine of the legal superiority of families or races, and proclaimed the equality of men before the law. Upon that they created a revolution and built the Republic. They were prevented by slavery from perfecting the superstructure whose foundation they had broadly laid. For the sake of the Union they consented to wait, but never relinquished the idea of its final completion. The time to which they looked forward with anxiety has come. It is our duty to complete their work."[26] Now was the "golden opportunity" to finish the "Second American Revolution." It would be one that might have made the Founding Fathers shudder, with its plans for massive redistribution of wealth and power. The events of Reconstruction more often called to mind the French Revolution, with the Jacobins assaulting the landed aristocracy and the Bourbons in counterrevolutionary reaction. But Radical Reconstruction was not to be a revolt of dispossessed masses rising from the social bottom against the established elite; this was a revolution from above and from outside the region carried out not by extralegal force but through the vastly expanded constitutional powers of the federal government, enforced by United States courts of law and, ultimately, by soldiers of the United States Army.

If the abolitionists had been dilatory and vague in discussing plans for emancipation and loath to use government power to further their ends, the Radicals in Congress now sprang to the task of this state-sponsored revolution with zeal. They displayed an enthusiasm for the use of government as an instrument for vast political, economic, and social change that was quite extraordinary even from our late-twentieth-century vantage point. The antebellum reformers' faith in moral suasion, along with their qualms about coercive human relations, had, it seemed, been drowned in the blood of a long, horrible war.

The goal of Radical Republicans, in brief, was to reconstruct the South in the image of the North, or its idealized self-image, for the South by their reckoning had become a negative image of what America should be. Underlying the Radical agenda was the premise, ingrained in many northern minds by years of antislavery propaganda, that the South constituted a fundamentally different type of society than the rest of America, one at odds with basic American principles of an egalitarian democracy. Resting on a debased race of servile, landless labor and ruled by a privileged landowning class, the social structure of the South, northern critics believed, had inhibited the economic development and spirit of social improvement that flourished naturally within free society elsewhere in America. Much of what had evolved after the American Revolution in the free states of the North — free labor, freehold farming, public schools, and other institutions — would therefore have to be imposed on the former slave states. "The whole fabric of southern society *must* be changed," Stevens explained. "How can republican institutions, free schools, free churches, free social intercourse exist in a mingled community of nabobs and serfs? If the South is ever to be made a safe republic let her lands be cultivated by the toil of the owners or the free labor of intelligent citizens." [27]

The main predicament for Radicals wanting to remake the South was that these free institutions would have to be forced upon states existing within a constitutional democracy that guaranteed to each state fundamental prerogatives of self-rule. Secession and war had suddenly opened radical new possibilities for the expansion of national authority at the expense of these states' rights. Well before Appomattox a rationale for radical social and political reconstruction had been in the making, beginning with theories that removed constitutional protection of rebellious states. The secessionists, by proclaiming their withdrawal from the Union, had handed the Radicals a powerful weapon. Soon after the war commenced, Thaddeus Stevens, Charles Sumner, and other Republicans in Congress began formulating arguments that the Confederate states had committed "state suicide" and that, once defeated, they were to be treated as "conquered provinces," whose former rights as states had been "forfeited." The rebellious states, Radicals proposed, were to be treated as territories under the authority of national government. Convenient though they were for postwar Republican plans, these arguments violated Lincoln's basic premise that the rebellion was illegitimate, that secession was impossible, and that the states continued to exist, though in the control of treasonous rebels. The Radicals, in effect, had accepted the southern rebels' claim that they had effectively withdrawn from the Union and therefore from the constitutional protection of states' rights within it.

Added to this circumvention of states' rights was another constitutional principle that vastly extended the range of federal power over the states. Radicals discovered in the Constitution hitherto obscure language by which the national government "guaranteed" each state a "republican form of government." This brief clause, Charles Sumner exclaimed, was a "sleeping giant" that granted Congress "supreme power over the states." Any state violating the principles of republican government, according to this doctrine of federal guarantee, would become subject to federal intervention. Furthermore, the Thirteenth Amendment granted Congress power to "enforce" the abolition of slavery by "appropriate legislation"—"words of peculiar energy," Charles Sumner noted in his speech justifying federal intervention.[28] Instead of a shield protecting the right of states to self-rule, the Constitution could serve as a powerful, intrusive instrument for the reform of southern institutions.

For Republicans in 1865 an immediate problem the South posed was a partisan threat to their hegemony in national government. During the war, the withdrawal of southern Democrats gave Republicans a rare opportunity to pass a wide range of legislation favoring northern business interests, to say nothing of the abolition of slavery. The entire Republican political agenda for the nation would have been stymied by southern Democrats had they been present in Congress. Now, according to Lincoln's and, later, President Andrew Johnson's moderate plan for "restoration" of the rebel states, an overwhelmingly Democratic South, united in enmity toward Republicans, was about to rejoin the Union. Moreover, it could claim greater power than ever, for the slave population that had been counted at a two-fifths discount for purposes of congressional representation would now yield full representation to the former slave states in the House of Representatives and the electoral college. Abolition could actually strengthen the national power of the former master class. The defeated rebels would send their elected representatives to statehouses and to the United States Congress; their votes would help decide who ruled the nation as president.[29] The slave-power conspiracy, it appeared to many, had been destroyed in war only to revive in more insidious and efficacious form.

Propelled by partisan anxiety and guided by a larger revolutionary vision of a South reconstructed for the benefit of all classes (except the treacherous planters), Republicans in Congress set out with a vast and multifaceted agenda for reform more sweeping than any seen before or since in American history. On one level was a political revolution. Radical Republicans sought to shift permanently the balance of power in the southern states away from the planter elite, and the coalition of white Conservative-Democrats that supported it, toward a new black yeomanry and a Republican coalition with former Whigs and anti-Confederate whites. One tactic aimed at excluding from political power (voting and office holding) all but unconditional Unionists, defined most rigorously as those who took the Ironclad Oath of loyalty, by which one swore never to have voluntarily aided the Confederate cause. Special provisions denied general pardons to major Confederate officials and those with twenty thousand dollars or more in property.[30]

While the South's former political leadership was being decapitated, a more dramatic change in the body politic came from below with the movement to guarantee voting rights of former slaves, who constituted a majority in parts of the Deep South. Black votes would vastly expand the foundation for a southern Republican Party, help protect other black civil rights, and, above all, continue the Republican Party in national power. The disfranchisement of many whites, coinciding with the enfranchisement of blacks, dramatically tilted the political tables in favor of the new black electorate in many states of the South.

As the electorate was radically reconstituted, blacks, together with whites from the North along with an element of native white southerners, formed a new southern wing of the Republican Party. This coalition dominated the new state constitutional conventions, rewrote the rules of politics, and greatly broadened the scope of government, all in ways that would benefit party followers and assure Republican dominance in the future. Provisions for reapportionment of representation, public education, internal improvements, and other progressive measures all pointed toward change in the purpose as well as the source of government power.

Radical Republicans also wished to transform the southern economy. Among the economic reforms some Radicals had entertained since early in the war were plans for the massive confiscation of land from disloyal southerners and the allotment of this and other public lands to former slaves. Beyond punishing the planter class, this proposal aimed at wholesale destruction of the plantation system and the creation of a society of small, efficient family farms. Thaddeus Stevens, the most enthusiastic proponent of land redistribution, suggested federal confiscation of some four hundred million acres, that land belonging to the wealthiest 10 percent. This would be allotted to freedmen in forty-acre plots and the rest, 90 percent of it, sold at public auction to finance war costs. Though never passed, the plans for confiscation remained the fullest expression of Radical designs for a reconstructed South.[31]

Another level of reform aimed at elevating freedmen in society. Republicans encouraged public schools for whites and blacks and, through private philanthropy, supported legions of schoolteachers and missionaries who went south to educate and uplift the freedmen. Through education, reformers hoped, former slaves (and poor whites) would become instilled with ambition for social and economic advancement, while, at the same time, education would provide some of the practical means of achieving their wants. Schools would stimulate the work ethic so essential to a free-labor system. Education would prepare the freedmen for citizenship and would make intelligent voters of young men. As in the common school systems of the North, public education was also promoted as a method of socializing children for a modern society, instilling punctuality, good order, self-discipline, obedience. In a variety of other ways, through government and private philanthropy, Republican policies sought to encourage stable marriage and family life among freedmen, promote temperance, support black churches, provide relief and medical care to the destitute, and generally help in the passage from a slave to free society. If the impulse behind these humanitarian reforms came largely from partisan goals of advancing a Republican electorate, they were nonetheless central to Radical hopes—and conservative fears—of racial equality.

By no means were all of these ideas for a reconstructed South converted into policy, nor were all the policies that were approved in law carried out effectively. But in its general outline, this was the political, economic, and social program Radical Republicans pursued in 1867. It was an agenda for political and social change as radical and far reaching as anything ever undertaken by the national government. Compared with the vast changes embraced by Radicals during Reconstruction, the Second Reconstruction that was launched a century later to desegregate the South seems quite modest in its reach.

At the end of four years of war, during which the Confederacy endured massive casualties, extreme hardship at the home front, demoralizing military invasions, and devastating destruction of property to a degree no Americans suffered before or since, the rebellious South accepted the verdict of the battlefield. They did so, for the most part, with stoic resignation. After Appomattox there were remarkably few guerrilla bands offering resistance, no pockets of irreconcilable opposition to reunion with the United States, and, in general, little left of any serious movement for southern independence. The memorials to the Lost Cause, the display of Confederate battle flags, and other gestures of respect for the rebellion that succeeding generations would offer, whatever they meant for the South's regional identity, became detached from any serious intent to revive the cause of secession.

If whites accepted southern independence as a Lost Cause, however, they would defend the principles of state autonomy and white supremacy that Radical Reconstruction imperiled with fierce and irreconcilable resistance. The prolonged contest between white southern conservatives and Republicans was more than a struggle over the control of the labor of former slaves. That was but part of a broader contest over the political and social status of blacks and whether they would be included within the circle of citizenship and equality with whites. Linked to that contest, of course, was the political struggle for control of the state in which Republicans sought victory by including blacks in the voting citizenry and white conservatives fought to exclude them.

The strategy conservative whites in the Deep South pursued immediately following emancipation was to utilize the power of the state to reestablish planters' control over their former slaves. Mississippi led the way in 1865 by devising a Black Code, a multifaceted legal instrument designed to force blacks to either sign year-long labor contracts or face arrest and fines (chiefly for vagrancy), which would be secured by the planters to whom the state would then bind over the prisoners to serve as an involuntary workforce. There were, in addition, a whole range of laws restricting black civil rights: the right to bear arms, assemble, and practice religion, among others. An apprenticeship law gave the state power to declare freed minors orphans and bind them over to a guardian, their former owners having first claim.[32] Where before the state sanctioned the power of the master over slave, now the state itself was the source of coercive power over black labor. It was partly in reaction to the Black Codes, which were seen as a defiant effort to return freedmen to virtual slavery, that Radical Republicans launched their program in 1867. They imposed military rule on the southern states and refused readmission to the Union until new constitutions guaranteeing the rights of black citizens were in place. Under federal mandate, the Black Codes were immediately rescinded. Now the contest over the control of labor and the status of black labor through the state became a struggle over control of the state itself. But with the weight of federal authority and military force on their side, alliances of black and white Republicans rose to power in one state after another largely on the strength of a new black electorate.

Southern whites fought hard to regain control of state governments. Though initially ill disposed to even acknowledge the legitimacy of black voting rights, more pragmatic minds persuaded the Democrats to pursue a strategy aimed at wooing a crucial segment of black voters away from the Republicans. They played on traditional themes of paternalistic dependence, fomented distrust toward "carpetbagger" Republican leaders, and lavished attention on "loyal" black partisans of the Democratic Party. Black voters were treated to barbecues, at which they were addressed by speakers, white and black, who testified to the abiding bonds between the races and warned of the dangers of the Republican intruders. Whatever ploys the Democrats and Republicans used to win black support, they were well within the bounds of the American political game as it had been played among northern ethnic groups for decades. There were other tactics developed in the postwar South that were less in keeping with those traditions, but they were not violent or illegal. In many places, for example, white Democrats would stand by the polls and write down the names of black Republican voters and publish their names in the local paper along with editorials urging landlords not to employ these "disloyal" blacks the following season. Fraudulent ballot counts and other improprieties became commonplace in closely contested southern elections. Such corruption was disturbing but hardly shocking to northerners who witnessed the scandals surrounding urban political machines. If these were seen as common symptoms of Democratic perfidy, they were as evident in Tammany Hall as in Mississippi.

What was truly shocking to Americans outside—and many within—the South was the hideous reign of terror carried out by the Ku Klux Klan and its various local imitators, such as the Knights of the White Camelia, that began with the onset of Radical Reconstruction and peaked in 1871. Here was a violent campaign involving murder, mutilation, whipping, and the burning of homes, schools, and churches. It took place far outside the bounds of law and well outside the traditions of even the most vicious political or labor conflicts seen up to that time in America. The Klan was engaged in a campaign of terror deliberately designed to intimidate black voters and to harass or murder Republican leaders. To be sure, many of the atrocities committed by the Ku Klux Klan and its ilk were acts of personal vengeance aimed at punishing individual blacks who were "out of their place." At times they seemed motivated by the more general goal of denigrating the status of blacks at a time when Republicans were struggling to elevate them. The Klan was never a highly structured organization; it was more a collection of very local dens who imitated one another rather than following a coherent plan. Democratic leaders did all they could to dismiss concern about the Klan by denying its existence or explaining it away as a series of disconnected personal conflicts. But the geographical pattern of violence that was concentrated in politically contested areas such as upstate South Carolina and northern Mississippi, the strategy of intimidating Republican voters and leaders, and the timing of Klan atrocities before and during elections all point to its purposeful role as the terrorist wing of the Democratic Party allied in a struggle to overthrow Republican rule.[33]

Republicans had constructed the legal framework for black equality within the constitutions of the states and nation, and, despite the campaigns of intimidation and violence, Republicans managed to gain control of southern states, send their people to Congress, and gain a foothold in local government as well. With the advent of Radical rule, white southern leadership shifted decisively from the moderate, conciliatory views that had often opposed secession and urged conciliation after Appomattox toward more extreme positions. Men who had pleaded for peace and were willing to accept defeat and reconcile with the Union were, in the face of black political power and Radical rule, now prepared to fight to the death for white supremacy and home rule. What the Klan and its Democratic allies were challenging was the legitimacy of Republican rule. "They [white southerners]," proclaimed one southern editor at the onset of Radical rule, "are not *ruled* by any governments they do not recognize as legitimate over them. . . . The white race of the South, have only to will the rule of the South; and there is no power on this continent, which can prevent it." [34]

Of course, there *was* a power that could enforce Republican rule and protect black rights. This power rested in state and, ultimately, federal government. The latter, with its enhanced constitutional powers that guaranteed due process and suffrage, took on final responsibility for defending black rights and Republican rule. To enforce the rule of constitutional law, the United States had its judicial system with its district attorneys to prosecute violators, judges to issue sentences, and federal marshals to carry out the law.

Whatever opposition and doubts persisted about the wisdom of their policies, the Republicans had managed within a relatively short period to redefine the legal status of more than four million former slaves and bring them — by law — within the circle of citizenship and equal rights. If all that were required to reform the South were laws, the Republicans had prescribed and administered legal remedies in bold fashion.

Of course, mere legislation was not in itself an adequate remedy. Laws generated within a popular democracy and officials elected in such a system are generally accepted as the legitimate expressions of the will of the people. Democracies, like all governments, ultimately rest on force, but enforcement is usually necessary only at the margins to ensure that all citizens respect the law and comply with it by reminding them through punishment of violators. What Republicans faced in the South, however, was massive resistance from a white citizenry that did not see Republican state governments or the black electorate as legitimate and was defiant of federal intrusion into what it considered the prerogative of the people of the states. Ultimately, the national government could enforce the law through the military might of its army, which had been garrisoned in parts of the South since 1867. White conservatives did all they could to show that Republican law and authority could be maintained *only* at the point of a bayonet.

How many troops would it take and for how long? By what means would southern whites accept the new order of things without the constant use or threat of force? What would it take to create the public opinion necessary for laws and government to be accepted? These were the questions Republicans and northerners of all persuasions were asking in the years before the end of Reconstruction in 1877. The show of federal force seemed only to strengthen white southern defiance, particularly when black soldiers were employed to enforce the law. When federal troops were withdrawn, conditions often grew worse. Republican governors were reluctant to make full use of state militia because few whites would enlist and the use of black militia threatened to bring all-out race warfare in such places as Mississippi and South Carolina.[35]

As horrified as they were at the atrocities in the South, northerners were growing indifferent to the plight of blacks or at least less willing to maintain their rights by force of arms. From the beginnings of the antislavery crusade, even radical abolitionists had focused moral attention on purging the Republic of sin, not on uplifting the slave or integrating freed blacks into the society as full and equal citizens. That latter goal had been advanced as a necessary political strategy of Republicans in a reconstituted Union and not solely out of humanitarian concern for the freed slaves. White supremacy may not have been as salient to northern political and social thought, but public opinion there was hardly united behind ideals of a biracial democracy in America. Furthermore, as Democrats excoriated Republicans for intervention in southern affairs, the rising political price for intervening on behalf of blacks offset the benefits of defending black citizenship in the South. President Grant referred to the change in northern public opinion in 1875 in response to the desperate pleas of fellow Republican Adelbert Ames, governor of Mississippi, who begged Grant to send U.S. troops to safeguard the coming state elections and prevent more racial violence: "[The] whole public are tired out with these annual, autumnal outbreaks in the South."[36] It was two years later that all federal troops were withdrawn and Reconstruction was brought to an end, part of the bargain made between Democrats and Republicans following the disputed presidential election of 1876.[37]

The history of Reconstruction would be told in terms first employed by conservative Democrats and later embedded in historical scholarship, always as a pessimistic lesson in the folly of reform and the incapacity of blacks for full citizenship. No other intellectual prop was so essential to the regime of Jim Crow than the "black legend" of Reconstruction. The American problem with the South, in the process, became redefined as "the Negro Question," and it was left largely to white southerners to answer for themselves with no intrusion from a nation exhausted by war and disillusioned with reform. As southern blacks prepared to endure their "dark journey" through the better part of a century of disfranchisement, violence, and segregation, conditions that were in many ways objectively worse than ever, America seemed willing to abandon any sense of national concern with the racial ills of a region or a nation. Nor would the nation be aroused to any feeling of moral urgency over the plight of former slaves. Their emancipation had required the condemnation of slavery and the South as intolerable national problems. Their oppression would require the complicity of a nation.[38]

Notes

I wish to thank David Carlton, Jacque Voegeli, and Larry Griffin for their many helpful and insightful comments on earlier versions of this essay.

1   Eric Foner, *Free Soil, Free Labor, Free Men: The Ideology of the Republican Party Before the Civil War* (New York, 1970).

2   Foner, *Free Soil.*

3   Robert W. Johannsen, ed., *The Lincoln-Douglas Debates of 1858* (New York, 1965), includes the text of the "House Divided" speech.

4   William Lloyd Garrison, from the *Liberator,* January 1, 1831, quoted in George M. Fredrickson, ed., *William Lloyd Garrison* (Englewood Cliffs, N.J., 1968), 23.

5   David J. Rothman, *The Discovery of the Asylum: Social Order and Disorder in the New Republic* (Boston, 1971).

6   Horace Bushnell, *Christian Nurture* (1847; reprint, New Haven, 1967); Philip J. Greven, *Spare the Child: The Religious Roots of Punishment and the Psychological Impact of Physical Abuse* (New York, 1990); idem, comp., *Child-Rearing Concepts, 1628–1861: Historical Sources* (Itasca, Ill., 1973).

7   Quoted in John L. Thomas, ed., *Slavery Attacked: The Abolitionist Crusade* (Englewood Cliffs, N.J., 1965), 24–25.

8   Quoted in Thomas, *Slavery Attacked,* 25.

9   Harriet Beecher Stowe, *Uncle Tom's Cabin, or Life among the Lowly* (1852; reprint, New York, 1962), 507.

10   Foner, *Free Soil.*

11   Quoted in Fredrickson, *Garrison,* 52–55.

12 Quoted in James M. McPherson, *The Struggle for Equality: Abolitionists and the Negro in the Civil War and Reconstruction* (Princeton, N.J., 1964), 33.

13 McPherson, *Struggle,* 33–38.

14 McPherson, *Struggle,* 65, 57.

15 McPherson, *Struggle,* 116.

16 McPherson, *Struggle,* 118.

17 James M. McPherson, *Battle Cry of Freedom: The Civil War Era* (New York, 1988), 494–95.

18 On combat motivation among northern and southern soldiers, see James M. McPherson, *What They Fought For, 1861–1865* (Baton Rouge, 1994).

19 McPherson, *Battle Cry,* 354–55, citing James G. Randall, *Constitutional Problems under Lincoln,* rev. ed. (Urbana, Ill., 1951), chaps. 12–16.

20 Quoted in McPherson, *Battle Cry,* 354.

21 McPherson, *Battle Cry,* 563–64.

22 Garry Wills, *Lincoln at Gettysburg: The Words That Remade America* (New York, 1992), 137–47.

23 Quoted in McPherson, *Battle Cry,* 558.

24 Eric Foner, *Reconstruction: America's Unfinished Revolution, 1863–1877* (New York, 1988), 67; Garrison quote in C. Vann Woodward, *The Burden of Southern History,* rev. ed. (Baton Rouge, 1968), 89–90. McPherson, in *Struggle for Equality,* makes the case for the ongoing commitment of other abolitionist leaders to the cause of equal rights.

25 On Radical theories of southern society, see, for example, Charles Sumner's Senate speech of February 5 and 6, 1866, reprinted in Harvey Wish, ed., *Reconstruction in the South, 1865–1877: First Hand Accounts of the American Southland after the Civil War by Northerners and Southerners* (New York, 1965), 110–11; Phillips quoted in McPherson, *Struggle,* 335.

26 Thaddeus Stevens, speech on Reconstruction, December 18, 1865, *Congressional Globe,* 39th Cong., 1st sess., 36: 74–75, reprinted in Wish, *Reconstruction in the South,* 96.

27 Quoted in Foner, *Reconstruction,* 236.

28 Foner, *Reconstruction,* 232–33; Sumner, speech of February 5 and 6, 1866, in Wish, *Reconstruction in the South,* 108–10.

29 Woodward, *Burden,* 95; C. Vann Woodward, *Reunion and Reaction: The Compromise of 1877 and the End of Reconstruction* (1951; reprint, New York, 1966), 14. "Their program," Woodward wrote of Lincoln and Johnson, "was restoration instead of reconstruction, and their method was conciliation instead of coercion."

30 Foner, *Reconstruction,* 183–85, 190–91. The pardon provisions were actually part of President Johnson's plan. They required individuals to petition the president for pardons. It was Johnson's own undermining of these restrictions, by generous approval of thousands of pardon petitions, that became a major grievance among Radicals.

31 Foner, *Reconstruction,* 235.

32 On the Mississippi Black Code, see William C. Harris, *The Day of the Carpetbagger: Reconstruction in Mississippi* (Baton Rouge, 1979).

33 Allen W. Trelease, *White Terror: The Ku Klux Klan Conspiracy and Southern Reconstruction* (Westport, Conn., 1971); Foner, *Reconstruction,* 425–44.

34 See Michael Perman, *Reunion without Compromise: The South and Reconstruction, 1865–1868* (Cambridge, Mass., 1973), 337–47, on "the irrelevance of the moderates"; Dan Carter, *When*

the War Was Over: The Failure of Self-Reconstruction in the South, 1865–1867 (Baton Rouge, 1985), also examines the failure of moderates. Quotation from *Charleston Mercury*, December 12, 1868, quoted in Perman, *Reunion without Compromise,* 339.

35   William Gillette, *Retreat from Reconstruction, 1869–1879* (Baton Rouge, 1979), 35.

36   Quoted in Gillette, *Retreat,* 157. Gillette explains the context of this quote, which shows more resolve in Grant than this excerpt suggests.

37   Woodward, *Reunion and Reaction.*

38   Neil R. McMillen, *Dark Journey: Black Mississippians in the Age of Jim Crow* (Urbana, Ill., 1989); C. Vann Woodward, *The Strange Career of Jim Crow,* 3d rev. ed. (New York, 1974).

∼ The South, the Supreme Court, and Race Relations, 1890–1965

JAMES W. ELY JR.

HISTORIANS HAVE DEBATED THE extent to which law and legal institutions in the South were distinctive.[1] Rather than participate in that dialogue, this essay seeks to examine a related topic: the South as an American problem in the context of race relations. The crucial importance of race throughout southern history is well known.[2] Indisputably the institution of slavery before the Civil War and the subsequent maintenance of racial caste divisions marked the region as unique in American society. The legal system acted in large measure as a club to enforce first slavery and then racial segregation. During much of the South's history the need to support white domination dwarfed other legal concerns.

This essay traces a marked change in both the national perception of and judicial attitudes toward regional control of race relations and civil rights between 1890 and 1965. In this era race relations were largely understood in regional terms, but thinking about the South's role underwent considerable transformation. Until the end of World War II the nation at large viewed race relations primarily as a regional problem to be handled on terms satisfactory to white southerners. Deference to the South was the guiding principle. The Supreme Court's treatment of racial issues reflected the larger currents of the time. After World War II, however, there was a renewed emphasis on civil rights. Heightened awareness of racial inequality by national political leaders and policymakers—propelled in part by increasing black protest and fear of potential international embarrassment—militated against formal segregation in the South.[3] The very social structure imposed by the white South came to be seen as a problem that required a national solution. In harmony with the gradually changing political and social environment following World War II, the Supreme Court abandoned its earlier hands-off approach and assumed an activist role in supervising race relations. Anticipating future legislative developments, the justices spearheaded the move to destroy segregation.

The Segregation Era

Sectionalism remained a potent force in American life during the Gilded Age. Recovering slowly from the ravages of the Civil War, an impoverished South continued to occupy a distinctive place in the polity. The restoration of white rule following the end of Reconstruction was a notable feature of the southern experience. As public opinion in the North abandoned Reconstruction, white supremacist sentiments gained ascendancy in southern politics. With the acquiescence of northerners, southern Democrats restricted black suffrage and imposed formal racial segregation on many social institutions.[4] Resort to violence to maintain the racial order was common. A dramatic outbreak of lynching swept across the South in the 1890s. Most lynch victims were black, and few lynchings were punished because local officials often colluded with the mobs. Racist social policies were accepted almost everywhere in the United States by 1900, but the South stood out with its insistence on the legalized color line to separate whites and blacks. Southern leaders relied on the doctrine of states' rights to provide legitimacy to their system of racial control. Seeking largely to be left alone, they were quick to defend state autonomy against perceived national encroachment.

A number of factors worked against judicial enforcement of racial equality. Racist assumptions permeated both popular attitudes and academic thought in late-nineteenth-century America. Leading scholars presented Reconstruction as both a political mistake and a constitutional error. On the other hand, sectional reconciliation between the North and the South was highly valued. Elite opinion makers were anxious not to exacerbate regional tension. In the late nineteenth century most Americans still looked to the states to determine social issues. The political branches of the federal government, the president and Congress, displayed no enthusiasm for an assault on legally imposed racial separation in the South.[5] Moreover, turn-of-the-century imperialism helped to undercut any lingering national sentiment critical of the white South. After the Spanish-American War the United States acquired overseas territories peopled by individuals with different racial and religious characteristics than the majority of American citizens. This new imperialism produced a situation in which the United States governed alien nonwhite peoples, and it tended to reinforce the belief that whites should naturally dominate society at home as well as abroad. Ironically, race relations in the South were not seen as a national problem during an era in which, by most standards, racial discrimination was at its worst.

These political and social realities severely restricted the Supreme Court in dealing with race relations. Furthermore, the justices by and large shared the prevalent racial outlook. By the 1890s the Court abandoned its earlier half-hearted attempts to construe the Fourteenth Amendment as a safeguard for the rights of blacks and acquiesced in the relegation of blacks to second-class citizenship.[6]

In the famous case of *Plessy v. Ferguson* (1896), the Supreme Court placed its seal of approval on the emerging pattern of racial segregation in the South.[7] Homer A. Plessy sought to invalidate Louisiana's separate-car law, which imposed criminal penalties on railroad passengers who went into a coach other than the one to which they were assigned according to race. Plessy assailed the separate-car statute as a violation of both the Thirteenth and Fourteenth Amendments. The Supreme Court, however, sustained the Louisiana law by a vote of seven to one. Justice Henry Billings Brown, who wrote the majority opinion, gave short shrift to the argument that railroad segregation violated the Thirteenth Amendment outlawing slavery. He simply maintained that a distinction based on race had "no tendency to . . . reestablish a state of involuntary servitude." Brown acknowledged that the purpose of the equal protection clause of the Fourteenth Amendment "was to enforce the absolute equality of the two races before the law." But he emphasized that laws requiring racial separation were widely regarded as within the state police power. To support this conclusion Brown specifically noted the practice of separate schools and laws forbidding racial intermarriage. Articulating a reasonableness test, Brown asserted that the Louisiana legislature was free "to act with reference to the established usages, customs and traditions of the people" in order to promote public peace. He then sharply questioned the premise that legislation could overcome deeply rooted racial distinctions:

> We consider the underlying fallacy of the plaintiff's argument to consist in the assumption that the enforced separation of the two races stamps the colored race with a badge of inferiority. If this be so, it is not by reason of anything found in the act, but solely be-

cause the colored race chooses to put that construction upon it. . . . The argument also assumes that social prejudices may be overcome by legislation, and that equal rights cannot be secured to the Negro except by an enforced commingling of the two races. We cannot accept this proposition. . . . Legislation is powerless to eradicate racial instincts or to abolish distinctions based upon physical differences, and the attempt to do so can only result in accentuating the difficulties of the present situation. If the civil and political rights of both races be equal, one cannot be inferior to the other civilly or politically. If one race be inferior to the other socially, the Constitution of the United States cannot put them upon the same plane.[8]

The upshot of *Plessy* was judicial affirmation that separate but equal facilities passed constitutional muster.

Justice John M. Harlan, in an impassioned dissent, assailed the Louisiana statute and forcefully contended that the three Reconstruction amendments banned racial discrimination. Endorsing the ideal of equal rights, Harlan maintained that the Thirteenth and Fourteenth Amendments "removed the race line from our governmental systems." Declaring the majority opinion to be as "pernicious" as the *Dred Scott* case, he broadly observed: "Our Constitution is color-blind, and neither knows nor tolerates classes among citizens. In respect of civil rights, all citizens are equal before the law. The humblest is the peer of the most powerful. The law regards man as man, and takes no account of his surroundings or of his color when his civil rights as guaranteed by the supreme law of the land are involved."[9] Despite its eloquence, Harlan's dissent was out of harmony with the racial sentiments of the age and fell on deaf ears.

Although a source of later controversy, *Plessy* attracted little notice at the time. Because the decision embodied popular attitudes, it was not a source of widespread protest. Nor did *Plessy* institute the racial caste system in the South. Laws that mandated separate schooling and travel facilities antedated *Plessy*. Yet the decision marked an important turning point in race relations. It legitimated segregation laws and opened the door to more intrusive state control of racial minorities. Moreover, *Plessy* signaled the Supreme Court's abandonment of any meaningful efforts to achieve racial equality.

Absent support from the political branches of the federal government, there was little the Court could do to stem the segregationist tide. But the justices can rightly be faulted for failure to enforce even the separate-but-equal standard.

In practice the public facilities available to whites and blacks grew increasingly unequal. The Supreme Court seemingly ratified this result in *Cumming v. Richmond County Board of Education* (1899). A Georgia county subsidized the student tuition at private high schools for white students but voted to convert the single black high school into a primary school. This move deprived the black high school students of any educational opportunity. Charging that the board's action denied equal protection of the laws, the black plaintiffs sought to enjoin the board from supporting the white schools. They evidently hoped that the board would respond to an injunction by reopening the black high school. In an opinion by Justice Harlan, however, the Court unanimously denied the requested relief. Notwithstanding his *Plessy* dissent, Harlan appeared to regard school segregation as an established fact. He uncharacteristically accepted at face value the school board's protestation that it acted for economic reasons and not to discriminate against blacks. Indeed, Harlan stressed that public education was a matter of state jurisdiction and that the federal courts should not intervene without clear evidence of a constitutional violation.[10] As a consequence of *Cumming*, public agencies could give a disproportionate share of benefits to whites so long as they could offer some rationale other than race.

The segregationist tide also engulfed private institutions. The Supreme Court proved unwilling to protect the right of a private school to conduct its business on a basis of racial equality. Berea College in Kentucky provided educational opportunities for both white and black students. In 1904 the Kentucky legislature enacted a law forbidding any person or corporation from operating a school in which students of both races were instructed together. Berea College argued that the legislation constituted an arbitrary interference with the right to pursue a lawful occupation. Writing for the Court in *Berea College v. Kentucky* (1908), Justice David J. Brewer, usually a defender of the rights of property owners, sidestepped the broad constitutional issues. Instead he concentrated on the authority of a state over the corporations it chartered. Brewer upheld the statute as an exercise of reserved power to amend corporate charters. The outcome is particularly glaring because, in other contexts, the justices were quite prepared to strike down state laws infringing the rights of corporate enterprise.

Likewise, the Supreme Court did not resist the growing movement in the South to disfranchise blacks. Southern legislatures employed numerous devices, such as the literacy and understanding tests as well as the poll tax, to restrict black political participation. Yet any exclusionary device that appeared even handed on its face was upheld by the Supreme Court despite evidence of discriminatory administration. In *Williams v. Mississippi* (1898), for instance, the Court unanimously approved Mississippi's literacy test and poll tax on grounds that these requirements applied to both white and black voters. Looking only at the text of the statute, the justices declined to examine the actual working of the literacy test and poll tax. Yet careful scrutiny would have revealed discriminatory administration of the suffrage provisions. Another challenge to the disfranchisement policy was presented in *Giles v. Harris* (1903). An Alabama black complained that he was denied registration because of his race and requested a federal court to order his registration. Speaking for a six-to-three majority, Justice Oliver Wendell Holmes declined to grant relief for technical reasons. Significantly, he added that the Court had little practical power to deal with racial disfranchisement. If whites were determined to keep blacks from voting, Holmes pointed out, putting the plaintiff's "name on a piece of paper [would] not defeat them." Relief from a political wrong committed by the people or a state, he declared, "must be given by them or by the legislative and political department of the government of the United States."[11] Although seemingly oblivious to the deteriorating legal and social position of blacks in the South, the justices were clearly mindful of the political realities that governed race relations.

Despite this bleak picture, the Supreme Court on infrequent occasion made an attempt to enforce the Reconstruction amendments. In *Bailey v. Alabama* (1911), for instance, the justices struck down a peonage statute under which an employee could be compelled to work in order to discharge a debt. Over the objection of Justice Holmes, the Court held that the statute imposed involuntary servitude in violation of the Thirteenth Amendment.[12] Moreover, in *Guinn v. United States* (1915), the Supreme Court invalidated a "grandfather clause" that discriminated against blacks by permitting whites to vote despite literacy and property qualifications if their ancestors could exercise the suffrage in 1866. This transparent evasion of the Fifteenth Amendment exceeded the bounds of judicial tolerance for southern suffrage laws.

With respect to the rights of property owners, the Supreme Court was similarly prepared to insist that national constitutional norms prevailed over southern racial practices. At issue in *Buchanan v. Warley* (1917) was the validity of residential segregation laws. Like many communities, Louisville, Kentucky, enacted an ordinance forbidding black persons from occupying houses in neighborhoods in which the majority of homes were occupied by whites.

A similar restriction against whites applied to neighborhoods where the majority of residents were black. Hence, the statute on its face appeared to impose equal burdens on both races. The city attempted to justify this measure as an exercise of the police power to promote racial harmony and safeguard racial purity. The Supreme Court unanimously rejected this contention. The justices first adopted a broad definition of property rights: "Property is more than the mere thing which a person owns. It is elementary that it includes the right to acquire, use, and dispose of it." [13] The Court then expressed skepticism about the racial purity rationale, pointedly observing that "the employment of colored servants in white families [was] permitted." The justices added that property might be acquired "by undesirable white neighbors." [14] The goal of eliminating racial conflict, they stressed, could not be achieved by destroying the right to dispose of property. It followed that this restriction on the right to alienate land constituted a deprivation of property without due process of law. In this case the judicial protection of property rights was instrumental in producing an important, if rare, victory against racial discrimination.

Notwithstanding these blows at certain discriminatory practices, judicial acquiescence in the racial order of the South persisted in the main during the 1920s and 1930s. In *Gong Lum v. Rice* (1927), the justices unanimously reaffirmed the validity of public school segregation. Following the *Buchanan* decision property owners increasingly turned to restrictive racial covenants as a means of maintaining residential segregation. In *Corrigan v. Buckly* (1926), the Supreme Court determined that such covenants were simply private agreements and did not constitute state action within the meaning of the Fourteenth Amendment. Nor did the Supreme Court aggressively challenge the continuing use of devices that effectively barred blacks from participation in the political process. For instance, the laws in several southern states permitted political parties to organize as private clubs and set their own qualifications for membership. Acting under such authority, the Democratic Party in a number of southern states prevented blacks from voting in their "private" primary elections. The justices validated this technique in *Grovey v. Townsend* (1935), holding that the political party was a private group and thus not subject to the restrictions imposed on state action under the Fourteenth and Fifteenth Amendments. Until World War II, then, both the nation and the Supreme Court saw racial issues as predominantly a southern matter and one to be adjusted regionally with a minimum of national oversight. As a consequence, the nation at large still did not see the South's handling of race relations as a problem.

Harbingers of Change

Notwithstanding the hands-off approach of the federal judiciary, gradual changes in the American polity during the 1930s and 1940s produced new attitudes concerning racial equality and the southern caste system. As a result, the South was increasingly placed on the defensive in the face of national criticism. These developments opened the door for a shift to a constitutional outlook that gave renewed emphasis to equality and paid less attention to traditional claims of state autonomy.

A variety of changes coalesced to foster a political and legal climate more receptive to the enforcement of equal rights. Massive black migration to the North during the early decades of the twentieth century meant that race relations could no longer be viewed as a peculiarly southern problem. The growing concentration of blacks in cities of the North also created a new political equation in which black voters wielded electoral power in closely contested northern states and thus had a direct impact on national elections. Moreover, Franklin D. Roosevelt's sweeping presidential victories reduced the Democratic Party's historical reliance on southern electoral votes.

The New Deal program, too, helped to set the stage for an erosion of state control over racial matters. Neither President Roosevelt nor his legislative program ever directly challenged segregation in the South. Indeed, Roosevelt would not even publicly endorse proposed antilynching legislation during the 1930s. New Deal labor legislation in practice often harmed blacks economically and caused displacement of black workers.[15] Some southern segregationists were stalwart backers of the New Deal, and Roosevelt depended on southern support in Congress to enact New Deal programs. But the centralizing approach of the New Deal nonetheless undercut the states' rights philosophy by encouraging people to seek national solutions to social problems. Roosevelt also appointed to the Supreme Court several justices sympathetic to civil rights.[16]

Another important catalyst for change was the entry of the United States into World War II. The United States ironically fought the Axis powers with segregated armed forces and experienced serious race riots in Detroit and Los

Angeles during 1943. There was pervasive discrimination in private employment.[17] Notwithstanding these realities, the war unleashed a powerful egalitarian impulse. Wartime popular culture stressed that racial discrimination was incompatible with American democracy. The atrocities committed by Nazi Germany and imperial Japan in the name of racial superiority did much to discredit all schemes of racial subordination and gave impetus to a reinvigorated civil rights drive.[18] World War II had an immediate impact on public opinion toward race relations in the North. In 1945, for instance, New York became the first state to establish a fair employment practices commission, and other northern states soon followed suit.

A powerful force for change was provided by the emergence of skillful litigation groups that formulated strategies to attack racial segregation. Foremost among these was the National Association for the Advancement of Colored People (NAACP), organized in 1909. Attorneys for the NAACP early targeted violations of due process in criminal trials. During the 1930s the NAACP also instituted several successful lawsuits seeking desegregation of graduate and professional school education. In *Missouri ex rel. Gaines v. Canada* (1938), the Supreme Court struck down the widespread southern practice of providing out-of-state scholarships for blacks seeking advanced education and indicated that the justices would look carefully at the equality of separate facilities. Success in this area encouraged the NAACP to pursue a litigation strategy aimed at winning equal salaries and facilities in public schools across the South.[19]

In the 1930s the Supreme Court also began to condemn the discriminatory administration of criminal justice in the South. Even a Court dominated by economic conservatives was unwilling to accept the racial status quo in this area.[20] The justices were responding to a series of egregious cases in which it appeared that black defendants were being railroaded by summary convictions after hasty trials. In *Powell v. Alabama* (1932), growing out of the notorious Scottsboro case, the Court mandated the appointment of defense counsel in capital trials. Subsequent convictions of the Scottsboro defendants were reversed on grounds that the Alabama jury selection procedures systematically discriminated against blacks.[21] Similarly, the justices in *Brown v. Mississippi* (1936) unanimously ruled that the use of coerced confessions in state criminal trials was a denial of due process.[22] The impact of this line of cases went beyond the important legal issues involved. The South's criminal justice system was held up to searching scrutiny and was seen by many as a national embarrassment. It was, moreover, just a short step from judicial oversight of criminal justice to judicial review of racial discrimination in other aspects of southern life.

Following World War II President Harry S. Truman placed civil rights squarely on the national political agenda.[23] In 1946 Truman created the Committee on Civil Rights to investigate racial discrimination and propose legislation. Two years later he issued an executive order eliminating segregation in the armed forces.[24] He also called for a federal fair employment practices commission and a ban on poll taxes. Modest by modern standards, the Truman program did not address the emotionally charged issue of separate schools. Southern lawmakers succeeded in blocking Truman's proposals in Congress. It was evident that Congress could not be counted on to bring about change in the South's racial policies.

Some southern political leaders split the Democratic Party in 1948 over the civil rights question and refused to support Truman's reelection bid.[25] Truman's upset victory not only diminished southern influence within the Democratic Party but also underscored the importance of black voters in national politics. In several closely divided states blacks provided Truman's margin of victory.[26] Aside from political considerations, Truman's interest in civil rights had important implications for judicial moves to achieve racial equality. The Truman administration made effective use of amicus curiae briefs, legal arguments filed by organizations other than parties seeking to influence the outcome of litigation. The administration filed amicus curiae briefs with the Supreme Court in a series of racial discrimination cases and urged the justices to strike down segregation in interstate transportation and higher education. For the first time since Reconstruction the executive branch displayed enthusiasm for equal rights and could be counted on to support judicial initiatives in this field.

Heightened concern about racial segregation was fueled, too, by the onset of the Cold War. United States officials were convinced that racial practices in the South harmed American foreign policy interests and compromised the nation's leadership in the struggle with the Soviet Union.[27] As early as 1948 the federal government pointed out the international implications of race relations in an amicus curiae brief filed with the Supreme Court. In its brief challenging school segregation in *Brown v. Board of Education* (1954), the government again emphasized Cold War tensions and the hostile international reaction to racial discrimination. "It is in the context of the present world struggle between freedom and tyranny," the brief declared, "that the problem of racial discrimination must be viewed."[28] Against the background of the Cold War it would have been very awkward for the Supreme Court, apart from other constitutional arguments, to place its seal of approval on formal racial segregation.

In keeping with the gradual evolution of social attitudes and the changing political realities, the Supreme Court in the 1940s forged new ground in the battle for equal rights. Overruling its previous decision on the white primary, the justices in *Smith v. Allwright* (1944) held that primary elections were an integral part of a state's election procedures.[29] Therefore all citizens had a right under the Fifteenth Amendment to participate in primary elections without racial discrimination. The Supreme Court continued to expand civil rights in *Morgan v. Virginia* (1946), striking down a Virginia statute that mandated segregation on carriers moving across state lines as an impermissible burden on interstate commerce.[30] In *Shelley v. Kraemer* (1948) the justices took aim at discriminatory barriers in housing. They ruled that state judicial enforcement of racial restrictive covenants constituted state action in violation of the Fourteenth Amendment.[31]

Despite these developments, the outcome in *Brown* was not a foregone conclusion. Sheltered by long-standing judicial precedent and the structure of federalism, the policy of separate schools in the South had acquired a large measure of constitutional legitimacy. Since segregated schools were at the heart of the South's caste systems white southerners were likely to resist fiercely any school desegregation directives. Still, there were enough portends of change to make astute southerners uneasy in the early 1950s. Public opinion outside the region and the federal courts were increasingly unwilling to accommodate southern exceptionalism on racial matters. In short, the South was now perceived as a problem, a region out of step with national norms.

The Second Reconstruction

The Supreme Court decision in *Brown v. Board of Education* that racial segregation in the public schools violated the equal protection clause of the Fourteenth Amendment sent accelerating shock waves across the South.[32] This decision inaugurated the modern civil rights era and heralded a comprehensive attack by the federal government on the segregated society of the South. The white South found itself on the defensive, with few effective political allies outside the region. Although receptive to *Brown,* public sentiment across the nation was apathetic and inclined to allow the South time to adjust to the new constitutional principles. The Supreme Court, fearful that immediate school desegregation might provoke hostility, equivocated with respect to the implementation of *Brown*. In 1955 the justices declared that desegregation should proceed with "all deliberate speed," an ambiguous formula that invited delay. But in a line of decisions the Court rapidly invalidated all legally approved forms of segregation, extending the *Brown* principle to state parks and public transportation.

Southern leaders responded to these judicial rulings by seeking to forge a united front in opposition to school desegregation.[33] They attempted to revive states' rights constitutionalism, which asserted that the states retained certain rights that could not be taken from them. Such thinking found expression in a series of resolutions by southern state legislatures that were designed to interpose state sovereignty between state residents and alleged improper exercises of federal power. The antebellum doctrine of interposition, derived from the theories of John C. Calhoun, had long been rejected as part of the constitutional tradition. Nonetheless, southerners appealed to history to justify on this basis state laws defending segregation.[34] Instinctively recognizing a sea change in northern attitudes, many southern leaders calculated that a constitutional approach would win more sympathy in the North than overt racial arguments in favor of segregation.

Building on this revival of states' rights sentiments, in 1956 Senator Harry F. Byrd of Virginia called for "massive resistance" to *Brown:* "If we can organize the Southern States for massive resistance to this order I think that in time the rest of the country will realize that racial integration is not going to be accepted in the South."[35] Senator Byrd was also one of the foremost sponsors of the Southern Manifesto of March 12, 1956, which attacked the Supreme Court's desegregation ruling "as a clear abuse of judicial power" and commended those states that had "declared the intention to resist forced integration by any lawful means."[36] As these outspoken pronouncements suggest, massive resistance rested on the contention that *Brown* lacked any constitutional basis. Southern leaders reasoned that the Supreme Court would be unable or unwilling to carry out its desegregation decree if confronted with uniform southern defiance. To achieve this end southern lawmakers enacted more than two hundred statutes and resolutions between 1955 and 1960 to hamper or prevent implementation of the *Brown* ruling. Although specific measures varied widely, states passed pupil assignment laws, cut off state funds from integrated schools, established private school tuition grants where public schools were closed, and repealed compulsory school attendance laws. Massive resistance reached a climax when Virginia closed schools facing desegregation in three localities in the fall of 1958.[37]

Notwithstanding widespread opposition to school desegregation among southern whites and an impressive array of laws intended to perpetuate separate schools, massive resistance proved to be a futile gesture. Several forces combined to undermine the efficacy of southern resistance to *Brown*. Blacks in the South began to mobilize and demand an end to segregation. The Montgomery bus boycott of 1955–57 vividly demonstrated the willingness of blacks to resist Jim Crow. The 1957 Little Rock crisis was another important watershed. President Dwight D. Eisenhower, despite his personal reluctance to endorse desegregation, made it clear that he was prepared to use the full power of the executive branch to enforce court orders against recalcitrant officials. Over the objection of southern politicians, Congress in 1957 enacted the first civil rights law since Reconstruction. In *Cooper v. Aaron* (1958) the Supreme Court reaffirmed *Brown* in sweeping terms. Thereafter the federal courts systematically voided the legal props supporting massive resistance. It proved impossible, moreover, for the southern states to maintain a common policy. A few states, including North Carolina, Florida, and Tennessee, began to accept school desegregation on a limited basis.[38]

No doubt many proponents of massive resistance genuinely believed in states' rights constitutionalism and resented federal intervention in what they regarded as a state matter. Distrust of outside control had long been a major theme in southern political life.[39] But in the eyes of northern opinion the states' rights doctrine was tainted by its close association with racial domination. The Little Rock confrontation and the threatened public school closings further alienated political sentiment outside the region. Northerners were scarcely of one mind with respect to issues involving race, but they agreed in progressively larger numbers that the status quo in the South was unacceptable. As sectional attitudes markedly diverged, the hope that massive resistance might prompt either a congressional restructuring of school policy or a judicial reconsideration of the topic was doomed. Yet without broad-based popular backing at the national level, there was no realistic possibility that individual states could withstand a Supreme Court edict.

During the early 1960s the standing of the white South in the constitutional polity deteriorated rapidly. After an initial period of caution, President John F. Kennedy embraced a program to promote desegregation. In 1963 he endorsed a comprehensive civil rights proposal to outlaw segregation in public accommodations. At the same time, blacks grew increasingly impatient with the leisurely implementation of *Brown* and other equal rights decisions. No longer willing to await judicial action, blacks increasingly turned to direct forms of protest. A wave of lunch counter sit-ins spread across the South in 1960–61. Freedom Riders challenged segregation in transportation facilities in 1961 and were brutally attacked by mobs in Alabama. Large-scale demonstrations protesting racial conditions broke out during 1963 in Birmingham and Danville.[40] Under mounting public pressure, Congress enacted the Civil Rights Act of 1964. This measure required equal access to public accommodations, outlawed employment discrimination, and authorized the federal government to withhold federal education funds from any school district that failed to desegregate. Vigorous enforcement of the funding provision brought about substantial progress toward integration of the public schools.[41]

There was always a political dimension to the Second Reconstruction. The sweeping social changes of the 1960s helped to transform the political landscape of the South. Congress destroyed barriers to black political participation. The Voting Rights Act of 1965 suspended literacy tests and strengthened federal protection of the right to vote.[42] The Twenty-fourth Amendment, ratified in 1964, barred poll tax requirements for voting in federal elections. The Supreme Court's reapportionment decisions, culminating in *Reynolds v. Sims* (1964), curbed the power of rural lawmakers in southern state legislatures. A two-party system gradually emerged to challenge the region's traditional domination by the Democrats. Blacks tended to vote heavily for Democratic candidates, and the number of black elected officials in the region grew markedly. Southern white voters, on the other hand, began to abandon the Democratic Party, first in national and then in state elections. The most striking evidence of the new political order came in presidential balloting. Between 1968 and 1992 the Republicans or third-party candidates captured the majority of southern states in every national election but one. Although Jimmy Carter of Georgia won a majority of southern states in 1976, even he failed to secure the backing of most southern whites and owed his victories in the South to black voters. Solid support from southern whites did much to ensure GOP control of the executive branch for most of this time.[43]

With the end of formal segregation and the political empowerment of blacks, southern society had been substantially reconstructed for a second time. The South no longer stood out as a singular region within the national community. The triumph of national constitutional norms also dealt a heavy blow to the viability of the states' rights tradition. Although problems lingered and many whites sought to evade desegregation, the South did not display striking departure from national policy on racial matters.

National Convergence

Racial issues continue to bedevil the United States. But after 1965 race was less frequently identified as a southern problem, and the South gradually ceased to be viewed as a pariah region. The disappearance of formal racial separation was an essential milestone in this process of regional convergence. Other developments, too, played a role in the blending of the South into the country as a whole. The wave of urban racial disturbances that occurred between 1964 and 1968, notably the major riots in Los Angeles (1965) and Detroit (1967), made apparent the national dimensions of racial tension in the United States. In the mid-1960s Martin Luther King Jr. turned his attention to combating racial segregation in Chicago with a campaign of rallies and marches.[44]

In the early 1970s the Supreme Court began to scrutinize de facto school segregation in northern cities. The flight of whites to the suburbs had left many urban school districts with largely black populations. Yet a move in the 1970s to desegregate northern urban schools by interdistrict busing with suburban communities aroused bitter white opposition reminiscent of the massive resistance era. Sensitive to public opinion, the Supreme Court in *Milliken v. Bradley* (1974) rejected the interdistrict remedy, thus shielding most suburbs from busing schemes. Not surprisingly, southerners were quick to detect a hint of insincerity in the professed northern commitment to school desegregation.[45]

The national dimension of the racial issue was underscored in other ways as well. As demonstrated by the aftermath of the first Rodney King verdict in 1992, the racial composition of criminal juries has become a sensitive matter across the nation.[46] Ironically, a 1993 study found that public schools in the South were the most racially integrated of any region in the country.[47] As circumstances changed, it became progressively more difficult to single out the South for moral blame. Indeed, as racial strife clearly became a national problem, one prominent observer asserted that northerners were adopting views traditionally associated with the South and decried the southernization of America.[48]

Changed goals espoused by civil rights advocates also contributed to a reduced focus on the South. Before 1965 the civil rights movement was primarily directed at southern law and policy and sought to achieve the principle of nondiscrimination. With the end of legally imposed segregation, civil rights leaders shifted gears and placed greater emphasis on race-conscious remedies, such as affirmative action in employment. Racial categories were even incorporated into legislation. The Voting Rights Act, for instance, was amended in 1982 to encourage racially proportional representation and the creation of predominantly black districts.[49] The new preferential programs have been highly controversial and are difficult to square with the vision of a color-blind Constitution.[50] For present purposes, however, it is important to bear in mind that the revamped civil rights agenda is national in scope and not regionally defined.

The image of the South in the American polity has changed markedly since 1890. This shifting perspective was largely a product of a transformation in northern attitudes after World War II as well as new political alignments. An attitudinal change, then, and not the objective circumstances of race relations in the region, caused the nation to redefine the racial system of the South as a problem. By the 1970s, however, the South was becoming less distinct from other sections of the country. With an increased convergence in the nation's approach to racial issues, the South was no longer seen as a retrograde region.

Notes

1 See, for example, Kermit L. Hall and James W. Ely Jr., eds., *An Uncertain Tradition: Constitutionalism and the History of the South* (Athens, Ga., 1989), and James W. Ely Jr. and David J. Bodenhamer, "Regionalism and American Legal History: The Southern Experience," *Vanderbilt Law Review* 39 (April 1986): 539–67.

2 James W. Ely Jr. and David J. Bodenhamer, "Regionalism and the Legal History of the South," in *Ambivalent Legacy: A Legal History of the South*, ed. David J. Bodenhamer and James W. Ely Jr. (Jackson, Miss., 1984), 4–7; Paul Finkelman, "Exploring Southern Legal History," *North Carolina Law Review* 64 (November 1985): 77–116, esp. 88–101.

3 See, generally, Walter A. Jackson, *Gunnar Myrdal and America's Conscience: Social Engineering and Racial Liberalism, 1938–1987* (Chapel Hill, 1990).

4 Morton Keller, *Affairs of State: Public Life in Late Nineteenth Century America* (Cambridge, Mass., 1977), 222–37; Edward L. Ayers, *The Promise of the New South: Life after Reconstruction* (New York, 1992), 132–59.

5 Melvin I. Urofsky, *A March of Liberty: A Constitutional History of the United States* (New York, 1988), 482–83.

6 John Braeman, *Before the Civil Rights Revolution: The Old Court and Individual Rights* (Westport, Conn., 1988), 68–76, 121; James W. Ely Jr., *The Chief Justiceship of Melville W. Fuller, 1888–1910* (Columbia, S.C., 1995), 155–60.

7   The best account of the *Plessy* litigation is Charles A. Lofgren, *The Plessy Case: A Legal-Historical Interpretation* (New York, 1987).

8   *Plessy v. Ferguson,* 163 U.S. 537, 543, 544, 550, 551 (1896).

9   *Plessy v. Ferguson,* 555, 559. For a discussion of Harlan's dissent, see Loren P. Beth, *John Marshall Harlan: The Last Whig Justice* (Lexington, Ky., 1992), 233–34.

10 J. Morgan Kousser, "Separate but *not* Equal: The Supreme Court's First Decision on Racial Discrimination in Schools," *Journal of Southern History* 46 (February 1980): 17–44. For a different view of Harlan's opinion in *Cumming,* see Andrew Kull, *The Color-Blind Constitution* (Cambridge, Mass., 1992), 125–30.

11 *Giles v. Harris,* 189 U.S. 475, 488 (1903).

12 Pete Daniel, *The Shadow of Slavery: Peonage in the South, 1901–1969* (Urbana, Ill., 1972), 65–81.

13 *Buchanan v. Warley,* 245 U.S. 60, 74 (1917). See Roger L. Rice, "Residential Segregation by Law, 1910–1917," *Journal of Southern History* 34 (May 1968): 179–99, and Richard A. Epstein, "Race and the Police Power: 1890 to 1937," *Washington and Lee Law Review* 46 (Fall 1989): 741–61, esp. 758–59.

14 *Buchanan v. Warley,* 81, 82.

15 David E. Bernstein, "Roots of the 'Underclass': The Decline of Laissez-Faire Jurisprudence and the Rise of Racist Labor Legislation," *American University Law Review* 43 (Fall 1993): 85–138, esp. 119–33.

16 Harvard Sitkoff, *A New Deal for Blacks: The Emergence of Civil Rights as a National Issue* (New York, 1978); Roger Biles, *A New Deal for the American People* (DeKalb, Ill., 1991), 172–92.

17 John Morton Blum, *V Was For Victory: Politics and American Culture During World War II* (New York, 1976), 182–220.

18 J. R. Pole, *The Pursuit of Equality in American History* (Berkeley, 1978), 256–57.

19 For the NAACP's legal campaign to advance civil rights, see Mark V. Tushnet, *The NAACP's Legal Strategy against Segregated Education, 1925–1950* (Chapel Hill, 1987). See also Robert L. Zangrando, *The NAACP Crusade against Lynching: 1909–1950* (Philadelphia, 1980).

20 Richard C. Cortner, *A "Scottsboro" Case in Mississippi: The Supreme Court and Brown v. Mississippi* (Jackson, Miss., 1986), 118–21; Bernstein, "Roots of the 'Underclass,' " 135.

21 Dan T. Carter, *Scottsboro: A Tragedy of the American South,* rev. ed. (Baton Rouge, 1979).

22 Cortner, *"Scottsboro" Case in Mississippi.*

23 See generally Donald R. McCoy and Richard T. Ruetten, *Quest and Response: Minority Rights and the Truman Administration* (Lawrence, Kans., 1973).

24 Richard M. Dalfiume, *Desegregation of the U.S. Armed Forces: Fighting on Two Fronts, 1939–1953* (Columbia, Mo., 1969), 132–74.

25 Nadine Cohodas, *Strom Thurmond and the Politics of Southern Change* (New York, 1993), 154–93.

26 Harvard Sitkoff, "Harry Truman and the Election of 1948: The Coming of Age of Civil Rights in American Politics," *Journal of Southern History* 37 (November 1971): 597–616.

27 Mary L. Dudziak, "Desegregation as a Cold War Imperative," *Stanford Law Review* 41 (November 1988): 61–120; Michael J. Klarman, "*Brown,* Racial Change, and the Civil Rights Movement," *Virginia Law Review* 80 (February 1994): 7–150, esp. 26–29.

28 Brief for the United States as Amicus Curiae, at p. 6, *Brown v. Board of Education,* U.S. Supreme Court Records and Briefs, Englewood, Colorado, Microcard Editions.

29 Steven F. Lawson, *Black Ballots: Voting Rights in the South, 1944–1969* (New York, 1976), 23–54.

30 Catherine A. Barnes, *Journey from Jim Crow: The Desegregation of Southern Transit* (New York, 1983), 46–51.

31 Clement E. Vose, *Caucasians Only: The Supreme Court, the NAACP, and the Restrictive Covenant Cases* (Berkeley, 1967).

32 Richard Kluger, *Simple Justice: The History of Brown v. Board of Education and Black America's Struggle for Equality* (New York, 1976); J. Harvie Wilkinson III, *From Brown to Bakke: The Supreme Court and School Integration, 1954–1978* (New York, 1979).

33 Klarman, "*Brown,* Racial Change, and the Civil Rights Movement," 97–118.

34 Herman Belz, "The South and the American Constitutional Tradition at the Bicentennial," in Hall and Ely, *Uncertain Tradition,* 45–49.

35 Quoted in James W. Ely Jr., *The Crisis of Conservative Virginia: The Byrd Organization and the Politics of Massive Resistance* (Knoxville, Tenn., 1976), 43.

36 Quoted in Ely, *Crisis of Conservative Virginia,* 43.

37 Ely, *Crisis of Conservative Virginia,* 73–89.

38 Robert Jerome Glennon, "The Role of Law in the Civil Rights Movement: The Montgomery Bus Boycott, 1955–1957," *Law and History Review* 9 (Spring 1991): 59–112; Tony Freyer, *The Little Rock Crisis: A Constitutional Interpretation* (Westport, Conn., 1986); David R. Colburn, "Florida Governors Confront the *Brown* Decision: A Case Study of the Constitutional Politics of School Desegregation, 1954–1970," in Hall and Ely, *Uncertain Tradition,* 326–55.

39 Klarman, "*Brown,* Racial Change, and the Civil Rights Movement," 109–11.

40 See, for example, William Chafe, *Civilities and Civil Rights: Greensboro, North Carolina, and the Black Struggle for Freedom* (New York, 1980), and James W. Ely Jr., "Negro Demonstrations and the Law: Danville as a Test Case," *Vanderbilt Law Review* 27 (October 1974): 927–68.

41 Gerald N. Rosenberg, *The Hollow Hope: Can Courts Bring About Social Change?* (Chicago, 1991), 46–54.

42 Lawson, *Black Ballots,* 307–52.

43 Earl Black and Merle Black, *The Vital South: How Presidents Are Elected* (Cambridge, Mass., 1992).

44 James R. Ralph Jr., *Northern Protest: Martin Luther King, Jr., Chicago, and the Civil Rights Movement* (Cambridge, Mass., 1993).

45 J. Harvie Wilkinson III, *From Brown to Bakke: The Supreme Court and School Integration: 1954–1978* (New York, 1979), 216–49.

46 Hiroshi Fukurai, Edgar W. Butler, and Richard Krooth, *Race and the Jury: Racial Disenfranchisement and the Search for Justice* (New York, 1993); Nancy J. King, "Racial Jurymandering: Cancer or Cure? A Contemporary Review of Affirmative Action in Jury Selection," *New York University Law Review* 68 (October 1993): 707–76.

47 *New York Times,* December 14, 1993. See *The Growth of Segregation in American Schools: Changing Patterns of Separation and Poverty Since 1968,* Harvard Project on School Desegregation (Cambridge, Mass., 1993).

48   John Egerton, *The Americanization of Dixie: The Southernization of America* (New York, 1974).

49   Abigail M. Thernstrom, *Whose Votes Count? Affirmative Action and Minority Voting Rights* (Cambridge, Mass., 1987). The Supreme Court in *Shaw v. Reno*, 113 Sup. Ct. 2816 (1993), cast doubt on the constitutionality of election districts designed to increase black representation solely on racial grounds. See also *Vera v. Richards* (S.D. Texas 1994), which struck down Texas's congressional districting as a violation of equal protection, declaring that districts designed to favor minority groups "bear the odious imprint of racial apartheid." Critics charge that such racial gerrymandering perpetuates segregation and institutionalizes racial division in the guise of civil rights.

50   Kull, *Color-Blind Constitution*, 182–224; Herman Belz, *Equality Transformed: A Quarter-Century of Affirmative Action* (New Brunswick, N.J., 1991).

∼ Since 1965: The South and Civil Rights

HUGH DAVIS GRAHAM

THE LITERATURE ON CIVIL RIGHTS and race relations since the 1960s is steeped in a fashionable gloom. Many histories of the civil rights movement describe the legislative reforms of the 1960s as essential but not fundamental, and some writers dismiss them as relatively easy and inconsequential. One textbook in African-American history, published in 1982 by black historians Mary Frances Berry and John Blassingame, devotes only four pages of the 485-page text to the civil rights movement and the reforms of the 1960s. Summarizing the Civil Rights Act of 1964 and the Voting Rights Act of 1965 in only three sentences each, Berry and Blassingame largely dismiss them with the observation that "political action did not improve the overall black condition."[1] In *The Struggle for Black Equality,* Harvard Sitkoff credits the Second Reconstruction of the 1960s with improvements in black education and political participation but finds persisting economic inequalities and concludes that a "Third Reconstruction, aiming for economic justice, is imperative."[2] William Chafe, looking back from the perspective of the mid-1980s, found little redistribution of political and economic power and concluded that the verdict on the Second Reconstruction "must be primarily negative."[3] In the progressively alienated writings of Derrick Bell, an African-American law professor at New York University and author of the standard textbook on race and American law during the 1980s, American society is seen as irredeemably racist at its core.[4]

Civil Rights Reform and the Continuitarians

These writers differ in the stress they place on inadequacy and failure in the civil rights reforms of the 1960s. All, however, emphasize a profound continuity in American life. Prior to the 1960s, scholars who emphasized continuity tended to be conservatives who approved American traditions of middle-class stability, limited government, free-market enterprise, and civic tolerance. During the 1960s, civil rights reformers demanded *dis*continuity. They attacked the legal foundations of the biracial caste system in the South and won unprecedented regulation by federal officials in both the public arena (education, government employment, elections) and the private sector (business accommodations, industrial and commercial employment, housing). After 1968, however, the trend toward Republican control of the presidency and, as a consequence, the increasing conservatism of the federal courts drove the civil rights coalition into an opposition role. The continuitarians of the post-1960s thus tended to be scholars of the Left, not the Right. Despite the Warren Court decisions and the legislation of the Kennedy-Johnson years, the continuitarians of the Left maintained, huge inequalities of race, sex, and class persisted in the distribution of income and political power in America.

From this perspective, the twin victories of "the Movement" in the 1960s — the Civil Rights Act of 1964 and the Voting Rights Act of 1965 — produced a premature celebration. The euphoria lasted less than one week. On August 11, 1965, only five days after President Lyndon Johnson signed the Voting Rights Act, a race riot broke out in the Watts section of Los Angeles that in a week of arson, looting, and police suppression claimed thirty-four lives (mostly black) and caused an estimated forty million dollars in property damage. Thirty years later, the story of civil rights policy since 1965 is commonly told either as a sad story of naive hopes and failed expectations or as a cynical tale of hypocrisy, betrayal, and profound national racism.[5]

The role of the South in this story remains a puzzle. Prior to 1965, the southern role was unambiguous. For centuries the South had been chief custodian to the nation's primal flaw of racial caste. Racism was therefore seen as an American problem because it was a southern problem. After World War II the South's Jim Crow system came under increasing attack; an embarrassment to the chief sponsor of the United Nations, it violated the American Creed of equal individual rights, hobbled the national economy, and was morally crippling to American leadership in the Cold War. From the 1860s to the 1960s,

civil rights reformers had sought to reconstruct the South by purging the cate-
gory of race from the world of public policy. The civil rights movement, in its
long campaign to bring a color-blind Constitution to the South, thus showed a
century of continuity. The national campaign to banish Jim Crow, resented by
white southerners and largely ineffective during the decade following *Brown
v. Board of Education,* built a powerful consensus outside the South that racial
distinctiveness had no legitimacy in law or policy.

With few exceptions the white South's elected representatives opposed the
antidiscrimination reforms of 1964 and 1965. Always successful in the past in
blocking significant threats to segregation, in the 1960s they faced a social
revolution, and as a consequence they suffered a rare and virtually total defeat.[6]
The year 1965 thus marks a watershed not only in civil rights policy but also in
the relationship between the South and the rest of the nation. The Watts riot
shifted the focus of racial attention sharply away from the South, which had
previously monopolized the racial spotlight. The four years of ghetto rioting
following Watts unmasked a legacy of white racism and discrimination that
was national in scope. The Kerner Commission, appointed by President Johnson in the wake of the Detroit riot of 1967, concluded that the entire nation
was "moving toward two societies, one black, one white—separate and unequal."[7] Increasingly, news stories about racial conflict and violence emanated
from outside the South—the turmoil over the Black Panthers, violent school
desegregation in Boston, national polarization over the *Bakke* "reverse discrimination" suit, the hostility between federal officials and civil rights leaders
during the Reagan administration, the growing concern in the 1980s over race
relations on the campuses, the debate over the black "underclass," the dangers
surrounding young black males, the Rodney King episode, the rising conflict
between African Americans and Latinos.[8]

Meanwhile, as racial conflict drew increasing national attention, writings
about the South swerved away from traditional racial themes. Memories of the
South's Jim Crow past were occasionally rekindled by events that fit traditional
patterns, for example, the political surge of David Duke in Louisiana. More
typically, however, writing about the South featured the Sunbelt economy, the
space explorations launched from Cape Canaveral and controlled from Houston, the political phenomenon of Jimmy Carter, the oil boom and the subsequent banking and real estate bust in Texas, the growth of the country music
industry in Nashville. Prior to 1965, the white South's defense of segregation
had monopolized the national discourse on race relations. After 1965, however,

the debate seemed to switch polarity. Civil rights leaders who had previously attacked racism as a southern phenomenon shifted their attacks northward and westward. This strategy led to an emphasis on the historical continuity of American racism, in the North and South alike. From the perspective of the North and West, a stress on continuity since the era of slavery was at best questionable in light of the federal shift to affirmative action requirements and the explosive growth of the black middle class since the 1960s. From the perspective of the American South, an emphasis on continuity seems contradicted by most of the evidence.

Consider the evidence for discontinuity offered by the policy revolution of 1964–65 and its consequences. Far from being a cosmetic improvement without significant structural implications for the distribution of money and power, the civil rights reforms of the 1960s provide a benchmark of change in American political life and especially in the history of the South. Within a decade the South witnessed four sharp breaks with its own past and with its past relationship with America, four major discontinuities that stand in sharp relief against the continuitarian backdrop of a perennially benighted and racist South. The first of these to occur involved the commercial heart of the caste system, the ban on racial mixing in restaurants, hotels, stores, and other privately owned places of public accommodation.

The Surprising Collapse of Segregation

When the racial violence in Birmingham in the spring of 1963 led President Kennedy to propose a civil rights bill aimed at the heart of segregation, its most controversial provision, Title 2, outlawed racial discrimination in public accommodations (hotels, motels, restaurants, department stores, theaters). When the civil rights bill neared passage in the spring of 1964, both passive noncompliance and violent resistance by segregationists were widely anticipated—an expectation well grounded in southern history and especially in recent experience. For this reason the administration's bill created a new agency, the Community Relations Service (CRS), based in the Commerce Department and assigned to conciliate disputes when Title 2 became law in the summer of 1964. I was working in Washington that summer as a training officer for the Peace Corps, and I was summoned to join hundreds of other white southerners in preparing to help the CRS calm desegregation disturbances in the South. To my great relief and to everybody's considerable surprise that

July, the massive desegregation of the South's tens of thousands of business establishments came off quietly and without a hitch. Segregationists resisted the implementation of Title 2, but their opposition took the form of lawsuits. In reply, the Warren Court that fall rushed through a unanimous ruling upholding Title 2 under the commerce clause. The Johnson administration, not knowing what to do with its unnecessary new agency, in 1966 transferred the CRS to the Justice Department, where it quietly withered from disuse. Why did white southerners in 1964 greet this lethal attack on Jim Crow with such law-abiding behavior? How do we square their response with a continuitarian view of the defiant and racially violent South?[9]

One explanation emphasizes conservative opposition to community violence on the part of southern business interests. Segregation ordinances reduced customer spending, and their enforcement often brought turmoil. Prior to 1964 southern businesses were often singled out for disruptive protests by both segregationists and integrationists, but Title 2 protected all commercial establishments by requiring the same behavior. Moreover, many of the larger southern enterprises, especially national department store chains and defense contractors such as Martin-Marietta in Georgia, were owned by non-southern firms that welcomed an end to local Jim Crow requirements. Finally, the rapid postwar growth of federal aid programs for hospital construction, roads, airports, and urban renewal had quietly created a network of mutual ties and interest-group coalitions between southern communities and Washington agencies. The benefits derived from these "iron triangles" and issue networks predisposed civic leaders toward cooperation with federal officials.[10] After a decade of "massive resistance" and escalating violence, local civic and commercial elites, including most southern newspapers, were united in supporting peaceful compliance.[11]

More important, perhaps, than the reasons for compliance were the lessons learned from it. When Jim Crow disappeared from the hotels and stores, old times there were quickly forgotten. Contrary to the continuitarian dogma of conservative Darwinists, stateways *did* change folkways, especially for a younger generation. Title 2 erased the social roles of segregated commerce from modern memory with astonishing speed and thoroughness. Southern students today, especially white students, find the practice of segregation virtually impossible to comprehend.

The Long Hot Summers and the Quiet South

The second discontinuity, setting the South apart not only from its own violent past but also from that of the rest of the nation, involves the wave of race riots that raged through American cities during the summers of 1964 through 1968. The South's appalling history of racial lynching was primarily a rural and small-town phenomenon, but the region was no stranger to urban race riots. The list of major southern and border race riots includes Wilmington, North Carolina (1898), Atlanta (1906), Houston (1917), Washington and Knoxville (1919), and Tulsa (1921). By the 1920s the South's contagion of lynching and urban riots had largely run its course, but the reason suggests more continuity than change. By the 1920s white racist violence in the South, often including government collusion or acquiescence, had so successfully terrorized defenseless black southerners that community leaders, especially business-oriented civic elites and organizations of white churchwomen, could curb white mob attacks without endangering the security of the caste system.

The race riots of the 1960s, however, were quite different. Like the Harlem riots of 1935 and 1943, the 1960s riots were black initiated, and they occurred largely outside the South. The major riots included, in 1965, Watts (Los Angeles); in 1966, Chicago, Cleveland, and Dayton; in 1967, Cincinnati, Detroit, Newark, and Jersey City; in 1968, Baltimore, Boston, Chicago, Cleveland, Hartford, Memphis, Philadelphia, Pittsburgh, San Francisco, Toledo, and Trenton. Aside from Memphis, which detonated after the local assassination of Martin Luther King on April 4, 1968, the major riots occurred outside the South. What *did* occur in the South were riot-demonstrations, similar to sympathy strikes, that typically grew out of student protests launched from black college campuses. They occurred in the South's African-American college towns: Atlanta (Atlanta University), Houston (Texas Southern), Jackson (Jackson State), Nashville (Fisk, Tennessee A&I), Greensboro (North Carolina A&T), Raleigh (Shaw). These "solidarity" riots were rarely very destructive in lives or property. Their leaders, unlike the blue-collar rioters of the northern ghettos, were sons and daughters of the black bourgeoisie.[12]

What lesson is taught by these differences in northern and southern rioting? They tell us forcefully that the civil rights laws of 1964 and 1965 produced a tangible payoff for black southerners. In riot-torn northern and western cities, where African Americans participated fully in the political process and enjoyed the protection of state and municipal antidiscrimination laws, the tension generated by civil rights protest was not released, as it was in the South, by exercising newly won freedoms to patronize previously off-limits hotels and restaurants, seek newly opened job opportunities, vote for candidates who sought black support and against those who did not. Southern blacks, however, exercised these newly guaranteed rights and felt their immediate benefits. Desegregation in public accommodations brought dignity to workaday routines in the South that had previously been marked by daily humiliation. Desegregation in employment opened to southern blacks for the first time a vast array of jobs that previously had been reserved for whites only. In an electorate enlarged by hundreds of thousands of black voters, the "Bull" Connors of the South could not, and did not, long survive.

The Voting Rights Act and the Detoxification of Southern Politics

The third major source of discontinuity was the Voting Rights Act and the political revolution that followed it. Whereas previous voting rights statutes had been ineffective (1957, 1960, 1964), the 1965 law earned a reputation as the most successful civil rights law in the twentieth century. Repeatedly amended and strengthened by large bipartisan majorities in Congress (in 1970, 1975, 1982), the Voting Rights Act enfranchised black southerners with unprecedented speed and effectiveness. By 1970 almost one million new African-American voters had been registered to vote in the South. Between 1964 and 1988 the proportion of voting-age blacks registered in the eleven southern states increased from 43.3 percent to approximately 64 percent. During the same period black registrants in the five Deep South states increased from 22.5 percent, a level of participation 47 percent lower than the white rate, to 65 percent, a level four points *higher* than the white rate.[13]

Enfranchisement armed blacks who previously had been defenseless against white segregationist legislatures, government agencies, juries, sheriffs, election officials, school boards, licensing and zoning and tax authorities. One immediate result was that white politicians quickly abandoned the rhetoric of racial demagoguery.[14] Veteran segregationist politicians such as Herman Talmadge of Georgia, George Wallace of Alabama, and Strom Thurmond of South Carolina openly courted black voters. Another result of massive black enfranchisement, though slower, was the racial integration of southern criminal justice systems, including police departments and juries. A third was the growth of black officeholders, both elective and appointive. The number of black elected officials in the seven southern states originally covered by the Voting Rights Act increased from fewer than 100 in 1965 to 3,265 in 1989.[15]

Most important, by purging southern politics of its racial poison, the Voting Rights Act freed not just black southerners but all southerners from a political bog that had mired the region in backwardness for generations. In a classic analysis of southern politics published in 1949, the political scientist V. O. Key Jr. described the South's four interlocking institutions of political sectionalism: racial segregation, disfranchisement of the black and white poor, malapportionment in favor of county-seat oligarchies, and a one-party system that stifled political competition. The combination, Key argued, trapped the region in an unresponsive polity that penalized most of its citizens (all blacks, nonaffluent whites, urban dwellers, and Republicans).[16] The judicial and legislative reforms of the 1960s effectively destroyed all four institutions of southern political sectionalism.

The result was not, however, what Key had hoped—a conversion of the underdeveloped South to a politics of New Deal liberalism. Southern governors and legislators did not significantly alter their traditions of low taxes and minimal social services. Nonetheless, the South after 1965 developed an effective two-party system in which black, white, urban, and certainly (indeed increasingly) Republican southerners participated freely. The result was a novelty unfamiliar to the generations of southerners before 1965: democratic politics at home in the states and cities and, in the nation, a kingmaker role for a region previously taken for granted.[17] The political system described by Key was a trap from which white southerners were incapable of rescuing themselves. Instead, white southerners were rescued by their black fellow southerners, as a beneficent by-product of rescuing themselves. Arguably the patron saint of southern (white) politics, Thomas Jefferson, should be joined in that role by Martin Luther King Jr.

The Bell-Shaped Curve of School Desegregation

The story of school desegregation in the South, our fourth source of fundamental change, introduces a strong note of ambiguity. By combining elements of both discontinuity (sharp breaks with the southern past) and convergence (the strengthening of common national patterns and the erosion of regional differences), it offers to neocontinuitarians such as Joel Williamson and Derrick Bell an argument that the southern shift from de jure to de facto segregation, forced on the South by the laws and court decisions of the 1960s, only clarified the national scope of America's bedrock commitment to white supremacy. The liberal policies of the 1960s, according to this argument, ironically strengthened the country's foundation of institutional racism by appearing to have reformed it. Thus discontinuity in the South is held to confirm a larger, national continuity of primordial American racism.

The bell-shaped curve of school desegregation in the South appears to offer some support for this argument. There is little disagreement that during the first phase of school desegregation, running from the *Brown* decision in 1954 to the enactment of the Elementary and Secondary Education Act of 1965, the federal courts acted cautiously and largely alone and hence produced only token results.[18] During the second phase, however, the courts, reinforced by federal agencies using the leverage of federal school aid to enforce the Civil Rights Act, began ordering school boards to achieve integration by busing for racial balance. Beginning in 1968, court-ordered busing produced dramatic results in the rural and small-town South, where both school busing and racially mixed housing were traditional. President Nixon, despite his public posturing against busing, quietly cooperated with the courts and quickened the dismantling of the South's dual school systems. By 1972, the proportion of black children attending all-black schools in the South had plunged from 68 percent in 1968 to 8 percent. By 1973 the South led the nation in school integration.[19]

In the third phase of school desegregation, however, the process reversed itself. Coinciding roughly with the shift from Nixon's presidency to the Ford administration, the third phase was characterized by rising national resentment against federal enforcement efforts and by demographic trends that sent the curve of school integration into a nationwide downward slide. In 1974 the Supreme Court under Chief Justice Warren Burger ruled in a suit from Detroit that suburban school districts not found in violation could not be required to help integrate city school systems. By 1974, desegregation efforts remained peaceful in the South but were violently resisted by white working-class parents in such cities as Boston and Denver. By 1975, the share of black children attending schools that were 95 percent or more black had declined in the South to 20 percent but had *risen* to 50 percent in the northern and western states. In 1976 and again in 1978, Congress passed legislation barring federal agencies from requiring busing for racial balance.

Following the election of Ronald Reagan in 1980, the literature on school desegregation shifted its focus from coercive methods to voluntary inducements, such as magnet schools, voucher systems, and privatization.[20] Residential patterns outside the South, where African Americans had migrated into increasingly black central cities, concentrated racial minorities in inner-city schools and accelerated the flight of whites, and subsequently of middle-class blacks as well, from deteriorating urban schools. In the South, where racial living patterns had historically been more mixed, the racial separation of housing and the housing-based resegregation of schools was slower. Nonetheless, by the late 1980s northern and southern cities were growing more alike in their racially separate patterns of housing and schools. They were also converging in their patterns of urban pathology, with a predominantly black "underclass" showing high rates of crime, imprisonment, school violence, alcohol and drug addiction, family instability, and deteriorating health.[21] The surprising civil rights successes of the post-1965 decade in the South, as demonstrated by the rapid collapse of the Jim Crow system, the relative absence of urban rioting, the detoxification of southern politics, and the rapid pace of school desegregation, lost momentum in the 1970s. By the 1980s, optimism was displaced by a growing pessimism over the future of race relations in America. Were we wrong to regard 1965 as a decisive watershed in southern history? Were the dramatic changes of the 1960s largely a surface phenomenon, yielding to deeper tides of racial animosity that flowed through the nation's history and knew no regional boundaries?

The Problem of Biracial Coalitions in the South

One way to begin to answer this question is to look more closely at the way black southerners were integrated into the region's political life after 1965. The best guarantee that the Second Reconstruction would not fail, as did the first, was a vigorous exercise of the power of black ballots. The federal courts, despite some narrowing of protections for minorities during the 1980s, raised no fundamental objections to the "disparate impact" model of affirmative action approved by the Burger Court.[22] In voting rights law, the courts rarely denied challenges by minority plaintiffs, and Congress consistently favored policies proposed by the Leadership Conference on Civil Rights.[23] The key to furthering the interests of African Americans in the South thus depended on the power of black ballots and the success of coalition building in competitive politics.

V. O. Key had hoped that the destruction of the four pillars of the South's traditional political system would end racial demagoguery, break the political dominance of rural minorities, and empower black citizens to bargain politically in a two-party system for the protections and benefits of government. In Key's analysis, widely shared by postwar students of American politics, the South's crippling problems of poverty and economic underdevelopment remained unaddressed because the region's have-not majority of working-class blacks and whites was split by racist appeals. Economic issues were regarded as "real," but racial issues were considered distracting and divisive. Mass enfranchisement should therefore enable biracial coalitions of the region's poor to win redistributionist social programs from government.

Key's liberal vision, however, was only partially vindicated by the results of the region's political revolution in the 1960s. Despite the success of the Voting Rights Act, in national elections since 1968 the South's black voters, constituting only 14 percent of the region's presidential electorate, have been outnumbered six to one by white voters. Furthermore, blacks reduced their bargaining power by voting predictably Democratic. A majority of southern whites, on the other hand, provided crucial support for Republican victories in national elections. At the state level, the impact of black political participation was more ambiguous. By 1975 the number of black elected officials in the South had risen to fourteen hundred. This represented an increase of 2,000 percent since 1965, although most officeholders held modest positions in small towns and counties of heavy black concentration. In contests for major metropolitan, congressional, and statewide offices, political demography favored white candidates.

Yet success in the new political environment, especially among Democratic candidates, required skill in the centrist art of moderation. Inviting black support at discreet arm's length, Democrats running for statewide office hoped to build majorities by combining the votes of loyalist blacks with at least 40 percent of the white vote. This delicate balancing produced a generation of surprising successes for moderate Democratic governors and U.S. senators, especially in a region that voted so persistently Republican in presidential elections. It also produced the era's only Democratic victories in presidential elections—Jimmy Carter in 1976 and Bill Clinton in 1992. Victories based on such indirect and centrist appeals, however, did not produce in southern states the kind of coalition bargaining, campaign promises, election mandates, and robust government programs that had inspired liberal Democrats since the New Deal and the Great Society.[24]

Why did the racial divisions of the past, although greatly attenuated, persist in southern political life after 1965, frustrating biracial coalition building and bipartisan bargaining? One reason was the growth of Sunbelt prosperity in the South, which eased populistic pressure for class solidarity across racial lines. Between 1969 and 1979 the incidence of poverty in the South fell from 41 to 30 percent among black families and from 11 to 7 percent among white families. Black families had thus made greater relative economic advances, but black southerners still remained four times more likely than white southerners to live below the poverty line.[25] Another source of racial division was disagreement over school busing, an issue that increasingly split the nation along racial lines. In 1974, when the Gallup poll asked blacks and whites in the North and South whether they favored or opposed "busing school children to achieve better racial balance in the schools," 75 percent of blacks supported busing whereas 72 percent of whites opposed it. In policy preferences, southern blacks remained far more liberal than southern whites. By substantial margins over white southerners, for example, blacks supported expanded government roles in providing employment, welfare, food stamps, medical insurance, aiding the cities, helping minorities, and passing the ERA.[26]

On the other hand, since the racial wars of the 1960s southern blacks have shown increasing identification with the South and have shared regional values across racial lines. Beginning in the mid-1970s blacks reversed their historical out-migration from the South. Between 1970 and 1980 the Northeast and the Midwest lost 342,000 black migrants and the South gained 209,000.[27] During the 1980s public opinion surveys using "feeling thermometer" questions demonstrated that southern blacks were warmly disposed toward certain symbols they shared with white southerners. One of these was the term *southerner* itself, a label that elicited negative reactions among southern blacks in the 1960s but was given a "warm" rating by 84 percent of black respondents in 1980.[28] Other symbols rated warmly by southern blacks and whites alike, and reflecting shared traditional values in southern culture, include the importance of religion, school prayer, patriotism, the military, and the environment.[29] Furthermore, with the rapid growth of the black middle class in the South since 1965 has come a convergence of white and black middle-class policy preferences concerning taxes, crime, school safety, college loans. If biracial populist coalitions are desirable in democratic politics, so too presumably are biracial coalitions supporting middle-class interests. Shared values and converging policy preferences between southern whites and blacks of all classes since the 1960s, however, have been dwarfed by a profound and widening split over one arena of public policy—minority preferences.

The Greatest Civil Rights Discontinuity: Minority Preference Policies

Continuitarians who minimize the significance of the civil rights reforms of the 1960s commonly fail to account for the greatest discontinuity of them all. The federal shift to minority preference requirements in civil rights enforcement occurred during 1969–71 under the Nixon administration. The causes for the shift are complex; they include the urgency generated by the urban rioting of 1965–68 and the skill of the civil rights coalition in lobbying legislators and agency officials. They also include the determination of the Nixon administration to split the labor–civil rights alliance, speed the growth of a more conservative black middle class, associate "racial quotas" in the public mind with the liberal legacy of the Democratic Party, and appeal to working-class resentment of court-ordered busing and "reverse discrimination."[30] These events helped produce a seismic shift in the American political landscape. It included the mass defection of southern and northern blue-collar whites from the New Deal coalition, the emergence of a Republican presidential majority and with it conservative trends in the executive and judicial branches, and a deep split in the civil rights coalition over the principle of constitutional color blindness.

In light of these events, the climactic years of Kennedy-Johnson reform, running from 1964 to 1968 (the Open Housing Act) and centering roughly on 1965, emerge as a watershed of the first magnitude. Prior to 1964, black southerners and their civil rights organizations for generations had placed their faith in a color-blind Constitution for all Americans. White southerners, together with their elected officials and governments, defended an opposite principle — that racial separation must govern public policy. The nation's nonsouthern majority, itself overwhelmingly white and holding the balance of political decision, shared the opinion of African Americans that racial distinctions in the law were incompatible with equal rights. This support by the national majority for constitutional principles of equal individual rights—the American Creed—remained latent until the 1960s. When it then was galvanized by the African-American civil rights movement, its support proved decisive.[31]

After 1968, however, black and white southerners switched sides. Majorities of black southerners, initially reluctant to abandon their traditional faith in legal color blindness, were persuaded by civil rights leaders to support race-conscious remedies to compensate for past discrimination. White southerners reversed their constitutional principles even more thoroughly and less reluctantly, switching allegiance by the 1970s from color consciousness to color blindness. In such a topsy-turvy world of reversed rationales, biracial coalitions remained as elusive as ever. Robert Botsch, in his study of working-class southerners during the 1970s, concluded that "the most troublesome issues with which the architects of a populist alliance must deal are those that raise the question of reverse discrimination." As the era of segregation receded into memory, white and black southerners with common class interests were divided once again, but in an opposite fashion, by government policies keyed to race. "Many white working-class southerners who are otherwise fairly moderate and tolerant on racial issues," wrote Botsch, "are greatly disturbed by what they perceive to be an effort by the national government to change the rules of the game so that the darkness of one's skin is more rewarded than is hard work."[32]

In the civil rights crisis of the 1960s, the issue was decided by the political pressure of nonsouthern whites, siding with black southerners and the goal of constitutional color blindness against white southerners and racial segregation. In the 1980s and 1990s, with southern blacks and whites switching positions, nonsouthern whites once again held the balance of national opinion. Had their beliefs also changed? In public opinion surveys since the 1950s, racial bias among white Americans has declined in all regions. These trends according to some critics are evidence of "superficial" tolerance masking "subtle" but deeply rooted racism. Recent survey research using experimental techniques, however, has shown that white opinion on racial issues has grown more pliable, less keyed to racial stereotypes, and better able through education to avoid racial double standards.[33] Studies of national opinion since the 1970s have shown wide support among whites as well as blacks for government assistance programs to aid minorities in education, jobs, health, and housing.[34] By enormous majorities, however, white Americans in all regions have rejected preferential treatment or racial quotas as a *means* of providing such aid. By a margin of four in every five, or more, white Americans in the 1980s and 1990s opposed minority preferences in jobs, racial quotas in college admissions, and school busing for racial balance. White women, though sharing with minorities a designation as protected-class beneficiaries in affirmative action programs, nonetheless registered the same 80 percent opposition level to minority preferences as did white men.[35] According to Paul Sniderman and Thomas

Piazza in their 1993 study *The Scar of Race,* white Americans are not unique in objecting to affirmative action preferences based on immutable traits. Opinion surveys in Australia, the United Kingdom, Germany, and Italy in 1987 showed large majorities of women as well as men objecting to giving women preferences in jobs and promotions. "Proposing to privilege some people rather than others, on the basis of a characteristic they were born with," Sniderman and Piazza write, "violates a nearly universal norm of fairness." [36]

The Irony of Freedom

The point is not to pick sides in the civil rights dispute over affirmative action. Rather, it is to emphasize how the very existence of the dispute presupposes advances and agreements in civil rights policy that were scarcely conceivable in the early 1960s. Consider the magnitude of these changes for the people of the South since 1965. Racial segregation was abolished in government, education, the world of commerce, and the job market (though not in housing, and not effectively in the schools). Blacks and whites participated fully in a system of vigorous two-party competition. A century of flight by African Americans from the southern region was reversed. By the 1980s the majority of black southerners no longer lived in poverty, and more than a quarter of the South's black families had incomes higher than the median income of southern white families.[37] Problems associated with the predominantly black underclass were attributed to national and even to international trends, including the decline of industrial employment in a global economy and job competition produced by massive immigration, rather than to regional peculiarities.

Even the deep divisions over racial preferences, which had seen white and black southerners suddenly swap their fundamental positions after a century of consistent advocacy, represented striking regional gains in race relations. Blacks demanding minority preferences could take for granted a virtually universal ban on invidious discrimination against them. Whites demanding equal-treatment policies were freed from the impossible burden of morally justifying a biracial caste system in America. Unlike the long era of segregation, when only the region's African Americans and a handful of southern white liberals occupied the moral high ground of opposing Jim Crow, in the post-1965 era both sides in the dispute over minority preferences brought to their cause a passion for principle and justice. Proponents of affirmative action appealed to historical realism, asking accelerated remedies to compensate for generations of systematic deprivation, whereby accumulated unfairness was frozen into white-controlled institutions. Proponents of constitutional color blindness appealed to the American Creed of individual rights and equal protection before the law, citing the unfairness of penalizing citizens guilty of no wrongdoing on account of immutable traits they were born with. Like the abortion controversy, in which fetal rights to life itself conflicted with the rights of innocent victims in cases of rape or incest, the dispute over minority preferences involved competing moral claims that resisted compromise and eluded consensus.[38]

When in the past have the people of the South, white and black alike, enjoyed such freedom to engage so fully in public discourse and the policy-making process, free at last of the tar baby of Jim Crow? After 1965, the region largely shed its ancient encumbrances: humiliation and powerlessness for blacks, guilt and national alienation for whites. The South was no longer defined by Americans primarily as a problem requiring remediation imposed by national authority. Southern patterns of race relations were no longer illegitimate and unstable because they were imposed by whites upon powerless blacks.

As we look toward the twenty-first century, prospects for race relations in the South remained clouded. Despite the rise of the region's black middle class, a stubborn racial gap persisted in education and income. Ironically, voting rights enforcement from Washington posed a new threat. Federal redistricting demands for "minority-majority" electoral districts threatened to resegregate the political parties. In a new form of racial gerrymandering, minority voters were packed into often strangely shaped districts to guarantee minority winners—a development encouraged not only by Democratic leaders beholden to the civil rights coalition but also by the Reagan and Bush administrations because it drove southern whites toward the Republican Party.[39] Nonetheless, the South's extraordinary history of social change since 1965 has given the region a unique asset: for blacks, a memory of civil rights gains unprecedented in magnitude and effectiveness; for whites, a removal of the corrupting whip hand of racial supremacy. For the generation of black and white southerners coming of age since the 1960s, the South's history brought not just the ancient burdens of tragedy, guilt, and defeat but also the winds of freedom.

Notes

1   Mary Frances Berry and John W. Blassingame, *Long Memory: The Black Experience in America* (New York, 1982), 194.

2   Harvard Sitkoff, *The Struggle for Black Equality, 1954–1980* (New York, 1981), 237. In a revised edition published in 1993, however, Sitkoff challenged the "dismissive view" of the civil rights movement and its accomplishments: "Black commentators disparaged it as 'bourgeois' or elitist, and belittled the reforms of the 1960s for failing to produce major structural changes or to overturn racism." "That view of the black struggle for equality and justice, of essentially *easy* and *inconsequential* triumphs," Sitkoff wrote, "is not the perspective of this book." Sitkoff, *The Struggle for Black Equality, 1954–1992* (New York, 1993), 232.

3   William H. Chafe, "One Struggle Ends, Another Begins," in *The Civil Rights Movement in America,* ed. Charles W. Eagles (Jackson, Miss., 1986), 147.

4   Derrick A. Bell Jr., *And We Are Not Saved: The Elusive Quest for Racial Justice* (New York, 1989); idem, *Faces at the Bottom of the Well* (New York, 1992).

5   See, for example, Manning Marable, *Race, Reform, and Rebellion: The Second Reconstruction in Black America, 1954–1990* (Jackson, Miss., 1991), 90–92, 200–210, and Joel Williamson, *The Crucible of Race: Black-White Relations in the American South since Emancipation* (New York, 1984), 509–10.

6   See Hugh Davis Graham, *The Civil Rights Era: Origins and Development of National Policy, 1960–1972* (New York, 1990). In the crucial Senate negotiations during the spring of 1964, the filibustering southerners largely removed themselves from the bargaining process, and as a consequence conservative interests were represented by the Republicans.

7   *Report of the National Advisory Commission on Civil Disorders* (New York, 1968), xii.

8   See, for example, Elijah Anderson, *Streetwise: Race, Class, and Change in an Urban Community* (Chicago, 1990); Andrew Hacker, *Two Nations: Black and White, Separate, Hostile, Unequal* (New York, 1992); Christopher Jencks, *Rethinking Social Policy: Race, Poverty, and the Underclass* (Cambridge, Mass., 1992); Jim Sleeper, *The Closest of Strangers: Liberalism and the Politics of Race in New York* (New York, 1990); Gerald David Jaynes and Robin M. Williams Jr., *A Common Destiny: Blacks and American Society* (Washington, 1989); and William Julius Wilson, *The Truly Disadvantaged: The Inner City, the Underclass, and Public Policy* (Chicago, 1987).

9   Title 2 was upheld in *Heart of Atlanta Motel v. United States,* 379 U.S. 241 (1964). See Hugh Davis Graham, *Civil Rights and the Presidency* (New York, 1992), 67–86.

10 Christopher Scribner, "Urban Renewal and Political Change in Birmingham," paper presented at the Tennessee Conference of Historians, University of the South, October 30, 1993.

11 See case studies in fourteen southern cities in Elizabeth Jacoway and David R. Colburn, eds., *Southern Businessmen and Desegregation* (Baton Rouge, 1982).

12 Hugh Davis Graham, "Civil Disorders: 1943–Present," in *Encyclopedia of Black America,* ed. W. A. Low and Virgil A. Clift (New York, 1981), 237–41; Hugh Davis Graham, "On Riots and Riot Commissions: Civil Disorders in the 1960s," *Public Historian* 2 (Summer 1980): 2–27.

13 Steven F. Lawson, *In Pursuit of Power: Southern Blacks and Electoral Politics, 1965–1982* (New York, 1985); Graham, *Civil Rights and the Presidency,* 141–42; Bernard Grofman and Chandler

Davidson, eds., *Controversies in Minority Voting: The Voting Rights in Perspective* (Washington, 1992), 42–44.

14 The statewide elections of 1970 produced a fresh class of progressive young governors—Dale Bumpers in Arkansas, Reubin Askew in Florida, Jimmy Carter in Georgia, Linwood Holton in Virginia—and subsequent elections in the 1970s added William Clinton in Arkansas, Richard Riley in South Carolina, Lamar Alexander in Tennessee.

15 David R. Goldfield, *Promised Land: The South since 1945* (Arlington Heights, Ill., 1987), 171–79; Dewey W. Grantham, *The Life and Death of the Solid South* (Lexington, Ky., 1988), 192–95. Chandler Davidson notes that in 1989 the 3,265 black elected officials constituted 10 percent of all elected officials in the seven states, whereas blacks constituted 23 percent of the voting-age population. See "The Voting Rights Act," in Grofman and Davidson, *Controversies in Minority Voting,* 43.

16 V. O. Key Jr., *Southern Politics in State and Nation* (New York, 1949). See Numan V. Bartley and Hugh D. Graham, *Southern Politics and the Second Reconstruction* (Baltimore, 1975).

17 Earl Black and Merle Black, *Politics and Society in the South* (Cambridge, Mass., 1987); idem, *The Vital South* (Cambridge, Mass., 1992).

18 J. Harvie Wilkinson III, *From Brown to Bakke: School Desegregation and the Supreme Court* (New York, 1979).

19 John Egerton, *School Desegregation: A Report from the South* (Atlanta, 1976).

20 See, for example, U.S. Department of Education, *Resegregation of the Public Schools: The Third Generation* (Washington, 1989); Christine H. Rossell, *The Carrot or the Stick for School Desegregation Policy: Magnet Schools or Forced Busing* (Philadelphia, 1990); and John E. Chubb and Terry M. Moe, *Politics, Markets, and America's Schools* (Washington, 1990).

21 Douglas S. Massey and Nancy A. Denton, *American Apartheid: Segregation and the Making of the Underclass* (Cambridge, Mass., 1993), esp. 60–82; Jaynes and Williams, *Common Destiny.*

22 For opposing views on this controversial issue, see Herman Belz, *Equality Transformed: A Quarter Century of Affirmative Action* (New Brunswick, N.J., 1991), and Alfred W. Blumrosen, *Modern Law: The Law Transfer System and Equal Employment Opportunity* (Madison, Wisc., 1993). Disparate impact theory held that a policy or practice (employment test, educational job or admissions requirement) was unlawful if it resulted in a statistical disparity between the minority population available (percentage of racial or ethnic minorities in the area workforce or application pool) and the minority population receiving the benefit (percentage of minorities hired, promoted, admitted). Under race-conscious affirmative action, the results-centered disparate impact standard replaced the procedurally oriented intent standard, which required equal treatment irrespective of racial or ethnic status and defined discrimination as an intentionally harmful act.

23 See Davidson, "Voting Rights Act," and Hugh Davis Graham, "Voting Rights and the American Regulatory State," in Grofman and Davidson, *Controversies in Minority Voting,* 7–51, 177–96.

24 Alexander P. Lamis, *The Two-Party South* (New York, 1984); Black and Black, *Vital South,* 213–40.

25 Thomas J. Naylor and James Clotfelter, *Strategies for Change in the South* (Chapel Hill, 1975).

26 George H. Gallup, *The Gallup Poll: Public Opinion, 1972–1977* (Wilmington, Del., 1978), 370–71.

27 Massey and Denton, *American Apartheid,* 60; Rex R. Campbell, "Return Migration of Black People in the South," *Journal of Politics* 39 (February 1979): 129–62.

28 Merle Black and John Shelton Reed, "Blacks and Southerners: A Research Note," *Journal of Politics* 44 (February 1982): 165–71.

29 Black and Black, *Vital South,* 234–35. The Blacks relied on the CBS News/*New York Times* exit polls of southern voters in the 1976–88 presidential elections and the National Election Study presidential-year surveys conducted by the Center for Political Studies of the University of Michigan. Several symbols produced warm responses from most southern blacks and cold responses from most southern whites—black militants, civil rights leaders, Jesse Jackson, Ted Kennedy, Democrats.

30 Graham, *Civil Rights Era,* esp. 233–54, 322–45.

31 Howard Schuman, Charlotte Steeh, and Lawrence Bobo, *Racial Attitudes in America: Trends and Interpretations* (Cambridge, Mass., 1985).

32 Robert E. Botsch, *We Shall Not Overcome* (Chapel Hill, 1980), 160.

33 Paul M. Sniderman and Thomas Piazza, *The Scar of Race* (Cambridge, Mass., 1993), 8–14, 35–87.

34 Schuman, Steeh, and Bobo, *Racial Attitudes in America;* Jaynes and Williams, *Common Destiny,* 113–60.

35 Seymour Martin Lipset, "Equal Chances versus Equal Rights," *Annals of the American Academy of Political and Social Science* 523 (September 1992): 63–74.

36 Sniderman and Piazza, *Scar of Race,* 134.

37 Black and Black, *Politics and Society in the South,* 295.

38 In a parallel debate of the 1970s that featured similar competition between incompatible core values, ERA feminists demanded absolute constitutional equality between the sexes, and antiratificationists demanded recognition and protection in public policy for the unique biological role of women.

39 For a critique of this strategy, see Linda Chavez, "Party Lines: The Republicans' Racial Quotas," *New Republic* 24 (June 1991): 14–16, and Abigail M. Thernstrom, "A Republican–Civil Rights Conspiracy," *Washington Post,* September 23, 1991. In 1993 the U.S. Supreme Court in *Shaw v. Reno* raised constitutional objections to race-based redistricting that remain unresolved.

∾ The South as an Economic Problem: Fact or Fiction?

ROBERT A. MARGO

ECONOMIC BACKWARDNESS AND POVERTY are central to the perception that the South was once an economic "problem" for the rest of the nation. Before the Civil War the South embraced slavery, an institution judged to be economically moribund as well as immoral. After the Civil War per capita incomes in the South converged only very slowly on the national average, allegedly because the region clung far too long to a single crop, cotton, which it produced with an exploitative and inefficient agricultural system, sharecropping, among other causes. Since World War II, per capita incomes in the South have risen sharply relative to the national average, and the southern economy has largely cast off its problem status.

In this essay I discuss various aspects of the economic development of the South that led to the perception (and reality) of economic backwardness. Economic historians have worked hard in the last two decades to clarify the details of southern economic development, and much of what they have discovered challenges conventional wisdom. In particular, I argue that the perception that the South failed to catch up economically before World War II is partly the result of a particular reference standard that is inappropriate to the historical circumstances southerners found themselves in after the Civil War.

The Southern Economy before the Civil War: Was It a Problem?

Since 1970 the South has largely been an economic success story; it is the rest of the country that has been the problem. The southern economy, especially its major urban centers such as Dallas, Houston, Atlanta, and Miami, has performed very well, give or take a few economic downturns. Other urban areas, such as Nashville, are poised on the edge of further growth. The South has the same shopping malls, the same fast-food restaurants, as the rest of the United States. Racial conflict, the quintessential southern social problem, is now a problem everywhere—like it always was, but the nation pretended otherwise.

For the first half of the twentieth century, however, the southern economy was definitely a problem, in the sense that southern per capita income fell significantly below that of the rest of the United States. What I wish to do first is to consider one explanation for southern economic backwardness: the South was poor around 1900 because it had embraced slavery, an economic system that was inefficient and unprofitable and that shifted resources away from such economic sectors as manufacturing, which defined economic development in the North and became identified with great wealth in the late nineteenth century.

The argument is as crusty as any in American history. Its roots are in the abolitionist movement, which adopted the argument when tactically expedient. But it was also embraced by a wide variety of historians in the early twentieth century, including Ulrich B. Phillips, perhaps the most famous southern historian of his era.[1]

The intellectual tide shifted in the late 1950s when two economists, Alfred Conrad and John Meyer, applied formal economic reasoning to the problem of determining the profitability of slavery.[2] Conrad and Meyer wrote down an equation for the rate of profit; collected data on slave prices, productivity, and "maintenance" costs (for example, food and clothing given to slaves); and, with the data, estimated a rate of return on investment in slaves. Their conclusion was that slavery was anything but unprofitable—indeed, on average, investments in slaves paid better than other alternative investments.

Subsequently, Yasukichi Yasuba demonstrated that slavery was not only profitable but also economically *viable*.[3] Viability is a more stringent condition than profitability. An investment may be profitable today but not viable in the long run. Viable means that it pays for the owner of a piece of capital to replenish it when it wears out (depreciates). In the case of slavery, viability means the slave owner was not better off manumitting slaves at birth or shortly thereafter; it paid, in other words, for the system to reproduce itself.

The next blow to the "slavery caused underdevelopment" thesis came when Richard Easterlin prepared a set of regional income estimates for the United States going back to 1840 (the earliest date for which suitable data survive).[4] Later in the essay I analyze Easterlin's data extensively. For now, I simply wish to note that Easterlin's estimates reveal that the South was *not* an economic laggard before the Civil War. True, per capita incomes were lower in the South than the national average, but the same was true in the Midwest. Further, the pace of economic growth was only slightly lower in the South than in the North during a period of exceptionally rapid overall economic growth.[5] At first glance, it seemed hard to square Easterlin's numbers with the notion that slavery was a poorly functioning economic system—although perhaps it still was, but the nonslave portion of the southern economy performed extremely well.

The scholarly debate reached intellectual frenzy with Robert Fogel and Stanley Engerman's cliometric research on the economics of slavery.[6] Fogel and Engerman's work was (and is) controversial, and it is not my intention to survey the battlefield and declare a victor. Rather, I wish to focus on one of their conclusions, which has stood up very well to critical scrutiny—the relative efficiency of slave agriculture.[7]

By "relative efficiency" I mean the following: imagine two farms, one with free labor, the other with slave labor. All other productive inputs—capital, land, and so forth—are the same. Which farm, on average, produces more agricultural output? Fogel and Engerman's startling answer was the slave farm. The productivity advantage of slave farms, however, was not universal. It existed only in certain crops (cotton, tobacco, sugar, rice), and it required a certain number of slaves to achieve (fifteen or so).

Although not all aspects of the productivity advantage can be traced to a specific source, one factor stands out, the *gang system* of organizing and directing agricultural slave labor. In the gang system, not unlike the factory system of England, tasks were subdivided and division of labor employed. Evidently the gang system was anathema to free labor; no free farms used it, as far as we know. Gangs could not be organized without a minimum number of slaves, which is why the productivity advantage of slave labor required a threshold (the fifteen slaves) in plantation size.

Three key implications follow from Fogel and Engerman's findings on relative efficiency. First, when coupled with evidence of viability, there is no reason to believe that slavery was dying of natural causes before the Civil War. Indeed, on economic grounds there is every reason to believe that slavery could have continued on after 1865 (as it did in Cuba, Puerto Rico, and Brazil). Second, the "sin" of slavery was spread far beyond the confines of southern plantations. Because slavery was relatively efficient, cotton was produced more

cheaply than it would have been otherwise. To a first approximation, the antebellum cotton market was competitive — many buyers, many sellers. In a competitive market, cost savings arising from efficiency gains are passed through
to consumers in the form of a lower price. Yankees, in other words, benefited
economically from slavery, as did the British and other European countries.
Third, the end of slavery involved more than a transfer of property rights from
slave owners to former slaves; some output was lost in the process. I will return to this point shortly.

If slavery was profitable, viable, and relatively efficient, is there any truth to
the notion that the "peculiar institution" damaged the South economically?
Certainly it damaged a large share of the region's population. The economic
costs for enslaved African Americans were enormous. There is no evidence
that slaves shared in pre–Civil War southern economic growth. Although
adult slaves appeared to have been relatively well fed by the standards of the
day, slave children were exceedingly malnourished.[8] The overwhelming majority of slaves lacked opportunities for upward mobility potentially available
to even the lowliest free laborer of the era. The vast majority of adult slaves
were illiterate, and adult illiteracy retarded the economic mobility of subsequent generations of African Americans well into the twentieth century.[9]

Can it be said that slavery retarded southern economic development in
other ways, in particular, by discouraging industrialization? After all, the
North developed manufacturing long before the South, and manufacturing
was the wave of modernity, not slavery. There is a grain of truth in the argument, but only a grain. With hindsight it is easy to criticize the South's failure
to industrialize, and to blame slavery for the failure, since it is the most obvious difference between North and South on the eve of the Civil War.

There are, however, two problems with the argument. First, slavery was not
incompatible with manufacturing per se. Slaves were successfully employed in
antebellum factories in Virginia and Alabama. The efficiency gains from slave
labor in agriculture, however, were so large that slaves were literally pulled
out of the cities (where the factories were) into the countryside.[10] Conditional
on slavery existing, free southerners would have been *worse off* economically
(lower per capita income) if the South had engaged in a massive industrialization push prior to the Civil War (because resources would have been misallo-
cated). The antebellum South's comparative advantage lay in agriculture, and
that advantage was enhanced (in certain crops) with the use of slave labor.

Second, while the incomes of free southerners did fall short of incomes in the North, the same can be said for many European nations in the nineteenth century. Indeed, many of these lagged behind the South, in terms of per capita income.[11] The problem of making such interregional or international comparisons is part of the general economic problem of "convergence," which I will return to later.

The Southern Economy, 1865–1940: What Was the Problem?

If southern poverty cannot be traced to poor economic performance under slavery, what can it be traced to? Some clues can be gleaned from Easterlin's income estimates for the immediate postbellum period (1860 to 1880). According to Easterlin's estimates, per capita incomes in the South fell drastically after the Civil War, relative to incomes elsewhere and, more surprisingly, in absolute terms. From 1880 to 1940, per capita incomes in the South grew about 0.3 percent faster than the rest of the country, but there still was a large regional gap in income on the eve of World War II.[12]

What caused the decline in southern incomes after the Civil War and why wasn't recovery swifter? The decline in income can be traced to several causes.[13] First, there was a tremendous fall in agricultural productivity. Simply put, the gang system disappeared shortly after the war, replaced by sharecropping and related forms of agricultural organization. With the loss of the gang system, however, came the end of the special efficiency advantage the South had enjoyed under slavery. Second, there was a decline in work effort among former slaves — as free workers, not surprisingly, they chose to work fewer hours and less intensively than they did as slaves (and not at all in gang-system agriculture).[14] Third, there was a slowdown in the rate of growth of demand for southern cotton, because other countries, such as India, emerged as alternative sources of supply.[15] Although scholarly debate continues to rage over the relative importance of these three factors, recent research suggests that the decline in agricultural productivity was the principal culprit.[16]

Note that one factor I omitted was destruction of physical capital during the war. Destruction of physical capital in the South was confined to a few areas (for example, Atlanta) and was repaired relatively quickly. The big loss was human capital — loss of life and wartime disabilities. Combined with similar losses in the North, these have been estimated to have been about several billion dollars (in 1860 dollars) — more than enough to buy the freedom of every slave *and* provide each former slave with forty acres and a mule.[17]

The slowness of southern recovery after the Civil War has fascinated historians for decades. For many, sharecropping is the smoking gun.[18] In place of slavery, sharecropping emerged as the dominant contractual form between landlords and farm workers. Sharecroppers agreed to work the land for a share of the crop — often 50 percent, but the share varied with what the landlord was willing to furnish the tenant (for example, fertilizer or a mule). A long intellectual tradition in economics suggests that sharecroppers had few incentives to work hard — after all, they got only a portion of the return from any increased effort — and fewer incentives to invest in the land or new technology. Moreover, landlords are said to have forced sharecroppers to grow excessive amounts of cotton, since cotton was readily marketable, thereby reducing the amount of food grown. Cotton "overproduction" was bad for the postbellum South, so the argument goes, because the demand for southern cotton was growing less rapidly than it had before the war.

The major difficulty with the sharecropping story is that it has little hard evidence to back it up. While there may have been some productivity disadvantages (certainly compared with the gang system), nothing actually proves that sharecropping per se was responsible for vast inefficiencies in agricultural production.[19] Although it is true that more resources were devoted to cotton production after the war, an upward trend was already in place in the 1850s, and the postbellum cotton boom can also be traced to the expansion of railroads. Markets were increasingly accessible to postbellum southern farmers, and they responded by growing more crops for export (that is, cotton), as farmers elsewhere in the United States did when faced with similar incentives.[20]

One popular story that deserves scrutiny invokes geographical inefficiencies in the allocation of labor and capital between the South and the rest of the nation. Simply put, the South had too little capital and too much unskilled labor — not a recipe for economic growth in an era that emphasized (as ours does) the substitution of capital and skilled labor for unskilled labor. The causes of the capital shortage are many and varied, but at the root was an inefficient financial sector.[21] The shortage of capital eased as the twentieth century progressed, but not enough to have made a big difference.

Low southern wages are not fully understood by economic historians. Migration from the South after World War II clearly raised southern wages, by reducing the supply of labor in the South relative to demand. But, even though migration from the South was extensive before the war, the question remains — why didn't southerners migrate northward in greater numbers earlier in the century?

One school of thought, associated with Gavin Wright, emphasizes bad timing. In the late nineteenth century, when industrialization was in full swing in the North, immigrants filled jobs in factories instead of southerners. Europeans succeeded, in other words, because they got there first. Once established, kinship networks sustained labor flows in both directions, creating an international labor market from which southerners were largely excluded. While this market was being created, southerners were "consumed by the turbulence of Reconstruction" precisely when "mass immigration was becoming an established part of the northern social fabric."[22] Busy with other things, southerners simply missed the boat.

Another school of thought emphasizes education. Better-educated southerners, black or white, were far more likely to move to the North than poorly educated southerners—and most southerners were poorly educated.[23] It may seem odd to focus on education, since the factory jobs Wright talks about did not require much schooling. However, illiteracy rates among European immigrants were lower than among southerners, and literacy, in any language, paid off in the New World, perhaps because exposure to schooling aided in assimilating workers into the nonfarm economy. The education story fits another fact: although unskilled wages were low, wages of skilled, educated labor were relatively high in the South. The South, in other words, had a shortage of skilled, educated labor.

Inadequate education was an especially serious problem for African Americans. Southern blacks suffered mightily under de jure segregation in the public schools. The schools were supposed to be "separate but equal" — "separate" they were, but "equal" was a farce, especially after African Americans were disfranchised throughout much of the former Confederacy around the turn of the century.[24] Jim Crow, of course, was not confined to schools; it infected all types of interactions between the races. Economic theory holds that discrimination is economically wasteful because resources (in this case, people) are not allocated to their highest-valued use. By embracing institutionalized racism the South sacrificed some economic growth, although how much is hard to know.

Southern Relative Backwardness and "Convergence"

Historians who accept any or all of the causes of southern relative backwardness presume that southern incomes could have converged far faster on the national average than they actually did after the Civil War. Losers of major wars sometimes do often catch up at remarkable rates — Japan and West Germany are the obvious examples. If the South had followed the same convergence pattern as Germany or Japan during the post-World War II period, the South would have been much richer in 1920 than it was actually observed to be.

Judged against the postwar experience of Western Europe or the Far East, the South definitely seems like a laggard. But such a comparison is inappropriate, for several reasons. The South was not the recipient of a Marshall Plan, which was a key factor in getting European recovery started after World War II. More fundamental, the evidently slow pace at which the South converged before World War II was not that unusual in the American experience. Today, differences across states in per capita incomes are relatively small, but the opposite has been true for much of American history.[25] During the period from 1880 to 1940 the South was attempting to catch a moving target — the North — which was busy establishing itself as the preeminent economy in the Western world.

Table 1 formulates the idea that the perceived slowness of southern recovery after the Civil War depends on what one assumes to be the reference standard. Column 1 of table 1 shows the actual level of southern per capita income relative to the national average between 1880 and 1960, in twenty-year increments. The other columns in the table show "predicted" or counterfactual levels of southern per capita income, again relative to the national average, over the same period.

The idea behind the counterfactual estimates is to imagine what the level of southern per capita income (relative to the national average) would have been had incomes in the South followed a particular pattern of economic convergence actually experienced in some reference group of nonsouthern states. The estimates in columns 2 and 3 of table 1 are based on a reference group consisting of per capita incomes in states in the Midwest relative to per capita incomes in states in the Northeast. On average, per capita incomes in midwestern states were lower than per capita incomes in northeastern states before World War II — the Northeast was a more developed economy, as it had been since the antebellum period.[26] But midwestern incomes managed to converge on northeastern incomes during the first half of the twentieth century. Taking the South's initial level of per capita income relative to the national average in 1880 as given (approximately 51 percent of the national average), suppose that southern incomes converged on the national average at the same pace at which midwestern incomes converged on the northeastern average over the 1880–1960 period. Under this hypothetical scenario, what would southern per capita income (relative to the national average) have been in each year? Col-

Table 1. Southern Per Capita Income as a Ratio of the
National Average: Actual versus Predicted (Counterfactual)

	Actual	Predicted Midwest/Northeast		Predicted Non-South
		Period	Average	Period
1880	.502	*	*	*
1900	.506	.594	.558	.655
1920	.604	.633	.616	.785
1940	.603	.589	.681	.819
1960	.762	.824	.753	.930
1970	.860	*	*	*
1980	.884	*	*	*
1990	.904	*	*	*

Sources: The column-1 figures for 1880, 1900, and 1920 are from Richard Easterlin, "Regional Growth of Income: Long-Term Tendencies," in *Population Redistribution and Economic Growth, United States, 1870–1950*, vol. 2, *Analysis of Economic Change*, ed. S. Kuznets, A. Miller, and R. Easterlin (Philadelphia, 1960); those for 1940 and 1960 are from Bureau of Economic Analysis, *State Personal Income by State: 1929–1982* (Washington, 1986); those for 1970–90 are from U.S. Department of Commerce, *Statistical Abstract of the United States, 1984* (Washington, 1983), 457, and U.S. Department of Commerce, *Statistical Abstract of the United States, 1992* (Washington, 1992), 439. *Notes:* See the appendix for details on the construction of this table. The "Actual" column gives southern per capita income as a ratio of national per capita income. The "Predicted" columns give the predicted value of southern per capita income as a ratio of national per capita income. The "Midwest/Northeast" columns are the regression sample consisting of states in the Midwest and the Northeast. The "Non-South" column is the regression sample consisting of all nonsouthern states. Period: predicted income is calculated from regressions of logarithmic growth rate of relative per capita income between 1880 and year t, t = 1900, 1920, 1940, and 1960. Average: predicted income is computed using the average of the convergence coefficients from the period regressions. The asterisk (*) indicates not applicable.

umn 2 (labeled Period) shows the counterfactual estimates using rates of convergence that vary across time periods defined by the beginning (1880) and ending dates (for example, the figure for 1940 uses the convergence rate over the period 1880 to 1940; the other periods are similarly defined). The counterfactual figures in column 3 (labeled Average) are computed using a single convergence rate averaged over the entire 1880–1960 period.

If southern economic performance is judged against the reference standard in column 2 or 3, the South is a laggard, but not much of one. Had the South followed the midwestern-northeastern pace of convergence between 1880 and

1900, southern per capita income relative to the national average would have been about 6 to 9 percentage points higher in 1900 than it actually was (for example, 59 percent of the national average, as shown in column 2, instead of the actual level of 51 percent, as shown in column 1). Evidently the southern economy "failed" between 1880 and 1900, but this failure can be partly attributed to the agricultural depression of the 1890s, which hit the South especially hard. In addition, it is important to note that by 1920 southern per capita income had largely caught up to where it is predicted it should have been—an actual level of 60 percent of the national average, compared with a counterfactual level of 62 percent. It is also noteworthy that the South largely held its own between 1920 and 1940, maintaining its relative level of per capita income at about 60 percent. Had the South instead followed the midwestern-northeastern 1920–40 convergence pattern shown in column 2, southern per capita income would have *declined* from 63 percent of the national average in 1920 to 59 percent of the national average in 1940.[27]

Column 4 of table 1 extends the reference group to cover all nonsouthern states, by adding in states in the West. Convergence is now computed in terms of any particular (nonsouthern) state's level of per capita income relative to the nonsouthern level of per capita income; thus the issue is, how quickly did poor nonsouthern states converge on the nonsouthern average? Here, finally, is evidence of substantial economic retardation in the South. Southern per capita income clearly converged on the national average between 1880 and 1940 at a slower pace than that at which states with below-average incomes outside the South converged on the nonsouthern average. Consider, for example, the figures for 1940. If the South had followed the nonsouthern convergence pattern, as shown in column 4, southerners would have earned about 82 percent of the national average income in 1940, compared with the actual figure of 60 percent, as shown in column 1. Using the non-South as the reference standard, then, southerners should have been about 37 percent richer (= 82/60) in 1940 than they actually were.

Two points are in order. First, even if the South had followed the nonsouthern convergence pattern, southerners still would have been very poor in the early twentieth century, compared with the rest of the nation. The Civil War dealt the South an extremely serious economic blow, and to have eliminated the regional income gap by, say, World War I, the southern economy would have had to perform a monumental feat. The point is *not* that backward agriculture, isolated labor markets, and bad schools are unimportant impediments to economic growth. Rather, the point is that if a group of non-southern states (for example, Minnesota and North Dakota) had been dealt an adverse economic "shock" about 1880 equal in magnitude to the impact of the Civil War on the southern economy, these states would have looked like a real economic "problem" to the rest of the nation for a long time. What really made the postbellum South *unique* as an economic problem was the size of the shock that the region had experienced, not an unusual inability to cope with such a shock. State and regional economies in the late-nineteenth- and early-twentieth-century United States, regardless of location, did not perform well enough to fully dissipate large-scale shocks (such as the one experienced by the Confederacy), even over the course of decades.

Second, including western states in the reference group stacks the deck against the South. Incomes in the West in the late nineteenth century were relatively high, primarily because mining and other industries devoted to the process of natural resources were highly profitable. Western incomes fell relative to the non-South average as resources shifted into the regions. If the South had been the beneficiary of a natural resource "shock" of similar magnitude after the Civil War (for example, the discovery of massive mineral deposits), there is no reason to suppose that southerners would have been slow to respond to the resulting economic opportunities. No such shock occurred, however, so the appropriate (counterfactual) experiment cannot be performed.

In sum, southern incomes converged slowly on the national average before World War II, but, by itself, the slow pace of convergence was not that unusual. The Midwest was not burdened by cotton overproduction, high rates of adult illiteracy, underfinanced school systems, and pervasive Jim Crow, yet poor midwestern states did not converge much faster on the richer Northeast than the South converged on the national average. In theory, one can easily speculate that the southern economy could have converged more quickly, but whether it reasonably could have is another matter.

Postwar Economic Growth in the South: What Problems Were Solved?

Today, the South's economic problems are not unique to it, for the region no longer appears economically backward, by national standards. Southern incomes still lag a bit, but regional gaps are vastly smaller than in 1940. As column 1 of table 1 demonstrates, convergence began in earnest after World

War II and occurred at a pace between 1940 and 1960 higher than predicted by my counterfactual estimates. In 1970, southern per capita income equaled 86 percent of the national average; by 1990, 90 percent of the national average.

What caused the increased pace of convergence after World War II? Chief among the long list of factors was the integration of southern labor markets into national markets. Although the process of labor market integration was under way before World War II, the war speeded up the process.[28] During the 1940s the United States experienced a substantial compression of its wage structure, partly as a consequence of war-related labor demands and partly engineered by government policy.[29] Wage differentials narrowed in many ways, one of which was regional. Labor market integration during and after World War II was especially important in the case of African Americans. Because of it (along with other factors) income differences between blacks and whites began to narrow, which was not true before World War II.

A second factor was productivity growth in southern agriculture, which accelerated with widespread mechanization in the 1950s. While it is true that mechanization, particularly in cotton agriculture, displaced agricultural labor, there is little doubt that, on the whole, agricultural productivity growth enhanced living standards for those remaining in the South.[30]

In addition to market integration and productivity growth, postwar southern development was aided by the Cold War: the South captured a goodly share of the federal defense budget, courtesy of able congressional maneuvering.[31] Spin-offs from the defense industry helped to spur growth in a number of southern cities, such as Houston and Huntsville. The development of reliable air-conditioning undoubtedly fueled urban economic development and raised nonfarm labor productivity, particularly in financial and business services. Precise measures of such effects, however, are hard to estimate.

Other factors of importance include vastly improved public schools and the civil rights movement. In terms of per pupil resources, public schools in the South still lag behind the rest of the nation, but the gap is far less than in the early twentieth century. For example, expenditures per pupil on teacher salaries in the South in 1920 were only 48 percent of the national average, whereas in 1991 they were 88 percent of the national average.[32] The improvement in the schools has contributed directly to income convergence, by augmenting the region's supply of skilled, educated labor. The region now boasts a growing black middle class. The emergence of a black middle class in the postwar South was aided by the earlier sacrifices of generations of black parents to educate their offspring against enormous odds and by state and federal antidiscrimination legislation associated with the civil rights movement.[33]

Conclusion

What, then, is the answer to the question posed in the title? The answer, I believe, is "some of both." Southern poverty was only too real historically, and the poor (and their descendants) are still with us. The scars caused by slavery and institutionalized racism were deep and long lasting. But the failure of the southern economy to converge rapidly before World War II is partly fiction. As my counterfactual estimates of per capita income demonstrate, the South could have done somewhat better, and the various factors discussed in the essay surely were impediments. However, the same counterfactual estimates also demonstrate that the southern economy would have had to perform vastly better than its regional counterparts elsewhere in the nation did to have closed the regional income gap, say, by World War I. Measured against the experience of the rest of the nation, the South has only recently emerged from its status as an economic problem. Measured against the experience of the developing world, the southern economy is a success story of major proportions. It took longer, with a few detours and wrong turns, but the South made it just the same.

Appendix: Computation of Table 1

The computation of table 1 took three steps. The first step was to put state per capita income estimates for the years 1880, 1900, 1920, 1940, and 1960 into computer-readable form. The second step was to estimate weighted least squares regressions of the form:

$$\ln g_{i,t-1880} = \alpha + \beta \ln r_{i,1880} + \epsilon,$$

where $\ln g_{i,t-n}$ is the logarithmic growth rate of state i's relative per capita income between 1880 and year t, $\ln r_{i,1880}$ is the logarithm of state i's relative per capita income in 1880, α and β coefficients, and ϵ is a random error term.[34] Four regressions were estimated, one for each year t ($t = 1900, 1920, 1940,$ and 1960). The regressions were weighted by the state population shares in year t.

The definition of "relative" depends on the sample for the regressions. In column 2 (labeled Period) and column 3 (labeled Average) of table 1, the sample consists of states in the Midwest and the Northeast (Easterlin's definitions of regions are used), and "relative" means relative to the average per capita income in the Northeast. In column 4 of table 1, the sample consists of all nonsouthern states, and "relative" means relative to the non-South average. The test for convergence is whether β is significantly negative; this, in fact, occurred in all the regressions.

The final step was to use the regressions to predict southern per capita income relative to the national average. For columns 2 and 4 of table 1, the procedure is as follows. I used the regression for year t to predict the growth rate of relative per capita income for each southern state between 1880 and year t. The variable $ln\ r_{i,1880}$ in this computation is now the logarithm of each southern state's per capita income in 1800 relative to the *national average*. Once the growth rate is known, it is straightforward to compute the state's relative per capita income in year t. The South-wide average is a weighted average of the state estimates (the weights are regional population shares in year t). In column 3 of table 1, the same procedure was followed except that α was set equal to zero, and β is the average of the β's from the year-specific regressions.

All data and the regression results are available on an IBM-formatted floppy disk from Robert A. Margo.

Notes

I am grateful to Stanley Engerman, Larry Griffin, two anonymous referees, and participants in the Robert Penn Warren Center for the Humanities for comments on earlier drafts and to Madhavi Venkatasen for excellent research assistance.

1   See Ulrich B. Phillips, *American Negro Slavery* (New York, 1918). For an extensive discussion of Phillips's argument (and evidence) that slavery was unprofitable and of the so-called Phillips school, see Robert W. Fogel and Stanley Engerman, *Time on the Cross: The Economics of American Negro Slavery* (Boston, 1974), 1:59–67.

2   Alfred Conrad and John Meyer, "The Economics of Slavery in the Antebellum South," *Journal of Political Economy* 56 (April 1958): 95–130. Kenneth M. Stampp, *The Peculiar Institution: Slavery in the Antebellum South* (New York, 1956), also concluded that slavery was profitable, although on less rigorous grounds.

3   Yasukichi Yasuba, "The Profitability and Viability of Plantation Slavery in the United States," in *The Reinterpretation of American History,* ed. Robert W. Fogel and Stanley Engerman (New York, 1971).

4   Richard Easterlin, "Regional Growth of Income: Long-Term Tendencies," in *Population Re-distribution and Economic Growth, United States, 1870–1950*, vol. 2, *Analysis of Economic Change*, ed. S. Kuznets, A. Miller, and R. Easterlin (Philadelphia, 1960).

5   According to Easterlin's estimates, per capita income in the South stood at 76 percent of the national average in 1840 and 72 percent in 1860; the corresponding figures for the Midwest are 68 percent in 1840 and 68 percent in 1860. Some scholars contend that Easterlin's esti-mates provide too rosy a picture of antebellum southern growth. Robert Gallman ("Slavery and Southern Economic Growth," *Southern Economic Journal* 45 [April 1979]: 1007–22), how-ever, has surveyed this debate and concludes that "a fair statement of the results of research on ante-bellum regional income [is that] the level of ante-bellum income was lower in the South" but "the Southern and Northern rates of growth were roughly the same" (1011).

6   Fogel and Engerman, *Time on the Cross*. For critiques of *Time on the Cross*, see Paul David et al., *Reckoning with Slavery* (New York, 1976). Robert W. Fogel, *Without Consent or Con-tract: The Rise and Fall of American Slavery* (New York, 1989), supersedes *Time on the Cross* but on the critical economic issues reaches similar conclusions.

7   See Robert W. Fogel and Stanley Engerman, "Explaining the Relative Efficiency of Slave Agriculture in the Antebellum South" and "Explaining the Relative Efficiency of Slave Agri-culture: Reply," in *Without Consent or Contract: Markets and Production, Technical Papers*, ed. R. Fogel and S. Engerman (New York, 1992), 1:241–303.

8   Richard Steckel, "A Peculiar Population: The Health, Nutrition, and Mortality of American Slaves from Childhood to Maturity," *Journal of Economic History* 46 (September 1986): 721–41.

9   Robert A. Margo, *Race and Schooling in the South, 1880–1950: An Economic History* (Chicago, 1990), chaps. 6, 7.

10 Claudia D. Goldin, *Urban Slavery in the American South, 1820–1860: A Quantitative History* (Chicago, 1976).

11 Measured in 1970 U.S. dollars, the per capita income of free southerners in 1860 was ap-proximately $570.00 — a level virtually identical to that achieved in Denmark, Germany, and France in 1870, and one *not* achieved in Sweden or Italy until after the turn of the twentieth century. The calculation of per capita income of free southerners assumes that slaves received incomes equal to their "maintenance" cost — that is, the cost of food, shelter, clothing, and so forth. Estimates of southern per capita income in 1860 are from Robert Fogel and Stanley Engerman, "The Economics of Slavery," in *The Reinterpretation of American Economic His-tory*, ed. R. Fogel and S. Engerman (New York, 1971), 335 (converted to 1970 dollars using the Warren-Pearson "All Commodities" wholesale price index, Series E-23, E-40, and E-52, in U.S. Department of Commerce, *Historical Statistics of the United States* [Washington, 1976], 199–201). Per capita income estimates for various European countries in the nineteenth cen-tury can be found in N. F. R. Crafts, *British Economic Growth during the Industrial Revolution* (New York, 1985), 54.

12 See Stanley Engerman, "Some Economic Factors in Southern Backwardness in the Nine-teenth Century," in *Essays in Regional Economics*, ed. J. Kain and J. Meyer (Cambridge, Mass., 1971), for a detailed discussion of the points in this paragraph.

13 On the sources of the decline in per capita income and agricultural productivity in the South

after the Civil War, see Roger Ransom and Richard Sutch, *One Kind of Freedom: The Economic Consequences of Emancipation* (New York, 1977); Claudia Goldin and Frank Lewis, "The Postbellum Recovery of the South and the Costs of the Civil War: Comment," *Journal of Economic History* 38 (June 1978): 487–92; and Claudia Goldin, " 'N' Kinds of Freedom," *Explorations in Economic History* 16 (January 1979): 8–30.

14   Ransom and Sutch, *One Kind of Freedom,* app. C.

15   Gavin Wright, "Cotton Competition and the Post-Bellum Recovery of the American South," *Journal of Economic History* 34 (September 1974): 610–35.

16   Jon R. Moen, "Changes in the Productivity of Southern Agriculture between 1860 and 1880," in Fogel and Engerman, *Without Consent or Contract: Markets and Production, Technical Papers,* 1:320–50.

17   Claudia Goldin and Frank Lewis, "The Economic Costs of the Civil War," *Journal of Economic History* 35 (June 1975): 299–326.

18   For a defense of the traditional thesis that sharecropping caused poverty, see Ransom and Sutch, *One Kind of Freedom.*

19   On efficiency aspects of sharecropping, see Stephen DeCanio, *Agriculture in the Postbellum South: The Economics of Production and Supply* (Cambridge, Mass., 1974); Ransom and Sutch, *One Kind of Freedom;* and Moen, "Changes," 330. Saying that sharecropping was not the problem is different from saying that *individual* sharecroppers had low productivity. Indeed, if sharecropping was such a terrible way to manage agricultural labor, it is difficult to understand why sharecropping persisted for so long. Joseph Reid, "Sharecropping as an Understandable Market Response: The Postbellum South," *Journal of Economic History* 33 (March 1973): 106–30, discusses the origins of sharecropping after the Civil War and the economic rationale for its persistence.

20   David Weiman, "The Economic Emancipation of the Non-Slaveholding Class: Upcountry Farmers in the Georgia Cotton Economy," *Journal of Economic History* 45 (March 1985): 71–93.

21   Ransom and Sutch, *One Kind of Freedom,* chaps. 6, 9.

22   Gavin Wright, *Old South, New South: Revolutions in the Southern Economy since 1865* (New York, 1986), 74.

23   Margo, *Race and Schooling,* chap. 7.

24   Margo, *Race and Schooling,* chaps. 2, 3.

25   Robert J. Barro and Xavier Sala-i-Martin, "Convergence," *Journal of Political Economy* 100 (April 1992): 223–51.

26   For example, according to Easterlin's estimates for 1920, per capita income in the west north central states (e.g., Minnesota) was only 66 percent of per capita income in the Northeast; in the Midwest as a whole (east and west north central states combined), per capita income was 76 percent of the northeastern average in 1920. By 1950, the ratio of midwestern per capita income to northeastern per capita income had risen to 0.92, or 92 percent. See Richard Easterlin, "Regional Income Trends, 1840–1950," in Fogel and Engerman, *Reinterpretation of American Economic History,* 40.

27   John Wallis, "Employment in the Great Depression: New Data and Hypotheses," *Explorations in Economic History* 26 (January 1989): 45–72, demonstrates that, measured by the growth

rate of employment, the South recovered more quickly from the Great Depression than the rest of the nation. This does not imply, of course, that the South escaped the depression — as the counterfactual estimates in column 3 of table 1 show, the depression per se slowed the pace of convergence between southern per capita income and the national average by roughly 7 percentage points (0.681–0.616, from column 3; recall that the figures in column 3 are computed using a convergence rate averaged over eighty years, which will smooth out the effects of economic cycles, such as the depression).

28   Wright (*Old South, New South,* chap. 7) shows that various New Deal programs, such as the National Industrial Recovery Act, the WPA (Works Progress Administration), and the Fair Labor Standards Act (specifically its minimum wage provisions), also helped to raise southern wages, in advance of World War II.

29   Claudia Goldin and Robert A. Margo, "The Great Compression: The Wage Structure in the United States at Mid-Century," *Quarterly Journal of Economics* 107 (February 1992): 1–34.

30   Richard Day, "The Economics of Technological Change and the Demise of the Sharecropper," *American Economic Review* 57 (June 1967): 427–49; John Cogan, "The Decline in Black Teenage Employment, 1950–1970," *American Economic Review* 72 (September 1982): 621–38.

31   Bruce J. Schulman, *From Cotton Belt to Sunbelt: Federal Policy, Economic Development, and the Transformation of the South, 1938–1980* (New York, 1991).

32   The 1920 figure was computed from U.S. Department of Commerce, *Statistical Abstract of the United States, 1922* (Washington, 1923), 104; the 1991 figure was computed from U.S. Department of Commerce, *Statistical Abstract of the United States, 1992* (Washington, 1993), 149, 151.

33   John Donohue and James J. Heckman, "Continuous versus Episodic Change: The Impact of Civil Rights Policy on the Economic Status of Blacks," *Journal of Economic Literature* 29 (December 1991): 1603–43.

34   The logarithmic growth rate between year t and 1880 is:

$$(\log \, [r_{i,t}/r_{i,1880}]) \, / \, (t - 1880),$$

where $r_{i,t}$ is state i's relative per capita income in year t. No adjustment is made for state differences in cost of living. It is doubtful, however, that such an adjustment would affect the regressions very much, since such differences were relatively small in the non-South.

∼ Blues for Atticus Finch:
Scottsboro, Brown, *and Harper Lee*

ERIC J. SUNDQUIST

PERCEPTIONS OF THE SOUTH AS an American problem have long been shaped by literary representations of the region created by authors on both sides of the Mason-Dixon line. In many of the most influential works, race and racial conflict have been at the heart of such representations, as indeed they have been at the heart of American social history. Harriet Beecher Stowe and Frederick Douglass, for example, are only the best known of numerous antebellum writers who waged war over slavery well before any shots were fired in the Civil War. In the post-Reconstruction era, national views of America's continuing racial dilemma and of the South alike were forcefully dictated by the popularity of Joel Chandler Harris's folkloric plantation tales and Thomas Dixon's racist novels celebrating the Ku Klux Klan, while black writers such as Charles Chesnutt and W. E. B. Du Bois, as well as later figures of the Harlem Renaissance, looked to the South and the formative experience of slavery in recovering the roots of African-American experience and arguing for black equality. And in employing antebellum time frames to engage contemporary racial contentions that were clearly national as well as regional in scope, Mark Twain established a paradigm of retrospective analysis followed by other writers who likewise subjected nostalgia for the plantation world to probing critique.

More recently, the monumental achievement of William Faulkner and the pathbreaking modern work of Richard Wright, Ralph Ellison, and Toni Morrison, to cite the most obvious, have kept the South at the forefront of consciousness in the nation's long drama of guilt and redemption over its twin birth in revolutionary democracy and racial slavery. As in the case of the Civil War itself, however, so in the case of the literature devoted to the mid-twentieth-century civil rights movement—in which one might expect the most overt confrontation with the South as an American problem—there has been a marked tendency to work at the crisis of American racial equality obliquely, to experiment with allegorical displacements and baroque characterization. One has only to think, for example, of William Melvin Kelley's *A Different Drummer* or Alice Walker's *Meridian,* two of the best African-American novels inspired by the civil rights era, to notice what unorthodox strategies have seemed necessary to represent adequately the upheavals and psychic costs of the struggle for black equality. Important as these novels are, though, they seem marginalia to the stately oratory of Martin Luther King Jr., memoirs by movement participants such as Anne Moody or Bobby Seale, allied autobiography by Malcolm X, Claude Brown, or Maya Angelou, and the great range of black music that told the story in other modes. Beside the influence and legacy of such work, permanent statements in the form of fiction have not been as commanding as one might expect.

At the same time, there remains the peculiar, unavoidable presence of Harper Lee's *To Kill a Mockingbird.* Published in 1960, a model of conventional plot and character, the novel is the most widely read twentieth-century American work of fiction devoted to the issue of race. The novel was an immediate best-seller, and several generations of American children have studied the novel at least once before leaving secondary school. For this reason it has defined for much of the nation—indeed, for much of the world, especially through its film version—the South as an American problem, a region unto itself yet at the same time an incarnation of the racial conflict that belongs to the whole of the United States rather than to southern states alone. In addition, the novel has remained a particular touchstone of white liberalism. Former Clinton campaign strategist James Carville, for example, has recalled *To Kill a Mockingbird* as the most important book of his life for the change it effected in his view of racial justice: "I just knew, the minute I read it, that [Harper Lee] was right and I had been wrong." Likewise, in arguing against the Confederate iconography of the current Georgia state flag, Governor Zell Miller recently cited the famous scene in which Scout's innocent banter disperses the mob come to lynch Tom Robinson as a model for his appeal to the state general assembly as "fathers and mothers, neighbors and friends" who had been taught in Sunday school to do the right thing.[1]

Despite the importance of such testimony, it is nonetheless tempting to ascribe the book's immense popularity, especially at the time of its publication, to its indulgence in comforting sentimentality and to assume that its fawning readership was overwhelmingly white. Even if that were true, one would still have to account for the novel's recorded impact on those whose sense of the righteous sprang from other sources. In his memoir of the civil rights movement, for example, James Farmer, head of the Congress of Racial Equality, recalls that in 1961, while he was under arrest with other Freedom Riders in Jackson, Mississippi, Roy Wilkins brought in two books "as gifts to help [him] pass the prison hours," one of them *To Kill a Mockingbird*.[2] Farmer did not record his opinion of the novel, but the significance of the gesture as an index of the book's popular appeal at the height of the civil rights protest is obvious.

Even though the novel continues to have a widespread influence on the imagination of many young Americans, however, it is today something of a historical relic—or better, an icon whose emotive sway remains strangely powerful because it also remains unexamined. It is something of a mystery, moreover, that the book has failed to arouse the antagonism now often prompted by another great novelistic depiction of the South as a national problem, *Adventures of Huckleberry Finn*, which arguably uses the word *nigger* with more conscious irony than does *To Kill a Mockingbird* and whose antebellum framework and moral complexity ought to be a far greater bulwark against revisionist denunciation. For all its admirable moral earnestness and its inventory of the historical forces making up white liberal consciousness in the late 1950s, Lee's novel might well have been entitled "Driving Miss Scout." That its basic answers to the questions of racial injustice appear almost irrelevant to the late-twentieth-century United States makes its cultural impact the more crucial to understand, not least because the novel pursues its ethical instruction with a cunning simplicity while at the same time implying that there *are* no simple answers, perhaps no answers at all.

In showing America's mid-century racial ambivalence in full bloom, *To Kill a Mockingbird* sweeps back through historical events whose culmination is in the watershed years of the late 1950s and early 1960s but that can hardly be understood within so narrow a time frame. Lee's novel is a document of historical crisis enfolded within a problem in literary representation, which in turn is built upon the interrelation between her strategies of fictive representation and the question of legal representation that is an issue in the novel itself and in the real world of jurisprudence and constitutional law to which Scout Finch's narrative frequently alludes. The novel offers an anatomy of segregation at the moment of its legal destruction. Insofar as it is a story that provisionally foresees the end of a long, bewildering, and violent phase of American history, it is a story of the South, the primary arena of desegregation, as a distillation of the nation, the atavistic and the everyday concentrated into a parable that brings no certainty that the end of segregation will be the end of racism.

Given its enduring appeal to deep wells of white American innocence, it may seem at first glance surprising how blunt is *To Kill a Mockingbird*'s examination of the South's "rape complex," as Wilbur Cash once called it. As a portrait of the South of the 1930s, the novel might be taken simply as a confirmation of the archetypal defense of lynching offered in the Senate by Alabama's J. Thomas Heflin: "Whenever a negro crosses this dead line between the white and negro races and lays his black hand on a white woman he deserves to die."[3] It could better be argued, however, that the appeal of the book, whose story is focused, after all, on the psychological and physical maturation of a young white girl with whom readers of the 1950s and 1960s are expected to identify, lies in its portrayal of a contemporary episode of the southern sexual "disease"[4] and in its invocation of the specter of "mongrelization" that was once more appearing in the oratorical and editorial protests that fueled southern reaction to *Brown v. Board of Education*. Behind the veneer of Scout Finch's first-person naïveté, Lee's novel defies, without destroying, conventional white southern fears of black sexuality, which drove the South, said Lillian Smith, to superimpose the semiotics of Jim Crow upon the white female body: "Now, parts of your body are segregated areas which you must stay away from and keep others away from. These areas you touch only when necessary. In other words, you cannot associate freely with them any more than you can associate freely with colored children."[5] Smith's characteristically acerbic description of the ethos of segregation brings together the two strong vectors of Lee's novel—its focus on childhood, the battleground of desegregation, and the rhetorical power of white womanhood, long the weapon of choice in racist arguments against equality.

Throughout the South *Brown* provoked new hysteria of the sort recorded in Mississippi circuit court judge Tom Brady's infamous broadside "Black Monday" (so called for the day the *Brown* opinion was issued), in which he summoned up the specter of alien invasion ("Communism disguised as 'new democracy' is still communism, and tyranny masquerading as liberalism is still tyranny") and prophesied that desegregation would unleash a new black threat to "the loveliest and the purest of God's creatures . . . [the] well-bred, cultured Southern white woman or her blue-eyed, golden-haired little girl." Sedition and the threat of racial corruption were everywhere: the year before Lee's novel was published, an Alabama state legislator who objected to the plot of a children's book entitled *The Rabbit's Wedding,* in which a white rabbit marries a black rabbit, succeeded not only in banning the subversive book from state libraries but in having copies burned as well.[6] Against the grain of its ineffable goodness *To Kill a Mockingbird* includes as well this powerful undertow of southern resistance and, in its half-disguise of violent racial realities, inscribes in an equally dangerous children's story the nightmare of America's own growing up.

The capital rape case of Tom Robinson tried by Atticus Finch occurs in 1935, set in a small-town Alabama courtroom that would inevitably have been reverberating with the impact of the ongoing trials of the young black men known as the Scottsboro Boys. Perhaps the most notorious modern criminal trials with race not technically but nonetheless fundamentally at issue, the ordeal of the young men charged with the rape of two white women, in a sequence of trials lasting from 1931 to 1937, put the South under sensational national scrutiny matched only by that aroused by the 1955 murder in Money, Mississippi, of Emmett Till, a fourteen-year-old Chicago boy accused of being fresh with a local white woman. Although it is conceivable that Lee's character Tom Robinson was inspired by the death sentence given a real-life black Alabama man named Tom Robinson in 1930 for his part in defending his family from a lynch mob, a story recounted in Arthur Raper's *Tragedy of Lynching,*[7] actual parallels to Tom's case were readily available, and Scottsboro was only the most egregious evidence that the kinds of justice administered by southern mobs and southern courts were often indistinguishable. From the southern point of view Scottsboro was a call to arms. Vanderbilt historian Frank Owsley, for instance, identified the Yankee intrusion into the sacred body of the South prompted by Scottsboro with the prior infamies of abolitionism and Reconstruction, when radical whites had encouraged black men "to commit universal pillage, murder and rape."[8] Outside the South, though, Scottsboro was emblematic of southern injustice and a litmus test of sectional paranoia, as was the Till case a generation later.

With mounting tension over civil rights activism augmented by the exoneration of Till's white killers, *To Kill a Mockingbird* was written, and subsequently read, in an atmosphere charged on the one hand by the impact of *Brown* and on the other by publicity about the revival of Judge Lynch in the South. Yet by dwelling on the narrative recollection of time past—"when enough years had gone by to enable us to look back on them," Scout tells us in setting the context for the book's action on the first page (3)—the plot deliberately casts backward to the era of Scottsboro, and Lee could easily have replaced her own epigraph from Charles Lamb ("Lawyers, I suppose, were children once") with Langston Hughes's "The Town of Scottsboro," one of several poems he devoted to the cause:

> Scottsboro's just a little place:
> No shame is writ across its face—
> Its court, too weak to stand against a mob,
> Its people's heart, too small to hold a sob.[9]

Hughes's Scottsboro might as well be Maycomb, where Tom Robinson is tried and quickly sentenced to death, or Sumner, Mississippi, where Till's murderers were tried and just as quickly acquitted. This doubled legal time frame is but one of several ways in which Lee, like Mark Twain before her, lays one era upon another in the retrospective narrative of Scout Finch, who looks back to a time when "people moved slowly . . . took their time about everything," when "there was no hurry, for there was nowhere to go" (5). Scout's nostalgia tells us about the operation of temporality in autobiography, about Lee's share in the long southern tradition of antimodernism, and about the power of mourning, commingled with defiance, in the reservoir of southern memory. But it tells us, more to the point, that we are reading at every moment an allegory of the South's own temporality and its public philosophy of race relations: "Go slow."

To Kill a Mockingbird is a novel of childhood, but one saturated in narrative consciousness of deeper regional and national time. Although it is not, strictly speaking, a historical novel, its careful deployment of familial genealogy, state history, and the romantic stereotypes of southern "breeding" create a context in which the pressure of contemporary time, with its threatened destruction of a white southern way of life, becomes urgent. The novel harks back to the 1930s both to move the mounting fear and violence surrounding desegregation into an arena of safer contemplation and to remind us, through a merciless string of moral lessons, that the children of Atticus Finch are the only hope for a future world of racial justice. Framed by the Boo Radley story, the book's racial "nightmare" (144) is to a noticeable degree made peripheral for young readers to the gothic tale of the "malevolent phantom" Boo (8) and the revenge of Bob Ewell. But Boo Radley's story is at the same time a means to displace into more conventional gothic territory the Finch children's encounter with "blackness" as it is defined by the white South and, more broadly, by white America. Associated from the outset with animal mutilation and black superstition (9), and with the laughter of Negroes passing in the night (55), Boo functions transparently as a harbinger of violated taboos and a displaced phantasm of racial fear, ultimately unmasked as the gentle, domesticated "gray ghost" of harmonious integration (13–14, 280). The novel's concluding Halloween sequence, with its brilliant prelude of the school pageant devoted to Alabama history and personified products of Dixie agriculture (dressed as a ham, Scout survives Bob Ewell's attack), tells us that the true danger comes from "white trash" ("Boo" evolves into the insidious "Bob"); and it offers the illusion that racial hysteria — the Klan, night-riding mobs, the White Citizens Council — can be likewise unmasked, humiliated, and brought to justice once the South disposes of its childish fears and moves forward into the post-*Brown* world.

To Kill a Mockingbird is a masterpiece of indirection that allows young readers to face racism through the deflecting screen of a frightening adventure story, just as it allows American readers to face racism through a tale that deflects the problem to the South. Embedded in an episodic story of wit and charm, and pursued through a series of remembered events that often channel serious racial issues into a puzzle of half-truths, children's games and pranks, and devious piety, the novel's lessons are as often held in abeyance as they are driven home by Lee's analogical strategies and her temporal displacement of the book's action into the lives of a pre-*Brown* generation. From the very outset of the novel Scout's reminders that we are reading a tale of the Depression-era South have the effect of suspending our judgment. The New Deal, however it may have helped southern blacks economically, posed little challenge to Jim Crow; though key civil rights legislative and judicial policy dates from the decade, the practice of segregation, and often of mob rule, remained largely untouched by the awakening of southern liberalism.[10]

There is thus everywhere available to the reader as an explanation of the book's dramatized racism and miscarriages of justice the argument that its action belongs to a bygone era. One effect of the temporal displacement, in fact, is to anchor the novel's social crises in a remembered world of general economic deprivation and cultural isolation. The Finch family is comparatively well off, of course, but the region's impoverished small farmers and sharecroppers, whether black or white, live still in the "shadow of the plantation," to borrow the title of Charles Johnson's important study of Black Belt Alabama in the 1930s, "dulled and blocked in by a backwardness which is a fatal heritage of the system itself." [11] Indeed, *To Kill a Mockingbird* itself so clearly harks back to the tradition of liberal exposés of southern racism, whose classic texts may be dated from the 1930s — works such as Johnson's *Shadow of the Plantation* (1934), Raper's *The Tragedy of Lynching* (1933), John Dollard's *Caste and Class in a Southern Town* (1937), Wilbur Cash's *The Mind of the South* (1941), and climaxing in a book with an even broader canvas, Gunnar Myrdal's monumental *An American Dilemma* (1944) — that the novel might almost be read as a kind of recapitulatory tribute to the tradition. Be that as it may, *Brown v. Board of Education* irrevocably changed things, and any novel dating from the rising crest of the civil rights movement must bear the consequences of its own nostalgia for a simpler, slower time, especially when that nostalgia is as tightly interwoven with the narrative's moral fabric as in the case of *To Kill a Mockingbird.*

The novel dwells on the problem of education, its relationship to the force of law, and the Finch children's assimilation to a network of southern social codes.[12] Combined with the contrast between the useless public schooling available to Scout and Jem and the righteous moral lessons they learn from Atticus, from their black cook Calpurnia, and from their regular witness of Maycomb's injustice, the book's nostalgia is a means to probe anxiety about desegregation in the post-*Brown* South and to remind its audience how fully the 1930s impinged upon the 1950s. Recalling a 1938 trip into rural Georgia, journalist Ralph McGill, a southern liberal in the Atticus Finch mold, might well have been describing both the pathetic Maycomb school portrayed by Lee and her implied judgment of the consequences for the South of its resistance to *Brown.* "There were poor schools in other regions of America," wrote McGill in 1963,

> but none had so many as the Southeast. And nowhere were there
> so many as shabby, barren, unpainted, bedraggled, disgracing their
> state and their country's flag raised daily on the school grounds. . . .
> That the South should hold on so desperately, with such pathetic,
> almost preposterous pride, to customs, traditions, and a so-called

way of life that kept them and their children from equal opportunity, which is the basic promise of their country, seemed even more irrational.[13]

When Harper Lee, like McGill, renders Alabama's compulsory education a farcical enterprise (30), she does so not simply to reflect upon the failures of time past, when black faces left no trace in the classroom. She also does so, one can suppose, in order to estimate the nation's contemporary legitimate interest in a federalized social practice that is, according to *Brown,* "the very foundation of good citizenship . . . a principal instrument in awakening the child to cultural values, in preparing him for later professional training, and in helping him to adjust normally to his environment."[14]

Equal education, said *Brown,* was the key to valued and meaningful membership in the nation, and the Court's decision made schools the crucible of change. Emmett Till's murder in 1955, the vicious treatment accorded the black students who integrated Central High School in Little Rock in 1957, and the abuse heaped upon African-American and white students in various communities who launched sit-in protests over the same period of time were reminders that the effects of *Brown,* good and ill alike, were to be felt especially by a younger generation, by children. In the commonsense words of McGill, *Brown* "was a decision about children. That's what the wise and moderate, long-overdue words of the nine justices were all about — the rights and opportunities of American children" and the principle that "the Constitution of the United States is as concerned with the rights of children as with those of their parents." In his most famous address, the speech made at the Lincoln Memorial on the occasion of the 1963 March on Washington, Martin Luther King Jr. likewise dreamed of that day when, "down in Alabama, with its vicious racists, with its governor having his lips dripping with the words of interposition and nullification, . . . little black boys and black girls [would] be able to join hands with little white boys and white girls as sisters and brothers."[15] The preoccupation of *To Kill a Mockingbird* with the moral education of children, its beguiling proposition that juries, police forces, and whole communities of sympathetic children (220, 157, 213) would make for a more just world, and, most famously, Scout's naive routing of the lynch mob that has come to drag Tom Robinson from jail — all are calculated to substantiate the ethical authority driving *Brown,* which said simply that all American children have an inalienable right to *equal* education.

In addition to dwelling for obvious reasons on the lasting impact upon children of segregation — creating in them, said the Court, "a lasting feeling of inferiority as to their status in the community that may affect their hearts and minds in a way unlikely ever to be undone" — the language of *Brown* also underscored the issue of temporality in its calculation of what *equal* meant in 1954. Whether to legitimize its heterodox appeal to social science rather than constitutional jurisprudence or simply to emphasize the long capitulation of federal rule to local southern practice, the opinion written by Chief Justice Earl Warren noted that "we cannot turn the clock back to 1868 when the [Fourteenth] Amendment was adopted, or even to 1896 when *Plessy v. Ferguson* was written." What Warren's formulation sought to do was justify the Court's dismissing historical interpretations of the Fourteenth Amendment as inconclusive and thus pave the way, not for a carefully reasoned destruction of separate but equal as a doctrine, but instead for a clean break with the constitutional past. *Brown* dealt with the racist underpinnings of *Plessy* by saying, in essence, that they were no longer relevant to the moral life of the mid-twentieth-century United States.[16] The peculiar nature of the *Brown* opinion was itself evidence that Warren had correctly foreseen the massive resistance that would arise in the South; and the notorious language of the Court's 1955 decree of implementation — "at the earliest practicable date . . . with all deliberate speed" — did not so much temporize as turn the issue over to executive and legislative enforcement, putting the spotlight on southern recalcitrance even as it gave it de facto sanction.[17]

But by what date, and with what speed? Fivescore years after the Emancipation Proclamation, King declared that he had stood in the lengthening shadow of Abraham Lincoln's failed dream quite long enough; and he admonished his vast audience that it was "no time to engage in the luxury of cooling off or to take the tranquilizing drug of gradualism." The gap between going slow and outright resistance was, in King's experience, painfully narrow, and since well before emancipation and the Civil War gradualism had served as a pretext for inaction and regression of the sort announced in the 1956 manifesto of resistance signed by many southern congressmen. Whereas *To Kill a Mockingbird* shot to the top of the nation's best-seller lists and was quickly adapted into its favorite movie, by 1960 only 6 percent of southern public schools had complied with *Brown*. Perhaps no one had a better sense of the likely cruelty of "deliberate speed" than Thurgood Marshall, the NAACP's lead attorney in the arguments for *Brown*. In the wake of the white rioting that accompanied

Autherine Lucy's attempt in 1956 to desegregate the University of Alabama (Harper Lee's alma mater), Marshall was asked if he did not believe in gradualism, to which he laconically replied: "The Emancipation Proclamation was issued in 1863, ninety-odd years ago. I believe in gradualism, and I also believe that ninety-odd years is pretty gradual."[18]

In his conversation with Jem after the miscarriage of justice that results in Tom Robinson's conviction, Atticus puts his own estimation of the crisis then on the horizon two decades away in a more pragmatic and revealing way: "Don't fool yourselves—it's all adding up and one of these days we're going to pay the bill for it. I hope it's not in you children's time" (221). Here as elsewhere, Atticus's assessment conflates the novel's time frames, at once forecasting the post-*Brown* world and yet delaying any resolution of its spreading political turmoil and street violence. Speaking from the other side of the color line, James Baldwin would similarly remark: "A bill is coming in that I fear America is not prepared to pay." However, his counsel to black Americans, whom he placed at the center of "this dreadful storm, this vast confusion," was to be ready to risk all—"eviction, imprisonment, torture, death"—in order to eradicate racism. "For the sake of one's children," Baldwin argued, "in order to minimize the bill that *they* must pay, one must be careful not to take refuge in any delusion—and the value placed on the color of the skin is always and everywhere and forever a delusion."[19] Although he too recognizes racism as a delusion, Atticus Finch stops short of asking for dramatic sacrifice in the name of justice. In fact, although he pleads directly to the readers of 1960, warning of a day of racial cataclysm rather than one of harmonious justice, Atticus, like Lee, seems satisfied with the "baby-step" (216) taken toward racial justice and appears to hope for a postponement of the fire next time.

In its constant dialectic between the era of Scottsboro and the era of mounting civil rights strife, the novel contains the unsettling prediction, so to speak, that the white southern children of the 1930s will have grown up into the white southern parents of the 1950s—supporters of interposition and massive resistance, members of the White Citizens Councils, those who spit on the Little Rock students or mobbed Autherine Lucy at Alabama and James Meredith at the University of Mississippi. Because Scout and Jem are, respectively, eight and twelve years old in 1935, they would be thirty-three and thirty-seven in 1960, in all likelihood parents faced with the decision of whether to support or resist school desegregation. The temptation for white readers to identify with the Finch children of the 1930s is thus counterpointed by the risk, nowhere clearly lessened by the novel's own predictions about their adult lives, that Scout and Jem may not have done the right thing when faced with a world of desegregation. Likewise, the book's minimal attempts to enter into African-American life, while they may be chalked up to the effects of Scout's limited point of view, which at times is manifestly racist — he's "just a Negro," she remarks to Dill when the latter weeps over Tom's abuse by the prosecutor (199) — or to Lee's attempt, comparable to that of Harriet Beecher Stowe in *Uncle Tom's Cabin,* to speak first of all to white America, or the moderate white South, must also be counted, if not as a failure of nerve, at least as an internalization of Jim Crow. In its sympathetic portrayal of Calpurnia and Tom, as well as a few secondary black characters, the novel was without question a step ahead of most popular white fiction of its era. Yet the whole psychological design of the narrative — its subliminal violation of racial (and gender) taboos and its guarded but nonetheless fierce satire on what Lee calls the "pink cotton penitentiary" of white southern womanhood (136) — sacrifices the legitimate exploration of an African-American perspective in order to enforce its searching critique of white liberalism in crisis. Of necessity, and with a diminution of power that would only become completely clear in historical retrospect, its narrative marginalization of black life functions as a form of segregation whose effect is to focus our attention not on region or state alone but on the nation come at last to its own southern crossroads.

Atticus Finch has been studied by attorneys for the quality of his moral character,[20] and his cinematic portrayal by Gregory Peck as a man of great tenderness and justice is so ingrained in American consciousness as to make him nearly impossible to imagine otherwise. If there is little question as to Atticus's integrity, however, his actions and his defense of Tom Robinson are seldom seen in any sort of historical context; and his own participation in the book's evasion of the hardest moral questions is usually ignored in favor of his commanding pedagogy. It is surely not hard to imagine that Atticus Finch, whether as portrayed by Peck or not, would be more easily recognized than Thurgood Marshall by the vast majority of Americans. Presented as the southern "good father," standing as he does in nearly mythic contrast to bad public fathers such as George Wallace, Ross Barnett, and Orval Faubus, Atticus is depicted as a grand hero to the book's black community, who stand in silent reverence as he passes from the courtroom after his futile but heroic defense of Tom (211).

Atticus Finch is a good lawyer, then, and a gentleman, but he is not a crusader. He takes Tom Robinson's case because he is appointed counsel (as required by 1930s statute in Alabama capital cases), is a man of professional ethics, and appears, moreover, to believe in defending Tom, even though he has no illusions about winning a rape case involving a black man and a white woman. Atticus ends his defense of Tom Robinson with a ringing declaration that the court of Maycomb County has available to it the same measure of justice one might seek from the United States Supreme Court—"in this country our courts are the great levelers, and in our courts all men are created equal" (205), he reminds his jury—but there is never one moment of doubt as to the verdict that will be returned. Scout puts it best: "Tom was a dead man the minute Mayella Ewell opened her mouth and screamed" (241). Against the certainty of defeat, Atticus Finch's heroic effort is all the more moving. In his integrity, humility, and common sense, Atticus is almost certainly meant to provide an alternative to the cranky fulminations about "Sambo," states' rights, and the Cold War voiced by Faulkner's liberal attorney, Gavin Stevens, in *Intruder in the Dust*. At the same time, however, Atticus too remains a man of the South, a moderately liberal insider. How else could he function as the symbolic conscience of his family and the white townspeople, those "with background" who privately "say that fair play is not marked White Only," who wish him to do the right thing on their behalf, but who otherwise scorn him as a "nigger-lover" (83–86, 108), who excuse themselves from jury duty, thus turning the decision over to "white trash," and who uphold at all human cost the grandiose myth of southern white womanhood (236)?

The course of Tom's ordeal and Atticus's defense is artfully constructed to exacerbate two mirroring paradoxes. First, Tom is placed in a deadly trap when he must either give in to Mayella Ewell's sexual advances or resist her, and then when he must either recant his story or accuse a white woman of lying. Driven to the impudence of declaring his fear that, no matter what he does, he will end up the victim of a judicial system in which mobs and juries are indistinguishable—"scared I'd hafta face up to what I didn't do," he meekly but archly replies to the prosecutor (198)—Tom is the personification of the daily apprehension that John Dollard found to be widespread among southern African Americans in the 1930s: "Every Negro in the South knows that he is under a kind of sentence of death; he does not know when his turn will come, it may never come, but it may also be at any time." [21] The second paradox, which is Scout's, the reader's, and finally the book's, is perfectly summed up in Atticus's admonition to his daughter, who has sought to defend him from the scorn of town and family alike: "[T]his time we aren't fighting the Yankees, we're fighting our friends. But remember this, no matter how bitter things get, they're still our friends and this is still our home" (76). The peculiar political morality that pervades the novel is incarnate in this expression of near paralysis, which at once identifies the race crisis as a *southern* problem—a matter of states' rights, ideally immune to renewed federal intervention—and describes it in terms that make decisive local action unthinkable. Even though Atticus Finch's own heroism may work to obscure this element of the book's lesson, the novel is, in fact, perfectly in accord with the southern view that the meaning of *Brown* was to be worked out internally. Just as the South closed ranks against the nation at the outset of desegregation—a reaction heightened by Mississippi's being thrust into the national spotlight by the Till case—so *To Kill a Mockingbird* carefully narrows the terms on which changed race relations are going to be brought about in the South.

Atticus's moral courage forms a critical part of the novel's deceptive surface. Whether to shield his children from the pain of racism or to shield Lee's southern readers from a confrontation with their own recalcitrance, Atticus, for all his devotion to the truth, sometimes lies. He employs indirection in order to teach his children about Maycomb's racial hysteria and the true meaning of courage, but he himself engages in evasion when he contends, for instance, that the Ku Klux Klan is a thing of the past ("way back about nineteen-twenty"), a burlesque show of cowards easily humiliated by the Jewish storeowner they attempt to intimidate in their sheeted costumes purchased from the merchant himself (147).[22] Such moments are not distinct from the book's construction of analogies for moral courage in the face of ingrained communal racism—for example, Atticus's killing of the rabid dog or Mrs. Dubose's breaking free of her morphine addiction—but rather part of it. Indirection and displacement govern both the novel's moral pedagogy and, in the end, its moral stalemate. The ethical example of Atticus Finch is heightened in exact ratio to the novel's insistence that, so far as Maycomb and Alabama are concerned, it is both inimitable and incomplete.

In the wake of losing Tom Robinson's case, Atticus suffers personal anguish and bitterness, but he reminds the children on this occasion and others that both juries and mobs in every little southern town are always composed of "people you know," of "reasonable men in everyday life," of "our friends" (157, 220, 146) and that racial injustice is a southern problem that must be solved from within by right-thinking white people. Atticus does not characterize the verdict as "spitting on the tomb of Abraham Lincoln,"[23] nor does he say of the jury: "If you ever saw those lantern-jawed creatures, those bigots whose mouths are slits in their faces, whose eyes pop out like a frog's, whose chins drip tobacco juice, bewhiskered and filthy, you would not ask how they can do it."[24] These remarks, which belong to Samuel Leibowitz, the principal defense attorney in several of the Scottsboro trials, cut through the decorous sanctimony of *To Kill a Mockingbird* and constitute as sharp an intervention into the novel as the comparable public reaction, outside the South, to the exoneration of the murderers of Emmett Till.

Vilified as the tool of the "Jew money from New York" that one prosecutor, during trial, said was bankrolling the representation of the Scottsboro Nine by the NAACP and the Communist Party,[25] the flamboyant Leibowitz came into the case in 1933, after its most significant development. His appearance as counsel was predicated on the case against Ozie Powell having been remanded back to Alabama after the historic Supreme Court reversal of the initial verdict in *Powell v. Alabama* in 1932. The Scottsboro cases are central to the novel not simply because Tom Robinson's trial is set perforce in their context, and not simply because the similarities between the accusations by, and cross-examinations of, the respective complaining white women, Victoria Price and Mayella Ewell, are of special note, but, more important, because *Powell* puts before us the very question of representation — of speaking or acting on behalf of another. In guaranteeing a constitutional right to counsel in certain capital cases, *Powell* for the first time partially incorporated the Sixth Amendment into the Fourteenth, thus nationalizing right to counsel as a matter of due process. The radical Left branded the decision a mere ruse to obtain an unchallengeable conviction on retrial, with the *Daily Worker* declaring that "the Supreme Court ha[d] taken great care to instruct the Alabama authorities how 'properly' to carry through such lynch schemes."[26] But *Powell* was arguably one of the most important decisions by the Court in the decades leading up to *Brown*, a contribution not only to criminal justice but to civil rights. Although the restrictions of *Powell* would not be entirely erased until *Gideon v. Wainright* in 1962 (which extended the federal constitutional guarantee of right to counsel to noncapital felony cases as well), the Court's opinion initiated a federal attack on previously insulated procedures of state criminal law and started a gradual revolution in constitutional restraints based on the Fourteenth Amendment that would continue through the century.[27] In the realm of criminal law *Powell* therefore nationalized rights under the Fourteenth Amendment in a way comparable to the education cases, beginning with *Missouri ex rel. Gaines v. Canada* in 1938, that opened the way to *Brown v. Board of Education* and finally destroyed the states' capacity to maintain legal Jim Crow.

By comparison to the role of education in *To Kill a Mockingbird,* right to counsel seems an abstruse issue—and one not overtly racialized. More critical might appear the other major Supreme Court decision to come out of the Scottsboro cases, *Norris v. Alabama,* which again overturned the convictions on the grounds that eligible African Americans had been systematically excluded from the jury pool. Like *Powell, Norris* further accelerated the dismantling of the post-Reconstruction rulings that had so long governed the immunity of state authority in determining civil rights protection.[28] Because it was decided in April 1935, in fact, *Norris* would have been at hand had Atticus Finch chosen to challenge the composition of the Maycomb County jury, arguing, for example, that Calpurnia, who teaches her son reading out of Blackstone's *Commentaries* (125), is a fit juror. But it is safe to assume that his efforts would have been as futile as those of Leibowitz at the lower court level. (One Scottsboro defendant, Haywood Patterson, whose case was remanded on a technicality at the same time as that of Clarence Norris, accurately described his unsympathetic all-white jury as "a nest of possums.")[29] Even though it has no such explicit racial dimension, *Powell* was nevertheless racialized in fact. The Court's opinion, written by George Sutherland, adverts to racial realism in its second sentence: "The petitioners, hereinafter referred to as defendants, are negroes charged with the crime of rape, committed upon the persons of two white girls."[30] The Court recognized, as the opinion indicates in several other instances, that the South's "rape complex" was more than a minor factor in the denial of due process.

Like Tom Robinson's case, the Scottsboro cases and the appeals leading to *Powell* magnified the simple question put to Atticus by Scout when she innocently asks: "What's rape?" (135). Atticus gives what to Scout is a bafflingly legalistic answer, one of the several occasions on which his own dicta for truth and honesty are violated. *To Kill a Mockingbird* gives two answers, one indicative of Scout's unlikely transcendence of the suffocating strictures of white southern womanhood, the other indicative of the comparable trap laid by the novel's historical frame of reference. To judge from Scout's acculturation over the course of the book, the South's inexhaustible penchant for ultimately referring every racial question to the mystical body of the white woman is not

eviscerated in the novel but, along with Maycomb's racial and class stratifica-
tions and the moral cowardice of the vast majority of its citizens, left more or
less in place. In the fiercely satiric missionary tea sequence, for example, Scout
must learn to be a "lady" amidst the rank hypocrisy of the town's leading
ladies, who complain that their black servants have become sulky in the aftermath of Tom's conviction, condemn not Mayella Ewell but Helen Robinson of
immorality, and tediously invoke the specter of the black rapist ("there's no
lady safe in her bed these nights" [232]). She must learn to be a lady by swal-
lowing her grief and protest when news of Tom's death during a prison escape
arrives in the very midst of this excruciating scene. Scout registers, without
protesting, her partial kinship with Tom's incarceration and readies herself to
"enter this world, where on its surface fragrant ladies rocked slowly, fanned
gently, and drank cool water," as she later recalls, without telling us from the
vantage of retrospect whether, in fact, she has ever escaped that world (233).[31]

Both the novel and Scottsboro asked what meaning "rape" might have if it
were only a rhetorical justification for lynching and lesser forms of prejudice
or for sectional resistance to the nationalization of constitutional rights. Past a
certain stage in the Scottsboro case, as in that of Tom Robinson, no one could
doubt the defendants' innocence; the question, rather, was the interpretation
of "rape" as a political disguise in the large wardrobe of southern racism and
the judicial procedure employed to codify a predetermined guilt. The facts
of *Powell* might have arisen in any number of criminal cases, but black-on-
white rape cases in some parts of the Jim Crow South were often guarantees
of the denial of due process—if the accused even got to arraignment and trial.
Anticipating the Till case two decades later, the initial Scottsboro case was distinguished by the fact that the court was anxious to preserve the appearance
of due process and avert a mob's vigilante justice. The antilynching crusader
Jessie Ames rightly noted, however, that a lynching of the defendants was
avoided only "at the expense of the integrity of the law."[32]

It is a tragic feature of the initial Scottsboro trial, then, that its speedy procedure at once averted (even if it actually reproduced) mob rule, created various
outrageous abridgments of due process, ultimately resulted in key Supreme
Court guarantees of criminal and civil rights, and yet brought justice to none
of the accused. As Atticus's futile defense of Tom Robinson proves, the beneficial effects of *Powell* were not immediately apparent in the courtrooms of
Alabama. The case bears on the novel not because it affects Tom's case, however, but because it makes clear how right to counsel and strategies of literary

representation are related. The right of black men and women to adequate representation in courts of criminal law usually meant, certainly in the segregated South, representation by white counsel—that is, representation by a white voice and argument of the kind idealized in the portrayal of Atticus Finch. That is to say, because the novel's power is tied to the national culture's propensity to embrace such liberal heroics, we must take note of its immersion in a legal moment at which the constricted frame of reference defining Tom Robinson's right to be represented could not help but enforce Harper Lee's moral appeal to white paternalism at the same time that it underscored her implicit insistence that the nationalization of civil rights, like that of criminal rights, could not be accomplished by judicial fiat. On key fronts in the battle over the Fourteenth Amendment, *To Kill a Mockingbird* thus describes exactly why the South would remain an American problem so long as it refused to admit that federal oversight and the Constitution took precedence over state and local custom.

In this respect, the mechanism by which Atticus's defense of Tom Robinson overlaps with Scottsboro at two points is worth special attention.

Samuel Leibowitz outraged the Alabama courtroom audience, the southern press, and several judges by his scathing dismantling of the testimony of Victoria Price, the principal witness after Ruby Bates recanted her story. His cross-examination called into question Price's virtue (he proved she had been a prostitute), her sexual experiences at the time in question (he showed she had voluntary intercourse with a white man less than twenty-four hours before the purported gang rape), and the state's worthless medical case (he forced examining doctors to admit that the evidence was useless: no motile sperm; no semen on her clothing; no vaginal injuries; and no scratches on her back, despite her claim of having been raped by six young men while lying barebacked in a train car loaded with chert). For her part, Victoria Price, who at first took apparent pleasure in what seemed at times a chatty recounting of the events, became increasingly sullen and vituperative in response to Leibowitz's grilling, not least when he feigned politeness.[33]

But neither his argument nor the evidence itself mattered. What Leibowitz failed to estimate correctly was that the trial, in the end, was about the South's right, as one prosecutor put it, to "protect the sacred secret parts of . . . the fair womanhood of this great State."[34] He miscalculated as well the degree to which Communism and the advocacy of black rights easily merged in the ritual scenario of violated southern womanhood. For instance, a 1934 leaflet issued by the Birmingham White Legion asked: "How would you like to awaken one morning to find your wife or daughter attacked by a Negro or a Communist?"[35] In the course of the first round of appeals, the Alabama State Supreme Court, although its motives may have been less than honest, rejected the adducement of Victoria Price's reputation as a prostitute, just as it rejected the appeal on the right-to-counsel and jury pool issues as well. If the Court observed a distinction important to women's rights, however, it too put the South's rape complex on display. Dismissing the appellants' complaint about the undue speed of the trial, the Court cited the celerity with which the assassin of President McKinley had been tried and executed in 1901. It applauded swift justice and, taking a page out of the speeches of Benjamin Tillman and the novels of Thomas Dixon, contended that "some things may happen to one worse than death." "[I]f the evidence is to be believed, one of these things happened to this defenseless woman, Victoria Price."[36] Or, as another prosecutor had replied in the second trial, when Leibowitz objected to his ranting about "niggers" and rape: "I ain't said nothin' wrong. Your Honor knows I always make the same speech in every nigger rape case." The judge in question concurred; and when he gave his instructions to the jury in a subsequent trial, he snarled out the word "r-r-rapist" in a gruesome tone.[37]

Although he takes none of Leibowitz's personal pride in doing so, Atticus Finch also politely but thoroughly humiliates Mayella Ewell on the stand, shredding her testimony, proving that she has been beaten (and probably raped) by her father, Bob Ewell, and in the process laying the ground for an appeal even as he virtually guarantees his client's conviction by the local jury. His brilliant cross-examination of Mayella more or less obviates the jury's verdict, which is predicated upon the simple assertion by a white woman and her father that a "black nigger" has been "ruttin" on her (173). Lee, of course, does not call into question Mayella's veracity by undermining her reputation for chastity but instead takes the greater risk — for which Tom must pay the heavier price — of making evident her own attempt to seduce an African-American man. It is necessary to the novel's excruciating effect that Mayella Ewell be a more sympathetic victim and a more compelling witness than Victoria Price. But it is also necessary that, like Victoria Price and like Carolyn Bryant, the principal defense witness in the trial of Emmett Till's killers, she lie in order to protect her father and to uphold the scaffolding of Maycomb County's rape complex. In Mayella's case, fittingly, there can be no medical evidence of rape because no doctor was called; but Atticus uses the evidence of her beating to prove that Robert E. Lee Ewell (to cite her father's actual name), not Tom Robinson, is guilty. He does so in a way important both to the novel's invocation of Scottsboro and to its own tactical usurpation of black voice, act, and identity.

Because he is disabled, his left arm shriveled from a cotton gin accident, Tom cannot have produced Mayella's injuries. There may be a particular allusion to Scottsboro here in that evidence brought forth in proof of the young men's innocence included the fact that one was crippled by syphilis to the point of sexual incapacity and another was nearly blind. All were poorly educated, and four of the nine were said to be mentally impaired. None of this necessarily counts against a charge of rape, of course, but as the Supreme Court reiterated in its *Powell* opinion,[38] it counts mightily in the rationale for right to counsel as a part of due process, for the physical or mental deficiency of the defendants was made a key part of the appeals in *Powell* both to undermine the probability of guilt and to bolster the more far-reaching constitutional argument. The cost to the humanity of the defendants, however, was not insignificant— no less so than the cost to our accurate perception of Emmett Till's humanity imposed by William Faulkner in a 1956 interview: "Maybe the purpose of this sorry and tragic error committed in my native Mississippi by two white adults on an afflicted Negro child is to prove to us whether or not we deserve to survive."[39] In what way Till was "afflicted" or how his murder might be construed as simply an "error" Faulkner, with his characteristic mixture of sympathetic insight and reactionary detachment, did not explain. Like Faulkner's peculiar construction of Till as a potential sacrificial victim, the question of physical or mental deficiency in the *Powell* decision bears analogically on the representation of blackness in *To Kill a Mockingbird*. It is not enough for Tom Robinson to be innocent. He must be unquestionably a "quiet, respectable, humble Negro" (192, 204). He must be pathetically innocent—a victim of Mayella's desperate loneliness and abuse, a strong man but emotionally incapable of resistance or violence, and comparable, as the novel's central metaphor puts it, to those innocent songbirds whose only job, a form of minstrelsy, is to "make music for us to enjoy . . . [to] sing their hearts out for us" (90).

In making Tom Robinson a contemporary version of Uncle Tom, the novel silences him and largely deletes from view his life and that of his family, but its reasons for doing so are not simplistic or one-dimensional. Lee's strategy of indirection sets in motion a dialectic between Atticus's voluble, nearly sacrosanct white voice and Tom's proscribed, muted black voice, and again between the 1930s, the world of Scottsboro and *Powell,* and the 1950s, the world of Selma and *Brown.* Of course the justification for Tom's own diffidence in the white man's world is clear enough if we call to mind the testimony of another Alabama sharecropper of the 1930s, Ned Cobb, whose story, under the pseudonym Nate Shaw, was recorded in the magnificent oral history *All God's Dangers.* In 1932, the same year as Scottsboro, Cobb was brought to trial for resisting sheriff's deputies who had come to confiscate illegally a neighbor's cotton crop. Recounting his own farcical one-day trial in the moving vernacular of his narrative—with its colloquial but still telling use of the term *nigger*—Cobb created an indelible picture of the legal and social silence imposed upon African Americans in his day:

> The nigger was disrecognized; the white man in this country had everything fixed and mapped out. Didn't allow no niggers to stand arm and arm together. The rule worked just like it had always worked: they was against me definitely just like they was against those Scottsboro boys. . . . The trials was just a sham, just a sham, both of em. I might tell em everything just like it was but they'd kick against me in court, in regards to my color, unless it come up this way: now a nigger could go in court and testify against his own color in favor of the white man, and his word was took. But when it come to speakin out in his own defense, niggers weren't heard in court. White folks is white folks, niggers is niggers, and a nigger's word never has went worth a penny unless some white man backed it up and told the same thing that the nigger told and was willin to stand up for the nigger. But if another white man spoke against the nigger and against the white man that was supportin him, why, they'd call that first white man "nigger-lover" and they wouldn't believe a word he said.[40]

We must imagine that, could Tom speak for himself, his interpretation of Alabama justice (if not his language) might be pretty close to Ned Cobb's. Because it filters Tom's story through the legal representation of Atticus Finch and the storytelling representation of Scout Finch, however, *To Kill a Mockingbird* denies Tom even this much of a voice in his story and therefore precludes a full portrait of the African-American struggle for justice. Here too, moreover, the novel's nostalgia screens out the urgency of the moment in which Lee was writing, for its frame of reference—its frame of representation, one might say—is not the world of Ned Cobb alone but also the world of Emmett Till.

∾ ∾ ∾

Thirty years and two thousand miles away from Tom Robinson, Eldridge Cleaver, minister of information for the Black Panthers, composed a harsh, violent refutation of the white South's racial fantasies when he recalled his 1955 breakdown in Soledad Prison upon learning of Emmett Till's lynching. His rage against yet another perversion of justice, said Cleaver, was the catalyst for his new philosophy that rape could be made into an "insurrectionary act," one explicable in the lines from his poem "To a White Girl":

> Your white meat
> Is nightmare food.
> White is
> The skin of Evil.
> You're my Moby Dick,
> White Witch,
> Symbol of the rope and hanging tree,
> Of the burning cross.[41]

Whatever injustice is answered by his rage, Cleaver's theory of rape was abhorrent. Yet his militant seizure of the historical myth of black male sexuality and his verse, in part an amalgam of James Weldon Johnson, Jean Toomer, Langston Hughes, and others, are a fair index of the conservatism of Harper Lee's novel—its palpable attempt both to register the reappearance of the South's rape complex in the Till case and to displace it into the time past of Scottsboro, to fold it into Scout's narrative but at the same time banish it to a nightmare from which the South might yet awake.

Cleaver was one of many African Americans, from Muhammad Ali to Henry Hampton, producer of *Eyes on the Prize,* who dated their civil rights activism—or, as in the case of Cleaver, their outlaw radicalism—to an awareness of the Till case. Medgar Evers, field secretary for the NAACP, risked his life to gather evidence and witnesses against Till's killers, and Anne Moody remembered that Till's murder made her hate both the whites responsible for the crime (the murder *and* the trial) and the blacks who did not rise against such injustice.[42] The Till case left an equal measure of well-directed activism and boiling debate in its wake for more than two decades to come, with Susan

Brownmiller and Angela Davis, among others, making it a point of departure for their critiques of the conjunction of racism and sexism and Toni Morrison choosing it as the subject for her only play, *Dreaming Emmett*.[43]

The most elaborate African-American response to Emmett Till was James Baldwin's 1964 play *Blues for Mister Charlie*. As Baldwin recognized, the special heinousness of the case came less from the self-evident miscarriage of justice or the gruesome publicity of the violence done Till (his mother demanded an open casket at his Chicago funeral, and photos of the disfigured corpse ran in *Jet* magazine) than from the cold-blooded display of southern defiance in the aftermath of the acquittal. In a famous 1957 interview conducted by William Bradford Huie for *Look* magazine, Till's murderers had freely admitted killing the boy and explained their actions in stereotypical terms. J. W. Milam argued that he and Roy Bryant had only intended to whip Till for his alleged insult to Bryant's wife and send him back to Chicago; but when Till purportedly bragged about his white girlfriends in the North, Milam did the only thing he could: "I counted pictures o' *three* white gals in his pocketbook before I burned it. What else could I do [but kill him]? No use lettin' him get no bigger!"[44] In reply to such white supremacist arrogance, Baldwin created not a cringing black victim but a smart-talking black man, born in the South but with a racial consciousness galvanized by life in the North, whose own brashness calls the white man's rhetorical bluff, mocking both the racist history of the Delta economy ("Coke! Me and my man been toting barges and lifting bales, that's right, we been slaving, and we need a little cool") and the white man's sexual anxiety ("The master race! You let me in that tired white chick's drawers, she'll know who's the master race!").[45] Baldwin, one might say, sought to provide a bridge from Bigger Thomas to Stokely Carmichael and Eldridge Cleaver, from the impotent rage of the pre-*Brown* years to the militant youth leadership, and increasing radicalism, of the civil rights movement when the Student Nonviolent Coordinating Committee and Black Power came to the fore.

Despite fascinating, surreal elements of stagecraft, Baldwin's play labors to conceptualize either white racists or white liberals in provocative terms, as though Baldwin simply found their fear unfathomable. His spokesman for liberal outrage, the journalist Parnell James, is no more effectual than Harper Lee's B. B. Underwood, who bangs out frantic editorials on racial injustice but secretly despises blacks. In *Blues for Mister Charlie*, no Atticus Finch appears, and Richard, like Emmett Till, is murdered in cold blood, albeit in deliberately stylized stage drama suffused with a sense of ritual repetition and debilitating weariness. But African-American characters speak at length and with passion in the play: Baldwin, like Cleaver, Moody, and others, found in Emmett Till a sufficient catalyst for his own reconstruction of the governing mythos of the white South, different in degree but not in kind from the governing mythos of white America.

From the perspective of the light it sheds on *To Kill a Mockingbird,* however, surely the most remarkable response to Till's death is Gwendolyn Brooks's sharp, strong refutation of the murder and its archive of white southern hatred in her poem "A Bronzeville Mother Loiters in Mississippi. Meanwhile, a Mississippi Mother Burns Bacon." Speaking from within the consciousness of one of the white killers' wives, Brooks imagines the growing revulsion the woman feels as the terror of her husband's act overtakes her. The illusion of his racial heroism shatters as she imagines Till's death even as her husband's bestial hands and lips clutch at her for satisfaction of his desire:

> She heard no hoof-beat of the horse and saw no flash of the shining steel.
> He pulled her face around to meet
> His, and there it was, close close,
> For the first time in all those days and nights.
> His mouth, wet and red,
> So very, very, very red,
> Closed over hers.

In the extended metaphor of the Fine Prince come to rescue his wife, the "milk-white maid," from the Dark Villain, Brooks rewrites a scene epitomized in *Birth of a Nation* but common to the racial rescue fantasies that made the Till travesty possible. Just as the mythology of heroism collapses into the truth of night riders and the Klan, so the protection against rape collapses into the expression of rape, its blood-red desire suffocating the woman's screams but linking her irrevocably to Till's mother:

> But his mouth would not go away and neither would the
> Decapitated exclamation points in that Other Woman's eyes.[46]

If it is generous to Carolyn Bryant (who, at least in public and in court, displayed no such conscience or cross-racial sisterhood), Brooks's poem, published in the same year as *To Kill a Mockingbird,* provides a further means to imagine Scout Finch grown up, for Brooks's daring leap into a counterracial and historical reality, because it has no parallel in the carefully circumscribed narrative of Scout Finch, forces us to ask if Harper Lee's adult narrator is capable of speaking in such a voice. It is a possibility that the novel neither denies nor confirms. Even if it is generated by the fictive adult consciousness of the 1950s, however, Scout's voice remains that of the child of the 1930s, which has the inevitable effect of placing it into a sectional as well as a temporal trap, at once lessening the moral force of its judgment and defining the novel itself as a manifestation of the South as an American problem. That such various representations of African-American self-assertion as those of Cleaver, Baldwin, and Brooks coexisted historically with *To Kill a Mockingbird*—but of course failed to reach even a fraction of Lee's vast audience—is a reminder that Atticus and Scout Finch may be less characters in a novel than the embodiment of the nation's profound, continuing, and frequently self-deluding need for racial salvation. If Harper Lee stops short of turning Tom's sacrifice into such a perfect agency for white redemption—as Faulkner had done with the sacrifice of Joe Christmas in his own Scottsboro-era novel, *Light in August*—the novel's desperate strategy of retrospection in effect stalls for time while black leaders capable of pushing beyond the spent forces of massive resistance and the liberal endgame of Atticus Finch come to the fore. As much as the farcical trial of Tom Robinson, of course, the conclusion of the novel also demonstrates that the law—most of all, the Constitution or the Supreme Court—may be incapable of rendering justice. The lesson latent within Atticus's willingness to cover up Boo's part in the killing of Bob Ewell is that circumvention of the law, even violent civil disobedience, may be necessary in order to create even an approximation of justice—though it remains a real question at the end of Scout's narrative whether the way of life in Maycomb has changed at all.

Tom Robinson's disabled arm is his legal alibi, but it is also the author's alibi—in the one case useless but in the other, for that very reason, perfect. Atticus must not only speak for him but also appropriate into his own ethical heroism Tom's masculinity and dignity as a black man, his very identity, much as the book itself appropriates Tom's African-American world to the ethical heroism of its white liberal argument. The reiterated moral of the novel—that to understand a person you must stand in his shoes or, better yet, "climb into his skin and walk around in it" (157, 218, 30)—is, in fact, called into question by its principal strategy of representation, which is in turn bound tightly to the limited, ventriloquized voice that African Americans are granted in the legal and customary world of the novel that belongs as much to 1950s America as it does to 1930s Alabama. *Powell v. Alabama* gave criminal defendants the right to legal representation as passionate and valuable as that afforded Tom Robinson by Atticus Finch. But in its very assault on states' rights and, by implication, on the doctrine of segregation, *Powell* also underlined the fact that the triumph of white liberalism might not be the end of racism.

It was Harper Lee's fortune to write at a moment when white America was ready for fictive salvation, and the risk she took cost her widespread scorn in the South for betraying her region and its way of life; but it was also her fate to write at a moment when other voices were being heard—in boycotts and demonstrations, in demands for enforcement of the law—and when other options for literary representation of the struggle for black justice were readily apparent. Just as the reach of Atticus Finch's integrity is circumscribed by his admonition that moral action must respect the prejudices of "our friends" and ultimately abide by local ethics, so the novel's undeniable power is circumscribed by its own narrative strategies.

It is no mistake, perhaps, that the white children of *To Kill a Mockingbird* never grow up. In Scout's retrospective narration, they remain ever poised for the hypothesis of desegregation. With the promised land of the post-*Brown* world ever on the horizon, Scout and Jem are timeless inheritors of the liberal vision even as Atticus Finch is its timeless exponent. Yet in choosing to contain Tom's story—the story of the black South—within the carefully controlled narrative consciousness of Scout and the idealized grandeur of Atticus Finch, Lee subordinated lasting vision to a moral expediency that remains familiar enough in late-twentieth-century America, as the racial problems of the South have become more commonly recognized as national problems. Locked into the paired narrative capacities of Atticus and Scout, Tom Robinson, and the social and historical African-American world for which he stands, are left without a true voice in their own representation, living still, in every rereading of the novel, under the South's death sentence and returning us to the admonition of James Baldwin in his essay on Faulkner and desegregation: "Any real change implies the breakup of the world as one has always known it, the loss of all that gave one an identity, the end of safety. . . . There is never time in the future in which we will work out our salvation. The challenge is in the moment, the time is always now." [47]

Notes

For helpful comments on this essay I would like to express my gratitude to colleagues in the 1992–93 faculty seminar sponsored by the Robert Penn Warren Center for the Humanities at Vanderbilt University and to audiences at Dartmouth College, West Virginia University, the University of Michigan, Northwestern University, the University of Southern California, the University of California at Riverside, and the Bread Loaf School of English. For research assistance, also supported by Vanderbilt University, I would like to thank Lisa Siefker Long.

1   James Carville, quoted in Garry Wills, "From the Campaign Trail: Clinton's Hell-Raiser," *New Yorker,* October 12, 1992, 93; Zell Miller, quoted in Celestine Sibley, "Miller Unfurls a Call for Justice and Honor," *Atlanta Constitution,* January 13, 1993, B, 2.

2   James Farmer, *Lay Bare the Heart: An Autobiography of the Civil Rights Movement* (New York, 1985), 14.

3   W. J. Cash, *The Mind of the South* (1941; reprint, New York, 1960), 117-19; J. Thomas Heflin, quoted in Harvard Sitkoff, *A New Deal for Blacks: The Emergence of Civil Rights as a National Issue* (New York, 1978), 267.

4   Harper Lee, *To Kill a Mockingbird* (1960; reprint, New York, 1982), 88. Further citations will be included in the text.

5   Lillian Smith, *Killers of the Dream,* rev. ed. (New York, 1961), 87.

6   Tom Brady, "Black Monday," in *The Eyes on the Prize Civil Rights Reader,* ed. Clayborne Carson et al. (New York, 1991), 93; Stephen J. Whitfield, *A Death in the Delta: The Story of Emmett Till* (Baltimore, 1988), vii, 10; David R. Goldfield, *Black, White, and Southern: Race Relations and Southern Culture, 1940 to the Present* (Baton Rouge, 1990), 76, 87.

7   Arthur Raper, *The Tragedy of Lynching* (Chapel Hill, 1933), 59-65; but cf. Robin D. G. Kelley, *Hammer and Hoe: Alabama Communists during the Great Depression* (Chapel Hill, 1990), who identifies the man as Tom Robertson, 81.

8   Frank L. Owsley, "Scottsboro: Third Crusade; Sequel to Abolitionism and Reconstruction," *American Review* 1 (January 1933): 267.

9   Langston Hughes, *Scottsboro Limited: Four Poems and a Play in Verse* (New York, 1932), n.p. It is noteworthy that the two best novels that may be said to be "about" Scottsboro, *To Kill a Mockingbird* and Arna Bontemps's *Black Thunder* (1936), a historical novel centered on the Richmond, Virginia, slave uprising led by Gabriel Prosser in 1800, speak pointedly to its principal issues without even mentioning the case.

10 Sitkoff, *New Deal for Blacks,* 102-215 passim; Morton Sosna, *In Search of the Silent South: Southern Liberals and the Race Issue* (New York, 1977), 60-87.

11 Charles S. Johnson, *Shadow of the Plantation* (1934; reprint, Chicago, 1969), 212.

12 Claudia Johnson, "The Secret Courts of Men's Hearts: Code and Law in Harper Lee's *To Kill a Mockingbird,"* *Studies in American Fiction* 19 (Autumn 1991): 129-39.

13 Ralph McGill, *The South and the Southerner* (1963; reprint, Athens, Ga., 1992), 244.

14 *Brown v. Board of Education,* 347 U.S. 493 (1954).

15 McGill, *South and the Southerner,* 245; Martin Luther King Jr., *A Testament of Hope: The Essential Writings and Speeches of Martin Luther King, Jr.,* ed. James M. Washington (San Francisco, 1986), 219.

16 *Brown v. Board of Education,* 347 U.S. 494, 492 (1954); Andrew Kull, *The Color-Blind Constitution* (Cambridge, Mass., 1992), 151-63; Richard Kluger, *Simple Justice: The History of Brown v. Board of Education and Black America's Struggle for Equality* (New York, 1976), 700-714.

17 *Brown v. Board of Education,* 349 U.S. 300-301 (1955). On massive resistance and the long-term effects of *Brown,* see, for example, Numan V. Bartley, *The Rise of Massive Resistance:*

Race and Politics in the South during the 1950s (Baton Rouge, 1969), and Michael J. Klarman, "How *Brown* Changed Race Relations: The Backlash Thesis," *Journal of American History* 81 (June 1994): 81–118.

18 King, *Testament of Hope*, 218; Thurgood Marshall, in *Eyes on the Prize*, Henry Hampton, producer, PBS Television.

19 James Baldwin, *The Fire Next Time* (New York, 1964), 138–40.

20 See Thomas L. Schaffer, "The Moral Theology of Atticus Finch," *University of Pittsburgh Law Review* 42 (Winter 1981): 181–224, and Timothy L. Hall, "Moral Character, the Practice of Law, and Legal Education," *Mississippi Law Journal* 60 (Winter 1990): 511–54.

21 John Dollard, *Caste and Class in a Southern Town* (New Haven, 1937), 359.

22 This deflection of attention from the Klan is all the more striking in view of Lee's transparent use of the rise of Hitler and European anti-Semitism as an ironic counterpoint to southern racism and the hypocrisy of American "democracy" (244–47). In the 1930s, despite black attempts to exploit parallels between racism and fascism, the white South routinely suppressed any conscious recognition of the suitability of the comparison. See Johnpeter Horst Grill and Robert L. Jenkins, "The Nazis and the American South in the 1930s: A Mirror Image?" *Journal of Southern History* 58 (November 1992): 667–94.

23 Quoted in Quentin Reynolds, *Courtroom: The Story of Samuel S. Leibowitz* (New York, 1950), 275.

24 Quoted in Dan T. Carter, *Scottsboro: A Tragedy of the American South*, rev. ed. (Chapel Hill, 1991), 244; Allan K. Chalmers, *They Shall Be Free* (New York, 1951), 51.

25 Carter, *Scottsboro*, 235.

26 *Daily Worker* quoted in Sitkoff, *New Deal for Blacks*, 225.

27 Francis A. Allen, "The Supreme Court and State Criminal Justice," *Wayne Law Review* 4 (summer 1958): 192–95; William Beaney, *The Right to Counsel in American Courts* (Ann Arbor, 1955), 151–57; Anthony Lewis, *Gideon's Trumpet* (1964; reprint, New York, 1989), 112–13, 197–220; David Fellman, *The Defendant's Rights Today* (Madison, Wis., 1976), 211–12.

28 *Norris v. Alabama*, 294 U.S. 587 (1935); Carter, *Scottsboro*, 322–24; Sitkoff, *New Deal for Blacks*, 227–28.

29 Haywood Patterson and Earl Conrad, *Scottsboro Boy* (New York, 1950), 37; Carter, *Scottsboro*, 324.

30 *Powell v. Alabama*, 287 U.S. 49 (1932).

31 The context of the scene, the ladies' sanctimonious discussion of African missions, only heightens Lee's great irony by bringing the black anticolonialist movements of the late 1950s into dialogue with America's civil rights movement. The church's failed mission in Africa — its participation in buttressing colonial depredations — is made comparable by Lee to the Christian hypocrisy of the Jim Crow South, each domain of white supremacist ideology an extension of the other.

32 Quoted in Sosna, *In Search of the Silent South*, 36.

33 Carter, *Scottsboro*, 81, 205.

34 Carter, *Scottsboro*, 344–45.

35 Kelley, *Hammer and Hoe*, 79.

36 *Weems v. State*, 224 *Alabama Reports* 526, 528, 536, 551 (1932).

37 Reynolds, *Courtroom,* 283–84; Carter, *Scottsboro,* 346.

38 Carter, *Scottsboro,* 45–46, 221–22; *Powell v. Alabama,* 52, 58, 69, 71.

39 William Faulkner, *Lion in the Garden: Interviews with William Faulkner,* ed. James B. Meriwether and Michael Millgate (Lincoln, 1968), 254.

40 Theodore Rosengarten, *All God's Dangers: The Life of Nate Shaw* (New York, 1974), 340.

41 Eldridge Cleaver, *Soul on Ice* (New York, 1968), 11–14.

42 Anne Moody, *Coming of Age in Mississippi* (New York, 1968), 129, 187; Whitfield, *Death in the Delta,* 58–59, 85–126.

43 Whitfield, *Death in the Delta,* 110–15.

44 William Bradford Huie, "What's Happened to the Emmett Till Killers?" *Look,* January 22, 1957, 64. See also Whitfield, *Death in the Delta,* 33–69, and William M. Simpson, "Reflections on a Murder: The Emmett Till Case," in *Southern Miscellany: Essays in History in Honor of Glover Moore,* ed. Frank Allen Dennis (Jackson, Miss., 1981), 177–200.

45 James Baldwin, *Blues for Mister Charlie* (New York, 1964), 98, 102.

46 Gwendolyn Brooks, "A Bronzeville Mother Loiters in Mississippi. Meanwhile, a Mississippi Mother Burns Bacon," in *Selected Poems* (New York, 1963), 75–80.

47 James Baldwin, "Faulkner and Desegregation," *Nobody Knows My Name* (New York, 1961), 100, 106.

∿ Black Southerners, Shared Experience, and Place: A Reflection

JIMMIE LEWIS FRANKLIN

EACH ESSAY IN THIS VOLUME EVOKES, in one manner or another, the central force of race in shaping and disseminating understandings of the South and its ills and injustices. Whether the "problem South" was understood to be slavery, resistance to the changes wrought by Reconstruction, Jim Crow practices and institutions, or opposition to the modern civil rights movement, the underlying and perennial issue clearly was race. Moreover, whether America's southern problem is discerned through an examination of the historical record or through the region's fiction, we look most closely for clues of its origins in race relations and racial happenings. Race, then, lies at the heart of the South as an American problem.

Race is also configured into cultural constructions of the problem South in another way, a way more subtle and too often overlooked. Understandings of "race" affected not only relations between blacks and whites but also the tensions among African Americans in the North, particularly between those who had settled there a generation or two earlier and those who had more recently migrated from the South. Between 1910 and 1960, almost four and half million blacks left the South for the North in search of greater freedom and economic opportunity.[1] The culture black southerners brought with them was an amalgamation of many elements both white and black, a product of region, reaction, and past experience.

∿ ∿ ∿

Scholars of the American South have long sought to discover the shaping influences of the region's culture. Although they have not reached any consensus about what it is, most have regarded the terms *South* and *southerner* to mean whites of the region and the cultural institutions they helped to mold. In recent years, however, historians and sociologists in particular have turned their attention to regional institutions and ways of behaving in the South that cut across racial lines—a biracial cultural process, even allowing for caste differences, that invariably made both blacks and whites *southerners*. The culture that we now know as "southern" was forged through the interactions of African Americans and whites in the region, interactions sometimes hostile in nature but grounded in the shared experiences of the land, climate, and agrarian life. Blacks changed whites in the South and were changed by them "in language, literature, and religion, in music and manners, and in cuisine and conjuring." [2]

The massive exodus of southern blacks that occurred in the early part of the twentieth century brought the "country-born and country-bred" to northern and midwestern cities, where they would ultimately have to contend with and respond to racism and neglect from northern whites. As Joel Williamson notes: "The North got at last what many Northerners had always feared would be the result of the death of slavery—an exodus of blacks to the North. The southern race problem of the nineteenth century became the national race problem of the twentieth, in part precisely because of the abandonment by the North of the Negro in the South." [3]

Once black southerners turned away from Dixie, they occasionally felt not only the cultural disdain of white northerners but also the bitter sting of rejection from a settled black middle class that wanted little contact with, or, in some cases, no part of, a "countrified" southern culture that came with the migrants. In this sense, southern blacks became a concern to northern African Americans. Particularly, it was the *southernness* of rural black migrants to the North that induced established African Americans in cities such as Chicago to perceive the need to distance themselves from, or to "guide" and "control," their newly arrived counterparts who continued "to sing, sell, eat, and dress as they had 'back home.'" [4] As the Chicago *Whip*, an African-American newspaper, remarked in 1920, "'It's no difficult task to get the people out of the South, but you have a job on your hands when you attempt to get the South out of them.'" [5] James Grossman, in fact, maintains that "Chicago's black middle class could see little redeeming value in southern black folk culture. Symbolizing the dependency and degradation of blacks in the rural South, it had no place in the modern northern city and only confirmed white stereotypes, thereby tarnishing the image that Chicago's black community wished to project." [6]

Many longtime residents blamed the transplanted migrants—called a "dirty, crude, and generally unpleasant" people—for potential threats to their social standing and responsibility, for threatening access to housing and jobs, and for running down middle-class African-American neighborhoods. Said one black professional, " '[T]he same class of Negroes who ran us away from Thirty-seventh Street are moving [to where Chicago's middle class now lives]. They creep along slowly like a disease.' "[7] The southern origins of recent migrants were also blamed for what was understood by established African Americans in the North to be ingrained habits of docility and servitude toward whites. In the early 1920s, for example, the Chicago *Defender* warned migrants against openly displaying dress signifying their southern background: " 'We are not in Southland and there is no mark of servitude that must be placed on a man or woman of color in these climes.' " A Chicago Urban League leaflet was equally pointed: " 'I will refrain from wearing dust caps, bungalow aprons, house clothing and bedroom shoes out of doors.' "[8] Thus "hostility toward most things Southern thus came to symbolize and exacerbate class tensions within black Chicago, but also drew upon notions about 'respectability' that crossed class lines."[9]

Older settlers among northern blacks had long since jettisoned whatever sense of place they may have had for the new opportunities they wished to pursue outside the South: each subsequent crest of black migrants from the South therefore only forced a reckoning with the painful past they left behind. Southern blacks who left for the North and brought with them a piece of their homeland found that they would have to bury it deeply to be accepted fully. Thus did the problem South extend into the lives of its most recent departees. Consequently, migrants "no more wished to be associated with Southern rural culture than did the Old Settlers."[10] They saw their native culture as a stigma, and even in the North they continued to experience their homeland—the South—as, once again, a restrictive boundary. Migrants often found it useful to shun what they had known and the land and kin they had left behind. Yet many found themselves unable easily to cast aside and turn away from their memories and indigenous culture. "It was difficult," in Grossman's words, "to cease being Southern sufficiently to meet standards set by the Northern bour-geoisie."[11]

Only more recently have African Americans begun to lay claim to their place in the South and to be permitted to savor the reciprocal relationship between southern culture and all those sharing in its creation. In 1966, Alice Walker, at the time living outside the South, spurned a writing fellowship in West Africa and went instead to Mississippi, realizing that she could "never live happily in Africa — or anywhere else — until [she] could live freely in Mississippi." [12] In response to Martin Luther King Jr.'s March on Washington speech, in which he encouraged the black masses to "go back to Mississippi," Walker said, "This may not seem like much to other Americans, who constantly move about the country with nothing but restlessness and greed to prod them, but to the Southern black person expecting to be run away from home — because of lack of jobs, money, power, and respect — it was a notion that took root in willing soil. We would fight to stay where we were born and raised and destroy the forces that sought to disinherit us." [13]

This sentiment was also ably captured by folklorist Ray Allen, who wrote of having accompanied a New York gospel quartet as it returned home after a performance in South Carolina. He was struck by what one of the quartet's members, drummer Jeff Richardson, said: "See, this is the place where everything was really created from — the South. They [rural African Americans] just moved North to expand." Richardson was himself not born in the South, but, in Allen's words, his "impassioned homage to the roots of his Southern faith" reflects an attitude that Allen labels "typical of many Northern African-Americans, young and old, who maintain strong cultural ties to the South." [14]

A number of contributors to this volume remark on how the meaning of the South has changed since the 1960s and how it continues to change. Their observations are pertinent here as well: African-American migrants to the North who once found their southernness rejected and consequently had to closet their roots now discover virtue in and admiration for the richness and vitality of the culture that blossomed from the southern experience they shared with whites.

But there is irony here, as there is in so much of what has constituted the South's American experience. Alice Walker tells of a friend from New York who came to Mississippi expecting to find " 'spiritual nourishment' " but instead found, in his words, " 'no nourishment . . . because Mississippi has changed. It is becoming truly American. What is worse, it is becoming the North.' " [15] So the implications of this essay extend beyond its ostensible topic — the biracial aspects of southern culture — to raise questions that go to the heart of this volume: assimilation and identity and the social construction of "Americanness" and "southernness." This essay may offer a convenient point of departure for scholars who wish to probe more deeply how cultural contestation and transformation in the American North represent yet another dimension of the South as an American problem.

Margaret Walker, the distinguished novelist and poet, occasionally writes and speaks of her relationship with the American South, especially Mississippi, where she lives and where she taught for more than three decades. Similar to many other blacks who experienced the South, Walker came to know firsthand the harsh reality of bitter racial oppression, including the callous mistreatment and death of close friends. Yet the writer draws much of her literary inspiration from a southern land that denied opportunity to African Americans, made a farce of justice, and proscribed the political, social, and economic rights of blacks. Margaret Walker's comments about the South and her intimate contact with the region tell us a great deal about Jim Crow, and they also reveal the many contradictions in southern life and the difficulty in comprehending its culture.

Walker's experiences in the American South have a significance that transcends narrow considerations of race and race relations. Her works paint a graphic picture of suffering and pain. Nevertheless, they also speak of a shared life between blacks and whites and the development of a southern sense of place, a sometimes elusive concept that defines a person in relation to the natural and human environment. In 1986 Walker told an interviewer that Mississippi was the "epicenter" of her life and that the South was the subject and source of all of her poetry. The Magnolia State, her statement suggests, did not belong only to white people; it was her place, too. Never one to take racial identity lightly, the occasionally blunt poet admitted to a strain of black nationalism in her soul. While that particular confession rings true to the experiences of many other black southerners, Walker also acknowledges that the South shaped her visual perceptions of art and her own artistry and that from childhood she had the feel of the South in her blood. "Warm skies and gulf blue streams," she writes, "are in my blood." [16]

The notion of a shared history between southern blacks and whites, so noticeable in Margaret Walker's statements, did not enjoy great popularity among historians and writers prior to the 1960s. Occasionally the mavericks, such as southern nemesis Wilbur Cash and a few others, wrote, to the chagrin of those around them, of the interwoven history of blacks and whites. They, however, were clearly the exception, not the rule. Perhaps no historian framed the issue in the period after the *Brown* decision with as much cogency as North Carolina historian George B. Tindall.

In his presidential address to the Southern Historical Association (SHA) twenty years ago, Tindall came hard to the point. "It is scarcely a new finding," he told his audience gathered in Atlanta, "that southerners white and black share the bonds of a common heritage, indeed a common tragedy, and often speak a common language, however seldom they may acknowledge it." Tindall's observation represented far more than a commentary on the syncretic character of southern culture. It also served — at least in the opinion of some who heard the address — as a stern rebuttal to those historians and sociologists in particular who looked upon black folk as a mere appendage to the South, persons who had made few if any contributions to the culture of the region. Like Tindall's address, this essay echoes the belief in a shared past between black and white southerners during the specific period of Jim Crow, but it goes further to relate that past to the idea of cultural syncretism and a sense of place. In the process, it inevitably confronts the difficult issue of black cultural distinctiveness and the argument for the existence of a special worldview among African Americans. It suggests that only through a more thorough examination of material culture, natural phenomena, and nonracial factors that affected the lives of black and white southerners can historians fully appreciate the full dimensions of a shared past.[17]

The view of shared historical development that took into account the unavoidable contact between black and white southerners and that leaned heavily upon the syncretic nature of culture, liberal though it appeared, did not satisfy many activist/reform-minded intellectuals. To comprehend African-American life, some argued, scholars had to examine black existence in the Jim Crow South through a totally different set of historical lenses. This group of intellectuals offered a stinging critique of previous scholarship, while stressing the distinctiveness of black culture. The pressure that they generated pointed toward a shift in historiographical focus — a shift that had direct links to the black consciousness movement of the 1960s and 1970s and to the attack on consensus scholarship. That movement, as August Meier and Elliott Rudwick correctly note, drew its strengths from the new social history and from the tendency to study oppressed groups "from the bottom up." While some historians with strong ideological leanings may overstate their case to achieve a meaningful dialectic within the academy in order to counter racist white views, most eschew polemical argument and ideology.[18]

In retrospect the emphasis on the distinctiveness of black cultural life that challenged the liberal view of a shared southern past is not surprising. The raging debate of the 1960s and 1970s over the issue only punctuated a broader discussion over ethnicity, race, and social values in American society that gained increasing currency in the years after World War II. Moreover, the discussion clearly reflected earlier battles over identity, separatism, and pluralism that stretched back to the pre–Civil War period of African-American history. Much more than before, however, the stridency of black nationalism during the period of the mid-1960s and early 1970s raised the question of shared values and challenged the contention that black southerners during the Jim Crow era could have possessed any regional attachment or a southern sense of place. The argument for the distinctiveness of black culture that ultimately turned on the special experiences of African Americans found articulate spokespersons in a variety of groups and academic fields. Sociologists in particular, with their inclination toward intellectual activism and a need for social change, leaned ideologically in that direction. Their views, not surprisingly, ran directly counter to the notion that pluralism did sometimes characterize areas of southern life.[19]

Sociologist Joyce A. Ladner's edited work *The Death of White Sociology,* for example, gives forceful currency to a cultural ethos among blacks that rejects—although subtly—the idea of a shared past. Ladner and others criticize the use of outdated social science theory and a sociology of knowledge that, when practically applied, denigrates black culture and relegates African Americans to an inferior social position. More important, they attack the parochial view of culture that dismisses African contributions as primitive and assigns a higher value to white institutions, art, and literature. Some of the contributors to Ladner's book view the cultural values that define racial identity within the historical black community as strikingly different from the views of white scholars and other intellectuals.[20]

If the relationship between scholarship and social action posited by the contributors to *Death of White Sociology* appeared new and disturbing to some, their critique of an anthropology and a sociology that utilized a comparative approach to culture clearly was not. Franz Boas and a few other anthropologists and sociologists had already shown the way, as Vernon J. Williams Jr. of Purdue University demonstrates in his fine study *From a Caste to a Minority.* For those of the Boasian school there existed distinct and widely differing cultures, but with none assigned a higher value than another. Because of the work of Boas and his followers, cultural relativism slowly began to gain ground after the first decades of the twentieth century.[21]

African-American scholars in particular, imbued with the idea of cultural relativism, revived the theme of the persistence of African cultural values set forth by anthropologist Melville J. Herskovits in the mid-1930s and the 1940s. They saw an essential connection between group solidarity and culture. With a vision shaped by the struggle for civil rights and with a desire to defeat efforts at white cultural hegemony, Ladner and others called for the creation of a more positive black identity and racial consciousness. In their judgment these were prerequisites for enjoying the privileges in a society free of racism. No longer should blacks accept the judgment of white scholars who measured them against an alien set of norms or refused to regard blacks as an integral part of the American scene.[22]

To comprehend what black contributors to Ladner's book wrote (at least relative to shared experience and place) requires in great part an understanding of their views on assimilation and on a black value system different from that of whites. With their intellectual guns often trained upon assimilationist-oriented blacks, they easily accepted sociologist E. Franklin Frazier's critique of the black middle class. With equal facility, they ignored or dismissed (at least momentarily) their disagreement with the distinguished scholar over intellectual matters related to African retentions and black family life. They accepted almost a priori Frazier's contention that the black middle class, especially black intellectuals, remained bent historically toward an assimilationist philosophy that, if followed, would ultimately result in the "annihilation" of African Americans "physically, culturally, and spiritually." Blacks also had to turn away from European cultural models and toward African values.[23]

Proponents of the distinctiveness of African-American culture differed over whether its source was fundamentally African or mainly a product of New World experiences. Most shared the opinion of political scientist Hanes Walton. In rejecting the contention that blacks supported American ideals in the same manner as whites, Walton maintained that the experiences of blacks had made them decidedly different from others around them. Even so, he did not attach himself to any pronounced view of African cultural heritage. Given his fundamental premise, however, Walton could not escape the conclusion that American blacks, especially black southerners, had been subjected to "a unique range of experiences endemic to the special position they occupied in society." Therefore, "even when they are performing common social roles they usually have uncommon experiences."[24]

An even clearer and decidedly more pronounced expression of this view came from Houston A. Baker Jr., past president of the Modern Language Association. Baker argued that blacks and whites had not shared to any significant degree the same physical environment or social experiences. Therefore, little reason existed to talk of common ground. The cultural distinctiveness of blacks gave them a worldview radically different from that of whites, especially white southerners. Baker stated sharply in 1971 that "the perspectives of black America and white America are as far apart as the captain's cabin and the quarters of 'black ivory' during the middle passage."[25]

The most striking and in many ways the most provocative commentary on African Americans' special worldview comes from native southerner Mack Jones. In his article "Political Science and the Black Political Experience: Issues in Epistemology and Relevance," Jones tackles far more than his title suggests. Every people, he argues, has a worldview that is a product of lived experience, and that particular experience "constitutes the lens through which the world of sense perception is reduced to described fact." Jones has as one of his principal concerns the construction of a useful paradigm for a political science that would serve the needs of black Americans struggling for equality. His philosophical commentary on the worldview of black Americans, however, brings him implicitly to the issue of culture and distinctiveness and to an attack on the notion of cultural syncretism. "Some might argue," he maintains, "that there is no black American worldview, but only a synthetic American worldview that reflects the racial and ethnic diversity that characterize the United States." He continues:

> Although it is consistent with the Great American Myth, that position is a bit fanciful. All people who perceive themselves as a distinct, historically determined people and who are perceived by others to be so have a corresponding worldview. The fact that there may be considerable similarities in the worldviews of proximate peoples indicates nothing more than that there is a certain correspondence between worldviews and lived experience, and that consequently people whose experiences overlap and are intertwined will manifest equally complementary worldviews. However, when proximate people are also adversaries, their worldviews will reflect the adversarial character of their relationship.[26]

African-American theory that stresses the uniqueness of black culture or the existence of a special worldview has a close link to the ideas of self-determination and nationhood. Cultural syncretism, shared experience, and pluralism do not excite those who see self-determination as a driving force in African-American history. Anthropologist John Langston Gwaltney's scholarship speaks directly to self-determinism among blacks. Gwaltney's study, *Drylongso: A Self-Portrait of Black America*, concentrates on blacks in urban areas and in the period after Jim Crow; however, in that study he generalizes that a sense of nationhood exists historically among black people and that it finds its roots not so much in "territoriality" but in the "profound belief in . . . [a] core black culture and in the solidarity born of a transgenerational detestation of . . . subordination."[27]

Historian Vincent P. Franklin expands on Gwaltney's theme in *Black Self-Determination*. According to Franklin, a set of core values—freedom, education, resistance, and self-determination—exists in the African-American community that readily appeals to the masses, if not to the black middle class. The shared experience of racial oppression, he holds, occupies the central position in defining the emerging value system of the black masses. Critics of *Black Self-Determination* readily noticed the book's intellectual tilt toward acceptance of nationalist and Pan-Africanist beliefs and its deemphasis of cultural syncretism. Given its conceptualization, the work could have conceded little to shared experiences of black and white southerners or to the development of a southern sense of place even had that been its mission.[28]

Unlike some advocates of a distinctive black culture, Franklin contends that African Americans' core values grew from experiences in the New World. American slavery served as the foundation for the cultural value system that black folk handed down to subsequent generations. Enslavement affected more than one generation of African Americans in the United States, and, therefore, certain values remained significant among the race from one era to the next and indeed became core values of the black American experience.[29]

The strong adherence to those values and to African-derived cultural expressions—such as music, folklore, and certain religious practices—testified to a continuing belief in self-determination. In the period after Reconstruction, blacks responded to the reality of white supremacy, which became the core value among whites that explained their ideas and institutional forms. The black masses, however, chose to maintain black institutions. They did that not only because they felt unwelcome in predominantly white public and private schools, churches, and other social organizations, but also because they believed blacks should control their own lives and affairs in a supposedly free environment. The black value system that continued to emerge represented a direct challenge to white nationalist ideology that sought to maintain a system of exploitation. Social distance between the races, if one reads correctly from *Black Self-Determination,* did not easily allow for shared experiences or for the development of a sense of place among blacks.[30]

Franklin saw self-determinist objectives reflected in black migration from the South, especially prior to 1900. Even though strong Pan-Africanist values may have characterized black movement from the South in the years before World War I, as Franklin suggests, it is difficult to assert categorically that they served as historical and cultural precedents for Marcus Garvey and African-American solidarity in the 1920s. Unquestionably, many blacks moved to the North or to all-black towns to escape white domination, but the reasons for leaving home were varied. The problem in studying black migration is that few scholars have examined systematically why many of the blacks best equipped to leave the South often did not; nor have they accounted for the relative lack of success of, say, Marcus Garvey's Back to Africa efforts in most parts of the region. This observation, of course, does not suggest that blacks willingly accommodated racist restrictions on their lives. The point is that cultural issues related to nonracial features of the American South and to regional attachment had a direct bearing on black southerners' decision to remain at home.[31]

Jim Crow and discrimination did provide a push for many black southerners to leave the South. Those negative forces also tugged at the cords of regional attachment, producing the kind of pull between cultures ("twoness") in blacks that W. E. B. Du Bois describes in *The Souls of Black Folk.* Given the intensity of the exchange over the nature of African-American culture, pluralism, and reform in the years after the 1960s, Du Bois's pronouncement could not escape close scrutiny and reinterpretation in an age when Eurocentrism and cultural pluralism have come in for a withering attack. For years, the black scholar's description of the problems created for blacks by living in a discriminatory society had stood as a classic statement on the themes of cultural alienation and attraction toward American culture and what meaning the black experience should have for all Americans.[32]

In a period characterized by deconstruction, which later revisionists may eventually label the age of literary nihilism, Du Bois ultimately came within sight of those on the watch for suspicious signs of cultural syncretism. In a recent essay, Molefi Kete Asante offers a significant, and sometimes provocative, statement on the issues of alienation, shared experiences of black and white southerners, and place. A native Georgian, Asante lived in Valdosta until his family moved to Nashville, where he grew to maturity. During his eighteen years in the South, he discovered that the region, like America in general, was black and white and that he stood powerless and excluded from any governing process. There existed in the South "black and white, two colors, two origins, two destinies, that is what intervened in the midst of reflections on place for a young African in the south of Georgia."[33]

Life in segregated Valdosta and the South tore at the vital fabric of black self-esteem, and it destroyed racial consciousness. Nevertheless, young Asante embraced his blackness; he did not reject it. One spoke to whites, he recalls, as if they were "strangers from another planet." Blacks regarded whites as natural enemies, enemies that could with a single word wreak havoc in one's life. They stood firm in keeping blacks from sharing space in almost every enterprise during the Jim Crow years. In a biting critique of Du Bois, Asante implies that the Massachusetts-born scholar must have felt a need "to be white or to be accepted by whites." Valdosta, Georgia, by contrast, had made his consciousness unitary and holistic, with a solid identity; therefore double consciousness did not constitute a problem for him! He wrote of his own identity:

> I was never affected by the Du Boisian double-consciousness. I never felt "two warring souls in one dark body" nor did I experience a conflict over my identity. Since I was a child I have always known that my heritage was not the same as that of whites. I never thought we came over here on the *Mayflower*. When I got up in the mornings to go to the cotton and tobacco fields, little white children got up to go fishing in the lakes or to camp.[34]

With his location centered squarely in the black community, Asante refuses to acknowledge a shared past with white southerners. "Did I think that I shared something with these whites?" he asked rhetorically. To put his argument succinctly, a person could have only one heritage despite the multiplicity of backgrounds that go into what is called heritage. In the end that person inherited a "unified field of culture, that is, one whole fabric of the past rather than split sheets or bits and pieces." Whatever the merits of that argument, Asante, unlike Margaret Walker, probably could never have found his epicenter in Georgia, Mississippi, or any other place in the American South. But Margaret Walker, too, was secure in her relation with the African-American community—she was no misoriented African but rather a person pulled by the attraction of place, family, and a complex cultural region called the South.

Black southerners who found their center in the black community but who re-shaped (without merely emulating) European cultural traits to fit aesthetic or survival needs or who shared common ways of doing things with whites were not necessarily "crazy." [35]

For most of the Jim Crow years black and white southerners shared the common experience of a life on the land, agrarian values, and a knowledge of a familiar material culture. Both races struggled for a way to live in harmony with the land and the environment; although neither could probably feel a part of the other's community, such a feeling is not necessarily a prerequisite for acquiring a sense of place. To many blacks, land in the rural South represented a terrible economic entrapment, a natural resource for sustaining economic subservience. Yet work on the land and its products played a significant part in an individual's personal view of worth and identity. Land, then, had a close association to the idea of place, even among those persons who failed to own it.

In an autobiographical work, Mississippian Chalmers Archer tells an ab-sorbing story of his family's involvement with the land, its meaning as a sym-bol of independence, and its relationship to a sense of place. Archer's book is no romanticized account of an American South that memory and time have softened. Here indeed is a story of travail and triumph, of sadness and sor-row. Here, too, is a close-up view of a family in its southern place pursuing daily routines with surroundings and household and food items recognizable by most people who lived in the region—lye soap, hoecakes, crackling bread, okra, peas, and beans. Kudzu vines dot the landscape, and black women (and white women as well) sweep yards clean in West African fashion. Here, also, are down-home blues and black folk serving a highly personal God in a mecha-nistic universe. Incidents of callous white indifference to black rights serve as vivid reminders of hypocrisy and inhumanity in the South, but Archer's readers can still appreciate the beauty of a land and a natural environment that both blacks and whites creatively used in common ways to temper the hardships of poverty and climate. [36]

Land exerted a powerful pull upon young Archer, and some of its effects were visible when he revisited the old homeplace in 1992. His family had lived in rural Holmes County, Mississippi, for more than a hundred years; when he returned to the family's old farm, appropriately called "The Place," he still had a "deep affection" for the land he had left behind. Something about the old Archer place—thoughts of family, remembered friendships, memories of special times, change of seasons, and the open spaces—kept calling him back.

The deep influence that the Mississippi terrain had on Archer calls readily to mind a similar effect it had on another southerner, Willie Morris, who in a conversation with his friend William Dunlap remarked that particular pieces of the landscape brought back to him a rush of memories that highlighted the significance of a sense of place.[37]

Land, of course, had important uses other than farming that fostered attachment, a sense of identity and place. In his excellent study *African-American Gardens and Yards in the Rural South,* Richard N. Westmacott examines shared characteristics and differences between black and white southerners that further our understanding of culture. Although he concentrates on contemporary gardens and yards, Westmacott interviewed persons whose parents owned property during the era of Jim Crow. Improvisation and creativity distinguish the gardens he studies, but Westmacott also uncovers features of West African life that blacks had retained. Gardening, he concludes, led to an attachment to place among both blacks and whites, even for those who did not own the land they worked. Among both races he finds the persistence of agrarian values that include independence, self-sufficiency, self-reliance, belief in the dignity of work, and attachment to family and community.[38]

The study of material culture during the last two decades has also provided scholars with a better understanding of place, cultural differences, and the common ground that black and white southerners came to share after emancipation. John M. Vlach, a leading student of material culture, contends that the syncretic process witnessed in so many African-American productions represented essentially a "technique for preserving one's identity, a method of intelligent and cogent problem-solving" under difficult conditions. African Americans have engaged in a continuing process to "reshape the old and the familiar into something contemporary and unique, to simultaneously express one's self and reinforce the image of the community." Improvisation reflected genuine creativity in black material culture.[39]

Black southerners, as the study of expressive and material culture clearly reveals, have very special historical experiences, but these differences should not obscure black people's relationship to a place and a history shared with others around them. A life existed behind the veil of segregation, pursued with such regularity and intensity and carried out in such aesthetic form that one can label it African American. Black people in the American South after the Civil War continued to reflect in their creations the cultures of West Africa — in music, art, architecture, religion, dress, language, food, folklore, family life, and many other areas as well. Regional attachment or sense of place may have been intimately related to actual living in the black southern community, as some contend, but black life also reflected the cultural syncretism that has generally characterized the histories of both the region and the country.[40]

Ralph Ellison, novelist and social critic who grew up in Oklahoma, echoed that point in his book *Going to the Territory.* The lives of the two races were so interwoven, he writes, that it was practically impossible to separate out certain features of their social and cultural life. Ellison notes perceptively that "by overlooking the blending and metamorphosis of cultural forms which is so characteristic of our society, we misconceive our cultural identity." Alabamian Pamela Grundy recognizes the prohibitive barriers imposed by a segregated South, but the reasonable proximity of whites and blacks under Jim Crow permitted neither to cast an airtight canopy over culture. She writes in *You Always Think of Home* that black and white lives wove together in "intricate design" crossing in homes, stores, and even sometimes on the grounds of friendship.[41]

Black and white southerners sometimes stumbled over a portion of their shared history at the strangest times and in the oddest places. Southerner James Alan McPherson, the Pulitzer Prize–winning African-American author, discovered a great deal about the subtle impact of culture at work only after moving to the Midwest. At the University of Iowa, where he teaches, McPherson observes an association between many black and white southerners, resulting from the "imperatives of a common cultural background" that had become "more pronounced once [they] were cut off from the institutional pressures that kept [their] racial identities paramount."[42]

Writer Willie Morris had a similar experience upon meeting the black novelist Richard Wright in Paris. The two quickly "hit it off" as Mississippians. Although Morris probably overstates the case in maintaining that the intermingling of whites and blacks in the South made possible the ease with which the two met, he was nearer the truth in proclaiming that knowing the same things, eating the same kind of food, and being abused by the same weather gave them something in common that spoke to the issues of identity and place. Wright, of course, had never misunderstood the American South, yet he remained conscious of the powerful impact of a culture that both blacks and whites had helped to create. The author of *Black Boy* and the powerful protest novel *Native Son* admits that in leaving the South to go North he "was taking part of . . . [it] to transplant in alien soil." Perhaps a sense of place had come with the territory.[43]

Shared experiences and a sense of place among blacks did not necessarily imply acceptance of an existing system of segregation and discrimination. When Hartman Turnbow, the hard-nosed, fearless civil rights fighter, told journalist Howell Raines of his intention to remain in Mississippi because he (Turnbow) knew his state, he spoke to the issues of both heritage and protest. Amateur poet the late Virginia Brocks-Shedd, never an apologist for racial ills during her career at Tougaloo College and the Piney Woods School in Mississippi, drew upon her life's experiences to write that she felt herself bound by "gentle southern spirits." She understood the relationship between identity, the land, and culture. In her "Southern Roads/City Pavement," Brocks-Shedd expresses the wish that southern roads would lead friends to her grave as she lay "covered in death under . . . precious southern soil." Turnbow and Brocks-Shedd are reminders that a strong black identity and a southern sense of place did not necessarily conflict with each other. Indeed, one could argue that attachment to place may have fostered a genuine spirit of protest in some black southerners.[44]

The career of Oklahoman Roscoe Dungee — to cite briefly only one example — gives considerable credence to this contention. Dungee's career links regional attachment to black rights and protest, and it also provides a look at the workings of natural phenomena, material culture, and imagination in the formation of a sense of place. His activities also stand in microcosm as a direct rebuttal to the idea prevalent in some circles that the middle class during the age of Jim Crow narrowly adhered to an assimilationist philosophy.[45]

Dungee went to Oklahoma Territory with his family in the late nineteenth century, and in 1915 he established the Oklahoma City *Black Dispatch,* which became the most important black newspaper in the Sooner State for more than half a century. He was the founder of the Oklahoma chapter of the National Association for the Advancement of Colored People (NAACP), and his dynamic and creative leadership enabled the organization to appear successfully before the United States Supreme Court on five separate occasions during the Jim Crow era. The *Guinn* case, which outlawed the Oklahoma "grandfather clause" in 1915, brought the NAACP its first major legal victory. Black culture, too, held great meaning for this crusading editor who consistently worked to improve black life and to strengthen community institutions. Blacks and American Indians, he constantly reminded his readers, played an important cultural role in the development of the state, and they could lay legitimate claim to its heritage. No hegemonic white culture co-opted his vision of full freedom for his people. He understood as well as most the meaning of the spirituals and the blues, and as an active member of the Association for the Study of Negro Life and History, he used both his newspaper and his considerable influence to keep the organization alive in his state.[46]

Dungee's career in Oklahoma does indeed reveal some ambivalence toward Oklahoma, but it also reflects what the editor thought about place. He repeatedly wrote of justice and injustice, democratic rights and societal wrongs, while, at the same time, he worked to promote a strong racial identity and racial solidarity. Nearly fifty years after he had come to Oklahoma Territory as a lad, he wrote reflectively about the Oklahoma place in an editorial he sometimes reprinted during the celebration of statehood day. Dungee's long commentary tells the story of a rough frontier land, where African Americans had come, much like their white counterparts, to realize their hopes and dreams. Oklahoma was home, and it represented a cultural landscape fashioned by blacks, whites, and American Indians who shared in bringing into existence the Sooner State.[47]

Roscoe Dungee, Margaret Walker, and other black southerners recognized that cultures could move in many directions at once. Although southern whites during the Jim Crow era did not readily accept the idea of the shared nature of their history with blacks or, for that matter, the existence of any meaningful culture among African Americans, they did borrow, mostly without attribution, African-American ways and material objects.[48]

John Edward Philips addresses this point in a thoughtful essay designed to synthesize the competing views of E. Franklin Frazier and Melville J. Herskovits. Philips writes that a significant amount of African culture still survives not only among blacks but also among whites as well. In his commentary on "white Africanisms" he retraces cultural areas that Herskovits examines in his studies of black culture during the mid-1930s and 1940s (namely, etiquette, music, religion, cuisine, and speech); he attempts to explain to a limited degree how those forms entered the white arena. Philips laments that, with only a few exceptions, scholars focus their attention in great part on unraveling the special character of African-American culture by looking at "African retentions (and thereby stressing the 'otherness' of black Americans)." While that approach yields some fruitful results, it prevents researchers from concentrating on the growth of a distinctive southern culture that involved considerable exchange between the races.[49]

Historians may never accurately determine the degree to which blacks in the

Jim Crow era responded to positive regional features of the South or the extent to which most blacks felt a deep sense of place. Historians are more certain, of course, of black people's rejection of oppression and of a civil religion that reinforced legalized segregation and discrimination. The responses of blacks in the post-*Brown* era to the idea of southernism, which sociologist John Shelton Reed writes about in *One South,* say something about the favorable effects of desegregation and its possible relationship to a sense of place. Those responses also tell historians about the movement of culture among groups and about some regional attachments that existed before the era of desegregation.[50]

Black southerners who went north to escape the Jim Crow South can now go home again. They are now partly accepted in the land that their parents and grandparents helped to build—back home to define and redefine southern institutions and the culture that gave the place its regional shape. The southern roads that drew the attention of Brocks-Shedd have led many of them back to the land where they can honor the memories of family and friends whose bodies lie buried deep within the southern soil, the soil that gave their lives a personal and collective identity, as it did other southerners. They return to a land where the exploits of folklore heroes such as Stagolee and John Henry once competed for attention among the masses and where the blues with their sorrowful notes and hope for the future helped their people make it through a southern night. Etched perhaps indelibly in their memories are the melodious sounds from mostly black Protestant churches in which the improvisation of black choirs and congregations made songs such as "Precious Lord," "This Little Light of Mine," and "Leaning on the Everlasting Arms" virtually religious anthems of the race.

The old place called the South, of course, no longer exists except in memory—that vital link to the past—but the cultural institutions and specific places still remain that made life meaningful for a people that survived with dignity and self-respect. Even some old country stores yet stand at isolated crossroads; a few smiling raconteurs still sit quietly under rusty cigarette or soft drink signs, sharing their folktales and mourning the passing of a once simple social order. New returnees may encounter difficulty finding Saturday night fish fries, all-week revivals, and church dinner on the grounds. But they still recognize their southern place, for the spirit of the past remains, fixed in memory by experiences that do not easily fade away.[51]

Within the last three decades, a large body of scholarship has enabled those returnees and scholars alike to comprehend better the complex culture of the

American South, a culture that blacks helped to mold and that they often shared with whites around them. Perhaps, as Nell Irvin Painter suggests, that is why African Americans now reflect a willingness to claim the South as their territory and why southern history must continue to take into account their past. If scholars record that past with the fidelity it demands, then future generations of black southerners, with keen historical awareness and an appreciation of their contributions to the South's cultural heritage, can say with Margaret Walker:

> I want my rest unbroken in the fields of southern earth; freedom to watch the corn wave silver in the sun and mark the splashing of a brook, a pond with ducks and frogs and count the clouds.
>
> I want no mobs to wrench me from my southern rest; no forms to take me in the night and burn my shack and make for me a nightmare full of oil and flame.
>
> I want my . . . song to strike no minor key; no fiend to stand between my body's southern song—the fusion of the South, my body's song and me.[52]

Notes

An earlier version of this essay was delivered on November 11, 1993, as the presidential address at the annual meeting of the Southern Historical Association in Orlando, Florida. I wish to thank four fine scholars and friends for their encouragement and constructive criticism of this article. They are Darlene Clark Hine, Arvarh E. Strickland, Donald L. Winters, and Jacque V. Voegeli.

1 Jack T. Kirby, *Rural Worlds Lost: The American South, 1920–1960* (Baton Rouge, 1987), 320.

2 Joel Williamson, *A Rage for Order: Black-White Relations in the American South since Emancipation* (New York, 1986), 29.

3 Williamson, *Rage for Order*, 205.

4 James Grossman, *Land of Hope: Chicago, Black Southerners, and the Great Migration* (Chicago, 1989), 138–54; Williamson, *Rage for Order*, 155.

5 Quoted in Grossman, *Land of Hope*, 154.

6 Grossman, *Land of Hope*, 151–52.

7 Grossman, *Land of Hope*, 153 (first quote). The statement from the black professional is from 139 (our insert).

8 Quoted in Grossman, *Land of Hope*, 150 (Urban League capitalization in original).

9 Grossman, *Land of Hope*, 153.

10 Grossman, *Land of Hope*, 153.

11 Grossman, *Land of Hope*, 153.

12 Alice Walker, *In Search of Our Mothers' Gardens* (New York, 1983), 163 (our insert).

13 Walker, *In Search of Our Mothers' Gardens,* 160–61.

14 Quoted in Ray Allen, "Back Home: Southern Identity and African-American Gospel Quartet Performance," in *Mapping American Culture,* ed. Wayne Franklin and Michael Steiner (Iowa City, 1992), 113 (Allen's insert in the Richardson quote).

15 Quoted in Walker, *In Search of Our Mothers' Gardens,* 169.

16 Kathleen Thompson provides a brief summary of Margaret Walker's career and work in Darlene Clark Hine, ed., *Black Women in America: An Historical Encyclopedia,* 2 vols. paged consecutively (New York, 1993), 2:1219–20. Walker's exchange with the poet Nikki Giovanni offers a good look at the Mississippi writer's philosophy. See Nikki Giovanni and Margaret Walker, *A Poetic Equation: Conversations between Nikki Giovanni and Margaret Walker* (Washington, 1974). The best source for understanding Walker's response to place is an interview by Jerry W. Ward Jr., "A Writer for Her People: An Interview with Dr. Margaret Walker Alexander," *Mississippi Quarterly* 41 (fall 1988): 515–27 (quotation on 515), and the poet's volume *This Is My Century: New and Collected Poems* (Athens, 1989). The quote in the last line of the second paragraph is from Walker's poem "Sorrow Home," which appears on p. 12 of that collection.

17 The quote is from the last page of George B. Tindall, "Beyond the Mainstream: The Ethnic Southerners," *Journal of Southern History* 40 (February 1974): 3–18; Lawrence W. Levine, *Black Culture and Black Consciousness: Afro-American Folk Thought from Slavery to Freedom* (New York, 1977), 444, and Leon F. Litwack, *Been in the Storm So Long: The Aftermath of Slavery* (New York, 1979), xi, also echo the theme of a common southern heritage of blacks and whites.

18 On the clash of white liberal views with those of blacks in their search for a usable past, see Fred Wacker, "The Fate of Cultural Pluralism within American Social Thought," *Ethnic Groups* 3 (June 1981): 125–38. August Meier and Elliott Rudwick, *Black History and the Historical Profession, 1915–1980* (Urbana, Ill., 1986), 229.

19 Black nationalism of the 1960s often conditioned the debate over distinctiveness. A useful background source is the introductory chapter in John H. Bracey, August Meier, and Elliott Rudwick, eds., *Black Nationalism in America* (Indianapolis, 1970), xxv–lx. This essay, of course, does not purport to deal specifically with the often discussed issues of southern identity and culture in any detail. Two instructive works, however, are C. Vann Woodward, "The Search for Southern Identity," in *The Burden of Southern History* (Baton Rouge, 1960), 3–25, and Immanuel Wallerstein, "What Can One Mean by Southern Culture?" in *The Evolution of Southern Culture,* ed. Numan V. Bartley (Athens, 1988), 1–13. A review of some of the scholarship on the question of black identity may be found in Seymour Parker and Robert Kleiner, "Status Position, Mobility, and Ethnic Identification of the Negro," *Journal of Social Issues* 22 (April 1964): 85–102.

20 Joyce A. Ladner, ed., *The Death of White Sociology* (New York, 1973).

21 Vernon J. Williams Jr., *From a Caste to a Minority: Changing Attitudes of American Sociologists toward Afro-Americans* (New York, 1989), 59–79, 84–98, 116–18.

22 Ladner, *Death of White Sociology,* xxiii–xxiv; see also Stanley H. Smith, "The Development of the Black Community," in *Group Identity in the South: Dialogue between the Technological*

and the Humanistic, ed. Harold F. Kaufman, J. Kenneth Morland, and Herbert H. Fockler (Starkville, Miss., 1975), 169–87.

23 For E. Franklin Frazier's biting critique of the black middle class, see his *Black Bourgeoisie* (Glencoe, Ill., 1957). The words quoted in the paragraph are from Frazier, "The Failure of the Negro Intellectual," in Ladner, *Death of White Sociology,* 65. An incisive comment on the black bourgeoisie and its critics, especially black separatists, is Raymond L. Hall, *Black Separatism in the United States* (Hanover, N.H., 1978), 250–51.

24 The Walton quote is from Caroline Torrance, "Blacks and the American Ethos: A Reevaluation of Existing Theories," *Journal of Black Studies* 3 (September 1990): 74.

25 The quote is from Houston A. Baker Jr., "Completely Well: One View of Black American Culture," in *Key Issues in the Afro-American Experience,* ed. Nathan I. Huggins, Martin Kilson, and Daniel M. Fox (New York, 1971), 1:22.

26 Mack Jones, "Political Science and the Black Political Experience: Issues in Epistemology and Relevance," *National Political Science Review* 3 (1992): 25–39; 7 (first quotation), 36 (second and third quotations).

27 John Langston Gwaltney, [ed.], *Drylongso: A Self-Portrait of Black America* (New York, 1980), xxvii.

28 V. P. Franklin, *Black Self-Determination: A Cultural History of the Faith of the Fathers* (Westport, Conn., 1984).

29 Franklin, *Black Self-Determination,* 4.

30 Franklin, *Black Self-Determination,* 6. Sterling Stuckey argues in *Slave Culture: Nationalist Theory and the Foundation of Black America* (New York, 1987), vii, 83, that the spirit of self-determination and black nationhood extended into the period after the American Civil War.

31 A variety of reasons compelled blacks to move to all-black towns. Two solid studies on the subject are Kenneth Marvin Hamilton, *Black Towns and Profit: Promotion and Development in the Trans-Appalachian West* (Urbana, Ill., 1991), and Norman L. Crockett, *The Black Towns* (Lawrence, Kans., 1979). The best study of black migration before World War I is William Cohen, *At Freedom's Edge: Black Mobility and the Southern White Quest for Racial Control, 1861–1915* (Baton Rouge, 1991). For a brief representative example of how blacks transferred their southern culture to the North, see Grossman, *Land of Hope,* 262–63.

32 W. E. Burghart Du Bois, *The Souls of Black Folk: Essays and Sketches* (Greenwich, Conn., 1961), 17.

33 Molefi Kete Asante, "Racism, Consciousness, and Afrocentricity," in *Lure and Loathing: Essays on Race, Identity, and the Ambivalence of Assimilation,* ed. Gerald Early (New York, 1993), 127–43.

34 Asante, "Racism, Consciousness, and Afrocentricity," 132, 134.

35 Asante, "Racism, Consciousness, and Afrocentricity," 37, 140, 142–43; for Asante's harsh indictment of "misoriented" Africans, see 143.

36 Chalmers Archer Jr., *Growing Up Black in Rural Mississippi: Memories of a Family, Heritage of a Place* (New York, 1992).

37 Archer, *Growing Up Black,* 3, 128, but especially the chapter entitled "The Place," 3–12. Black Mississippian Clifton L. Taulbert had a reaction to the land similar to Archer's. See his *Once upon a Time When We Were Colored* (Tulsa, 1989), 2–4. Morris's comment is from Willie

Morris, *Homecomings* (Jackson, Miss., 1989), xii.

38 Richard Noble Westmacott, *African-American Gardens and Yards in the Rural South* (Knoxville, 1992). Harvard psychologist Robert Coles comments on the attachment of poor people to the land and place in Tony Dunbar, *Our Land Too* (New York, 1969), x. Stuart A. Marks's study, *Southern Hunting in Black and White: Nature, History, and Ritual in a Carolina Community* (Princeton, N.J., 1991), is the only work of its type that focuses on similarities and differences in black and white gaming practices in the South. It has much to say about history, the natural environment, and place.

39 John Michael Vlach, *By the Work of Their Hands: Studies in Afro-American Folklife* (Ann Arbor, 1991), 4–6. The reader should also consult the same author's *The Afro-American Tradition in Decorative Arts* (Cleveland, 1978), 1–5.

40 An excellent discussion of the origins of African-American culture is Mary Frances Berry and John W. Blassingame, *Long Memory: The Black Experience in America* (New York, 1982), 3–32. See, too, John H. Dormon and Robert R. Jones, *The Afro-American Experience: A Cultural History through Emancipation* (New York, 1974), 1–21. One cannot ignore Sidney W. Mintz and Richard Price, *The Birth of African American Culture: An Anthropological Perspective* (Boston, 1992). Various theories of African-American culture are examined with great clarity in Amuzie Chimezie, "Afro-Centricity and Ethnicity: Definitive Concepts of Culture," *Western Journal of Black Studies* 7 (winter 1983), 216–28.

41 Ralph Ellison, *Going to the Territory* (New York, 1986), 125. Pamela Grundy, *You Always Think of Home: A Portrait of Clay County, Alabama* (Athens, 1991), 109. For a view similar to Ellison's related to American history generally, see the work by Albert Murray, *The Omni-Americans: New Perspectives on Black Experience and American Culture* (New York, 1970). See also Murray's description of his return to his hometown of Mobile, Alabama, in his *South to a Very Old Place* (New York, 1971), 135–91. An incisive article on southern writers and regional identity is William L. Andrews, "In Search of a Common Identity: The Self and the South in Four Mississippi Autobiographies," *Southern Review* 24 (winter 1988), 47–62. Margaret Jones Bolsterli wrote in *Born in the Delta: Reflections on the Making of a Southern White Sensibility* (Knoxville, 1991), 66, that "if truth were told, there were more frequent paths of communication than people wanted to recognize."

42 James Alan McPherson, "A Region Not Home: The View from Exile," in *The Prevailing South: Life and Politics in a Changing Culture*, ed. Dudley Clendinen (Atlanta, 1988), 204.

43 Morris, *Homecoming*, xxi. Richard Wright, *Black Boy: A Record of Childhood and Youth* (New York, 1945), 284. For a related comment, see Gayle Graham Yates, *Mississippi Mind: A Personal Cultural History of an American State* (Knoxville, 1990), 80–84, 229–30.

44 Howell Raines, *My Soul Is Rested: Movement Days in the Deep South Remembered* (New York, 1977), 19–20. Virginia Brocks-Shedd's poem "Southern Roads/City Pavement . . . ," written in Jackson in 1983, is in my possession. Pages are unnumbered.

45 No published biography of Roscoe Dungee exists. See a brief description of him in my *Journey toward Hope: A History of Blacks in Oklahoma* (Norman, 1982), 29, 54–57, 76, 102–3, 115–16, 163, 198–99.

46 Dungee played an important role in helping establish the NAACP Conference of Branches structure that gave state groups considerable control over their local activities. Indeed, some

Oklahomans believe that he developed the idea. Although historians have trouble document-
ing that fact, the frequency with which Oklahoma went before the United States Supreme
Court testified to Dungee's effectiveness in that state.

47   The editorial appears in the Oklahoma City *Black Dispatch,* April 22, 1939.

48   Lawrence Levine has written with keen insight on the movement of culture in various directions in two chapters of his recent book. See "The Unpredictable Past: Reflections on Recent
American Historiography" and "The Historian and the Culture Gap" in Lawrence W. Levine,
The Unpredictable Past: Explorations in American Cultural History (New York, 1993), 3–13,
14–31.

49   John Edward Philips, "The African Heritage of White America," in *Africanisms in American
Culture,* ed. Joseph E. Holloway (Bloomington, Ind., 1990), 225–39. For a reflective comment on the sharing of cultures among groups, see Alice Barkley's interview with Professor
Charles Long, director of the Center for Black Studies at the University of California, Santa
Barbara, "Who Are the Many? What Is the One?" *Touchstone Magazine* 22 (1993): 7–11. The
obvious borrowing by whites of black musical forms needs no documentation. However,
most people do not readily associate African Americans with country music, or whites with
the blues. Paul Hemphill has written of the considerable influence blacks had on country
music in his book *The Nashville Sound: Bright Lights and Country Music* (New York, 1970),
161–68. Some whites also played and enjoyed blues before the recent period of American history. In the 1980s and 1990s, however, blues became very dependent commercially on white
audiences. See the superb chapter "The Blues Is a Lowdown Shakin' Chill" in James C. Cobb,
The Most Southern Place on Earth: The Mississippi Delta and the Roots of Regional Identity
(New York, 1992), 276–305; and for the influence blacks and whites had on each other in an
earlier period, see Edward L. Ayers, *The Promise of the New South: Life after Reconstruction*
(New York, 1992), 377–98. Southern music—especially blues, country, spirituals, and jazz—
and special ways of preparing food have been noticeable identifying symbols of the region.
See John Egerton, with Ann Bleidt Egerton and photographs by Al Clayton, *Southern Food:
At Home, on the Road, in History* (New York, 1987), 16–17, 26–27, 34–35, 110, 148–49. The
designation "soul food" for southern cooking has as much to do with the sociology of race
relations as with the methods of preparation.

50   John Shelton Reed has addressed the issue of the South and southern distinctiveness in a
number of his works. The most useful for the essay here is *One South: An Ethnic Approach to
Regional Culture* (Baton Rouge, 1982), 113–18 (chap. 8, with Merle Black).

51   The black writer Arna Bontemps made his way back to the South in the mid-1960s. See
his "Why I Returned," *Harpers* 230 (April 1965): 177–82. A study by Daniel Johnson, "Black
Return Migration to a Southern Metropolitan Community: Birmingham, Alabama," Ph.D.
diss., University of Missouri, 1973, 39, showed that "race *per se* did not figure prominently
among the reasons given for returning to the South." However, one should not generalize
about return migration from a specific example. Yet Johnson's study does say something
about the lure of southern culture and about the gradual disappearance of legalized segregation and racism. The image of the South in the two paragraphs above is based on my
personal contact with black returnees to the South and on my partly autobiographical ad-

dress "A Southern Sense of Place: Notes of a Native Son," April 15, 1993, Tuscaloosa, Alabama (University of Alabama Press pamphlet, Tuscaloosa, 1993), 12–13.

52 See Nell Irvin Painter, " 'The South' and 'the Negro': The Rhetoric of Race Relations and Real Life," in *The South for New Southerners,* ed. Paul D. Escott and David R. Goldfield (Chapel Hill, 1991), 42–66. Thadious M. Davis has come as close as anyone to understanding the connection between the African-American experience and place in a brief but superbly executed article entitled "Expanding the Limits: The Intersection of Race and Region," *Southern Literary Journal* 20 (spring 1988): 3–11. The reader may profit from the published proceedings of two specific conferences on place: Peggy W. Prenshaw and Jesse O. McKee, eds., *Sense of Place: Mississippi* (Jackson, Miss., 1979), and S. Mort Whitson, ed., *Sense of Place in Appalachia* (Morehead, Ky., 1988). Margaret Walker's lines are from "Southern Song" in *This Is My Century,* 11.

～ Race and Southern Literature: "The Problem" in the Work of Louis D. Rubin Jr.

MICHAEL KREYLING

IN OUR SEMINAR, WE ALL tried to argue, as Larry Griffin does in the introduction to our conversations, that the "problem of the South" is multifaceted. Indeed, Joyce Chaplin investigates the problems of climate, David Carlton the problems of economic circumstance; my contribution was to argue that the problem was one of literary construction: types, tropes, typologies, and so on. But, as these essays tend to show, we always come back to race as the problem in and of the South. Robert Margo's numbers might be interpreted to argue that poverty and a lag in economic "progress" are more illusion than fact. However, after reading Eric Sundquist's fine, hard essay "Blues for Atticus Finch," the problem is back: Emmett Till is really dead, and he is not the only African American to have perished in the name of law, or the community, or the sanctity of the southern this or that.

Herein lies a southern problem—perhaps not so urgent as the legal issues discussed by James Ely or Sundquist but just as stubborn. If a literary history represents a group's experience, values, myths over time, what is the South's literary history to be? One of the Agrarian fathers, John Crowe Ransom, asked the question much more elegantly in "Antique Harvesters":

> what shall this land produce?
> A meager hill of kernels, a runnel of juice?

A common sense of place, in answer to Ransom's punning questions, is often invoked as the foundation of the literary history of the South; some version of Woodward's "burden" formula is most frequently applied as history. Jimmie Franklin's melancholy essay suggests (*asserts* might be the appropriate verb) that because (or in the name) of race there is no common language on which to construct a literary history for the South. Separate experiences, separate worldviews make any lunge for the overarching story a kind of hegemonic power grab. The white (male) literary historian of the South—like Atticus Finch, as Sundquist exposes him—is no paragon but rather a genteel paternalist waving a gag order for all other voices. What shall this land produce?

The problem facing the literary historian of the South is that the significant southern literary figures of this century—those with the means, motive, and opportunity to write southern literary history (the Fugitive-Agrarian brotherhood and its heirs and successors in the New Criticism)—have shown little or no desire to come to terms with race, opting instead for literary criteria that all but disallow African-American expression and experience from the realm of art or cultural significance. George B. Tindall was not the first nor the last to note that the Agrarian manifesto of 1930 (*I'll Take My Stand*) deliberately aimed to manifest "regional loyalties in situations dissociated from an emphasis on the issue of race."[1]

It was not to be actual African-American experience to which the literary mind of the South must pay attention but, according to Allen Tate, the "image" of that lived experience in the (white) mind: "All great cultures have been rooted in peasantries, in free peasantries, I believe, such as the English yeomanry before the fourteenth century: they have been the growth of the soil. . . . The white man got nothing from the Negro, no profound image of himself in terms of the soil."[2] And in the latter obligation, the African American, again according to Tate, failed. "Image" became a kind of password. Literature was made of images; on the other hand, life was filled with experiences. If one's art was perceived by the literary powers to be too full of experiences (as was Richard Wright's—to anticipate this argument—or Douglass's, or Du Bois's), it was barred from the territory of literature: silenced, like Tom Robinson in the Maycomb courtroom, for whom even the most genteel and oblique self-reference is his death warrant.

Because Tate and his cohorts among southern literary critics have proclaimed themselves victors, history has given way to image. Wilbur J. Cash, not immune to the power of image himself, nevertheless saw the problems in a people whose collective "mind . . . is continuous with the past."[3]

"The past," Cash argued, is not the same as "history," and those who elevate the former neglect the latter. Specifically, Cash trenchantly observed, if history is composed of experience rather than image,

[p]rimarily this group [the Agrarians] was one which turned its gaze sentimentally backward. Its appearance just as the South was moving toward the crisis of the depression, just as Progress was apparently sweeping the field, just as the new critics and writers were beginning to swing lustily against the old legend and the old pattern, was significant. In a real fashion these men were mouthpieces of the fundamental, if sometimes only subterranean, will of the South to hold to the old way: the spiritual heirs of Thomas Nelson Page. And their first joint declaration, *I'll Take My Stand*, was, like their earlier prose works in general, essentially a determined reassertion of the validity of the legend of the Old South, an attempt to revive and fully restore the identification of that Old South with Cloud-Cuckoo Town, or at any rate to render it as a Theocritean idyll.[4]

"Idyll," "legend," "old," "old," "old": Cash's rhetorical game plan is easy to see — "swing lustily" at the same lobs, hit the ball into the open court, win the match for "Progress," "crisis," in short, for history.

Almost no one played southern literary history by Cash's rules. The "old pattern" of the New Critics held sway until the recent age of "theory," which Jimmie Franklin fears is an age of "literary nihilism." Whether theory is nihilistic or not, its advent has opened cracks in heretofore solid literary edifices. Southern literary study seems to have resisted theory with particular fervor. To be sure, theory (like any "new" strategy for looking at the familiar — like the New Criticism itself in the 1930s and 1940s) is a threat. But to what?

American literary historian Lawrence Buell has examined the problems in writing and in accepting literary history as a truth-bearing genre. What he has said of American literary history goes double for southern:

> The anxiety provoked by such factors [as changes in the ways literary history is understood and in the personnel who write it] may weigh harder on Americanists than on British literature specialists because of certain complications endemic to the former field, which for one thing relies for its self-definition more heavily on extratextual claims about the distinctiveness of the nation's social structure, physical environment, and so forth. Therefore Americanists may be destined to make a particularly conflicted contribution to the debate over how to do literary history in a time of undoing.[5]

There is no better, that is, more instructive, "case of the conflicted contributor" than Louis D. Rubin Jr. No one has done more to "naturalize" the literary critical techniques of New Criticism (which forbade the "extratextual") to the politics and thematics inherent in Agrarianism itself and in his own time. And no one has done more (not even the Agrarian fathers) to try to accommodate "the distinctiveness of the [region's] social structure" to the needs of a redemptive literary-historical narrative that specifically addressed the problem of race as the chief, albeit negative, mark of distinctiveness. Beginning in the early 1950s (at a "time of undoing" for the South) and continuing into the 1990s, Louis Rubin has forged, modified, and polished a truce between the image of the South and the American South as a problem in American history.

In a couple of rather severe essays, literary critic Paul A. Bové has accused Agrarianism and its devotees of transforming a "politics into the political quietism or conservatism of New Critical orthodoxy" that effectively "forgot" any and all connections to history by stressing the formal, aesthetic qualities of literary works over their social and cultural conditions.[6] "PROFESSIONAL SOUTHERNERS," Bové's name for the usual suspects, spread cultural amnesia.[7] The rules of the game as, for instance, Brooks and Warren's *Understanding Fiction* (originally published in 1943) sets them forth, call almost all of the cultural/historical context out of bounds. This, Bové asserts, makes the court too narrow, the game too easy for the powers that be. Clearly, Bové feels there is a bill to pay: a charge with interest for racial apartheid in the South as a region. Bové may well be one of those literary historians who, to quote Buell, see the text primarily as a "sociogram" to preserve and protect power.[8]

There is, however, something in Bové's allegation, for before there was an Agrarian literary history, there was a strategy for protecting its sanctity. In "Remarks on the Southern Religion," Tate's essay in *I'll Take My Stand* (1930), his "remarks" adumbrate a literary theory by painting the line between "history" and "image," by ruling out as nonsouthern and unthinkable anything hybrid. If "horsepower" is unthinkable as a notion because it conjoins the concrete (the horse) and the abstract (the concept of power), how can literary history (as a similarly "hybrid genre") be thought, much less written?

"Take the far more complex image of history, if indeed it may be called an image at all," Tate writes.[9] Images constitute the vocabulary of the stable, traditionalist, religious community: the ideal condition of life-in-the-group as the Agrarian formula would have it. As integers of traditional thought, images do not bond well to any grammar. A mind thinking in images is not, Tate suggests, apt to think historically as well, at least not historically in such a way as to be long-viewing or narrativizing: "These more concrete minds may be said to look at their history in a definite and now quite unfashionable way. They look at it as a concrete series that has taken place in a very real time—by which I mean, without too much definition, a time as sensible, as full of sensation, and as replete with accident and uncertainty as the time they themselves are living in, moment by moment."[10] History, as the meaning-conferring act of the human mind in the Enlightenment tradition, tries to impose a narrative long view on the "moment by moment." By definition, then, history is a game nobody inside the gates wishes to play. "[I]f you take history not as an image or many images, you have to take it as an idea, an abstraction, a concept," Tate complains, using the fierce Agrarian either/or rule.[11] Readers familiar with Tate and the Agrarian dogma will recognize "idea," "abstraction," "concept" as the poisonous heresy of the deracinated modern mind. Like Cartesian zombies, these moderns think in the long view, arrogantly granting precedence to the abstract series over the concrete moment. They (we—Tate even included himself) see horsepower rather than the horse, empty structures of experience rather than the "whole, separate, and unique" moment.[12] In a replay of the debate between Edmund Burke and Thomas Paine in the 1790s, Tate enrolled the South on the side of Burke.

Bové's indictment, though summary, is not wholly without merit. The problems facing a southern literary historian writing from the inside (where else?) were formidable. Louis Rubin saw the tip of the paradox in the problematic relationship between an empirical historical entity (the South) and the claim of ontological distinctiveness for aesthetic works produced by its artists. In an early essay, he notes with apparent equanimity that "the modern South has produced a distinguished body of criticism based squarely on the premise of the entire autonomy of the individual story and poem."[13] The problem of making a collection of "entire autonomies" into a coherent literary canon troubled the Agrarian fathers not at all, for with few exceptions they held the South itself to be an ontological constant guaranteeing the unity of the individual work. Rubin often paid homage to this critical by-law, but his tendency was almost always equally, and surreptitiously, historical. Under the rhetorical cover of common sense and reasonableness, Rubin built a southern literature that the Fugitive-Agrarian disciples could not have made. He began, after all, in the decade (1950s) James Ely describes in his essay as years of landmark change and massive resistance.

Rubin's precursors had produced volumes such as Beatty and Fidler's *Contemporary Southern Prose* (1940), dominated by essays and reviews arguing the ideological virtues of unreconstructed southernism (a kind of massive resistance before its time), and Tate's *A Southern Vanguard* (1947), a rather loose collection of essays, poems, and stories submitted to a literary contest in memory of John Peale Bishop. Works available for classroom and scholarly use, such as *Southern Prose and Poetry for Schools,* compiled by Edwin Mims (the bane of the Fugitives) and Bruce Payne in 1910, were clearly unacceptable: most of them contained propaganda aimed at affirming the New South agenda — horsepower rather than the horse. There was no comprehensive work that developed a literary-historical plot and based its critical discipline on the principle of textual autonomy until Rubin undertook the project.

How successfully could a canon of autonomous works form or be formed into a history, a narrative? The New Criticism would need a fundamental adjustment to support a literary history, and none of its originators seemed poised to make it. Ransom, as the decade of the 1930s waned, divorced himself from poetry and the politics of the region, to the dismay of some of the original brethren. He got into "theory." Tate, interested in history to the extent that it could be made to disclose its sweeping conceptual principles, likewise showed little or no interest. Davidson, from his roost as Vanderbilt professor and book reviewer, wrote essays on the current state of southern literature; he might have taken on the work of literary history, but his energies were consumed in social and political controversy. Warren, because of his devotion to History and history (the big fateful pattern and the individual event), seems a likely candidate for the work. He was, but he put his massive energies into an anthology of American literature for the classroom. By virtue of individual personalities and circumstances, and by virtue of the stress on the autonomy of the text, the Agrarians/New Critics never actually accomplished a literary history.

We can get an inkling of what a southern literary history under the unadjusted Agrarian/New Critical auspices might have been from the work of Richard Weaver (1910–63). Educated at the University of Kentucky, Vanderbilt, and Louisiana State University, Weaver was a rhetorician and a philosopher of the

South whose work in its totality constitutes a literature-based history of the cultural ideal of the South.

Weaver's 1943 Ph.D. dissertation at Louisiana State University (directed by Agrarian associate and New Critic Cleanth Brooks and signed by another, Robert Heilman) is a comprehensive study of the intellectual work of the conservative southern mind from the defeat in 1865 to the brink of the First World War. It was published posthumously in 1963 as *The Southern Tradition at Bay.* Weaver's purpose in his dissertation is to validate, by means of traditional literary-historical study, the existence of a "metaphysical dream"—a sort of Platonic idea of southernness, a shared superstructure of consciousness and value—common not only to the elite of a certain culture in the American South but also to Western-Christian culture in its loftier manifestations from the Golden Age of Greece, the Renaissance of Dante, and, to a certain extent, the Protestant renaissance of John Milton. The plan would fit Tate's outline of South-as-religion. Cash, Weaver's contemporary, would have placed it in Cloud-Cuckoo Town. Weaver's blueprint, in other words, had a definite design and a definite past. As it migrated freely through history, it was immune to historical qualification and shaping.

In the 1940s and 1950s, when activists for American literary history were claiming a national "renaissance" in the mid-nineteenth century of Melville, Hawthorne, Whitman, and Thoreau (and when Rubin was working in this particular vineyard for Robert Spiller), Weaver cast a much wider net. Not only did he insist on a southern literary-historical genealogy that went back to the Christian Gospels, but he also insisted on a fairly inflexible and closed intellectual approach to that canon. In "Aspects of the Southern Philosophy," the second essay in Rubin and Jacobs's symposium *Southern Renascence* (1953), Weaver argues, echoing Tate's theory as well as his title, that the southern way of thinking about itself and the world is essentially religious. Rubin was to take up a defense of the same position twenty years later in his essay "Fugitives as Agrarians: The Impulse behind *I'll Take My Stand*" (1972). Weaver extends Tate's pronouncement by filling in particulars. *The* southern philosophy, or way of thinking, both Tate and Weaver explain, resists analytical operations of thought in all cases—resists on the grounds that analysis is in fact a miscarriage of the highest purposes and obligations of the human mind. *The* southern mind apprehends holistically, piously, in a way that is consistent with "the form in which the messages of the great religions come."[14] Ransom, hedged about with subtle ironies, had touched this sacred stone in "Antique Harvest-ers." For Weaver, however, there is no irony; the genuine southerner's relation to his time and place is either an act of faith or an act of apostasy. The South itself is revealed as one of the "great religions." Its canon, like the canons of the great religions, is fixed, inspired by the metaphysical dream, sufficient unto itself without historical setting.

There are problems in speculating on the contents of a literary canon as Richard Weaver might have imagined it; he did not completely assemble one. He was, after all, a rhetorician and a historian of the Idea, not of multiple ideas, much less of events and texts. And he died suddenly. The true South for Weaver was immune from class struggle and the turmoil of romantic indi-vidualism. Race scarcely entered his mind, except as an insurrection trumped up by Yankee agitators and social scientists. In the post–World War II times James Ely describes, Weaver spent most of his considerable energy baiting the liberal position and its proponents. In the end, like his Agrarian mentors, Weaver was more interested in the image of the South than he was in the his-tory of the South.

This reinforced consensus, though, is not exactly the one Louis Rubin, start-ing out in American studies in the 1950s, adopted. As several of his works show, Rubin is an admirer and sympathetic interpreter of H. L. Mencken, the one-man wrecking crew of the Bozart. One cannot, it seems, serve both Mencken and the religiously tilted literary-historical poetics of Weaver and the Agrarian tradition—at least, not for long. As an early champion of Thomas Wolfe, Rubin also had trouble trying to crash the Agrarian parade. The Agrari-ans' preference for aesthetic formalism in poetics banished Wolfe's hairy novels to literary nowhere. One of Rubin's own contributions to *Southern Renascence,* "Thomas Wolfe in Time and Place," argues for the expansion of the fledg-ling modern southern canon to accommodate Wolfe: "It was these Nashville Agrarians of *I'll Take My Stand* who in large measure formulated the credos and the critical foundation basic to most modern Southern literature. Partici-pating membership in the Nashville group, however, is hardly a requirement for the Southern author."[15] Nor, need it be said, for the southern literary his-torian. Crashing the sanctuary was more difficult than negotiating a truce with the Agrarian–New Critical axis. In following years, as Rubin published many of his consolidating books of essays, he altered strategy from beating his ad-versaries to joining them, forging what amounts to a truce between the simple imperative of history and "these Nashville Agrarians" who seemed to want to deny it.

~ ~ ~

The History of Southern Literature (1985), chief editor of which is Louis Rubin, stands as the skyscraper on the landscape of southern literary history, and it was erected in a kind of charmed obliviousness to its circumstances: it was erected (echoing Buell) in "a time of undoing." As a glance at the field of southern literary study will show, *HSL* is more inclusive of southern literary history than anything that preceded it. There have been symposia, readers, anthologies of various breeds, but nothing before has given southern literary history so much legitimacy in one volume. It even supersedes Jay Hubbell's *The South in American Literature* (1953) by extending its survey into modern and contemporary ground, by withdrawing southern literary study from the larger field of "American literature" (inasmuch as no such compromise is carried in the latter title, nor is any detectable in the editorial policy and practice), and by transferring the handling of southern literature from the scholars to the critics.[16]

Few will dispute the claim that Rubin is the primary architect and developer of southern literary study in this century and that *HSL* is his monument. Some have added ornament, or even a wing, to the basic structure, but the blueprint is Rubin's, extended or polished or interpreted by the "Rubin generation," many of whom are Chapel Hill Ph.D.'s, and by the fraternity of friends whom Rubin has often acknowledged.[17]

Sometimes, though, from inside the building we cannot really tell what the structure looks like. To an outsider (one who, like Rubin himself, never had a course in southern literature or southern history in college or graduate school) coming upon the project complete, its "madeness" seems all too evident. Certain features that the original builders and tenants consider "natural" or "given" (e.g., sense of place, a Woodwardian sense of historical burden, an innate sense of narrative) to me seem problematic. In an age Buell characterizes as affording, if not enforcing, "a plurality of available historicisms," all "natural" attributes become conventions dependent on prior texts and situations, themselves dependent, and so on.[18] The ontological certainty of "South" seems less automatic now than it did during the heyday of construction and expansion.

Rubin himself is a source of some clues into design choices. In "The Way It Was with Southern Literary Study: A Reminiscence," Rubin shows, I think, that he has been a self-conscious (albeit not wholly consistent) reconciling, liberal tendency in fluctuating rapport with the essentially conservative (if not reactionary-and-proud-of-it) right wing of southern literary history plotted by the Agrarian/New Critical group in the 1940s and 1950s.

Rubin takes as his foundation assumption that a realistic positivistic relationship between human history and aesthetic works is the place where literary criticism begins. Lawrence Buell, in a different but related context, has described the foundation assumption of Rubin's vintage: "Literary history's mission was once well understood. Its task was to conjoin intrinsic and extrinsic, literary texts and their historical settings, in narrative that represented history's actual course. Literary history was a hybrid but recognizable genre that coordinated literary criticism, biography, and intellectual/social background within a narrative of development."[19] The Fugitive-Agrarian narrative, insofar as one is adumbrated in this group's several works, is not developmental but disintegrative: things fall apart as history brings change to an original, utopian state of organic stability. Rubin faced the challenge of reconciling intrinsic with extrinsic, when the extrinsic was mostly race and the intrinsic was trained to ignore it. He revived the word *image* but coupled it with *history* and synonyms.

In "The Curious Death of the Novel: Or, What to Do about Tired Literary Critics," Rubin states the premise that art is "the ordering of human experience into a meaningful pattern, dependent not on its faithfulness to 'real life' but on the validity of its own representation for its impact."[20] Southern literature gets its validation as image from an order made meaningful by the work itself. This suprahistorical identity is not contingent on "real life" or actual history, although it might make use of it as raw material. Aesthetic works by southern authors (e.g., novels, short stories, plays, poems, some forms of biography and criticism itself) carry an added or supercharged degree of order because they are generated by a community that itself borders on the suprahistorical, that (like a religion) is *more* than the sum of its parts. In subject matter as well as in form, southern literature reflects the "active and palpable *force*" of the community in which the individual producers have their lives.[21]

In fact, such work increases in literariness in proportion as its agreement with the "community" tightens and its reliance on historical fact decreases. Studying communal literature communally renews the communal bond: "[W]hy do southern writers write the way they do?" Rubin asks in the preface to *William Elliott Shoots a Bear.* "If one grants that there is and has been a body of literature identifiable as southern, then what is there about the place and the time that has played so noticeable a role in shaping the literature?"[22] Rubin's starting position is very slippery; he finds bedrock where others find a hall of mirrors. In granting that there is a "literature identifiable as southern," have we not already all but allowed distinctiveness in the society? Do we not, by the circular dynamics of this argument, substitute the effect for the cause and risk dismissing or mistaking certain problematic literary work for reasons that will never be known? I think so; this is not the sociological process of "contestation" that Larry Griffin sees. This is, rather, the amnesia that Bové decries.

Take, as an example of this closing hermeneutical circle, the following excerpt from Robert B. Heilman's "The Southern Temper." This is the essay in definition that leads off *Southern Renascence* and, reprinted, bats second in *South: Modern Southern Literature in Its Cultural Setting* (1961). Heilman's assertion of natural and seamless continuity from southern society to southern literature lies deep in the DNA of southern literary study: "The sense of the concrete, as an attribute of the fiction writer, is so emphatically apparent in Faulkner, Warren, and Wolfe, so subtly and variously apparent in Porter, Welty, and Gordon, and so flamboyantly so in someone like Capote (who hardly belongs here at all) that everybody knows it's there."[23] Since everybody knows it's there, nobody need really define what "it" is. "It" is the constantly affirmed center of a discourse protected from inquiry. Because of Heilman's reliance on this center, then, "the sense of the ornamental" and its apparent opposite "functionalism" in literary criticism can *both* signify the southern temper.[24] Furthermore, the southern temper can be denoted by a sense of the concrete and by a sense of the symbolic even though these two terms appear to be opposites.[25] There is a fundamental conservatism in a critical discourse that is immune to certain kinds of questions; it enforces "quietism," another of Bové's complaints. As Quentin Compson might have muttered in a similar situation: "You would have to be born there . . . to know what 'it' was, and then you wouldn't have to ask."

It is not as if the "through-the-looking-glass" character of Heilman's essay and of *Southern Renascence* in general was lost on its original audience. Its skeptical reception is forgotten when, as Bové charges, "professional southerners" are in charge of remembering. Norman Podhoretz (as a New York Intellectual in the early 1950s, he represented one of the chief coteries vying with "professional southerners" for mastery of the intellectual culture of the United States) pegged the political aspects of *Southern Renascence* immediately in a review Rubin was slow to forget.[26] "One would like to think," Podhoretz begins, "that the whole thing [*Southern Renascence*] is a case of innocent literary misjudgment. But we are already dealing here not with a group of people so impressed by Southern literature that they feel impelled to study it, but rather with something closer to a political movement."[27] And that political movement can have, in Podhoretz's view, no other object than to thwart change in the legal and social relations between the races in the South. To see such a political agenda in literary criticism was to show evidence of the virus of modernity in one's temperament.

Southern literary history, during its early years with Rubin, struggled with the challenge of race just as Tate and others had tried to fight off accusations of fascism. Rubin tried to address the challenge of defending a conservative poetics as a reactionary politics. But he saw it as subject matter, not as a language of its own. Podhoretz saw race as an issue of rhetoric, protected at the highest levels: "But the Faulknerian attitude to the Negro problem—that it is a deep moral turbulence in the blood of the South which can only work itself out in agony, guilt, and expiation—soon becomes a received idea, and the urgency disappears."[28]

Reading a defense of the racial status quo as a function of literary representation, a historical experience filtered through a construction process called "Faulknerian" after its foremost, but not its only, practitioner, moves it, Podhoretz implies, from the arena of historical-political action into a frame of aesthetic contemplation where "the urgency disappears." The canon-building function of *Southern Renascence* is, Podhoretz argues, ideologically conservative whether or not any of the contributors confess a particular political stance, and it works to "disappear" the need for social action by absorbing history into the literary, the "Faulknerian." In such territory as this lies the "problem" of southern literary history, for it is in attempting to see and discuss such a situation that Rubin's literary history displays the blinding injuries sustained in the collision of image and history. Eric Sundquist is very trenchant in his exposure of the "go slow" racial wish fulfillment of *To Kill a Mockingbird*; Podhoretz was more biting in his accusations of the entire literary-historical southern statement.

Rubin's writings occupy a complex position in this political confrontation, both loyal to the (unstated) conservative agenda *and* inclined toward change. Serving the former goal, his work strives toward the establishment of the South as an "image," a keyword in the New Critical lexicon denoting a condition of existence, or mode of being immune to historical contingency and the call to action. In an essay of 1956, "The Historical Image of Modern Southern Writing," Rubin collapses distinctions separating the various meanings of "history," "the past," "the South," "real." "History — defeat, the war, the past — in the South these were not abstractions," he writes. "To a child growing up in the South, they were very real. Southerners knew that history was not merely something in books."[29] And yet, for the writers of the southern renascence, Rubin explains, "the image of the war and the past," their birthright, was all they had in place of firsthand history.[30] They could only know it secondhand, as an image carried mainly in books. And, as the current events of the 1950s made clear, the book image was preferable to the historical reality.

Rubin's sense of the play of history in the southern imagination is linked very closely to Allen Tate's concept of the simultaneity of past and present in the mind of the modern southerner:

> The writers of the Southern renascence were able to re-create the life around them, about which they were writing, not simply because they were blessed with somewhat superior powers of description. They saw it as if they had been gifted with a kind of historical perspective, which translated what they saw in terms of what *had been* as well as what now was. . . . The present was focused into perspective by the image of the past lying behind it. Their own contemporary life was seen not only for its own sake but as formed and influenced by the life that had preceded it.[31]

It is not always so easy to measure the relative weights of the southern past as "image" and "contemporary life." More often than not, in practice, Rubin tends to privilege representations of the present viewed through the "focus" of the tragic past as legitimate southern literature. For instance, Rubin credits the Faulknerian voice of Chick Mallison or Quentin Compson as a legitimate southern voice on (in the former case) the question of federal intervention in southern ways of community life or (in the latter) the oppressive nearness of the heroic past, not because of overt racism but because of the "Faulknerian" self-conflict in either voice. As we shall see, Richard Wright's or Ralph Ellison's conflicted voices are more problematic to this theory.

This bind seems clearer in another "image" essay, "An Image of the South," that Rubin contributed to a collection of essays he coedited with James J. Kilpatrick, *The Lasting South: Fourteen Southerners Look at Their Home* (1957). The subtitle is no accidental echo of *I'll Take My Stand* and of its authors, the original Twelve Southerners. Political change in the 1950s (this collection had been begun only months after the announcement of *Brown v. Topeka* in May 1954) threatened the "image" of the South and had made it unlikely that such agreement on a "specific platform and bill of particulars" as the original Twelve had enjoyed would be possible in 1957, yet the editors claimed that "the South's identity [was] worth preserving" in the aftermath of *Brown* and a few months before the troubles at Central High School in Little Rock.[32]

"A good deal of what is contained in this book," Kilpatrick and Rubin write in their preface, "relates to [the segregation issue]," [33] even though no single essay specifically addresses it. The fourteen southerners might hold differing views on the issue; in fact, "the editors themselves" hold different views, although Kilpatrick, in the final essay of the book, "Conservatism and the South," is the only one to state his position. Not surprisingly, he is against judicial dismantling of "separate but equal." [34] His statement leaves Rubin as the liberal by default. It is from this Quentinesque position that he, once again, attempts to clarify the "image" of the South.

In "An Image of the South," Rubin walks the fine line between change and reaction. Bowing to the traditional conservatism of the southern "community," Rubin laments that "[t]he South is in danger today of losing its most precious possession, that regional quality, and the enemy is just as much within as without." [35] The Cold War rhetoric of "enemies within" signals the deployment of the South in the rhetorical battles of the Red-fearing 1950s—not the last time it would be so used (see below). The conservative strophe of *The Lasting South* was followed, in 1960, by the liberal antistrophe of *The Southerner as American,* nine essays by "Southerners, born, reared, and largely trained in the South," who were linked by the fear that the contemporary segregation crisis would repeat the secession crisis of a century earlier.[36]

The Reconstruction crisis was more likely to repeat than secession. The collective impact of the essays of *The Lasting South* is to line up the southern "community" for a broadside attack on its deracinated mirror image: postwar American "society," a mixture of visible and invisible threats, of aliens and weak patriots, of losers of China and pinko softies on Communism, of lonely crowds and hidden persuaders in business. The South was nothing like that, according to Rubin. The southerner naturally got "to know and enjoy almost everyone in his community, because by the very nature of small town life he [was] thrown in with them day after day, at work and at play." [37] Body snatchers could not succeed in the southern community, and the combine of jurists and sociologists at work on the body of the community could prescribe nothing but poison.

"New York" is the familiar image of the place where the nefarious forces of destruction nest. As a counterimage to the South, Rubin claims, "New York" shows no desire to "encumber" itself with a history.[38] Preferring southern myth to any alternative program of existence, the Rubin of *The Lasting South* argues that the South's relatively narrow range of social activities and few but happy social classes lead to an intensity of relationship among all members of the "imaged" community. Any infiltrator would be instantly recognized. And even though there was a class hierarchy in the South, Rubin claims that no jealousy or friction created a basis for class conflict.[39] The plantation economy, Rubin goes further to assert, entailed very little mobility in buying and selling or in actual migrations from place to place.[40] The broad, indirect hint seems clear: the southern community is the American answer to the Marxist paradigm of society as locked in class conflict and mortgaged to capitalistic forces. Why would a nation in danger, as the United States was in the midst of the Cold War, want to tamper with the internal systems of a region that could be its salvation? The emphasis on the image of the South induces an amnesia that makes it possible to forget, for instance, that in the actual South the buying and selling of human beings as slaves was pivotal to the plantation economy and rendered the "community" as capitalistic as any coven of Wall Street traders in wheat or varnish or cotton futures — as James Oakes argues in this collection. Under the power of the Image, the South in the 1950s becomes, then, not a historical result or outcome of social problems dating from the beginnings of chattel slavery in North America but rather a timeless or mythic struggle between the ever integrative "community" and the ever disintegrative modern society.

Race is always the spoiler, though, the historical slap on the face that breaks the amnesia, the hold of myth. Ironically, Rubin admits that the precursors who handed down the well-wrought image of the South also transmitted the sin. His own tortured position owes something, if not all, to the racial past that is so vital to the South's identity: "Had the Southerner been willing, in the 1910's, the 1920's, the 1930's, to adjust his thinking to the Negroes' growing development and to make the necessary accommodations, a situation need never have arisen where a Supreme Court could declare that 'separate' and 'equal' were contradictory terms."[41] The southerners of those decades were the sponsors of the southern renascence, those who created that image, that unity, that idea of the South that Rubin feels called upon to defend in other parts of his essay. The Twelve Southerners had indeed woven a nifty web of ideological heritage: they caught even those who wished to perpetuate their work.

The entrapment is easier to see if we look at Rubin's guardianship of the southern canon, his revisions and admissions, and the credentials he insisted on. The hinge was always race.

To be sure, *Southern Renascence* did include an essay by a black critic, Irene Edmunds on Faulkner. But that did not keep the volume as a whole and the literature it stood for from escaping charges of parochialism and special pleading. Willard Thorpe, in *American Literature,* did not mention the presence or absence of race in the table of contents or essays, but he did find fault in too much Fugitive-Agrarian "logrolling."[42] The anonymous reviewer in *The Nation* was more direct, faulting the volume for omitting "younger" authors (presumably those younger than Warren or Welty, who were in their early forties at the time) and "Negro authors" altogether.[43]

The issue was sensitive. Rubin had at least two masters to serve: the massed presence of his precursors in southern literature (who had left no recipe for including African-American authors among the southern community and who were still very much alive) and the gradually building conviction that some change had to occur. In a subsequent essay in his "image" series, "Southern Literature: The Historical Image," Rubin tried to reconcile the forces contending within himself and in the emerging field of southern literature.

On the one hand, as a literary modernist by temperament and training, Rubin had held certain beliefs about the separate spheres of literature and "ideological convictions" that were more prevalent then than now.[44] He read the chief black American author of the day, Richard Wright, as impeded by "social purpose" that diverted his fiction from "aesthetic grounds" into propaganda.[45] In the 1950s the word *propaganda* carried a stronger charge than it does today. Wright's membership in the Communist Party, as well as the manifest denial, in all of his works, of the splendor of the southern community black or white, made his admission to the canon impossible. Elsewhere in the same essay, however, Rubin found that Erskine Caldwell's "ideological convictions" did not offset Jeter Lester's "individuality" as a southerner and as a literary creation.[46] By the skin of his (Caldwell's) teeth, and by some surreptitious politicking with the language of literary criticism, Caldwell—who also flirted with Communism and Communists—was admitted into the canon when many of

Rubin's own brother critics excluded him. The problem of African-American membership appeared to be resolved with the appearance of Ralph Ellison's *Invisible Man* (1952). Here was a "Negro novelist," Rubin wrote, who could keep the emphasis on "novelist" and who could deploy the full regalia of the literary modernist movement *and* address "recent social and political developments."[47] That Rubin (and so many of his readers) did not read the manifest and complex politics of *Invisible Man* is one of the "problems" of southern literary history (and of American literary history more generally) that invite indictments such as Bové's. Nor did enough of them read Ellison's essays in controversy, eventually collected in *Shadow and Act* (1964). If they (we) had, there would have been less temptation to see *Invisible Man*, in New Critical terms, as untainted by politics or sociology.

One African-American writer in the canon, on the grounds of literary merit however problematic, established a precedent. Others could now be seen, usually in retrospect, as forerunners struggling toward the plateau of literature through the brier patch of social, political, cultural "setting." The enterprise of developing southern literary history is a retrospective process; we build a past from the present with certain devices and desires. In the anthologies Rubin was later (1970, 1979) to edit himself or with associates, African-American writing gained an ever increasing presence: first Booker T. Washington (Rubin, like many of his fellows, saw Du Bois not so much as author but rather as NAACP "agitator"),[48] Chesnutt, Ellison; then Douglass, James Weldon Johnson, Hurston, Wright, and others.

While the reigning teaching anthology for southern literature courses in college, the Beatty-Watkins-Young *Literature in the South* (1952; rev. 1968) kept a sort of silence on the issue of race (Washington was permitted to speak, but Douglass had to wait for the revised edition), Rubin kept the subject on the table. In "Notes on a Rear-Guard Action" (1964), he surveys the history of southern literature (much of which he had assembled) from the vantage point of the death of William Faulkner in the summer of 1962 and the enrollment of James Meredith at Ole Miss the following fall. His device in this essay is to enlist the Abraham of southern and American literature, Faulkner, in the cause of moderate-to-liberal involvement in the acknowledgment of race in the southern community of ideas. This essay was written at a difficult time for southern literature, for the pressure to join the bandwagon of change had impacted heavily on the southern writer, reducing the range of choices he or she felt possible and narrowing the acceptable sweep of "the tradition." These were the years of the Voting Rights Act of 1964, of freedom marches and assassinations, of Eudora Welty's "Must the Novelist Crusade?" (1965) and its answer "no."

Rubin's response as the leading literary historian of the South is indirect. He does not advocate a specific position on the political issue; that would violate his own rule of separation of the literary and the political. Rather, he constructs a southern literary past using the lives and works of selected literary men whose positions in the South (and on the South) might serve cumulatively as a model for the present. Using the prestige of the major figure of the present (Faulkner), Rubin undertakes to recover corresponding major figures in the ante- and postbellum periods of southern literary history—Poe and Clemens—whose examples establish the "tradition" of passionate ambivalence in situations of racial conflict involving the community. This design creates and perpetuates the Faulknerian, that is, problematic, tradition of feeling a lot but doing little when race and the image of the South collide.

Rubin's engagement with Poe, and through Poe with the "tradition" of Coleridgean unity as at its core southern, is a long and intricate story; Rubin has come back to it relatively recently in *The Edge of the Swamp* (1989). Here, let me just outline the engagement with Clemens as literary-historical entr'acte to his treatment of Faulkner, the civil rights witness.

Having established, as the central metaphor of his southern literary history, the posture of ambivalent contortion—the contrapposto he mentions repeatedly from Tate's "double focus" description of the modern southern writer ("*The Fugitive*, 1922–1925: A Personal Recollection Twenty Years After")—Rubin deploys it retrospectively in search of precedents. Cable, for example, had it in a limited supply ("Politics and the Novel: George W. Cable and the Genteel Tradition" [1970]). William Elliott, in the Old South, had it not at all because he was too invested in the ideological treasury of his society ("William Elliott Shoots a Bear" [1974]). Clemens, though, had it to the max. In his editorial introduction to the postbellum period in *Southern Writing: 1585–1920*, which he edited with Richard Beale Davis and C. Hugh Holman, Rubin places Clemens at the head of the congregation of writers of that period. His Clemens is the ambivalent South-hater of *Life on the Mississippi*, in love with the Edenic place but ready to dynamite the false front built by Walter Scott imitators. Unlike any other southern writer before Faulkner, Rubin claims in " 'The Begum of Bengal': Mark Twain and the South" (1975), Clemens brought "critical scrutiny" to bear upon the sacred "pieties" of southern life and cultural experience, but *from within* the passionate community of the South. In that way he

(Clemens) anticipated the great twentieth-century icon of southern divided-
ness, Quentin Compson, who said quite a lot about his deep moral turbulence
but did little except to kill himself when faced with the necessity of living in a
world of history.[49] One could also propose that "discovering" the "tradition"
of internal, passionate, conflicted love-hate *also* creates space for Rubin himself, as the literary historian of the South and in the South. Not surprisingly,
one of the warmest and fuzziest of modern southerners, Atticus Finch, takes
the same passionately conflicted position; Sundquist dissects him telling Scout
to hate the sin of lynching but to love the community that perpetrates it.

The Clemens-Twain-Faulkner-Quentin quartet figures centrally in Rubin's
solo anthology, *The Literary South* (1979). Through this complexly negotiated
southern identity—Clemens viewed retrospectively from the decades of social
turmoil in the South and through the prestige of the southern Nobel laure-
ate—Rubin constructs a psychomachia for southern literary history that pre-
serves the Agrarian/New Criticism edifice *and* admits race as synecdoche of
history.

In "Notes on a Rear-Guard Action," the critic uses Faulkner directly, not
through Quentin or another of his character-surrogates, to enact southern literature's "attitude" toward its own historical circumstances. For Rubin, Faulkner had marked the trail with *Light in August*. The powerful ambiguity of Joe
Christmas gives the requisite flesh and blood (the realistic mimesis) to the issue
of race and to the attitude of the southern critic: split between honor for the
stable and time-hallowed community and the moral imperative of equality,
the southerner (critic or writer) identifies with Joe Christmas, for whom race
is doom even though, with finesse, it might have been avoided. In this novel
Rubin could show that "the way that the book is written and what it shows"
are coincident.[50] Shifting to the collective pronoun, Rubin also shifts from the
descriptive to the prescriptive. *Light in August* traces a pattern all genuine
southerners *should* recognize and follow: "Both the right and the difficulty of
doing right were very sharp realities, and we could not ignore their existence.
So we worked out, as all human beings would naturally do, some very elaborate compromises with our integrity, and we persuaded ourselves that these
would suffice."[51] On one side of the fine line is allegiance to the "we," the community that provides the guaranteeing mimetic reference for all meaning. On
the other side is a kind of apostasy or estrangement, an alienation from "time
and place" that means death for the artist. Faulkner is the way out of the di-

lemma, for from the novel Rubin shifts to a resurrected Faulkner who "would have put on his coat and tie and hat and gone over to the campus, and stood quietly alongside of James Meredith," not at all unlike Atticus facing down his underclass neighbors at the Maycomb jailhouse.[52] What we know of Faulkner from biographies and his letters (and, as long as we are choosing a team from his characters, from Gavin Stevens and Chick Mallison) strongly suggests that he probably would not have desired to be involved in the desegregation of Ole Miss. But the pull of his literary gravity makes his imaginary attendance necessary; no other personification of the "community" will do.

The election of Jimmy Carter as president in 1976 did much to change (or to mark a change) in the meanings of southern community and southern history. Rubin responded to the change in *The American South: Portrait of a Culture* (1980), a collection of essays by several authors commemorating the admission of the South to the American mainstream—propaganda, of a sort, originally assembled for the United States Information Agency, proclaiming a South triumphant over the worst crimes of its apartheid. Whereas the part of race had been a cause of dispute in earlier works, in *The American South* there is no whiff of reaction. We are all rowing in the same direction. Several African-American authors contribute essays on African-American writing, and Rubin devotes most of his introduction to a reweaving of race, community, and image.

The pattern tends to decentralize race and to substitute community—to move history aside for myth. Rubin regrets the expense of so much antebellum southern intellectual energy on politics and oratory devoted to the defense of slavery. Not that John C. Calhoun, the major offender, was morally wrong: he was simply ignorant of the historical limitations on slavery. Expansion out of the South "could not possibly be made economically feasible" in Rubin's historical view, and so all of Calhoun's proslavery treatise writing amounts to a waste of his energies and the community's attention.[53] He was not evil, just a windbag.

The core of the community's "self-definition" was so strong that it survived Calhoun and the rest. It survived civil war too. "If southern sectional identity were dependent on slavery, then the loss of the war and the end of slavery should have destroyed that identity," Rubin proposes. "It did not."[54] Reasoning retrospectively from his idea of the community of palpable force, Rubin reinforces the southern myth by removing, or demoting, slavery from the list of reasons the Confederacy as a nation went to war. Behind this claim is the unstated one that historical interests have always been subordinate to metaphysical ones in the defining of the South.

Nor has the southern community held onto itself as an aristocratic remnant in a modern democracy. Whereas other conservative political-cultural movements of the twentieth century (e.g., T. S. Eliot's views as summarized in *Notes Toward a Definition of Culture* and the Action Française) were avowedly elitist, the Agrarian movement in the South, "by virtue of its roots in the southern community," was neither aristocratic nor snobbish. Furthermore, "[i]ts community assumptions saved it from intellectual hatred. It had no role for antisemitism or any other sort of xenophobia, either in its principles or its dynamics. . . . At heart it was not even pro- (or anti-) segregation, though the expected fealty was paid to that staple of white southern enterprise, for race relations were tangential to its concern, which was an assertion of the value of the humane community in protest and rebuke to dehumanization and materialistic, acquisitive society."[55] The southern Agrarians were closer soul brothers to another antebellum American writer, Henry David Thoreau, than to Calhoun. Both, I think, would have been surprised at the seating arrangement. And what literary historian now can elide the politics of Agrarianism and "the human community"? How does one "see" and rebuke "dehumanization and materialistic, acquisitive society" and not see the dehumanization of black human beings during slavery and since by a society so acquisitive and materialistic as to put dollar values on human beings and sell them for profit?

Rubin's sanguine, nostalgic revision of the Agrarian movement seems at least partially undermined by one of the essays in *The American South*. Blyden Jackson's personal memoir "Growing Up Black in the Old South and the New: Or, Mr. Wheat Goes with the Wind" exposes the elaborate network of southern conventions and rituals that kept the African American as effectively subordinate after emancipation as before. Jackson's experience of growing up black in the American South is closer to the one described by Ellison in *Invisible Man* than it is to the imagined sense of the southern community praised in Rubin's peroration.

Rubin's more recent work seems to continue in the vein of nostalgic detoxification of the southern image. Was slavery the cornerstone to southern identity, materially or psychologically, or both? No. Was the Agrarian ideology elitist (as some contemporary revisionists have claimed) or even fascist (as more extreme critics alleged in the 1930s)? No and No. Was southern public resistance to desegregation in the 1950s and 1960s a deep and determined sign of the majority's will to resist change? No. In *The Edge of the Swamp* (1989) Rubin goes so far as to recant Quentin's famous rejoinder to his roommate: "You cant [*sic*] understand it [the South]. You would have to be born there."

Ostensibly a reading of Simms, Poe, and Timrod, *The Edge of the Swamp* is also continuous with Rubin's decades-long attempt to weave literary and historical modes of expressing and knowing the South. Prominent among the items on his agenda in this book is an argument against Lewis Simpson on the one hand (whose work on southern literature and history Rubin finds insufficiently grounded in the particulars of time and place) and Eugene Genovese on the other (whose work proposes a South altogether too particularly capitalist and materialist).[56] Rubin prefers the sacred but accessible middle ground, which for him supports a South consistent with "historical common sense and human nature."[57]

What this effectively means is that the community definition of the South becomes ensconced as the one and only "natural" path to the South itself. The mind naturally apprehends the South this way, Rubin argues, and therefore is not stampeded by, to use two examples, the hypothesis of the South as an aristocratic enclave or the prominence of racial guilt at the core of the southern self. The plantation, Rubin asserts, was in essence and in fact a middle-class operation that Americans north and south would have recognized as such.[58] "Historical common sense" tells us that it was the antebellum equivalent of the big house in the suburbs. And the antebellum southern slave owner was no seething cauldron of racial guilt and hate; he (not she) was no different from a present-day tobacco grower who would plow his crop under if there were another way to make a living.[59]

Perhaps Rubin's reaction to the poles of southern discourse, as he sees them, is ill considered. To reduce history to such a low common denominator as "common sense" risks sapping it of its potential to illuminate the present. If the past *was* the present except for accessories, why be curious about it? Even though the dilution of history-as-difference enhances Rubin's "community" concept, by leading to the claim that southerners of whatever century would recognize one another as brethren, his assertion of the commonality of past and present in fact reduces the South to banality: slaves = sticks of tobacco, the quarters = the urban ghetto. There is the real amnesia.

Notes

1   George B. Tindall, "The Central Theme Revisited," in *The Southerner as American*, ed. Charles Grier Sellers Jr. (Chapel Hill, 1960), 126.

2   Allen Tate, "The Profession of Letters in the South," in *Essays of Four Decades* (Denver, 1968), 525.

3   W. J. Cash, *The Mind of the South* (New York, 1941), x.

4   Cash, *Mind of the South*, 389–90.

5   Lawrence Buell, "Literary History as a Hybrid Genre," in *New Historical Literary Study: Essays on Reproducing Texts, Representing History,* ed. Jeffrey N. Cox and Larry J. Reynolds (Princeton, N.J., 1993), 217.

6   Paul A. Bové, *Mastering Discourse: The Politics of Intellectual Culture* (Durham, N.C., 1992), 115.

7   Bové, *Mastering Discourse*, 116.

8   Buell, "Literary History," 223.

9   Allen Tate, "Remarks on the Southern Religion," in *I'll Take My Stand: The South and the Agrarian Tradition,* by Twelve Southerners (New York, 1930), 160.

10   Tate, "Remarks," 160.

11   Tate, "Remarks," 160.

12   Tate, "Remarks," 162.

13   Louis D. Rubin Jr., *South: Modern Southern Literature in Its Cultural Setting* (Garden City, N.Y., 1961), 11.

14   Richard Weaver, "Aspects of the Southern Philosophy," in *Southern Renascence*, ed. Louis D. Rubin Jr. and Robert Jacobs (Baltimore, 1953), 14–15.

15   Louis D. Rubin Jr., "Thomas Wolfe in Time and Place," in Rubin and Jacobs, *Southern Renascence*, 290–91.

16   Louis D. Rubin Jr., "The Way It Was with Southern Literary Study," *Mississippi Quarterly* 43 (spring 1990): 149 ff.

17   The "Rubin generation" was first used by Jefferson Humphries in his introduction to *Southern Literature and Literary Theory* (Athens, Ga., 1990), vii–xviii. Rubin denied the existence of such a generation in "A Letter to the Editor," *Mississippi Quarterly* 45 (spring 1992): 189–93. A partial list of the scholars and critics who have been associated with Rubin either as his students or as colleagues at Chapel Hill is impressive: Thadious Davis, Fred Hobson, Anne Goodwyn Jones, Lucinda MacKethan, Susan Snell, Robert Phillips. If one adds the names of those whose books have appeared in series Rubin has edited for Louisiana State University Press, the list grows like Topsy—and includes the author of this essay. Since it is now the case that scholars whom Rubin has helped to train at the University of North Carolina are now training others, it might be more correct to speak of a Rubin dynasty.

18 Buell, "Literary History," 217.

19 Buell, "Literary History," 216.

20 Louis D. Rubin Jr., "The Curious Death of the Novel: Or, What to Do about Tired Literary Critics," in *The Curious Death of the Novel: Essays in American Literature* (Baton Rouge, 1967), 15.

21 Memo and syllabus pertaining to "The Southern Novel and the Southern Community," an NEH Summer Institute at the University of North Carolina, Chapel Hill, 1989, 1.

22 Louis D. Rubin Jr., *William Elliott Shoots a Bear: Essays on the Southern Literary Imagination* (Baton Rouge, 1975), ix.

23 Robert B. Heilman, "The Southern Temper," in Rubin and Jacobs, *Southern Renascence,* 3.

24 Heilman, "Southern Temper," 7.

25 Heilman, "Southern Temper," 8–9.

26 He remembered in *The Curious Death of the Novel* and in subsequent comments.

27 Norman Podhoretz, "Southern Claims," *Partisan Review* 21 (January–February 1954): 119.

28 Podhoretz, "Southern Claims," 122.

29 Louis D. Rubin Jr., "The Historical Image of Modern Southern Writing," *Journal of Southern History* 22 (May 1956): 150.

30 Rubin, "Historical Image," 150.

31 Rubin, "Historical Image," 154 (emphasis in original).

32 Louis D. Rubin Jr. and James J. Kilpatrick, eds. *The Lasting South: Fourteen Southerners Look at Their Home* (Chicago, 1957), n.p.

33 Rubin and Kilpatrick, *Lasting South,* x.

34 Kilpatrick, "Conservatism and the South," in Rubin and Kilpatrick, *Lasting South,* 203.

35 Louis D. Rubin Jr., "An Image of the South," in Rubin and Kilpatrick, *Lasting South,* 2.

36 Sellers, *Southerner as American.*

37 Rubin, "Image of the South," 4.

38 Rubin, "Image of the South," 3.

39 Rubin, "Image of the South," 7.

40 Rubin, "Image of the South," 6.

41 Rubin, "Image of the South," 11.

42 Willard Thorpe, review of *Southern Renascence,* in *American Literature* 26 (January 1955): 575.

43 "Southern Authors," *The Nation,* October 17, 1953, 317.

44 Louis D. Rubin Jr., "Southern Literature: The Historical Image," in *South,* 12.

45 Rubin, "Southern Literature," 19.

46 Rubin, "Southern Literature," 12.

47 Rubin, "Southern Literature," 13, 20 ff.

48 Rubin, *Lasting South,* 12.

49 Rubin, *William Elliott,* 58–59.

50 Rubin, *Curious Death,* 139.

51 Rubin, *Curious Death,* 145.

52 Rubin, *Curious Death,* 149.

53 Louis D. Rubin Jr., ed., *The American South: Portrait of a Culture* (Baton Rouge, 1980), 4.

54   Rubin, *American South*, 4.

55   Rubin, *American South*, 12.

56   Louis D. Rubin Jr., *The Edge of the Swamp: A Study in the Literature and Society of the Old South* (Baton Rouge, 1989), 17 ff, 26.

57   Rubin, *Edge of the Swamp*, 41.

58   Rubin, *Edge of the Swamp*, 39.

59   Rubin, *Edge of the Swamp*, 43–44.

∾ The End of the South as an American Problem

JOHN EGERTON

FOR AS LONG AS THE LOWER reaches of the North American continent have been commonly referred to as "the South"—which is to say, since the reigning white overlords of the region started rallying their forces in defiance of the national will about 150 years ago—this obstreperous section of the United States has been a puzzle, a preoccupation, and a problem to the nation and to itself.

Before that, in the seventeenth and eighteenth centuries, as the United States slowly emerged from colonial dependency to assert its nationhood through revolution, a sense of common purpose inspired unity and obscured regional differences. The colony-cum-state of Virginia was not so much southern as central during the early period (1789–1824), when it produced four of the first five presidents of the United States. The thirteen colonies that became the charter states of the new nation were coastal jurisdictions stretching from New England to Georgia; the rest of the country, including its southern extension—the future states from Tennessee and Alabama westward to Texas—was then variously called the frontier, the territories, the West.

What was to become our South got its identity and its cohesion in the first half of the nineteenth century as the young nation fell into deepening internal conflict over the economic, political, social, and moral questions surrounding slavery. Many other distinctions contributed to the cultural divergence of the region; climate and geography ordained a society more rural and agricultural than urban and industrial, and its ethnic makeup, its class structure, and its political, educational, and religious institutions all developed a character and personality quite unlike those in the North. But these were minor and inconsequential differences compared with those that had to do with race—with white and black, European and African, free and slave.

In the early decades of the nineteenth century, as the slave trade was curtailed and slavery was abolished in the North, the white leaders of the southern states drew ever closer to one another in their defense of this social system and their determination to extend it into the western states and territories. It was then, in the 1840s and beyond, that the South became an American problem, a problem so grave and threatening that 250 years of shared history would not be enough to prevent a shattering civil war.

Far from resolving the animosities and smoothing over the differences that separated the North and the South, the War Between the States set into stone a pattern of conflict and invidious comparison that would not be worn away by another century of passing time. The victors followed conquest with economic and political domination, as victors invariably do, but they lacked the wisdom, the patience, and the vision to bring about genuine democratic reform. When their misguided self-righteousness could produce no model for the attainment of racial and social equality in a vanquished population not far from being half white and half black, the forces of occupation withdrew, leaving the remnant confederacy of reactionary Bourbons to resume their old way of life.

The bargain that ended Reconstruction left economic power in the hands of the northern victors but returned political and social power to the southern white men who had held it previously or to their successors in privilege. In short order, they disfranchised the black minority and systematically imposed segregation and inequality by law. The myth of "separate but equal" development not only assured the general disadvantage of black citizens but also perpetuated the inferiority of the South in the national scheme of things. In continuation of this well-established pattern, the South would remain an American problem right on into the twentieth century. When the Great Depression laid the United States low and ushered in Franklin D. Roosevelt and his New Deal recovery programs in the 1930s, the South was flat on the bottom of the national economic heap.

In order for the white South to explain and justify and accept its lowly status in twentieth-century America, it had to believe that the "good life" of the aristocratic Old South had been destroyed by invading barbarians from the North; there couldn't be a "Lost Cause" without an enemy to lose it to. And the rest of the country, agitated and obsessed as it often was with its own real or imagined "demons"—the Native American remnant, the immigrant hordes, robber barons, corrupt politicians, gangsters, religious fanatics, and various radical elements — needed the South, or some such convenient dumping place, to gaze upon with smug condescension. (If the South had won the war, no doubt it would have done the same.)

As time went on, a sense of permanent estrangement came to characterize the relationship between the region and the nation; long after the wounds of war had scarred over, there remained this separation, this distance. White men of power and privilege, in the North as well as the South, apparently perceived their self-interest to be best served by a certain arm's-length coolness. Each side saw itself as different/better and the other as different/worse. But if there was mutuality in the arrangement, there was also one-sided advantage; the South had blindly played into the North's hands, accepting continued isolation and bottom-rung inferiority as the price it would willingly pay for a free hand in perpetuating Jim Crow segregation and white supremacy.

Considering all this historical baggage, it's no wonder that the Dixieland states came to be seen as a national irritant, a festering sore on the body politic — and not much wonder, either, that the nation couldn't summon the will or the nerve to lance the boil. Trite as it may be to say it, the old saw rings true: if the South hadn't existed, the nation would have had to invent it.

The depression still had not ended when World War II began; in fact, it was the economic and social stimulus of the war itself, more than any other force, that jolted the South and the nation into a volatile new world of peril and promise. But in the postwar era, the South once again missed a golden opportunity to begin a self-prescribed process of healing and reform, and it was thus unprepared when its own black minority, inspired by religious leaders and legal experts devoted to the biblical and constitutional promises of justice and equality, finally demanded redress in the courts and in the streets.

And so the much criticized and still rebellious region continued to be pictured as something of an embarrassment to the United States until the mid-1960s, when new federal laws and court decisions finally destroyed the "separate but equal" myth. The scene of domestic conflict then began to shift to various stages elsewhere in the country, and the scourge of injustice and inequality that had for so long been interpreted as the South's affliction inexorably came to be seen as the nation's.

Throughout two and a half centuries of slavery and another of segregation, the nonsouthern people of the United States were conditioned to assume moral high ground, from whence to gaze down judgmentally upon the backward South as a benighted nether region of pervasive inferiority. But since the mid-1960s, that air of superiority has almost completely evaporated. Now, with the country as a whole beset by racial, ethnic, social, and cultural conflict, it may be more accurate to say that *America* is an American problem—and the South could turn out to be not so much the perpetual source of the trouble as a contemporary key to the solution.

The preponderance of evidence amassed in the essays in this volume affirms the South's negative image throughout most of the long sweep of American history, contradicting the largely positive impression commanded by this avowedly democratic and demonstrably powerful nation. Particularly in the years from 1860 to 1945 was this so. The eleven rebellious states that made up the Confederacy were not rescued from their plight by secession or civil war, by Union occupation or Reconstruction, by segregation, depression, or two world wars. There were, of course, a privileged few southerners who lived quite comfortably in the years between 1870 and 1930, and a larger number who made up the budding middle class of merchants, yeoman farmers, and skilled professionals, but the overwhelming majority, white and black, were simply poor—often miserably, desperately, inescapably poor. Consider this profile of the region in 1930, just before the New Deal appeared on the scene:

Of the approximately thirty million southern people, seven of every ten were Caucasians (the vast majority of them Anglo-Saxon Protestants), and the rest were partially or fully of African descent. Two-thirds of this population lived on farms or in villages of a few hundred people, and two-thirds of all those rural residents were tenant farmers or sharecroppers whose annual cash income wavered between negligible and nonexistent. Exceedingly fortunate—and exceedingly rare—was the family that could count on a thousand dollars of spendable income annually.

They were serfs, pure and simple—that is, the ones who were able to find and hold any job, however menial. They sorely lacked the rudimentary necessities of food, clothing, and shelter. If they had anything at all to drive, it was apt to be an overworked mule, not a tractor or a truck or a car. In return for their backbreaking labor to produce such inedible goods as cotton, tobacco, and coal, they earned at most only a dollar or two a day—and their bosses quickly got it back at the commissary or the company store.

They lived for the most part in houses we would now characterize as hovels—unpainted and uninsulated shacks with no gas for heating or cooking, no electric lights, no running water, no telephones, radios, fans, or window screens. Both the quantity and quality of health care available to them left much to be desired. They suffered far more from disease, mental illness, malnutrition, and starvation than citizens elsewhere in the country. Mothers and babies were twice as likely to die in childbirth in Alabama or Louisiana as in Connecticut or Nebraska or Oregon; similar disparities characterized the fatality rate for most other hazards, from alcoholism and venereal disease to workplace accidents and murders. Women and children were as likely to be found working long hours in the fields and textile mills as they were to be at home or in school.

Politics and religion served as the two principal spectator sports, and an endless parade of demagogues and charlatans kept the masses astir with alternating exhortations to blind faith and know-nothing fanaticism. Bigotry and intolerance flourished in the South, not only against blacks but also to the detriment of Catholics, Jews, foreigners—and of course Yankees. Virtually every form of violence was far more prevalent there than elsewhere: North Carolina had ten times as many murders per capita as New York; of the twenty-seven hundred lynchings reported in the United States between 1890 and 1930, four out of every five took place in the South, and the vast majority of the victims were black men.

The public and civic life of the region was for most people a barren and monotonous void. Libraries, schools, and colleges were effectively reserved for the privileged—when they existed at all—and in the best of circumstances they were deficient in resources and inferior in quality. Millions of southern laboring men and women were illiterate, and their children, having little or no exposure to newspapers, magazines, and books, were doomed to bear the same handicap. Only white men (and in rare instances, white women) served as law enforcement officers, judges, jurors, or jailers. White women in general were allowed few opportunities to assert their individuality, though they were not an oppressed class in the same way that blacks were. Jails and prisons were more like medieval dungeons than so-called correctional institutions.

Not even one in every five adults regularly cast ballots or otherwise participated in the political process, and elected officials often took advantage of their long and unchallenged incumbency to compile careers marked by incompetence, favoritism, or outright corruption. In fact, if there is one indictment above all others that can be fairly applied to the South in the first half of the twentieth century, it is the abject failure of its politicians to lead and serve with positive distinction. Notwithstanding a few statesmen here and there, they were on the whole unworthy of the people to whom they had sworn allegiance, and they deserve the judgment and condemnation of history for keeping the South hopelessly poor, economically dependent on the North, racially divided internally, and all but immobilized by a selectively reconstructed remembrance of its checkered past.

All in all, the contrast between life in Dixie and life in other regions of the country in those years was conspicuous, accentuated by bad attitudes on both sides—by brash, haughty Yankees and proud, resentful rebels. There were a few creative endeavors at which southerners did often excel (talking, writing, cooking, and music making come quickly to mind), but the lingering stereotypes that seemed to cling to southern people of both races like ticks on a hound were devoid of any positive elements. The derogatory images could be painful and infuriating, but the harsh reality was torment enough: six or seven decades after the Civil War, the South still had the look and feel of an antebellum peasant society—an isolated, race-obsessed, class-riven, violent, intolerant, educationally deficient, hand-to-mouth society that was rapidly losing its best and brightest citizens in the north-bound migration stream.

It was virtually mandatory in southern white society in those days to celebrate the Lost Cause of the Confederacy and to ignore or deny altogether the manifest consequences of insistent and persistent white supremacy. Native sons and daughters courted the wrath and rejection of their peers if they dared to point out that segregation imposed a competitive disadvantage on almost all southerners vis-à-vis other Americans. Not until the New Deal days was there the remotest prospect of reform—and even then, the issue of racial discrimination was cautiously averted, and measurable improvements in the lives of the South's poverty-stricken majority were painfully slow in coming.

Finally, in 1938, the National Emergency Council issued its "Report to the President on Economic Conditions of the South," downplaying the fact that a committee of white southerners had actually drafted and refined the document. In a letter to that committee before it began its deliberations, President Roosevelt subscribed to a point of view that was widely shared outside the South and would be quoted frequently in the years to come. "It is my conviction," he declared, "that the South presents right now the Nation's No. 1 economic problem—the Nation's problem, not merely the South's." (Almost no one knew, then or later, that the president's letter, including that explicit assessment, had been drafted for him by a white southerner, New Deal attorney Clifford Durr of Montgomery, Alabama.)

The white South in 1938 was not ready for social change, to say nothing of racial equality. That very report on economic conditions spelled out all sorts of disparities between southern and nonsouthern peoples, but it studiously avoided all but the most oblique references to race and had absolutely nothing to say about discrimination per se. In Birmingham that fall, some fifteen hundred delegates — progressive whites and blacks of every economic class — organized the Southern Conference for Human Welfare to address the social problems southerners faced, but they were soon assailed as left-wing radicals and Communist fellow travelers by the reactionary ruling class, and the reformers would never attract enough committed allies to be seen as a mass movement.

It was also in the fall of 1938 that Roosevelt got a strong dose of conservative reality at the polls. In the national elections midway through his second term in the White House, the president could not prevent the progressive wing of the Democratic Party from sustaining heavy losses, as the Republicans captured more than seventy seats in both houses of Congress. Ironically, the housecleaning was energized by a reactionary revolt among southern Democrats who had become implacable enemies of FDR and his reformist New Deal philosophy. World War II may have been all that saved Roosevelt himself from defeat in 1940 and again in 1944.

Lest it be thought that the more enlightened North was doing a far better job than the South in extending democracy to African Americans and other racial minorities, a glance at the abundance of evidence to the contrary is in order. By 1940, more than three million of the nation's thirteen million black citizens were living outside the South, most of them having joined the great exodus from Dixie to escape the hazards and terrors of everyday life in the region. Life in the North — the vaunted Promised Land — was in some ways better for the southern immigrants, but segregation and lack of opportunity followed them wherever they went.

There was only one African American — a member of the House of Representatives from Chicago — serving in the U.S. Congress in the 1930s, and there wouldn't be but one more until 1954. Discrimination in employment and housing was a serious problem almost everywhere blacks began to relocate. In Boston, Philadelphia, Chicago, and most cities across the North, de facto segregation was commonplace in hotels, restaurants, and other public accommodations. California, Oregon, Michigan, and Colorado were among numerous states with laws prohibiting intermarriage. In the District of Columbia, seat of our national government and repository of our documents of liberty, segregation was almost as rigid as it was in Atlanta or Birmingham or Memphis. All branches of the armed forces were segregated, and the service academies were virtually all white. The Red Cross at first barred black blood donors outright and then segregated the contents of its blood banks. Even such reputed founts of wisdom and knowledge as Princeton University were lily white to the marrow of their bones, and so were many state universities.

Still, nobody did it quite like the South. Most of its churches preached white supremacy, its educational institutions practiced it, its businesses and industries swore by it, its police and courts enforced it, its state and local laws spelled it out in so many words. Contrary to the assertions of many, it was not the unlettered and unpolished masses of white southerners who invented and insisted on segregation; rather, it was the exalted guardians of the public trust, backed up by the leadership of such mainline groups as the medical and bar associations, the chambers of commerce, the civic clubs — and all of those with the acquiescence, if not the outright encouragement, of their lodge brothers at the national level.

The South's political, economic, spiritual, and intellectual leaders rarely spoke or acted, even in private, against the prevailing laws and customs of segregation and white supremacy. All the more conspicuous and admirable, therefore, were the notable exceptions to this pattern — a relative handful of men and women, black and white, who tried all through the thirties, forties, and fifties to introduce positive reforms into the region. Their collective biography is an inspiring story in its own right. Different though they were from one another, they all ended up on the side of progressive social change, opposite the reactionary men and women who were willing to pursue any course, no matter how extreme, in order to keep the South from surrendering its undemocratic claim to segregation and white supremacy.

Although there is hardly enough space here for more than a partial roll call, it does seem appropriate, even essential, to name some of the people whose long-ago visions of a reformed South have turned out to be closer to the evolving makeup and character of the region than have the backward-looking gazes of their adversaries.

From the beginning of the thirties, and even earlier, a few organizations managed to generate an interest in southern social problems by engaging in activities that raised questions about racial and socioeconomic inequality. Some, such as the Commission on Interracial Cooperation in Atlanta and the Southern Tenant Farmers Union in rural Arkansas, were founded and based in the region; others, such as the National Association for the Advancement of Colored People and the Julius Rosenwald Fund, were headquartered in the North. All of these groups were led either by native southerners or by people whose experiences had given them an intimate knowledge of social problems in the southern and border states.

In this early scattering of activists and reformers was a mixture of well-known and little-known individuals: James Weldon Johnson, Howard A. Kester, Walter White, H. L. Mitchell, W. E. B. Du Bois, Will Alexander, Charlotte Hawkins Brown, Myles Horton, Charles H. Houston, Edwin Embree, Thurgood Marshall, Don West, Mary McLeod Bethune, Claude Williams, Charles S. Johnson, Jessie Daniel Ames, Langston Hughes, James Dombrowski, and others.

The Southern Conference for Human Welfare in 1938 and the Southern Regional Council in 1944 brought more progressives to the fore as the South gradually awakened from its long post–Civil War slumber. Frank Porter Graham, Benjamin Mays, Lucy Randolph Mason, Grace T. Hamilton, Aubrey Williams, Gordon B. Hancock, Clark Foreman, Horace Mann Bond, Virginia F. Durr, Osceola McKaine, Guy B. Johnson, Rufus Clement, Witherspoon Dodge, Albert Dent, and Dorothy Rogers Tilly were among the most visible of these.

All through the thirties and forties and into the fifties, there were southern-born novelists and journalists living in and outside the region who used the power of the written word to nudge the South toward reform. Richard Wright, Erskine Caldwell, Zora Neale Hurston, Lillian Smith, John H. McCray, W. J. Cash, J. Saunders Redding, James Agee, Robert L. Vann, Stetson Kennedy, Robert S. Abbott, William Faulkner, Roscoe Dunjee, Thomas Sancton, Ted Poston, Ralph McGill, Ralph Ellison, Hodding Carter, P. B. Young, Virginius Dabney, Arna Bontemps, and Jonathan Daniels all contributed in greater or lesser degree to this effort.

As it happens, these short rosters include roughly equal numbers of whites and blacks; the parity is symbolic of the stake both races have had in progressive social reform throughout southern history. Richard Wright said it succinctly for all African Americans in 1941: "If we perish, America will perish."

And as Martin Luther King Jr. and others, black and white, would declare a quarter century later, the freedom of black southerners was inseparably linked with the liberation of every American, for segregation and inequality held us all in bondage.

A few southern public servants, elected and appointed, could be counted with these others on the side of favoring a reformation in the states of the Old South. The rules of segregation assured that this list at first would be made up almost exclusively of white males: Congressman Maury Maverick of Texas, Senator Claude Pepper of Florida, Supreme Court justice Hugo L. Black of Alabama, federal district judge J. Waties Waring of South Carolina, Governors Ellis Arnall of Georgia and James E. Folsom of Alabama, Virginia state assemblyman Francis Pickens Miller, and a few others. Federal appeals court judge William H. Hastie became the first African American to join this small circle when he was appointed to the bench by President Roosevelt in 1937. (FDR also named black "advisers" to a number of administrative posts in the New Deal and chose Benjamin O. Davis Sr., a career soldier, to be the first black general in the U.S. Armed Forces.)

Academia contributed indirectly to the cadre of reformers. Howard University in Washington, under its longtime president Mordecai Johnson, was by most assessments the premier model of both scholarship and social responsibility among black institutions; on its standout faculty were such respected activist-scholars as historian Rayford W. Logan, political scientist Ralph J. Bunche, sociologist E. Franklin Frazier, and poet Sterling Brown. The University of North Carolina was a similar beacon on the white side, with playwright Paul Green, the university press under W. T. Couch, and the social science faculty under Howard W. Odum getting the most attention—they and the university's liberal president, Frank Porter Graham.

The great black exodus from Dixie in the depression and war years robbed the South of an abundance of talent, from major league baseball star Jackie Robinson and all the professional athletes who came after him to Louis Armstrong and the scores of musicians who made jazz and swing the most popular music of the thirties and forties. The South spawned other noted northern black leaders, too: labor activist A. Philip Randolph was from Florida, singer-actor Paul Robeson had ancestral roots in North Carolina, District of Columbia human rights advocate Mary Church Terrell was born in Memphis, and Channing Tobias, a native of Georgia, was a respected figure in the YMCA and other public-interest organizations. Florida native James Weldon Johnson was the first black executive director of the NAACP.

The white South also sustained heavy migration losses throughout most of the century separating the Civil War from the civil rights movement. For countless hundreds of creative and talented men and women, life elsewhere in the country simply offered more opportunity and more promise than life in the repressive environment of the segregated South.

All these people with southern origins and with visions of a southern reformation held out the promise of change even in the somber days of rigid segregation that filled the entire first half of the twentieth century. Because their views were consonant with the democratic ideals so deeply embedded in American history—and because fortune has thus far looked kindly on this imperfect nation—the progressive southerners ended up on the "right" side of that history, on the side of the one nation indivisible, with liberty and justice for all. Thomas Jefferson, articulate southern gentleman that he was, had long since given us the words to proclaim our freedom—among them the "self-evident truth" that all men (and presumably women) are created equal. The attainment of that ideal remains for us still—southerners and all Americans—the great unmet challenge of our life as a nation.

In many ways, the South and its people, black and white, still suffer from their long history of racial discrimination. But the tide of legalized segregation was turned between 1954 and 1965, and since then the region has made significant social and economic strides. Two profoundly symbolic events in the 1960s indelibly marked the turning. The first was on August 28, 1963, when a quarter of a million people at the Lincoln Memorial in Washington—and millions more on television—heard the Reverend Martin Luther King Jr., a black native of Georgia, deliver his spellbinding "I Have a Dream" oration. The second was on March 15, 1965, when a joint session of the United States Congress and a vast television audience heard President Lyndon B. Johnson, a white native of Texas, invoke the words of the civil rights anthem "We Shall Overcome" in putting the full weight of his office behind passage of the 1965 Voting Rights Act.

With quickening speed over the past thirty years, the South has cast off the fetters of racial and regional inferiority and taken its rightful place in the national circle of citizenship. Economic and racial problems that once were considered paramount have diminished to such an extent that many people of both races in and outside the region now see the South as a more appealing place to live than any other part of the country. The so-called Sunbelt—an image-conscious, quasi-mythical new Promised Land—now beckons investors, young fortune seekers, retirees, and even many of the migrants and exiles who left in anger years ago. This is no longer a shunned address, a dreaded destination; in fact, the very term *Sunbelt* has an intentional glow, an enticing sheen, in favorable contrast to the new and negative tag that clings to some parts of the North: the "rust belt."

The extent of some changes is simply astonishing. In 1940, most of the southern states effectively denied the ballot to all except a token few black citizens, but now, blacks in the South register and vote in percentages that closely parallel those of whites. Fifty years ago, there were virtually no black elected public officials in the South at any level, and fewer than a hundred nationwide, but by 1994 there were more than eight thousand in the country, and seven of every ten—more than fifty-five hundred—were the chosen representatives of voters in the southern and border states. Those same states elected more than half of the forty African-American members (thirty-nine Democrats, one Republican) of the 103d Congress, which took office in 1993—and not a single one of them perished in the 1994 midterm-election landslide that gave the Republicans controlling majorities in both houses. (Some were jeopardized, however, by pending lawsuits challenging the configuration of the majority-black districts from which they come.) Blacks have also been elected in recent years to serve as mayors of many of the South's largest cities, and one, Douglas Wilder, was voted in as governor of Virginia in 1989.

The South's public schools were completely segregated by law until the Supreme Court declared such statutes unconstitutional in 1954; forty years later, biracial or multiracial enrollment was a more commonplace characteristic of the schools in this region than it was in most other parts of the nation. And in the categories of employment and housing, two more fundamental indicators of societal stability, southerners in general and black southerners in particular could look back on a fairly consistent pattern of both relative and absolute progress since segregation was outlawed.

These four factors—politics, education, employment, and housing—are like the legs that support a solid table; when properly constructed, they should bring about stability, balance, and equity. Without in any way suggesting that the South has built a perfect table, it seems fair to say that it has strengthened every leg for all its citizens over the past fifty years. The beleaguered South that Franklin Roosevelt saw as the nation's most pressing domestic problem in 1938 is now at least as functional as the other regions; indeed, the condition of its economic and social health elicits a certain note of envy in many states from New England to the West Coast.

But the South, of all places, should know better than to assume an attitude of prideful arrogance over this ironic turn of events. However much solid improvement there has been in the region's record of providing more and better job opportunities, schools, housing, and political clout for all its citizens, the fact remains that the continuing problems in these areas—and in health, welfare, public safety, and other sectors as well—are serious, chronic, and national in scope.

Unemployment, underemployment, homelessness, and hopelessness plague millions of southerners, no less than other Americans. The South has its share of bad schools, too—and a great many that are still segregated. The struggle of every American to grow up in safety and good health, to get a decent education, to find a satisfactory place to live, to have a rewarding career, and to be a productive citizen is at least as much of a challenge in Georgia or Louisiana as it is in Connecticut or Illinois. The bittersweet bounty of television and other technological wonders of the modern age is by no means confined to one class or race or region; their blessings and curses fall willy-nilly on one and all. The violent and destructive drug culture that now plagues so much of contemporary American life is pitilessly indiscriminate, wreaking devastation in rural areas as well as cities, in wealthy communities as in poor ones—and in the South no less than the rest of the country. The daily exchange of verbal cannon fire over the issues that divide Americans these days—gun control, abortion, crime and punishment, racial and ethnic and gender hostility—is every bit as bombastic in the South as in the North.

Even in the realm of politics—probably the most transformed of all our basic institutions in its assurance of genuine equity—the South has not found a short-cut route to a democratic utopia. Instead, those who work for political change frequently find themselves linked to others of every stripe who, like the proverbial sausage makers, labor with uneven success at the messy, ugly, thankless, and all too often fruitless task of lawmaking.

The South's political history in the last half of the twentieth century is profoundly puzzling in many ways. Consider, for example, this anomaly: the blacks and white liberals who challenged the reactionary Democrats in the generation before the civil rights movement won their case—but never won control of the party machinery or the electorate. Conservative Democrats and Republicans (the latter a minuscule and virtually powerless fragment when segregation was in full blossom) have managed through most of this period to maintain the upper hand in southern politics at every level, from the local courthouses to the halls of Congress. The fall of segregation in the South was a victory for liberalism but not for liberals. (One explanation for this paradox surely must be that the defeat of segregation was not a defeat of individual segregationists; their racism may be in remission, but it flares up at the slightest provocation.)

And then there is this to ponder: the South has provided the last three Democratic presidents of the United States (and four of the last five, if you count Harry Truman, a border-state politician whose Kentucky ancestors fought for the Confederacy). All of them sprang from Baptist roots in the rural South. All were patterned in the traditional, mainstream mold of the centrist national Democrats (liberal or progressive, by southern standards), and they paid their dues as loyal servants of the party. What's more, the committed efforts of Harry Truman, Lyndon Johnson, Jimmy Carter, and Bill Clinton to bind up the nation's racial wounds and close the book on inequality have been far more extensive and more productive than the initiatives of almost all our other presidents, going back to George Washington (the one exception being the Kentuckian Abraham Lincoln). Yet throughout their tenure in office, the modern southern presidents aroused—still arouse—more angry opposition from conservative southern whites than from just about anyone else.

What could be more enigmatic than the eternal vicissitudes of politics? The eternal ambivalence of white southerners, perhaps. After almost a half century of incremental reforms in race relations—reforms that were generated from within and without by blacks and whites, liberals and progressives and even a few conservatives—the unabashedly racist and reactionary Democrats who once ruled the South with an iron hand have long since gone with the wind, evaporated into space like a faded nightmare. They were followed in office by a wave of moderate to progressive "New South" governors and members of Congress, three of whom went on to the presidency. But now, in one more twist of irony, there is a new generation of political leaders in the region—not the reformers who turned the South away from white supremacy, but the national Republicans, whose last successful venture below the Mason-Dixon line was a campaign to end, by force of arms, a racially motivated rebellion of white conservatives well over a century ago.

These political conundrums can perhaps be explained in part as classic examples of the South's chronic propensity for self-inflicted harm. To put it simply: even when it wins, it loses. A more positive—and less cynical—interpretation is that only the most extreme fringe element of political candidates any longer pledges allegiance to racial bigotry; the vast majority are compelled to acknowledge the inclusiveness of contemporary political discourse. This is a direct legacy of the hard-won Democratic reforms of the past sixty years. All of the southerners who have occupied the White House for the Democratic Party since the end of World War II brought with them a worldview, as much pragmatic as philosophical, that the idealistic principles of American democracy had to become a living reality for every citizen. To their credit, virtually all black southerners and a substantial proportion of whites now share that vision, or so the public opinion polls and the campaign promises of most candidates tell us.

But if the rhetoric of politicians is no longer blatantly racist, the reality of separation and estrangement is increasingly evident in almost every segment of American society, and disturbing new manifestations of racial and ideological conflict regularly press painfully upon the public consciousness, like a persistent toothache. In a curious and unexpected way, the South has at last reached parity with the rest of the nation, if only because whatever shortcomings and failings the region still has are now at least as evident in the East and Midwest and West as they are there.

All of which begs another question: Does the South have collective qualities of character and personality arising from its history that might now be summoned to point the nation toward higher ground? It seems prudent not to overstate such a claim. After all, this is the same South that in the past so vigorously defended slavery, that invented segregation, that resisted even the most modest attempts to nourish simple justice. Furthermore, the South traditionally has been identified with political, religious, economic, and social conservatism—and conservatism by definition has more to do with resisting change than with stimulating it. The conservative Republican avalanche of 1994 was nowhere more powerful than in the South, and southern members of Congress were among the principal instigators of it.

As the United States gropes for a central path to unity within the broad landscape of diversity, however, it is worth remembering that the social and ideological bomb that blew the South and the nation apart in the first place was triggered by a misguided faith in racial chauvinism, in white supremacy—and that is a subject that southerners white and black have been compelled existentially to face.

Their common history has linked them inseparably; whether friend or foe, they are kinfolk—spiritual and cultural first cousins, if not brothers and sisters, husbands and wives. Southern whites assumed advantage over southern blacks, but neither race was shielded from the consequences of poverty, oppression, discrimination, and defeat. They endured and survived a history that set them apart together on a tributary of the American mainstream, and there their lives were similarly shaped by proximity. Their speech, their music, their food and drink, their work, their entertainment, their religion, their rites of passage into birth and marriage and death—all these were recognizably alike, albeit not identical.

Racially different southerners were not strangers; they knew one another on sight and often by name. Whether or not they could acknowledge it comfortably, they shared a place, an identity, a culture. In the best of circumstances, a measure of affection and trust developed between them—and in that slender reed of caring and knowing there is an element of hope, a seed of possibility that could transcend the limits of liberal and conservative ideology.

The end of the South as an American problem does not signal the end of social and cultural conflict in the United States. It could mean, however, that this region, with its long history of internal conflict, is now in a better position to steer the country closer to its ideals, if only because the people of the South know from bitter experience how disastrous the policy of segregation and enforced inequality was—for whites as well as blacks, for men and women of every station, and for the entire nation no less than its once rebellious southern states.

∿ Contributors

David L. Carlton, associate professor of history at Vanderbilt University, teaches the history of the South. His book *Mill and Town in South Carolina* deals with the impact of the rise of the textile industry in South Carolina. He is currently working on a study of economic development in North Carolina in the late nineteenth and twentieth centuries.

Joyce E. Chaplin, associate professor of history at Vanderbilt, specializes in colonial American history with a particular interest in the South. Her book *An Anxious Pursuit: Innovation in Commercial Agriculture and the Idea of Modernity in South Carolina, Georgia, and British East Florida, 1730–1815* was recently published by the University of North Carolina Press. She is currently working on English natural histories of America and the influence of scientific theory of English views of the New World.

Don H. Doyle, professor of history at Vanderbilt, teaches American social history. His book *New Men, New Cities, New South* deals with the rise of an urban business class. He is currently working on a history of Lafayette County, Mississippi, the basis for William Faulkner's Yoknapatawpha saga.

John Egerton is a Nashvillian who for thirty years has written about the South and the changes it has gone through. Among his books are *A Mind to Stay Here, Generations,* and *The Americanization of Dixie.* His latest book, *Speak Now Against the Day,* is about the generation of southerners just before the civil rights movement.

James W. Ely Jr., professor of law and history at Vanderbilt, teaches in the School of Law; he has a special interest in the legal history of the South and has published numerous books and articles on the subject. His most recent book is *The Chief Justiceship of Melville W. Fuller, 1888–1910.* He is currently working on a book dealing with the legal history of the railroad industry.

Jimmie Lewis Franklin, professor of history at Vanderbilt, specializes in African-American history. He has written on a variety of subjects in southern history. His most recent book, *Back to Birmingham,* is a biography of Birmingham mayor Richard Arrington. The former president of the Southern Historical Association, he is now engaged in a study of black southerners and "sense of place."

Hugh Davis Graham, Holland N. McTyeire Professor of History at Vanderbilt, has published numerous articles and books on the American South, among them *Southern Politics and the Second Reconstruction* (with Numan Bartley). His recent book, *The Civil Rights Era,* was a jury nomination for the 1991 Pulitzer Prize in history.

Larry J. Griffin, professor of sociology and political science at Vanderbilt, teaches southern studies and has published numerous articles on the subject. He is currently engaged in a study of lynching and averted lynching in the South.

Michael Kreyling, professor of English at Vanderbilt, teaches southern literature and has published two books on Eudora Welty and, more recently, *Figures of the Hero in Southern Narrative.* He is currently focusing on southern literary culture after World War II.

Robert A. Margo, professor of economics at Vanderbilt, teaches American economic history. He has published widely on aspects of African-American education, including *Disfranchisement, School Finance, and the Economics of Segregated Schools in the United States South, 1890–1910* and *Race and Schooling in the South, 1880–1950.* He is currently working on a book dealing with wages and labor markets before the Civil War.

James Oakes, professor of history at Northwestern University, is the author of *The Ruling Race* and *Slavery and Freedom.* He is currently writing a book called *Created Equal? A Social History of American Political Thought.*

Eric J. Sundquist, professor of English at UCLA, has written numerous books and articles on southern literature, including *Faulkner: The House Divided,* and, recently, *To Wake the Nations: Race in American Literature* and *The Hammers of Creation: Folk Culture in Modern African-American Fiction.* He is currently investigating the literature and other cultural expressions of the modern civil rights movement.

~ Bibliography

Newspapers

Carolina Messenger, 1808
Charleston Mercury, 1868
New York Times, 1993
Oklahoma City Black Dispatch, 1939

Official Records and Documents

Brown v. Board of Education, 347 U.S. 493, 494, 492 (1954).

Brown v. Board of Education, 349 U.S. 300–301 (1955).

Brown v. Board of Education, U.S. Supreme Court Records and Briefs, Englewood, Colorado, Microcard Editions.

Buchanan v. Warley, 245 U.S. 60, 74, 81, 82 (1917).

Giles v. Harris, 189 U.S. 475, 488 (1903).

Heart of Atlanta Motel v. United States, 379 U.S. 241 (1964).

Norris v. Alabama, 294 U.S. 587 (1935).

Plessy v. Ferguson, 163 U.S. 537, 543, 544, 550, 551, 555, 559 (1896).

Powell v. Alabama, 287 U.S. 49 (1932).

Shaw v. Reno, 113 Sup. Ct. 2816 (1993).

Vera v. Richards (S.D. Texas 1994).

Weems v. State, 224 *Alabama Reports* 526, 528, 536, 551 (1932).

Articles, Memoirs, and Miscellaneous Writings

Allen, Francis A. "The Supreme Court and State Criminal Justice," *Wayne Law Review* 4 (summer 1958): 191–204.

Allen, Ray. "Back Home: Southern Identity and African-American Gospel Quartet Performance." In *Mapping American Culture*, ed. Wayne Franklin and Michael Steiner. Iowa City, 1992.

Andrews, William L. "In Search of a Common Identity: The Self and the South in Four Mississippi Autobiographies," *Southern Review* 24 (winter 1988): 47–62.

Applebome, Peter. "New South and Old." *New York Times*. July 31–August 3, 1994.

Archdale, John. *A New Description of That Fertile and Pleasant Province of Carolina*. In *Narratives of Early Carolina, 1650–1708*, ed. Alexander S. Salley Jr. New York, 1911.

Arsenault, Raymond. "The End of the Long Hot Summer: The Air Conditioner and Southern Culture." *Journal of Southern History* 50 (November 1984): 597–628.

Asante, Molefi Kete. "Racism, Consciousness, and Afrocentricity." In *Lure and Loathing: Essays on Race, Identity, and the Ambivalence of Assimilation*, ed. Gerald Early. New York, 1993.

Baker, Houston A., Jr. "Completely Well: One View of Black American Culture." In *Key Issues in the Afro-American Experience*, ed. Nathan I. Huggins, Martin Kilson, and Daniel M. Fox. New York, 1971.

Baldwin, James. "Faulkner and Desegregation." In *Nobody Knows My Name*. New York, 1961.

Baltimore to King Charles I, August 19, 1629. Public Record Office, Colonial Office 1.5, Kew.

Banes, Ruth A. "Southerners up North: Autobiographical Indications of Southern Ethnicity." In *Perspectives on the American South*, ed. James Cobb and Charles Wilson. Vol. 3. New York, 1985.

Barkley, Alice. "Who Are the Many? What Is the One?" Interview with Professor Charles Long, director of the Center for Black Studies at the University of California, Santa Barbara. *Touchstone Magazine* 22 (1993): 7–11.

Barro, Robert J., and Xavier Sala-i-Martin. "Convergence." *Journal of Political Economy* 100 (April 1992): 223–51.

Bartik, Timothy. "Is There a Southern Ascendancy? Reflections on a Century-Old Question." Remarks on panel discussion, Vanderbilt Alumni Reunion, 1988. *Vanderbilt Magazine* 73 (fall 1988): 7–13.

Belz, Herman. "The South and the American Constitutional Tradition at the Bicentennial." In *An Uncertain Tradition: Constitutionalism and the History of the South*, ed. Kermit L. Hall and James W. Ely Jr. Athens, Ga., 1989.

Bernstein, David E. "Roots of the 'Underclass': The Decline of Laissez-Faire Jurisprudence and the Rise of Racist Labor Legislation." *American University Law Review* 43 (fall 1993): 85–138.

Bingham, Richard. Preface to *A True Reporte, Of the late discoveries . . . ,* by George Peckham. London, 1583.

Black, Merle, and John Shelton Reed. "Blacks and Southerners: A Research Note." *Journal of Politics* 44 (February 1982): 165–71.

Blumer, Herbert. "Social Problems as Collective Behavior." *Social Problems* 18 (winter 1971): 298–306.

Bontemps, Arna. "Why I Returned." *Harper's*, April 1965, 177–82.

Brady, Tom. "Black Monday." In *The Eyes on the Prize Civil Rights Reader*, ed. Clayborne Carson, et al. New York, 1991.

Brocks-Shedd, Virginia. "Southern Roads/City Pavement." In possession of Jimmie Franklin. 1983.

Brooks, Gwendolyn. "A Bronzeville Mother Loiters in Mississippi. Meanwhile, a Mississippi Mother Burns Bacon." In *Selected Poems*. New York, 1963.

Buell, Lawrence. "Literary History as a Hybrid Genre." In *New Historical Literary Study: Essays on Reproducing Texts, Representing History*, ed. Jeffrey N. Cox and Larry J. Reynolds. Princeton, N.J., 1993.

Butler, John. "Magic, Astrology, and the Early-American Religious Heritage, 1600–1760," *American Historical Review* 84 (April 1979): 317–46.

Campbell, Rex R. "Return Migration of Black People in the South." *Journal of Politics* 39 (February 1979): 129–62.

Canup, John. "Cotton Mather and 'Criolian Degeneracy.'" *Early American Literature* 24 (1989): 20–34.

Carlton, David L. "Paternalism and Southern Textile Labor: A Historiographical View." In *Race, Class, and Community in Southern Labor History: Selected Papers, Seventh Southern Labor Studies Conference, 1991*, ed. Gary M. Fink and Merle E. Reed. University, Ala., 1994.

———. "The Revolution from Above: The National Market and the Beginnings of Industrialization in North Carolina." *Journal of American History* 87 (September 1990): 445–75.

———. "Urbanization." In *Encyclopedia of the Confederacy*. Vol. 4. New York, 1993.

Carlton, David L., and Peter A. Coclanis. "Capital Mobilization and Southern Industry: The Case of the Carolina Piedmont." *Journal of Economic History* 49 (March 1989): 73–94.

———. "The Uninventive South? A Quantitative Look at Region and American Inventiveness." *Technology and Culture* 36 (April 1995): 220–44.

Carr, Lois Green, and Lorena S. Walsh. "Changing Lifestyles and Consumer Behavior in the Colonial Chesapeake." In *Of Consuming Interests: The Style of Life in the Eighteenth Century*, ed. Cary Carson, Ronald Hoffman, and Peter J. Albert. Charlottesville, 1994.

Carrigan, Jo Ann. "Privilege, Prejudice, and the Strangers' Disease in Nineteenth-Century New Orleans." *Journal of Southern History* 36 (November 1970): 568–78.

Chafe, William H. "One Struggle Ends, Another Begins." In *The Civil Rights Movement in America*, ed. Charles W. Eagles. Jackson, Miss., 1986.

Chaplin, Joyce E. "Tidal Rice Cultivation and the Problem of Slavery in South Carolina and Georgia, 1760–1815." *William and Mary Quarterly*, 3d ser., 49 (January 1992): 59–61.

Chavez, Linda. "Party Lines: The Republicans' Racial Quotas." *New Republic*, June 1991, 14–16.

Chimezie, Amuzie. "Afro-Centricity and Ethnicity: Definitive Concepts of Culture." *Western Journal of Black Studies* 7 (winter 1983): 216–28.

Cobb, James C. "Beyond Planters and Industrialists: A New Perspective on the New South." *Journal of Southern History* 54 (February 1988): 45–68.

Cogan, John. "The Decline in Black Teenage Employment, 1950–1970." *American Economic Review* 72 (September 1982): 621–38.

Colburn, David R. "Florida Governors Confront the Brown Decision: A Case Study of the Constitutional Politics of School Desegregation, 1954–1970." In *An Uncertain Tradition: Constitutionalism and the History of the South*, ed. Kermit L. Hall and James W. Ely Jr. Athens, Ga., 1989.

Conrad, Alfred, and John Meyer. "The Economics of Slavery in the Antebellum South." *Journal of Political Economy* 56 (April 1958): 95–130.

Curtin, Philip D. "Epidemiology and the Slave Trade." *Political Science Quarterly* 83 (June 1968): 190–216.

Davidson, Chandler. "The Voting Rights Act." In *Controversies in Minority Voting: The Voting Rights in Perspective*, ed. Bernard Grofman and Chandler Davidson. Washington, 1992.

Davis, Steve. "The South as 'the Nation's No. 1 Economic Problem': The NEC Report of 1938." *Georgia Historical Quarterly* (summer 1978): 119–32.

Davis, Thadious M. "Expanding the Limits: The Intersection of Race and Region." *Southern Literary Journal* 20 (spring 1988): 3–11.

Day, Richard. "The Economics of Technological Change and the Demise of the Sharecropper." *American Economic Review* 57 (June 1967): 427–49.

Degler, Carl. "Thesis, Antithesis, Synthesis: The South, the North, and the Nation." *Journal of Southern History* 53 (February 1987): 3–18.

DeSaussure to Ezekiel Pickens, September 10, 1805. Henry William DeSaussure Papers, South Caroliniana Library. Columbia, S.C.

Donohue, John, and James J. Heckman. "Continuous versus Episodic Change: The Impact of Civil Rights Policy on the Economic Status of Blacks." *Journal of Economic Literature* 29 (December 1991): 1603–43.

Douglass, Frederick. "What to the Slave Is the Fourth of July?" In *The Frederick Douglass Papers*, ed. John W. Blassingame. Ser. 1, vol. 2. New Haven, 1982.

Dudziak, Mary L. "Desegregation as a Cold War Imperative." *Stanford Law Review* 41 (November 1988): 61–120.

Earle, Carville V. "Environment, Disease, and Mortality in Early Virginia." In *The Chesapeake in the Seventeenth Century: Essays on Anglo-American Society*, ed. Thad W. Tate and David L. Ammerman. Chapel Hill, 1979.

Easterlin, Richard. "Regional Growth of Income: Long-Term Tendencies." In *Population Redistribution and Economic Growth, United States, 1870–1950*. Vol. 2, *Analysis of Economic Change*, ed. S. Kuznets, A. Miller, and R. Easterlin. Philadelphia, 1960.

———. "Regional Income Trends, 1840–1950." In *Reinterpretation of American Economic History*, ed. Robert Fogel and Stanley Engerman. New York, 1971.

Ely, James W., Jr. "Negro Demonstrations and the Law: Danville as a Test Case." *Vanderbilt Law Review* 27 (October 1974): 927–68.

Ely, James W., Jr., and David J. Bodenhamer. "Regionalism and American Legal History: The Southern Experience." *Vanderbilt Law Review* 39 (April 1986): 539–67.

———. "Regionalism and the Legal History of the South." In *Ambivalent Legacy: A Legal History of the South*, ed. David J. Bodenhamer and James W. Ely Jr. Jackson, Miss., 1984.

Engerman, Stanley. "Some Economic Factors in Southern Backwardness in the Nineteenth Century." In *Essays in Regional Economics*, ed. J. Kain and J. Meyer. Cambridge, Mass., 1971.

Epstein, Richard A. "Race and the Police Power: 1890 to 1937." *Washington and Lee Law Review* 46 (fall 1989): 741–61.

Finkelman, Paul. "Exploring Southern Legal History." *North Carolina Law Review* 64 (November 1985): 77–116.

Finley, Moses I. "Slavery." In *International Encyclopedia of the Social Sciences*, ed. David Sills. New York, 1968.

Fischer, David Hackett. "Climate and History: Priorities for Research." *Journal of Interdisciplinary History* 10 (spring 1980): 821–30.

Fogel, Robert W., and Stanley Engerman. "The Economics of Slavery." In *The Reinterpretation of American Economic History,* ed. Robert Fogel and Stanley Engerman. New York, 1971.

———. "Explaining the Relative Efficiency of Slave Agriculture in the Antebellum South" and "Explaining the Relative Efficiency of Slave Agriculture: Reply." In *Without Consent or Contract: Markets and Production, Technical Papers,* ed. Robert Fogel and Stanley Engerman. Vol. 1. New York, 1992.

Franklin, Jimmie L. "A Southern Sense of Place: Notes of a Native Son." University of Alabama Press pamphlet. Tuscaloosa, 1993.

Fuller, Richard, and Richard Myers. "The Natural History of a Social Problem." *American Sociological Review* 3 (June 1941): 320–29.

Gallman, Robert. "Slavery and Southern Economic Growth." *Southern Economic Journal* 45 (April 1979): 1007–22.

Garrison, William Lloyd. From the *Liberator,* January 1, 1831. Quoted in *William Lloyd Garrison,* ed. George M. Fredrickson. Englewood Cliffs, N.J., 1968.

Glennon, Robert Jerome. "The Role of Law in the Civil Rights Movement: The Montgomery Bus Boycott, 1955–1957." *Law and History Review* 9 (spring 1991): 59–112.

Goldfield, David R. "The Urban South: A Regional Framework." *American Historical Review* 86 (December 1981): 1009–34.

Goldin, Claudia. "'N' Kinds of Freedom." *Explorations in Economic History* 16 (January 1979): 8–30.

Goldin, Claudia, and Frank Lewis. "The Economic Costs of the Civil War." *Journal of Economic History* 35 (June 1975): 299–326.

———. "The Postbellum Recovery of the South and the Costs of the Civil War: Comment." *Journal of Economic History* 38 (June 1978): 487–92.

Goldin, Claudia, and Robert A. Margo. "The Great Compression: The Wage Structure in the United States at Mid-Century." *Quarterly Journal of Economics* 107 (February 1992): 1–34.

Graham, Hugh Davis. "Civil Disorders: 1943–Present." In *Encyclopedia of Black America,* ed. W. A. Low and Virgil A. Clift. New York, 1981.

———. "On Riots and Riot Commissions: Civil Disorders in the 1960s." *Public Historian* 2 (summer 1980): 2–27.

———. "Voting Rights and the American Regulatory State." In *Controversies in Minority Voting: The Voting Rights in Perspective,* eds., Bernard Grofman and Chandler Davidson. Washington, 1992.

Grill, Johnpeter Horst, and Robert L. Jenkins. "The Nazis and the American South in the 1930s: A Mirror Image?" *Journal of Southern History* 58 (November 1992): 667–94.

Hahn, Steven. "Class and State in Postemancipation Societies: Southern Planters in Comparative Perspective." *American Historical Review* 95 (February 1990): 75–98.

Hall, Timothy L. "Moral Character, the Practice of Law, and Legal Education." *Mississippi Law Journal* 60 (winter 1990): 511–54.

[Hayes, Edward, and Christopher Carleill]. "A Discourse Concerning a Voyage . . ." (1592). In *New American World: A Documentary History of North America to 1612,* ed. David B. Quinn et al. London, 1979.

Heilman, Robert B. "The Southern Temper." In *Southern Renascence,* ed. Louis D. Rubin Jr. and Robert Jacobs. Baltimore, 1953.

Higgs, Robert Higgs. "American Inventiveness, 1870–1920." *Journal of Political Economy* 79 (May–June 1971): 661–67.

Hilgartner, Stephen, and Charles Bosk. "The Rise and fall of Social Problems: A Public Arenas Model." *American Journal of Sociology* 94 (July 1988): 53–78.

Hobson, Fred. "The Savage South: An Inquiry into the Origins, Endurance, and Presumed Demise of an Image." *Virginia Quarterly Review* 61 (summer 1985): 377–95.

Hollman, C. Hugh. "The Southerner as an American Writer." In *The Southerner as American*, ed., Charles Grier Sellers Jr. Chapel Hill, 1960.

Huie, William Bradford. "What's Happened to the Emmett Till Killers?" *Look*, January 22, 1957, 63–68.

Johnson, Claudia. "The Secret Courts of Men's Hearts: Code and Law in Harper Lee's *To Kill a Mockingbird*." *Studies in American Fiction* 19 (Autumn 1991): 129–39.

Johnson, Daniel. "Black Return Migration to a Southern Metropolitan Community: Birmingham, Alabama." Ph.D. diss., University of Missouri, 1973.

Johnson, Gerald. "The Horrible South." *Virginia Quarterly Review* 11 (April 1935): 201–17.

Jones, Mack. "Political Science and the Black Political Experience: Issues in Epistemology and Relevance." In *Ethnic Politics and Civil Liberties*, ed. Lucius J. Barker. Vol. 3 of *National Political Science Review*. New Brunswick, N.J., 1992.

Kemmerer, Donald L. "Financing Illinois Industry, 1830–1890." *Bulletin of the Business Historical Society* 26 (June 1953): 97–111.

Kendrick, B. B. "The Colonial Status of the South." In *The Pursuit of Southern History: Presidential Addresses of the Southern Historical Association, 1935–1963*, ed. George Tindall. Baton Rouge, 1964.

Kilpatrick, James J. "Conservatism and the South." In *The Lasting South: Fourteen Southerners Look at Their Home*, ed. Louis D. Rubin Jr. and James J. Kilpatrick. Chicago, 1957.

King, Martin Luther, Jr. "Letter from the Birmingham Jail." In *Why We Can't Wait*. New York, 1964.

King, Nancy J. "Racial Jurymandering: Cancer or Cure? A Contemporary Review of Affirmative Action in Jury Selection." *New York University Law Review* 68 (October 1993): 707–76.

Klarman, Michael J. "Brown, Racial Change, and the Civil Rights Movement." *Virginia Law Review* 80 (February 1994): 7–150.

———. "How *Brown* Changed Race Relations: The Backlash Thesis." *Journal of American History* 81 (June 1994): 81–118.

Koeniger, A. Cash. "Climate and Southern Distinctiveness." *Journal of Southern History* 54 (February 1988): 21–44.

Kousser, J. Morgan. "Separate but not Equal: The Supreme Court's First Decision on Racial Discrimination in Schools." *Journal of Southern History* 46 (February 1980): 17–44.

Kreyling, Michael. Memo and syllabus pertaining to "The Southern Novel and the Southern Community," an NEH Summer Institute at the University of North Carolina. Chapel Hill, 1989.

Kupperman, Karen Ordahl. "Fear of Hot Climates in the Anglo-American Colonial Experience." *William and Mary Quarterly*, 3d ser., 41 (April 1984): 213–40.

———. "The Puzzle of the American Climate in the Early Colonial Period." *American Historical Review* 87 (December 1982): 1262–89.

"The Life and Labours of Richard Eden." In *First Three English Books in America,* ed. Edward Arber. Birmingham, 1885.

The Life of St. Brendan (c. 1520). In *New American World: A Documentary History of North America to 1612,* ed. David B. Quinn et al. London, 1979.

Lipset, Seymour Martin. "Equal Chances versus Equal Rights." *Annals of the American Academy of Political and Social Science* 523 (September 1992): 63–74.

Marshall, Thurgood. *Eyes on the Prize.* Produced by Henry Hampton. PBS Television.

McPherson, James Alan. "A Region Not Home: The View from Exile." In *The Prevailing South: Life and Politics in a Changing Culture,* ed. Dudley Clendinen. Atlanta, 1988.

Mencken, H. L. "The Sahara of the Bozart." In *Prejudices: Second Series.* New York, 1920.

Merrens, H. Roy, and George D. Terry. "Dying in Paradise: Malaria, Mortality, and the Perceptual Environment in Colonial South Carolina." *Journal of Southern History* 50 (November 1984): 533–50.

Meyer, David R. "Emergence of the American Manufacturing Belt: An Interpretation." *Journal of Historical Geography* 9 (April 1983): 145–74.

———. "The Industrial Retardation of Southern Cities, 1860–1880." *Explorations in Economic History* 25 (October 1988): 366–86.

Mitchell, Samuel. "The Nationalization of Southern Sentiment." *South Atlantic Quarterly* 7 (April 1908): 107–13.

Moen, Jon R. "Changes in the Productivity of Southern Agriculture between 1860 and 1880." In *Without Consent or Contract: Markets and Production, Technical Papers,* ed. Robert Fogel and Stanley Engerman. Vol. 1. New York, 1992.

Oglethorpe, James. "Letters from James Oglethorpe." Georgia Historical Society, Collections. 3:142. Savannah, 1848.

Olsen, Mancur. "The South Will Fall Again: The South as Leader and Laggard in Economic Growth." *Southern Economic Journal* 49 (April 1983): 916–32.

Owsley, Frank L. "Scottsboro: Third Crusade; Sequel to Abolitionism and Reconstruction." *American Review* 1 (January 1933): 267–68.

Pagden, Anthony. "Identity Formation in Spanish America." In *Colonial Identity in the Atlantic World, 1500–1800,* ed. Nicholas Canny and Anthony Pagden. Princeton, N.J., 1987.

Painter, Nell Irvin. "'The South' and 'the Negro': The Rhetoric of Race Relations and Real Life." In *The South for New Southerners,* ed. Paul D. Escott and David R. Goldfield. Chapel Hill, 1991.

Parker, Seymour, and Robert Kleiner. "Status Position, Mobility, and Ethnic Identification of the Negro." *Journal of Social Issues* 22 (April 1964): 85–102.

Philips, John Edward. "The African Heritage of White America." In *Africanisms in American Culture,* ed. Joseph E. Holloway. Bloomington, 1990.

Pierson, George. "The Obstinate Concept of New England: A Study in Denudation." *New England Quarterly* 28 (March 1955): 3–17.

Podhoretz, Norman. "Southern Claims." *Partisan Review* 21 (January–February 1954): 119–23.

Potter, David M. "The Enigma of the South." *Yale Review* 51 (October 1961): 142–51.

———. "The Historical Development of Eastern-Southern Freight-Rate Relationships." *Law and Contemporary Problems* 12 (summer 1947): 416–48.

Reed, John Shelton. "The South's Mid-life Crisis." In *My Tears Spoiled My Aim and Other Reflections on Southern Culture*. Columbia, Mo., 1993.

Reid, Joseph. "Sharecropping as an Understandable Market Response: The Postbellum South." *Journal of Economic History* 33 (March 1973): 106–30.

The relation of the right honourable the Lord De-La-Warre (1611). In *New American World: A Documentary History of North America to 1612*, ed. David B. Quinn et al. London, 1979.

Rice, Roger L. "Residential Segregation by Law, 1910–1917." *Journal of Southern History* 34 (May 1968): 179–99.

Rubin, Louis D., Jr. "The Curious Death of the Novel: Or, What to Do about Tired Literary Critics." In *The Curious Death of the Novel: Essays in American Literature*. Baton Rouge, 1967.

———. "The Historical Image of Modern Southern Writing." *Journal of Southern History* 22 (May 1956): 147–66.

———. "An Image of the South." In *The Lasting South: Fourteen Southerners Look at Their Home*, ed. Louis D. Rubin Jr. and James J. Kilpatrick. Chicago, 1957.

———. "A Letter to the Editor." *Mississippi Quarterly* 45 (spring 1992): 189–93.

———. "Southern Literature: The Historical Image." In *The South, Modern Southern Literature in Its Cultural Setting*, eds. Louis D. Rubin Jr. and Robert Jacobs. Garden City, N.J., 1961.

———. "Thomas Wolfe in Time and Place." In *Southern Renascence*, ed. Louis D. Rubin Jr. and Robert Jacobs. Baltimore, 1953.

———. "The Way It Was with Southern Literary Study." *Mississippi Quarterly* 43 (spring 1990): 147–62.

Rutman, Darrett B., and Anita H. Rutman. "Of Agues and Fevers: Malaria in the Early Chesapeake." *William and Mary Quarterly*, 3d ser., 33 (January 1976): 31–60.

Schaffer, Thomas L. "The Moral Theology of Atticus Finch." *University of Pittsburgh Law Review* 42 (winter 1981): 181–224

Schorer, Mark. "The Necessity of Myth." In *Myth and Mythmaking*, ed. Henry A. Murray. New York, 1960.

Scranton, Philip. "Varieties of Paternalism: Industrial Structures and the Social Relations of Production in American Textiles." *American Quarterly* 36 (summer 1984): 235–57.

Scribner, Christopher. "Urban Renewal and Political Change in Birmingham." Paper presented at the Tennessee Conference of Historians, University of the South, October 30, 1993.

Sellers, Charles Grier, Jr. "The Travail of Slavery." In *The Southerner as American*, ed. Charles Grier Sellers Jr. Chapel Hill, 1960.

———. "Who Were the Southern Whigs?" *American Historical Review* 59 (January 1954): 335–46.

Sibley, Celestine. "Miller Unfurls a Call for Justice and Honor." *Atlanta Constitution*, 13 January 1993, B2.

Simpson, William M. "Reflections on a Murder: The Emmett Till Case." In *Southern Miscellany: Essays in History in Honor of Glover Moore*, ed. Frank Allen Dennis. Jackson, Miss., 1981.

Sitkoff, Harvard. "Harry Truman and the Election of 1948: The Coming of Age of Civil Rights in American Politics." *Journal of Southern History* 37 (November 1971): 597–616.

Smiley, David. "The Quest for the Central Theme in Southern History." *South Atlantic Quarterly* 71 (summer 1972): 307–25.

Smith, Daniel Blake. "Mortality and Family in the Colonial Chesapeake." *Journal of Interdisciplinary History* 8 (winter 1978): 403–27.

Smith, John. *Advertisements For the unexperienced Planters of New-England, or any where* (1631). In *The Complete Works of Captain John Smith (1580–1631) in Three Volumes,* ed. Philip L. Barbour. Vol. 3. Chapel Hill, 1986.

———. *The Generall Historie of Virginia, New-England, and the Summer Isles . . .* (1624). In *The Complete Works of Captain John Smith (1580–1631) in Three Volumes,* ed. Philip L. Barbour. Vol. 3. Chapel Hill, 1986.

Smith, Stanley H. "The Development of the Black Community." In *Group Identity in the South: Dialogue between the Technological and the Humanistic,* ed. Harold F. Kaufman, J. Kenneth Morland, and Herbert H. Fockler. Starkville, Miss., 1975.

"Southern Authors." *Nation,* October 17, 1953, 317.

Spector, Malcolm, and John Kitsuse. "Social Problems: A Re-Formulation." *Social Problems* 21 (fall 1973): 145–59.

Stammp, Kenneth M. "The Southern Road to Appomattox." In *The Imperiled Union: Essays on the Background of the Civil War.* New York, 1980.

"A State of the Province of Georgia, Attested upon Oath, in the Court of Savannah, November 10, 1740" (1742). In *Tracts and Other Papers, Relating Principally to Origins, Settlement, and Progress of the Colonies in North America, from the Discovery of the Country to the Year 1776,* ed. Peter Force. Washington, 1836.

Steckel, Richard. "A Peculiar Population: The Health, Nutrition, and Mortality of American Slaves from Childhood to Maturity." *Journal of Economic History* 46 (September 1986): 721–41.

Stevens, Thaddeus. Speech on Reconstruction, December 18, 1865, Congressional Globe, 39th Cong., 1st sess. In *Reconstruction in the South, 1865–1877: First Hand Accounts of the American Southland after the Civil War by Northerners and Southerners,* ed. Harvey Wish. New York, 1965.

Sumner, Charles. Senate speech of February 5 and 6, 1866. In *Reconstruction in the South, 1865–1877: First Hand Accounts of the American Southland after the Civil War by Northerners and Southerners,* ed. Harvey Wish. New York, 1965.

Tailfer, Pat, et al. *A True and historical narrative of the Colony of Georgia . . .* (1741). In *Tracts and Other Papers, Relating Principally to Origins, Settlement, and Progress of the Colonies in North America, from the Discovery of the Country to the Year 1776,* ed. Peter Force. Vol. 1. Washington, 1836.

Tate, Allen. "The Profession of Letters in the South." In *Essays of Four Decades.* Denver, 1968.

———. "Remarks on the Southern Religion." In *I'll Take My Stand: The South and the Agrarian Tradition,* by Twelve Southerners. New York, 1930.

Thernstrom, Abigail M. "A Republican–Civil Rights Conspiracy." *Washington Post,* September 23, 1991.

Thorpe, Willard. Review of *Southern Renascence. American Literature* 26 (January 1955): 575.

Tindall, George B. "The Benighted South: Origins of a Modern Image." *Virginia Quarterly Review* 40 (spring 1964): 281–94.

———. "Beyond the Mainstream: The Ethnic Southerners." *Journal of Southern History* 40 (February 1974): 3–18.

———. "Business Progressivism: Southern Politics in the 1920s." In *The Ethnic Southerners.* Baton Rouge, 1976.

———. "The Central Theme Revisited." In *The Southerner as American,* ed. Charles Grier Sellers Jr. Chapel Hill, 1960.

———. "Mythology: A New Frontier in Southern History." In *The Idea of the South: Pursuit of a Central Theme,* ed. Frank Vandiver. Chicago, 1964.

Torrance, Caroline. "Blacks and the American Ethos: A Reevaluation of Existing Theories." *Journal of Black Studies* 3 (September 1990): 72–86.

Wacker, Fred. "The Fate of Cultural Pluralism within American Social Thought." *Ethnic Groups* 3 (June 1981): 125–38.

Wallerstein, Immanuel. "What Can One Mean by Southern Culture?" In *The Evolution of Southern Culture,* ed. Numan V. Bartley. Athens, Ga., 1988.

Wallis, John. "Employment in the Great Depression: New Data and Hypotheses." *Explorations in Economic History* 26 (January 1989): 45–72.

Walsh, Lorena S., and Russell R. Menard. "Death in the Chesapeake: Two Life Tables for Men in Early Colonial Maryland." *Maryland Historical Magazine* 69 (summer 1974): 211–27.

Ward, Jerry W., Jr. "A Writer for Her People: An Interview with Dr. Margaret Walker Alexander." *Mississippi Quarterly* 41 (fall 1988): 515–27.

Warner, John Harley. "The Idea of Southern Medical Distinctiveness: Medical Knowledge and Practice in the Old South." In *Science and Medicine in the Old South,* ed. Ronald L. Numbers and Todd L. Savitt. Baton Rouge, 1989.

Wear, Andrew. "Making Sense of Health and the Environment in Early Modern England." In *Medicine in Society: Historical Essays,* ed. Andrew Wear. Cambridge, 1992.

Weaver, Richard. "Aspects of the Southern Philosophy." In *Southern Renascence,* ed. Louis D. Rubin Jr. and Robert Jacobs. Baltimore, 1953.

Weiman, David F. "The Economic Emancipation of the Non-Slaveholding Class: Upcountry Farmers in the Georgia Cotton Economy." *Journal of Economic History* 45 (March 1985): 71–93.

———. "Staple Crops and Slave Plantations: Alternative Perspectives on Regional Development in the Antebellum Cotton South." In *Agriculture and National Development: Views on the Nineteenth Century,* ed. Lou Ferleger. Ames, Iowa, 1990.

Wills, Gary. "From the Campaign Trail: Clinton's Hell-Raiser." *New Yorker,* October 12, 1992, 92–101.

———. "The Words That Remade America: Lincoln at Gettysburg." *Atlantic,* June 1992, 57–79.

Wilson, Samuel. *An Account of the Province of Carolina, in America* (1682). In *Narratives of Early Carolina,* ed. Salley. 168.

Woolgar, Steve, and Dorothy Pawluch. "Ontological Gerrymandering: The Anatomy of Social Problems Explanations." *Social Problems* 32 (February 1985): 214–27.

Wright, Gavin. "Cotton Competition and the Post-Bellum Recovery of the American South." *Journal of Economic History* 34 (September 1974): 610–35.

Yasuba, Yasukichi. "The Profitability and Viability of Plantation Slavery in the United States." In *The Reinterpretation of American History,* ed. Robert W. Fogel and Stanley Engerman. New York, 1971.

Monographs and Collections

Acosta, Joseph. *The Naturall and Morall Historie of the East and West Indies*. Trans. E[dward] G[rimestone]. London, 1604.

Alexander, Margaret Walker. *This Is My Century: New and Collected Poems*. Athens, Ga., 1989.

Anderson, Elijah. *Streetwise: Race, Class, and Change in an Urban Community*. Chicago, 1990.

Arber, Edward, ed. *The First Three English Books on America*. Birmingham, 1885.

Archer, Chalmers, Jr. *Growing Up Black in Rural Mississippi: Memories of a Family, Heritage of a Place*. New York, 1992.

Ayers, Edward L. *The Promise of the New South: Life after Reconstruction*. New York, 1992.

Baldwin, James. *Blues for Mister Charlie*. New York, 1964.

———. *The Fire Next Time*. New York, 1964.

Barlowe, Roger. *A briefe summe of geographie*. London, 1541.

Barnes, Catherine A. *Journey from Jim Crow: The Desegregation of Southern Transit*. New York, 1983.

Bartley, Numan V. *The Rise of Massive Resistance: Race and Politics in the South during the 1950s*. Baton Rouge, 1969.

Bartley, Numan V., and Hugh Davis Graham. *Southern Politics and the Second Reconstruction*. Baltimore, 1975.

Beaney, William. *The Right to Counsel in American Courts*. Ann Arbor, 1955.

Bedini, Silvio A. *Thomas Jefferson: Statesman of Science*. New York, 1990.

Bell, Derrick A., Jr. *And We Are Not Saved: The Elusive Quest for Racial Justice*. New York, 1989.

———. *Faces at the Bottom of the Well*. New York, 1992.

Belz, Herman. *Equality Transformed: A Quarter-Century of Affirmative Action*. New Brunswick, N.J., 1991.

Berger, Peter, and Thomas Luckmann. *The Social Construction of Reality: A Treatise in the Sociology of Knowledge*. New York, 1966.

Berry, Bill, ed. *Located Lives: Place and Idea in Southern Autobiography*. Athens, Ga., 1990.

Berry, Mary Frances, and John W. Blassingame. *Long Memory: The Black Experience in America*. New York, 1982.

Bertelson, David. *The Lazy South*. New York, 1967.

Beth, Loren P. *John Marshall Harlan: The Last Whig Justice*. Lexington, Ky., 1992.

Beverley, Robert. *The History and Present State of Virginia* (1705). Ed. Louis B. Wright. Chapel Hill, 1947.

Biles, Roger. *A New Deal for the American People*. DeKalb, Ill., 1991.

Billings, Dwight B. *Planters and the Making of a "New South": Class, Politics, and Development in North Carolina, 1865–1900*. Chapel Hill, 1978.

Black, Earl, and Merle Black. *Politics and Society in the South*. Cambridge, Mass., 1987.

———. *The Vital South: How Presidents Are Elected*. Cambridge, Mass., 1992.

Bluestone, Barry, and Bennett Harrison. *The Deindustrialization of America*. New York, 1982.

Blum, John Morton. *V Was For Victory: Politics and American Culture During World War II*. New York, 1976.

Blumrosen, Alfred W. *Modern Law: The Law Transfer System and Equal Employment Opportunity.* Madison, 1993.

Bolsterli, Margaret Jones. *Born in the Delta: Reflections on the Making of a Southern White Sensibility.* Knoxville, 1991.

Bontemps, Arna. *Black Thunder.* 1936. Reprint, Boston, 1968.

Botsch, Robert E. *We Shall Not Overcome.* Chapel Hill, 1980.

[Boulton, Richard]. *A Compleat History of Magick, Sorcery, and Witchcraft.* London, 1715.

Bourne, William. *A regiment for the sea.* London, 1580.

Bové, Paul A. *Mastering Discourse: The Politics of Intellectual Culture.* Durham, N.C., 1992.

Boydston, Jeanne. *Home and Work: Housework, Wages, and the Ideology of Labor in the Early Republic.* New York, 1990.

Boyle, Sarah Patton. *The Desegregated Heart: A Virginian's Stand in the Time of Transition.* New York, 1962.

Bracey, John H., August Meier, and Elliott Rudwick, eds. *Black Nationalism in America.* Indianapolis, 1970.

Bradford, William. *Of Plymouth Plantation, 1620–1647.* Ed. Samuel Eliot Morison. New York, 1953.

Braeman, John. *Before the Civil Rights Revolution: The Old Court and Individual Rights.* Westport, 1988.

Brahm, William Gerard, De. *History of the Province of Georgia with Maps of Original Surveys.* Wormsloe, 1849.

Burnham, Walter Dean. *Critical Elections and the Mainsprings of American Politics.* New York, 1970.

Bushnell, Horace. *Christian Nurture.* 1847. Reprint, New Haven, 1967.

Carlton, David L. *Mill and Town in South Carolina, 1880–1920.* Baton Rouge, 1982.

Carmer, Carl. *Stars Fell on Alabama.* 1934. Reprint, New York, 1952.

Carter, Dan T. *Scottsboro: A Tragedy of the American South.* Rev. ed. Chapel Hill, 1991.

———. *When the War Was Over: The Failure of Self-Reconstruction in the South, 1865–1867.* Baton Rouge, 1985.

Carter, Hodding. *The Angry Scar: The Story of Reconstruction.* New York, 1959.

Cash, W. J. *The Mind of the South.* New York, 1941.

Chafe, William. *Civilities and Civil Rights: Greensboro, North Carolina, and the Black Struggle for Freedom.* New York, 1980.

Chalmers, Allan K. *They Shall Be Free.* New York, 1951.

Chaplin, Joyce E. *An Anxious Pursuit: Agricultural Innovation and Modernity in the Lower South, 1730–1815.* Chapel Hill, 1993.

Chubb, John E., and Terry M. Moe. *Politics, Markets, and America's Schools.* Washington, 1990.

Cleaver, Eldridge. *Soul on Ice.* New York, 1968.

Cobb, James C. *Industrialization and Southern Society, 1877–1984.* Lexington, Ky., 1984.

———. *The Most Southern Place on Earth: The Mississippi Delta and the Roots of Regional Identity.* New York, 1992.

———. *The Selling of the South: The Southern Crusade for Industrial Development, 1936–1980.* Baton Rouge, 1982.

Coclanis, Peter A. *The Shadow of a Dream: Economic Life and Death in the South Carolina Low Country, 1670–1920*. New York, 1989.

Cohen, William. *At Freedom's Edge: Black Mobility and the Southern White Quest for Racial Control, 1861–1915*. Baton Rouge, 1991.

Cohodas, Nadine. *Strom Thurmond and the Politics of Southern Change*. New York, 1993.

Commager, Henry Steele. *The American Mind: An Interpretation of American Thought and Character since the 1880s*. New Haven, 1950.

Conkin, Paul K. *The Southern Agrarians*. Knoxville, 1988.

Cortner, Richard C. *A "Scottsboro" Case in Mississippi: The Supreme Court and Brown v. Mississippi*. Jackson, Miss., 1986.

Crafts, N. F. R. *British Economic Growth during the Industrial Revolution*. New York, 1985.

Crockett, Norman L. *The Black Towns*. Lawrence, 1979.

Cronon, William. *Changes in the Land: Indians, Colonists, and the Ecology of New England*. New York, 1983.

Cuningham, William, comp. *The Cosmographical Glasse . . . .* London, 1559.

Dalfiume, Richard M. *Desegregation of the U.S. Armed Forces: Fighting on Two Fronts, 1939–1953*. Columbia, Mo., 1969.

Dalzell, Robert F., Jr. *Enterprising Elite: The Boston Associates and the World They Made*. Cambridge, Mass., 1987.

Daniel, Pete. *The Shadow of Slavery: Peonage in the South, 1901–1969*. Urbana, Ill., 1972.

David, Paul, et al. *Reckoning with Slavery*. New York, 1976.

DeCanio, Stephen. *Agriculture in the Postbellum South: The Economics of Production and Supply*. Cambridge, Mass., 1974.

Dees, Morris, with Steve Fiffer. *A Season for Justice: The Life and Times of Civil Rights Lawyer Morris Dees*. New York, 1991.

Degler, Carl. *The Other South: Southern Dissenters in the Nineteenth Century*. Boston, 1982.

———. *Place over Time: The Continuity of Southern Distinctiveness*. Baton Rouge, 1977.

Doerflinger, Thomas. *A Vigorous Spirit of Enterprise: Merchants and Economic Development in Revolutionary Philadelphia*. New York, 1986.

Dollard, John. *Caste and Class in a Southern Town*. New Haven, 1937.

Dorman, Robert L. *Revolt of the Provinces: The Regionalist Movement in America, 1920–1945*. Chapel Hill, 1993.

Dormon, John H., and Robert R. Jones. *The Afro-American Experience: A Cultural History through Emancipation*. New York, 1974.

Doyle, Don H. *New Men, New Cities, New South: Atlanta, Nashville, Charleston, Mobile, 1860–1900*. Chapel Hill, 1990.

Du Bois, W. E. B. *The Souls of Black Folk: Essays and Sketches*. Greenwich, 1961.

Dunbar, Tony. *Our Land Too*. New York, 1969.

Edsall, Thomas B., and Mary D. Edsall. *Chain Reaction: The Impact of Race, Rights, and Taxes on American Politics*. New York, 1991.

Egerton, John. *The Americanization of Dixie, the Southernization of America*. New York, 1974.

———. *School Desegregation: A Report from the South*. Atlanta, 1976.

Egerton, John, with Ann Bleidt Egerton and photographs by Al Clayton. *Southern Food: At Home, on the Road, in History.* New York, 1987.

Elkins, Stanley. *Slavery: A Problem in American Institutional and Intellectual Life.* 3d rev. ed. Chicago, 1976.

Ellison, Ralph. *Going to the Territory.* New York, 1986.

Ely, James W., Jr. *The Chief Justiceship of Melville W. Fuller, 1888–1910.* Columbia, S.C., 1995.

———. *The Crisis of Conservative Virginia: The Byrd Organization and the Politics of Massive Resistance.* Knoxville, 1976.

Escott, Paul, and David Goldfield, eds. *Major Problems in the History of the American South.* Vol. 1, *The Old South.* Lexington, Mass., 1990.

Farmer, James. *Lay Bare the Heart: An Autobiography of the Civil Rights Movement.* New York, 1985.

Faulkner, William. *Intruder in the Dust.* New York, 1948.

———. *Lion in the Garden: Interviews with William Faulkner.* Ed. James B. Meriwether and Michael Millgate. Lincoln, 1968.

Faust, Drew Gilpin. *The Creation of Confederate Nationalism: Ideology and Identity in the Civil War South.* Baton Rouge, 1988.

Fellman, David. *The Defendant's Rights Today.* Madison, 1976.

Finley, Moses I. *Ancient Slavery and Modern Ideology.* New York, 1980.

Fogel, Robert W. *Without Consent or Contract: The Rise and Fall of American Slavery.* New York, 1989.

Fogel, Robert W., and Stanley Engerman. *Time on the Cross: The Economics of American Negro Slavery.* Boston, 1974.

Foner, Eric. *Free Soil, Free Labor, Free Men: The Ideology of the Republican Party before the Civil War.* New York, 1970.

———. *Reconstruction: America's Unfinished Revolution, 1863–1877.* New York, 1988.

Ford, Lacy K., Jr. *Origins of Southern Radicalism: The South Carolina Upcountry, 1800–1860.* New York, 1988.

Franklin, Jimmie L. *Journey toward Hope: A History of Blacks in Oklahoma.* Norman, 1982.

Franklin, V. P. *Black Self-Determination: A Cultural History of the Faith of the Fathers.* Westport, 1984.

Frazier, E. Franklin. *Black Bourgeoisie.* Glencoe, Ill., 1957.

Fredrickson, George M. *White Supremacy: A Comparative Study in American and South African History.* New York, 1981.

Freehling, William W. *Prelude to Civil War: The Nullification Controversy in South Carolina, 1816–1836.* New York, 1965.

Freehling, William W., and Craig M. Simpson, eds. *Secession Debated: Georgia's Showdown in 1860.* New York, 1992.

Freyer, Tony. *The Little Rock Crisis: A Constitutional Interpretation.* Westport, 1986.

Fukurai, Hiroshi, Edgar W. Butler, and Richard Krooth. *Race and the Jury: Racial Disenfranchisement and the Search for Justice.* New York, 1993.

Gallup, George H. *The Gallup Poll: Public Opinion, 1972–1977.* Wilmington, Del., 1978.

Gans, Herbert J. *The Urban Villagers: Group and Class in the Life of Italian-Americans.* Glencoe, Ill., 1962.

Gay, Peter. *The Enlightenment: An Interpretation*. Vol. 2, *The Science of Freedom*. New York, 1969.

Genovese, Eugene D. *The Political Economy of Slavery*. New York, 1965.

————. *The World the Slaveholders Made: Two Essays in Interpretation*. New York, 1969.

Gerbi, Antonello. *The Dispute of the New World: The History of a Polemic, 1750–1900*. Trans. Jeremy Moyle. Pittsburgh, 1973.

Gerster, Patrick, and Nicholas Cords, eds. *Myth and Southern History*. Vol. 2, *The New South*. Urbana, Ill., 1989.

Gillette, William. *Retreat from Reconstruction, 1869–1879*. Baton Rouge, 1979.

Giovanni, Nikki, and Margaret Walker. *A Poetic Equation: Conversations between Nikki Giovanni and Margaret Walker*. Washington, 1974.

Gispen, Kees, ed. *What Made the South Different?* Jackson, Miss., 1990.

Goldfield, David R. *Black, White, and Southern: Race Relations and Southern Culture, 1940 to the Present*. Baton Rouge, 1990.

————. *Cotton Fields and Skyscrapers: Southern City and Region, 1607–1980*. Baton Rouge, 1982.

————. *Promised Land: The South since 1945*. Arlington Heights, Ill., 1987.

Goldin, Claudia D. *Urban Slavery in the American South, 1820–1860: A Quantitative History*. Chicago, 1976.

Goodwyn, Lawrence. *Democratic Promise: The Populist Moment in America*. New York, 1976.

Grafton, Anthony, with April Shelford and Nancy Siraisi. *New Worlds, Ancient Texts: The Power of Tradition and the Shock of Discovery*. Cambridge, Mass., 1992.

Graham, Hugh Davis. *Civil Rights and the Presidency*. New York, 1992.

————. *The Civil Rights Era: Origins and Development of National Policy, 1960–1972*. New York, 1990.

Grantham, Dewey W. *The Life and Death of the Solid South*. Lexington, Ky., 1988.

Greene, Jack P., ed. *The Diary of Colonel Landon Carter of Sabine Hall, 1752–1778*. Charlottesville, 1965.

Greven, Philip J., comp. *Child-Rearing Concepts, 1628–1861: Historical Sources*. Itasca, Ill., 1973.

————. *Spare the Child: The Religious Roots of Punishment and the Psychological Impact of Physical Abuse*. New York, 1990.

Grofman, Bernard, and Chandler Davidson, eds. *Controversies in Minority Voting: The Voting Rights in Perspective*. Washington, 1992.

Grossman, James R. *Land of Hope: Chicago, Black Southerners, and the Great Migration*. Chicago, 1989.

The Growth of Segregation in American Schools: Changing Patterns of Separation and Poverty Since 1968. Harvard Project on School Desegregation. Cambridge, Mass., 1993.

Grundy, Pamela. *You Always Think of Home: A Portrait of Clay County, Alabama*. Athens, Ga., 1991.

Gutman, Herbert G. *Work, Culture, and Society in Industrializing America*. New York, 1976.

Gwaltney, John Langston, [ed.] *Drylongso: A Self-Portrait of Black America*. New York, 1980.

Hacker, Andrew. *Two Nations: Black and White, Separate, Hostile, Unequal*. New York, 1992.

Hahn, Steven, and Jonathan Prude, eds. *The Countryside in the Age of Capitalist Transformation: Essays in the Social History of Rural America*. Chapel Hill, 1985.

Hall, Kermit L., and James W. Ely Jr., eds. *An Uncertain Tradition: Constitutionalism and the History of the South*. Athens, Ga., 1989.

Hall, Raymond L. *Black Separatism in the United States.* Hanover, N.H., 1978.

Hamilton, Kenneth Marvin. *Black Towns and Profit: Promotion and Development in the Trans-Appalachian West.* Urbana, Ill., 1991.

Hammond, John. *Leah and Rachel, or, the Two Fruitfull Sisters Virginia, and Mary-Land.* London, 1656.

Hareven, Tamara K. *Family Time and Industrial Time.* Cambridge, Eng., 1982.

Harris, William C. *The Day of the Carpetbagger: Reconstruction in Mississippi.* Baton Rouge, 1979.

Hartwell, Henry, James Blair, and Edward Chilton. *The Present State of Virginia, and the College* (1697). Ed. Hunter Dickinson Farish. Williamsburg, 1940.

Hartz, Louis. *The Liberal Tradition in America: An Interpretation of American Political Thought since the Revolution.* New York, 1955.

Hemphill, Paul. *The Nashville Sound: Bright Lights and Country Music.* New York, 1970.

Hermanus, Philip, comp. *An excellent Treatise teaching howe to cure the French-Pockes . . . .* London, 1590.

Hesseltine, William, and David Smiley. *The South in American History.* 2d ed. Englewood Cliffs, N.J., 1960.

Hill, Samuel S., Jr., ed. *Religion and the Solid South.* Nashville, 1972.

Hine, Darlene Clark, ed. *Black Women in America: An Historical Encyclopedia.* New York, 1993.

Hobson, Fred. *Tell about the South: The Southern Rage to Explain.* Baton Rouge, 1983.

Hughes, Langston. *Scottsboro Limited: Four Poems and a Play in Verse.* New York, 1932.

Humphries, Jefferson. *Southern Literature and Literary Theory.* Athens, Ga., 1990.

Hunter, James Davison. *Culture Wars: The Struggle to Define America.* New York, 1991.

Isaac, Rhys. *The Transformation of Virginia, 1740–1790.* Chapel Hill, 1982.

Jackson, Walter A. *Gunnar Myrdal and America's Conscience: Social Engineering and Racial Liberalism, 1938–1987.* Chapel Hill, 1990.

Jacoway, Elizabeth, and David R. Colburn, eds. *Southern Businessmen and Desegregation.* Baton Rouge, 1982.

Jaynes, Gerald David, and Robin M. Williams Jr. *A Common Destiny: Blacks and American Society.* Washington, 1989.

Jefferson, Thomas. *Notes on the State of Virginia* (1785). Ed. William Peden. Chapel Hill, 1955.

Jencks, Christopher. *Rethinking Social Policy: Race, Poverty, and the Underclass.* Cambridge, Mass., 1992.

Jennings, Francis. *The Invasion of America: Indians, Colonialism, and the Cant of Conquest.* Chapel Hill, 1975.

Johannsen, Robert W., ed. *The Lincoln-Douglas Debates of 1858.* New York, 1965.

Johnson, Charles S. *Shadow of the Plantation.* 1934. Reprint, Chicago, 1969.

Jones, Hugh. *The Present State of Virginia, from Whence Is Inferred a Short View of Maryland and North Carolina* (1724). Ed. Richard L. Morton. Chapel Hill, 1956.

Keller, Morton. *Affairs of State: Public Life in Late Nineteenth Century America.* Cambridge, Mass., 1977.

Kelley, Robin D. G. *Hammer and Hoe: Alabama Communists during the Great Depression.* Chapel Hill, 1990.

Key, V. O. *Southern Politics in State and Nation.* New York, 1949.

Killian, Lewis. *White Southerners*. New York, 1970.

King, Martin Luther, Jr. *A Testament of Hope: The Essential Writings and Speeches of Martin Luther King, Jr.* Ed. James M. Washington. San Francisco, 1986.

Kirby, Jack T. *Rural Worlds Lost: The American South, 1920–1960*. Baton Rouge, 1987.

Kluger, Richard. *Simple Justice: The History of Brown v. Board of Education and Black America's Struggle for Equality*. New York, 1976.

Kull, Andrew. *The Color-Blind Constitution*. Cambridge, Mass., 1992.

Ladner, Joyce A., ed. *The Death of White Sociology*. New York, 1973.

Lamis, Alexander P. *The Two-Party South*. New York, 1984.

Lasch, Christopher. *The True and Only Heaven: Progress and Its Critics*. New York, 1991.

Lawson, John. *A New Voyage to Carolina* (1709). Ed. Hugh Talmage Lefler. Chapel Hill, 1967.

Lawson, Steven F. *Black Ballots: Voting Rights in the South, 1944–1969*. New York, 1976.

———. *In Pursuit of Power: Southern Blacks and Electoral Politics, 1965–1982*. New York, 1985.

Lee, Harper. *To Kill a Mockingbird*. 1960. Reprint, New York, 1982.

Leiter, Jeffrey, Michael D. Shulman, and Rhonda Zingraff, eds. *Hanging by a Thread: Social Change in Southern Textiles*. Ithaca, N.Y., 1991.

Leventhal, Herbert. *In the Shadow of the Enlightenment: Occultism and Renaissance Science in Eighteenth-Century America*. New York, 1976.

Levine, Lawrence W. *Black Culture and Black Consciousness: Afro-American Folk Thought from Slavery to Freedom*. New York, 1977.

———. *The Unpredictable Past: Explorations in American Cultural History*. New York, 1993.

Lewis, Anthony. *Gideon's Trumpet*. 1964. Reprint, New York, 1989.

Lindstrom, Diane. *Economic Development in the Philadelphia Region, 1810–1850*. New York, 1978.

Litwack, Leon F. *Been in the Storm So Long: The Aftermath of Slavery*. New York, 1979.

Lofgren, Charles A. *The Plessy Case: A Legal-Historical Interpretation*. New York, 1987.

Malcolm X, with the assistance of Alex Haley. *The Autobiography of Malcolm X*. New York, 1965.

Marable, Manning. *Race, Reform, and Rebellion: The Second Reconstruction in Black America, 1954–1990*. Jackson, Miss., 1991.

Margo, Robert A. *Race and Schooling in the South, 1880–1950: An Economic History*. Chicago, 1990.

Marks, Stuart A. *Southern Hunting in Black and White: Nature, History, and Ritual in a Carolina Community*. Princeton, 1991.

Massey, Douglas S., and Nancy A. Denton. *American Apartheid: Segregation and the Making of the Underclass*. Cambridge, Mass., 1993.

McCoy, Donald R., and Richard T. Ruetten. *Quest and Response: Minority Rights and the Truman Administration*. Lawrence, 1973.

McGill, Ralph. *The South and the Southerner*. 1963. Reprint, Athens, Ga., 1992.

McLaurin, Melton. *Celia: A Slave*. Athens, Ga., 1991.

———. *Separate Pasts: Growing Up White in the Segregated South*. Athens, Ga., 1987.

McMillen, Neil R. *Dark Journey: Black Mississippians in the Age of Jim Crow*. Urbana, Ill., 1989.

McPherson, James M. *Abraham Lincoln and the Second American Revolution*. New York, 1990.

———. *Battle Cry of Freedom: The Civil War Era*. New York, 1988.

———. *The Struggle for Equality: Abolitionists and the Negro in the Civil War and Reconstruction*. Princeton, 1964.

————. *What They Fought For, 1861–1865*. Baton Rouge, 1994.

Meier, August, and Elliott Rudwick. *Black History and the Historical Profession, 1915–1980*. Urbana, Ill., 1986.

Mintz, Sidney W., and Richard Price. *The Birth of African American Culture: An Anthropological Perspective*. Boston, 1992.

Moody, Anne. *Coming of Age in Mississippi*. New York, 1968.

Moore, Barrington. *Social Origins of Dictatorship and Democracy: Lord and Peasant in the Making of the Modern World*. Boston, 1966.

Morgan, Edmund S. *American Slavery, American Freedom: The Ordeal of Colonial Virginia*. New York, 1975.

Morris, Willie. *Homecomings*. Jackson, Miss., 1989.

————. *North toward Home*. New York, 1967.

Murray, Albert. *The Omni-Americans: New Perspectives on Black Experience and American Culture*. New York, 1970.

————. *South to a Very Old Place*. New York, 1971.

Myrdal, Gunnar. *An American Dilemma: The Negro Problem and Modern Democracy*. New York, 1944.

National Emergency Council. *Report on the Economic Conditions of the South*. Washington, 1938.

Naylor, Thomas J., and James Clotfelter. *Strategies for Change in the South*. Chapel Hill, 1975.

Newby, I. A. *Jim Crow's Defense: Anti-Negro Thought in America, 1900–1930*. Baton Rouge, 1965.

Oakes, James. *The Ruling Race: A History of American Slaveholders*. New York, 1982.

————. *Slavery and Freedom: An Interpretation of the Old South*. New York, 1990.

O'Brien, Michael. *The Idea of the American South, 1920–1941*. Baltimore, 1979.

Patterson, Haywood, and Earl Conrad. *Scottsboro Boy*. New York, 1950.

Patterson, Orlando. *Freedom: Volume 1: Freedom in the Making of Western Culture*. New York, 1991.

————. *Slavery and Social Death*. Cambridge, Mass., 1982.

Perman, Michael. *Reunion without Compromise: The South and Reconstruction, 1865–1868*. Cambridge, Mass., 1973.

————. *The Road to Redemption: Southern Politics, 1869–1879*. Baton Rouge, 1984.

Phillips, Ulrich B. *American Negro Slavery*. New York, 1918.

————. *Life and Labor in the Old South*. Boston, 1951.

Pole, J. R. *The Pursuit of Equality in American History*. Berkeley, 1978.

Potter, David. *The South and the Sectional Conflict*. Baton Rouge, 1968.

Prenshaw, Peggy W., and Jesse O. McKee, eds. *Sense of Place: Mississippi*. Jackson, Miss., 1979.

Raines, Howell. *My Soul Is Rested: Movement Days in the Deep South Remembered*. New York, 1977.

Ralph, James R., Jr. *Northern Protest: Martin Luther King, Jr., Chicago, and the Civil Rights Movement*. Cambridge, Mass., 1993.

Ramsay, David. *A Dissertation on the Means of Preserving Health in Charleston and the Adjacent Low Country*. Charleston, 1790.

————. *A Review of the Improvements, Progress and State of Medicine in the Eighteenth Century*. Charleston, 1800.

————. *A Sketch of the Soil, Climate, Weather, and Diseases of South-Carolina*. Charleston, 1796.

Randall, James G. *Constitutional Problems under Lincoln*. Rev. ed. Urbana, Ill., 1951.

Ransom, Roger, and Richard Sutch. *One Kind of Freedom: The Economic Consequences of Emancipation.* New York, 1977.

Raper, Arthur. *The Tragedy of Lynching.* Chapel Hill, 1933.

Reed, John Shelton. *The Enduring South: Subcultural Persistence in Mass Society.* Chapel Hill, 1986.

———. *One South: An Ethnic Approach to Regional Culture.* Baton Rouge, 1982.

———. *Southerners: The Social Psychology of Sectionalism.* Chapel Hill, 1983.

Report of the National Advisory Commission on Civil Disorders. New York, 1968.

Reynolds, Quentin. *Courtroom: The Story of Samuel S. Leibowitz.* New York, 1950.

Riley, James C. *The Eighteenth-Century Campaign to Avoid Disease.* New York, 1987.

Rittenhouse, David. *The Virginia Almanack for the Year of Our Lord God 1776.* Williamsburg, [1775].

Romans, Bernard. *A Concise Natural History of East and West Florida.* London, 1775.

Rosenberg, Gerald N. *The Hollow Hope: Can Courts Bring About Social Change?* Chicago, 1991.

Rosengarten, Theodore. *All God's Dangers: The Life of Nate Shaw.* New York, 1974.

Rossell, Christine H. *The Carrot or the Stick for School Desegregation Policy: Magnet Schools or Forced Busing.* Philadelphia, 1990.

Rothman, David J. *The Discovery of the Asylum: Social Order and Disorder in the New Republic.* Boston, 1971.

Rowan, Carl. *South of Freedom.* New York, 1952.

Rubin, Louis D., Jr., ed. *The American South: Portrait of a Culture.* Baton Rouge, 1980.

———. *The Edge of the Swamp: A Study in the Literature and Society of the Old South.* Baton Rouge, 1989.

———. *South: Modern Southern Literature in Its Cultural Setting.* Garden City, N.Y., 1961.

———. *William Elliott Shoots a Bear: Essays on the Southern Literary Imagination.* Baton Rouge, 1975.

Rubin, Louis D., Jr., and James J. Kilpatrick, eds. *The Lasting South: Fourteen Southerners Look at Their Home.* Chicago, 1957.

Schulman, Bruce J. *From Cotton Belt to Sunbelt: Federal Policy, Economic Development, and the Transformation of the South, 1938–1980.* New York, 1991.

Schuman, Howard, Charlotte Steeh, and Lawrence Bobo, *Racial Attitudes in America: Trends and Interpretations.* Cambridge, Mass., 1985.

Sellers, Charles Grier, Jr. *The Market Revolution: Jacksonian America, 1815–1846.* New York, 1991.

———, ed. *The Southerner as American.* Chapel Hill, 1960.

Settle, Dionyse. *A true reporte of the laste Voyage into the West and Northwest regions . . . by Capteine Frobisher.* London, 1571.

Shumaker, Wayne. *The Occult Sciences in the Renaissance: A Study in Intellectual Patterns.* Berkeley, 1972.

Silver, Timothy. *A New Face on the Countryside: Indians, Colonists, and Slaves in South Atlantic Forests, 1500–1800.* Cambridge, 1990.

Singal, Daniel Joseph. *The War Within: From Victorian to Modernist Thought in the South, 1919–1945.* Chapel Hill, 1982.

Sitkoff, Harvard. *A New Deal for Blacks: The Emergence of Civil Rights as a National Issue.* New York, 1978.

————. *The Struggle for Black Equality, 1954–1980.* 1981. Reprint, New York, 1993.

Skocpol, Theda. *Protecting Soldiers and Mothers: The Political Origins of Social Policy in the United States.* Cambridge, Mass., 1992.

Sleeper, Jim. *The Closest of Strangers: Liberalism and the Politics of Race in New York.* New York, 1990.

Smith, Henry Nash. *Virgin Land: The American West as Symbol and Myth.* 1950. Reprint, Cambridge, Mass., 1970.

Smith, Lillian. *Killers of the Dream.* New York, 1949.

Sniderman, Paul M., and Thomas Piazza. *The Scar of Race.* Cambridge, Mass., 1993.

Sosna, Morton. *In Search of the Silent South: Southern Liberals and the Race Issue.* New York, 1977.

Southern, David. *Gunnar Myrdal and Black-White Relations: The Use and Abuse of "An American Dilemma," 1944–1969.* Baton Rouge, 1987.

Stammp, Kenneth M. *The Peculiar Institution: Slavery in the Antebellum South.* New York, 1956.

Stewart, James Brewer. *Holy Warriors: The Abolitionists and American Slavery.* New York, 1976.

Stowe, Harriet Beecher. *Uncle Tom's Cabin, or Life among the Lowly.* 1852. Reprint, New York, 1962.

Stuckey, Sterling. *Slave Culture: Nationalist Theory and the Foundation of Black America.* New York, 1987.

Taulbert, Clifton L. *Once upon a Time When We Were Colored.* Tulsa, 1989.

Taylor, Charles. *Sources of the Self: The Making of the Modern Identity.* Cambridge, Mass., 1989.

Taylor, George Rogers, and Irene D. Neu. *The American Railroad Network, 1861–1890.* Cambridge, Mass., 1956.

Thernstrom, Abigail M. *Whose Votes Count? Affirmative Action and Minority Voting Rights.* Cambridge, Mass., 1987.

Thomas, John L., ed. *Slavery Attacked: The Abolitionist Crusade.* Englewood Cliffs, N.J., 1965.

Thomas, Keith. *Man and the Natural World: A History of the Modern Sensibility.* New York, 1983.

————. *Religion and the Decline of Magic.* London, 1971.

Thornton, J. Mills. *Politics and Power in a Slave Society: Alabama, 1800–1860.* Baton Rouge, 1978.

Tichi, Cecelia. *New World, New Earth: Environmental Reform in American Literature from the Puritans through Whitman.* New Haven, 1979.

Tindall, George B. *The Ethnic Southerners.* Baton Rouge, 1976.

Tinling, Marion, ed. *The Correspondence of the Three William Byrds of Westover, Virginia, 1684–1776.* Charlottesville, 1977.

Tise, Larry. *Proslavery: A History of the Defense of Slavery in America, 1701–1840.* Athens, Ga., 1987.

Trelease, Allen W. *White Terror: The Ku Klux Klan Conspiracy and Southern Reconstruction.* Westport, 1971.

Tushnet, Mark V. *The NAACP's Legal Strategy against Segregated Education, 1925–1950.* Chapel Hill, 1987.

Twelve Southerners. *I'll Take My Stand: The South and the Agrarian Tradition.* New York, 1930.

Urofsky, Melvin I. *A March of Liberty: A Constitutional History of the United States.* New York, 1988.

U.S. Department of Commerce. *Historical Statistics of the United States.* Washington, 1976.

U.S. Department of Commerce. *Statistical Abstract of the United States, 1922.* Washington, 1923.

U.S. Department of Commerce. *Statistical Abstract of the United States, 1992.* Washington, 1993.

U.S. Department of Education. *Resegregation of the Public Schools: The Third Generation.* Washington, 1989.

Ver Steeg, Clarence L. *Origins of a Southern Mosaic: Studies of Early Carolina and Georgia.* Athens, Ga., 1975.

Vlach, John Michael. *The Afro-American Tradition in Decorative Arts.* Cleveland, 1978.

——— . *By the Work of Their Hands: Studies in Afro-American Folklife.* Ann Arbor, 1991.

Vose, Clement E. *Caucasians Only: The Supreme Court, the NAACP, and the Restrictive Covenant Cases.* Berkeley, 1967.

Walker, Alice. *In Search of Our Mothers' Gardens.* New York, 1983.

Warner, John Harley. *The Therapeutic Perspective: Medical Practice, Knowledge, and Identity in America, 1820–1885.* Cambridge, Mass., 1986.

Waters, Pat. *The South and the Nation.* New York, 1969.

Weaver, Richard. *The Southern Tradition at Bay: A History of Postbellum Thought.* New Rochelle, N.Y., 1968.

Westmacott, Richard Noble. *African-American Gardens and Yards in the Rural South.* Knoxville, 1992.

Whitfield, Stephen J. *A Death in the Delta: The Story of Emmett Till.* Baltimore, 1988.

Whitson, S. Mort, ed. *Sense of Place in Appalachia.* Morehead, Ky., 1988.

Wiener, Jonathan M. *Social Origins of the New South: Alabama, 1860–1885.* Baton Rouge, 1978.

Wilkinson, J. Harvie, III. *From Brown to Bakke: The Supreme Court and School Integration, 1954–1978.* New York, 1979.

Williams, Vernon J., Jr. *From a Caste to a Minority: Changing Attitudes of American Sociologists toward Afro-Americans.* New York, 1989.

Williamson, Joel. *The Crucible of Race: Black-White Relations in the American South since Emancipation.* New York, 1984.

——— . *A Rage for Order: Black-White Relations in the American South since Emancipation.* New York, 1986.

Wills, Garry. *Inventing America: Jefferson's Declaration of Independence.* Garden City, N.Y., 1978.

——— . *Lincoln at Gettysburg: The Words That Remade America.* New York, 1992.

Wilson, Charles Reagan, and William Ferris. *The Encyclopedia of Southern Culture.* Chapel Hill, 1989.

Wilson, William Julius. *The Truly Disadvantaged: The Inner City, the Underclass, and Public Policy.* Chicago, 1987.

Wood, Gordon S. *The Radicalism of the American Revolution.* New York, 1992.

Wood, Philip J. *Southern Capitalism: The Political Economy of North Carolina, 1880–1980.* Durham, N.C., 1986.

Woodward, C. Vann. *American Counterpoint: Slavery and Racism in the North-South Dialogue.* Boston, 1971.

——— . *The Burden of Southern History.* Rev. ed. Baton Rouge, 1968.

——— . *Origins of the New South, 1877–1913.* Baton Rouge, 1951.

——— . *Reunion and Reaction: The Compromise of 1877 and the End of Reconstruction.* 1951. Reprint, New York, 1966.

————. *The Strange Career of Jim Crow.* Rev. ed. New York, 1974.

Workman, W. D. *The Case for the South.* New York, 1960.

Wright, Gavin. *Old South, New South: Revolutions in the Southern Economy since 1865.* New York, 1986.

Wright, Louis B., ed. *The Prose Works of William Byrd of Westover: Narratives of a Colonial Virginian.* Cambridge, Mass., 1966.

Wright, Richard. *Black Boy: A Record of Childhood and Youth.* New York, 1945.

Yates, Frances A. *The Occult Philosophy in the Elizabethan Age.* London, 1979.

Yates, Gayle Graham. *Mississippi Mind: A Personal Cultural History of an American State.* Knoxville, 1990.

Zangrando, Robert L. *The NAACP Crusade against Lynching: 1909–1950.* Philadelphia, 1980.

Zinn, Howard. *The Southern Mystique.* New York, 1964.

∼ Index

Abolitionism, 5, 17–18, 24, 44, 45, 98–99, 102–13, 165; and liberalism, 96; and American Anti-Slavery Society, 102, 106–7, 113; and "free-soilers," 103; and secession, 108–9. *See also* Radical Republicans

Acosta, Jose de, 63–64

Adventures of Huckleberry Finn (Twain), 183

African-American Gardens and Yards in the Rural South (Westmacott), 223

African Americans: and emancipation, 5, 254; migration of, to North, 6, 13, 41, 49–50, 133, 210–12, 220, 268; and political protest, 6, 139; and freedom in postbellum South, 40–41; and colonization outside U.S., 99, 104; and Liberia, 104; emancipation of, 111–12; and slave insurrections, 112; voting rights of, 116–17, 119, 130, 154, 160, 270; in Mississippi, 119; disfranchisement of, 127, 131–32, 136; violence against, 127, 139, 185, 193; and education, 130, 170; and debt peonage, 131; and political power, 133–35, 151–52, 154–56, 270; and criminal justice, 134, 151, 201; and discrimination in jury selection, 134, 196; in Virginia, 136; and race riots, 140, 146; in middle class, 148, 156, 175–76, 217, 219; and student protests, 150; and voter registration, 151; and development of underclass, 154; migration of, to cities, 154; in elected positions, 155; voting as Democrats, 155; migration of, to South, 156; and labor market integra-

tion, 175; and legal representation, 198; and Pan-Africanism, 220; in literature, 235, 249–50; in Congress, 265, 270; and segregation in North, 265–66; banned from donating blood, 266; in federal judiciary, 268; and higher education, 268. *See also* Civil rights; Civil rights movement; Disfranchisement; Racism; Segregation; White supremacy

Agrarians, 3–4, 42, 235–55 passim

Agriculture, 47, 57, 168, 173, 175. *See also* Cotton; Economic conditions; Sharecropping

Airs, Waters, Places (Hippocrates), 63

Alabama: disfranchisement of blacks, 131; jury selection, 134; fear of miscegenation, 185

Allen, Ray, 213

All God's Dangers, 201

American Creed and white southerners, 36

American Dilemma, An (Myrdal), 14

American Literature (Thorpe), 249

American pluralism, 43

American South: Portrait of a Culture, The (Rubin), 253–55

American studies, 35–37, 39

Ames, Adelbert, 122

Ames, Jessie, 197

Archdale, John, 69, 74

Archer, Chalmers, 222–23

Asante, Molefi Kete, 220–21

"Aspects of the Southern Philosophy" (Weaver), 240